Smithsonian Folkways Recordings

AMERICAN
MUSICAL
TRADITIONS

Smithsonian Folkways Recordings

American Musical Traditions

Volume

3

British Isles Music

Jeff Todd Titon

Bob Carlin

SCHIRMER REFERENCE

GALE GROUP

THOMSON LEARNING

New York • Detroit • San Diego • San Francisco
Boston • New Haven, Conn. • Waterville, Maine
London • Munich

Schirmer Reference
1633 Broadway
New York, NY 10019

Gale Group
27500 Drake Rd.
Farmington Hills, MI 48331

Library of Congress Cataloging-in-Publication Data

American musical traditions / [general editors] Jeff Todd Titon, Bob Carlin.
    P.   cm.
"Published in collaboration with The Smithsonian Folkways Archive."
Includes bibliographical references, discographies, videographies, and index.
Contents: v. 1. Native American music—v. 2. African American music—v. 3. British Isles music—v. 4.
    European American music—v. 5. Latino and Asian American Music.
ISBN 0-02-864624-X (set)
1. Folk music—United States—History and criticism—Juvenile literature. 2. Music—United States-History and criticism
    —Juvenile literature. 3. Ethnomusicology—Juvenile literature. [1. Folk music—History and criticism. 2. Music—History
    and criticism.]
I. Titon, Jeff Todd, 1943-   II. Carlin, Bob.

ML3551.A53 2001
781.62'00973-dc21

TABLE OF CONTENTS
VOLUME 3

TABLE OF CONTENTS
VOLUMES 1, 2, 4, AND 5

VOLUME 1: NATIVE AMERICAN MUSIC

VOLUME 2: AFRICAN AMERICAN MUSIC

VOLUME 4: EUROPEAN AMERICAN MUSIC

CENTRAL/SOUTHERN EUROPEAN—ACADIAN/FRENCH MUSIC

CENTRAL/SOUTHERN EUROPEAN—ITALIAN MUSIC

GERMAN/EASTERN EUROPEAN MUSIC

VOLUME 5: LATINO AMERICAN MUSIC AND ASIAN AMERICAN MUSIC

INTRODUCTION TO *AMERICAN MUSICAL TRADITIONS*

Jeff Todd Titon

This five-volume work presents an American musical mosaic. Folklorists and ethnomusicologists whose research centers on musical traditions in the United States wrote authoritative essays specifically for *American Musical Traditions*. We solicited additional materials from the Smithsonian Institution's Center for Folklife and Cultural Heritage, particularly from Smithsonian Folkways Recordings and the Smithsonian Folklife Festival. Keyed to musical examples and illustrations on both the Smithsonian Folkways website and the Brown University website (addresses below), *American Musical Traditions* presents a combination of words, sounds, and images so readers can hear, as well as read about, much of the music under discussion.

It goes without saying that at the start of the twenty-first century, every community in the United States has music. But this has been true for as long as the continent has been settled by humans; among the Native Americans, music (and dance) has always played an important role in ceremony and recreation.

My great-grandparents grew up in a world in which people who wanted to hear music had to learn to sing and play it themselves. Today televisions, videocassette recorders, radios, and compact disc players can be found in most American households, along with collections of recordings. All of these are products of the twentieth-century revolution in electromechanical musical reproduction, permitting anyone to hear music on demand without performing it.

In addition to the old methods of distributing music, a dizzying array of new digital formats and delivery methods, including mini-disc, CD-R, CD-RW, mp3, and DVD, along with the World Wide Web, are bringing music into the new century, while musical performance itself is being reconceived with the help of electronic equipment, sampling, and computers. Today, of course, music from all over the globe is available at the flip of a switch or movement of a computer mouse. But every community also has its live music makers. Music is taught and learned in the public schools, in music academies, and by private teachers. Community bands and orchestras, informal chamber music groups, singer-songwriters with guitars, basement or garage rock and country bands, singers of all stylistic persuasions—these music makers can be found in just about every community, large or small.

Outside the mainstream there is another kind of music, one that members of certain populations regard as their own. While contemporary popular music is set in the present and strives for novelty and sales, and while classical music looks to the future and strives for originality, this other music, which in this book we call "traditional," is almost always linked to the past and bounded in certain ways. The traditional music we have in mind usually arises in connection with ethnic or regional identity, and sometimes it is connected to an original homeland outside the United States. The groups that possess traditional music often

attach it to particular (named) people and places, with ties to an older generation of source musicians from whom it has been learned.

Traditional music has sometimes been called folk music, but in university circles today the word "folk" carries troublesome baggage (such as nationalism, purity, and noblesse oblige) and so the younger generation of scholars tends to avoid it. Today the word "traditional" often substitutes for "folk," but "tradition" can be a troublesome word as well. Scholars have shown that it is naive to consider traditions a set of ancient, sacred rules, like the American Constitution, that we must interpret reverentially. Traditions turn out to be far more flexible than we ever imagined. After all, traditions must adapt to the present moment or they will fail; and more than a few traditions turn out, on inspection, to be the invention of things we want to believe about the past but that have little or no basis in fact. For example, the contemporary sound of "Irish traditional music"—represented by popular Irish bands featuring uillean pipes, fiddles, wooden flutes, guitars, tin whistles, citterns, bouzoukis, and bodhrans, a sound that is marketed as "Celtic music" and is sometimes pictured with ancient mists and druidic artifacts on album covers—turns out to be only a few decades old. The periodic revival of Celtic culture seems to be a tradition itself, one that the poet William Butler Yeats invoked more than a hundred years ago in *The Celtic Twilight*.

Today it is easy to debunk invented traditions wherever an ancient pedigree is foolishly sought, and music seems particularly susceptible to this kind of search. Yet when the dust settles we see that all living traditions bend the past to the present in order to continue into the future. Regarded in the present as manifestations of the past, they are thought to carry some authority (or not carry it) by virtue of that association.

In the upper Midwest, for example, where Germans, Swedes, Finns, and Norwegians settled more than a hundred years ago, many communities have retained, and revived, and in so reviving further developed, musical traditions that are recogniz-

ably their own. The same is true of other ethnic immigrant populations in different parts of the country. It is a mistake to think that traditions are rigid. Change, it seems, is built into most musical traditions. African Americans created music styles such as the blues, spirituals, jazz, and soul music, all featuring improvisation. Hip-hop, the most modern musical manifestation of this improvised cultural tradition, has its roots in the oral poetry of the African American "toast" (Jackson 1974) and in a lengthy tradition of vernacular dance. In African American musical traditions, innovation is the norm.

Geographical region, ethnic population, and musical style have guided most research into American vernacular musical traditions. This work reflects those boundaries. Volume 1 presents Native American music; Volume 2 offers African American music; Volume 3 concentrates on the music of the British Isles, including Ireland, in America. These are the three areas that have received the most attention from musical scholars. In the last thirty years or so, research has increasingly focused on the music of European and Asian immigrant ethnic groups. Volume 4 therefore presents music from European American immigrant communities, including those from France, Italy, Germany, Poland, Czechoslovakia, Hungary, Sweden, Norway, and Finland; and Volume 5 offers music from the Spanish-speaking communities as well as Asian American music. Readers who wish to learn more about how and where ethnic groups settled in the United States are referred to James Paul Allen and Eugene James Turner, *We the People: An Atlas of America's Ethnic Diversity*, and to the *Harvard Encyclopedia of American Ethnic Groups*.

Organizing these volumes according to ethnic groups must not leave the impression of a rigid, balkanized United States of tight-knit musical enclaves. Classical music is available to all. Few consider this Western art music to have ethnic boundaries. Popular music that comes from the media is also open to all. While many musical communities do take stewardship of music they identify as their own, their people also participate in the mainstream of America's popular

music styles that do not reflect the perspective of any single group. In addition, they may adopt practitioners who learn their traditional music but who did not grow up in their communities.

Although the Navajo, for example, continue to practice their traditional ceremonial and recreational music, they compose music in new modes reflecting influences from contemporary gospel music, Hollywood film music, acoustic guitar–based singer-songwriter music, and New Age music, among others. Yet the most popular music on the reservations is country music, and Navajos regularly form country and rock bands.

Nor should we think of traditional music as extending unchanged back through time. The accordion, a musical staple for several generations among Hispanic musicians on the Texas-Mexican border, was borrowed from German immigrants to that region. The guitar, regarded by some as the American folk instrument par excellence, gained its great popularity only in the twentieth century. And the five-string banjo, identified today with hillbillies and bluegrass musicians, derives from an African instrument that, along with the African American population, significantly changed the sound and style of vernacular dance music in the American South. Although this work emphasizes those styles of music that the various ethnic musical communities consider to be their own, we do not wish to claim that this is the only, or necessarily the principal, music with which the people in these communities are involved.

These volumes are not meant to cover each and every musical tradition. It would be impossible to do so; first because this work is not large enough, and second because the scholarship available is uneven in coverage. There are many more musical communities than scholars surveying the subject. We have selected representative communities and musical genres to give an idea of the range of traditional music in the United States. Some of this research is current, representing musical communities today; some is historical and represents musical communities in the past. The writing

includes two main perspectives: essays on communities and examples of their music, and interviews or profiles of particular musicians and musical groups. Although this is a large work, we do not claim to be comprehensive or definitive; thus we invite further research. Because each volume has an introductory essay describing its contents, in what follows I will discuss the origin and development of the project as a whole.

From the outset, this reference work was conceived to reflect recent research by folklorists and ethnomusicologists on the one hand, and the holdings of the Smithsonian Institution's Center for Folklife and Cultural Heritage on the other. Since the early 1970s, public-sector folklorists, ethnomusicologists, and their academic colleagues have surveyed ethnic and regional music-making in many communities across the United States. Often sponsored by arts councils, cultural organizations, and community initiatives, and in many cases underwritten by the Folk Arts Division of the National Endowment for the Arts, the American Folklife Center of the Library of Congress, and the Smithsonian's Center for Folklife and Cultural Heritage (formerly the Office of Folklife Programs), from about 1977 to 1995 folklorists could be found in nearly every one of the fifty states, surveying folklife and expressive culture (including music) and documenting and presenting the products of this research. Those products were unprecedented in number and quality. Fieldnotes, booklets, recordings, videos, festivals, tours, exhibits, and apprenticeships most often were targeted back into those communities rather than meant for archives or a central data bank.

Cutbacks and reorientation in public funding for the arts, however, coupled with the lack of formal, ongoing, institutional support, have redirected public-sector workers' efforts toward heritage and tourism. Thus, it seemed an appropriate moment to ask these fieldworkers and arts administrators to contribute essays to a project that would gather some of this work together. Accordingly, in 1995 I sent out a prospectus for this work along with invitations to all

the state folklorists and ethnomusicologists listed in the *Public Folklore Newsletter* as well as to numerous academic colleagues, inviting topics, entries, and proposals for additional contributors. It was a long process, but several people responded positively and the fruits of their labors are evident throughout these volumes, as their contributions make up a substantial proportion of this work. Obtaining them and guiding their direction was my main task. Co-editor Bob Carlin's primary job was to select materials from the Smithsonian Institution for these volumes.

Many contributors to this project also worked, at one time or another, for the Smithsonian Folklife Festival, formerly known as the Festival of American Folklife (FAF); and therefore we could draw upon that work for their contributions to this volume. The Smithsonian Folklife Festival is an ongoing, multicultural, international event, staged annually since 1967 in the nation's capital on the mall between the Lincoln Memorial and Washington Monument. It is the largest and by far the most expansive, longest-lasting folk festival in the United States. Typically it runs for two weeks during late June and early July and features a few hundred singers, musicians, dancers, storytellers, crafters, and other folk artists in an outdoor museum setting meant to celebrate the diverse folkways of the United States and other lands. The Festival presents these folk artists on stages, in tents, and in open-air locations where they perform and demonstrate for an audience of tourists amid a celebratory atmosphere. During the more than thirty years that the FAF has run, the staff has implemented a cultural policy that involves more than merely a demonstration and preservation theater. Theirs is a vision of a multicultural world living in harmony, celebrating mutuality while learning from different traditions.

From the outset, the festival planners understood the importance of documentation as well as presentation. Every event that took place on every stage was recorded by festival staff. Festival recordings and related materials are housed in the Ralph Rinzler Folklife Archives and Collections at the Center for Folklife and Cultural Heritage, Smithsonian Institution. Each year an elaborate program booklet is prepared for the public. It contains essays introducing many of the individuals and the communities featured at the festival. Written by the folklorists and ethnomusicologists who had researched the music, crafts, and other expressions of folklife for the annual presentations, these essays are both authoritative and accessible. Often they are the best short introductions to the musics of particular ethnic and regional communities; we have drawn liberally on them for this volume. The Smithsonian's other contribution derives from the materials in Smithsonian Folkways Recordings.

Folkways Recordings, begun in 1948 by Moses Asch, reflected the very broad tastes of its founder. From the Folkways catalog you could hear everything from the demonstration collection of world music recorded at the turn of the twentieth century for the Berlin Archiv to the music of Leadbelly, Woody Guthrie, and Pete Seeger, as well as the famous Harry Smith *Anthology of American Folk Music,* recently reissued by Smithsonian Folkways.

But Asch did not stop there. Modern poetry in the voices of the authors, bird songs, and even the sounds of factory work fell within the recorded output of this eclectic operation. Folkways was one of very few record companies in the 1940s and 1950s publishing folk music from American communities, including Native American and European immigrants, along with the British American and African American music that collectors had been emphasizing throughout the twentieth century. Many, but not all, of these albums came with copious (and only lightly edited) documentation by the field researchers and other experts, in the form of notes slipped into the double-channeled Folkways album cover. Folkways recordings cost a little more than most, but they provided more, too; and in many instances they provided the only recordings available representing various populations on the planet. During the folk revival of the late 1950s and early 1960s, Folkways was the first to

present the traditional music of Roscoe Holcomb, Wade Ward, Doc Watson, and others from the southern Appalachian Mountains. Much of their material is of enormous historical value and, for that reason, we have preserved the original text that accompanied their works.

In 1987, the Smithsonian's Folklife division acquired Folkways Recordings and hired Anthony Seeger to direct the operation. (In 2001 Seeger was replaced by Daniel Sheehy, formerly the Director of the Folk Arts Program, National Endowment for the Arts.) Smithsonian Folkways kept all of the back catalog in print (it can be ordered at any time from their website), and they have produced more than a hundred new albums; we have drawn liberally on those with American subjects for this work. Finally, we have gone outside of commissioned articles and Smithsonian materials to obtain other well-documented descriptions of musical communities where they were needed to fill in gaps. We present the whole as a spicy stew, a mosaic, and a mix that we think will appeal and stimulate the reader's appetite for more.

LINKS TO WEBSITES

On occasion, the essays in *American Musical Traditions* discuss recordings that are part of the vast Smithsonian Folkways library, particularly those essays that were originally Smithsonian materials. The relevant Folkways catalog number for the recordings appears in each essay's headnote, when available, or elsewhere in the essay. Readers may then visit the Internet's World Wide Web to listen to those recordings; in many cases, they are available for direct purchase online after they have been previewed. The Smithsonian recordings, in both Liquid Audio and RealAudio format, may be downloaded from the Smithsonian Folkways website, which is found at http://www.si.edu/ folkways. There, readers should click on the "Liquid Audio" link to go directly to the Smithsonian's catalog of recordings.

In addition, I am building my own site at Brown University to house links to record-

ings and other materials that are not part of the Folkways collections. As *American Musical Traditions* was going to press, the site was still under construction, but content is being added. It can be located at http://www.stg.brown.edu/MusicAtlas.

VOLUME 3: BRITISH ISLES MUSIC

This third volume of *American Musical Traditions* brings together research on American music drawn from various British Isles traditions. The volume is organized more or less geographically from northeastern traditions through the southeastern traditions, and then to the west. It ends with a separate section on Irish American music, which has maintained a distinct identity separate from other British Isles traditions. These chapters mix general overviews on musical **genres** and styles with essays about specific local traditions and those that spotlight key performers.

GLOSSARY AND INDEX

Each volume of *American Musical Traditions* includes a glossary of terms used in that volume and an index that includes citations to all five volumes in the series. Throughout the essays and sidebars in each volume, certain terms appear in boldface, indicating that the term is fully defined in the glossary at the back of the book. The glossary also includes "See" and "See also" references to make locating the appropriate term easier. The index in each volume is comprehensive—that is, it includes citations to all five volumes of *AMT,* not just the individual volume. Numerals followed by a colon and then the page number are used to indicate in which volume a citation appears. In addition, page references in bold refer to a main essay or sidebar on that topic and page references in italics refer to photos; maps are clearly indicated. Index sub-topics are indented beneath the main topic. For example, an index citation for drums might look like this:

Drums, 1:23–28, 2:54, 3: 125
  double-barreled drum, 2:76
  in Native American ceremonies, 1:48
  in calypso music, 5:35
  spread of across the Great Plains 1:98 (*map*)

ACKNOWLEDGMENTS

We gratefully acknowledge the assistance of the Smithsonian Institution's Folklife division, the National Endowment for the Arts' Folk Arts Program, the Scholarly Technology Group of Brown University, and Schirmer Reference in making this project possible. We thank the many artists and musicians who cooperated with the researchers who wrote the entries, as well as the researchers themselves who are named in this book as contributors. Special thanks to the authors of the introductions to each volume: Burt Feintuch, David Evans, Thomas Vennum, Philip Nusbaum, and Tom Van Buren. Thanks to Art Rosenbaum for his wonderful cover designs. In addition, we would like to thank Richard Carlin for overseeing this project and keeping it on track during his tenure at Schirmer. Thank you to Charlotte Heth for her expert review of the Native American volume. Finally, we are grateful to those in the Smithsonian Institution who helped with this project. Anthony Seeger and the staff of Smithsonian Folkways made their archives available to us. Diana Parker, director of the Smithsonian Folklife Festival, and Richard Kurin, head of the Smithsonian's Office of Folklife and Cultural Heritage, helped us obtain additional information related to the musical communities represented down through the years at the Festival.

We would also like to thank our editors including Deborah Gillan Straub, Stephen Wasserstein, and Brad Morgan, as well as the members of Gale's production and design staff, including Wendy Blurton, Evi Seoud, Mary Beth Trimper, Randy Bassett, Barb Yarrow, Pam Reed, Christine O'Bryan, Tracey Rowens, Cindy Baldwin, Margaret Chamberlain, and others who provided able assistance.

BIBLIOGRAPHY

Allen, James Paul; and Turner, Eugene James. (1988). *We the People: An Atlas of America's Ethnic Diversity*. New York: Macmillan.

Jackson, Bruce, compiler. (1974). *"Get Your Ass in the Water and Swim Like Me!": Narrative Poetry from the Black Oral Tradition*. Cambridge: Harvard University Press.

Thernstrom, Stephan. (1980). *Harvard Encyclopedia of American Ethnic Groups*. Cambridge: Harvard University Press.

INTRODUCTION: BRITISH ISLES MUSIC

Burt Feintuch

Burt Feintuch is professor of folklore and English at the University of New Hampshire, where he also directs the Center for the Humanities. From 1991 through 1995 he edited the Journal of American Folklore.

If you could hear the music the authors describe in this section on American musical traditions rooted in the British Isles, what would it sound like? To begin with the obvious, were it vocal music, it would be performed in English. Other languages from England, Scotland, Wales, and Ireland have had varying degrees of currency in the United States, but they are almost entirely gone from the music cultures and musical **genres** discussed here. And because English is the nation's dominant language, it transcends sets of genres and varieties of performance sharing particular historical derivations. So, we have to go beyond language to think about what unites these musics.

That brings us to voice. Regardless of whether this music is sung or played on **instruments**, a quality that we might term "single-voicedness" characterizes it. The voice—human or instrumental—seems to be the focus, the strongest presence, in these musical traditions. In genres such as **ballads**, where the story is the heart of the performance, a single voice narrates. The voice is animated by **melody**, but the text is the thing, and the singer serves to give voice to that text. When groups sing in these traditions, they are predisposed to sing as one voice. Think of the precision of tight **bluegrass** harmonies, the dignity of Shaker **hymns**. The melodies tend to be regular, metrical. Counter-melodies are rare, and **unison** singing is common. Even, as in the example of the Old Regular Baptists **lining out** hymns, where the performance dynamic includes a **songleader**, the tendency is for the group to join in with the leader as soon as they recognize the line and to sing together. As a result, the sound, while ragged at the ends, melismatic (when several distinct tones—usually three or more—are used to carry a single syllable), and tolerant of a certain amount of individual interpretation, adds up to something pretty close to one voice.

Or think of the sound of a **string band**— **fiddles**, **banjos**, **guitars**, and other instru-

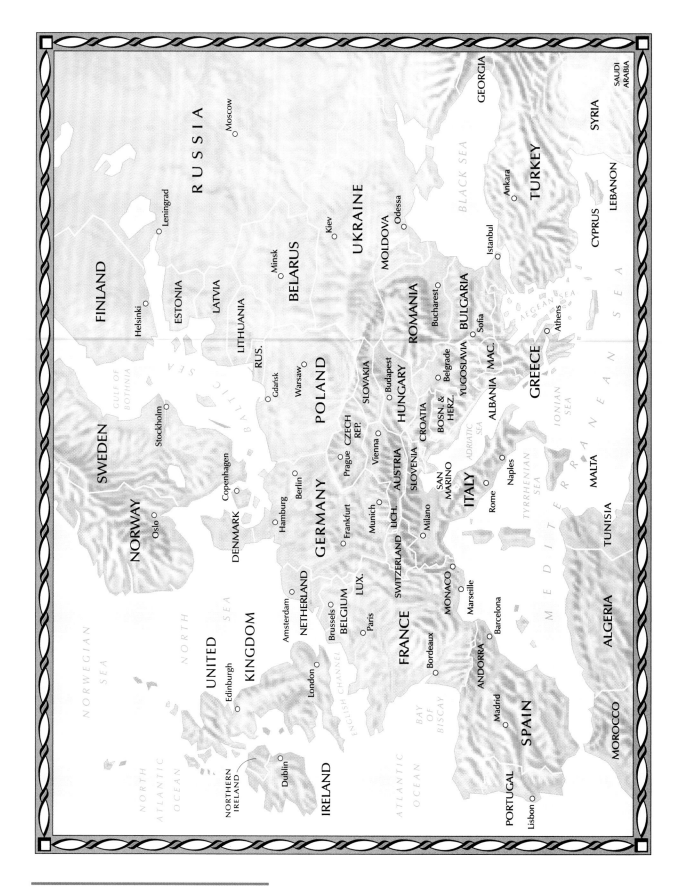

European Music Traditions

ments blazing away at dance music. The aesthetic there, it seems, is still a single-voiced one, where melody is what matters, even if the individual instruments take their own routes through the tune, some playing a version of the melody line, others providing rhythmic support for the melody. Most Irish instrumental music in the United States is based on this pattern as well. There, it's the tune that matters. Instruments in a session or accompanying dance may have a variety of roles and capabilities, but they hang together, and the tune is the thing. The closer we get to musical **forms** that most clearly reflect the influences of other musics or formal composers—**Western swing**, say, with its intimation of **jazz** timing, or the part-singing of some **shape-note** hymnody—the less pronounced the single-voicedness of the music is. But if it's music rooted in the British Isles, voice, story or text, and melody are likely to dominate in performances, whether **secular** or sacred, song or tune.

The musical traditions in this volume form the root of one of the oldest European musical cultures in the new world, the result of colonization by various populations from the British Isles. Over time, the music rooted in the British Isles began creative interactions with other musical traditions in the cultural mosaic that became the United States. As a result, although we use "British Isles" to categorize this volume's music, readers should understand that cultural interactions among many groups molded these musics in style and genre. At the start of the twenty-first century it is difficult to argue for a "pure stream" of British Isles music in the United States, but the musical traditions we label that way include genres and styles that many Americans continue to identify as quintessential examples of U.S. vernacular music.

Although the historical record is sketchy, it is safe to say that in their earliest embodiments the British Isles traditions in the new world were not significantly different from what the colonists had known at home. Over time, thanks to new cultural circumstances, the older music tended to develop its own distinctively American forms and styles of performance. In some cases, it localized and

remained vital in certain places only, as in the example of some forms of hymnody. It developed regional styles and **repertoires**, as any survey of U.S. fiddle music would demonstrate. In other cases it inspired or blended with other forms of musical creativity en route to the creation of new styles and genres. As twentieth-century musical innovations, bluegrass and Western **swing** exemplify that trend of innovation. But some of the old forms lost their vitality and exist today only in very marginal circumstances or as revived or preserved traditions. That is largely the case of the ballad, the **narrative song** that is one of the oldest forms of European music in the new world. All of the musical traditions in this volume thrived well into the twentieth century, though, and at the start of the twenty-first, many of them are still thriving if not always strongly represented in mass culture.

It is tempting to think of all of the British Isles music as early arrivals in North America. But some of the musical traditions in this volume came with more recent waves of immigrants. The Irish music that thrives in some U.S. cities is largely a twentieth-century development here, thanks to patterns of transatlantic immigration, and in some places, such as Boston and New York, its vitality is bound up with the continuing fact of immigration. Cape Bretoners in the Boston area play the Scottish-influenced music of their homeland, having gone to the "Boston states" out of economic necessity. Immigrant communities, no matter what their background, frequently use music as an important way to maintain social ties and to represent identity, and while many Americans stereotypically associate British Isles traditions with a long-vanished colonial English majority culture, some of the musical traditions this volume presents thrive in contemporary communities of immigrants.

Now complicate matters more by factoring in both the mass media and cultural diversity. Even the oldest of the musical traditions in this section exist, or existed, thanks in part to print. For example, the ballad, a genre deeply rooted in western European **oral tradition**, is inextricably tangled

up with printed **broadsheets**, both in Britain and the United States, where printers routinely published and sold song texts on **broadsides** into the early twentieth century. But the advent of inexpensive means of packaging and reproducing music—popular-culture phenomena such as **minstrel shows** and sheet music at first, but particularly sound recordings and radio in more recent years—had the dual effect of spreading many sorts of music beyond their localities and inspiring much cultural creativity. Beyond Native American traditions, one could argue that culture contact, especially, but not solely, between European and African Americans, gave us all distinctively American musical forms and that the mass media supercharged cultural exchange, accelerating it and raising the economic stakes.

Nearly all of this music was local at first, even if it was familiar in many different localities. Ballad singing, now nearly gone, was part of domestic life, a way to connect people and social values in the contexts of work and play. Based on English and Scottish templates, this form flourished in the United States, and a distinctive body of narrative folk songs developed in various American regions. Play-parties and dances were based in local communities, often part of household life, as in New England **kitchen rackets**.

Reflecting social change, over time many of these secular music traditions, especially dancing, moved from the home to more public events such as community picnics, **frolics**, and other local gatherings held at grange halls and schoolhouses. These domestic and community musical events provided some of the most important opportunities for musical exchanges between African American and white musicians, especially before the Civil War, when black musicians often entertained whites, especially by playing for dancing, at corn shuckings, balls, and other events. Although much American country dance was originally based on English and French patterns, it went on to assume regional forms in the United States, and in some places dance style and the music that accompanies it are both inflected by African American aesthetics and performance styles.

See glossary for definition of boldfaced terms

The commercialization of entertainment also furthered cultural exchange, even if from today's vantage point the entertainment itself seems permeated by racism. Black-face minstrelsy probably introduced the banjo to white musicians, where it became, for a brief time, a voguish instrument in genteel circles before developing its current association with **old-time** and bluegrass musics. Industrial and entrepreneurial developments transformed the banjo from a homemade, often rudimentary, instrument to a technically advanced, and sometimes highly adorned, musical instrument. These developments, coupled with the advent of mass merchandising, also led to the invention of the **autoharp**, the integration of the **mandolin** into string band music, the popularization of the guitar, and other new developments. Entrepreneurship created new commercial ventures such as public dances, which also fostered cultural exchange.

The early recording industry had a huge impact on the British Isles traditions. On one hand, early commercial recordings documented vernacular styles of music from various American regions. Some early recordings seem to have captured repertoires and performance styles that were direct reflections of an older British Isles set of traditions. On the other hand, the emergence of the recording industry encouraged new musical creativity, leading to twentieth-century popular forms based on the stylistic and generic conventions of older musical forms. Bluegrass is a case in point. Based on older string band music, with a strong dose of upland Southern religious singing traditions, it also shows a strong African American influence, especially rhythmically. Bill Monroe, who invented bluegrass, credited the influence of a Black guitar player from western Kentucky, Arnold Schultz. For a time, bluegrass was a regional popular music, very much commercialized in its performance settings and in its connection to radio and the recording industry. Over time, it transcended much of its regional base, and today it has an international following. Western swing is a parallel example, incorporating older fiddle

music styles with the swing music of its day, and reflecting the complicated cultural mix of its southwestern birthplace, where German American, Mexican American, and African American musicians (not to mention many others) influenced the creation of a number of regional popular musics. As the social base of much American music moved away from intimate local settings, new forms of commercially viable music—**rockabilly** and **honky-tonk**, for instance—built on the foundations of those community-based musics, playing a major role in the emergence of dominant forms of American popular music.

The availability of recording technology also gave impetus to the work of scholars and enthusiasts interested in documenting musical traditions. By the latter part of the nineteenth century, local enthusiasts, scholars, and others were publishing the results of songhunting field research. Early on, the ballad was a powerful draw, and many published collections feature ballads discovered in field research, typically in either the southeast or in New England. Sound recording technology allowed fieldworkers to document musical sounds and performances. Archival collections such as the Archive of Folk Song, established in 1928 at the Library of Congress (now the Archive of Folk Culture), developed as major repositories of sound recordings of a wide range of musical traditions.

Fieldworkers documented many examples of music rooted in the British Isles—remarkable fiddle players as well as occupational songs from loggers, cowboys, and miners, for example—as Americans came to understand that many of these musical traditions were vital in various communities. Some regional musics grew to be emblematic, featured at events such as early folk festivals, which often celebrated (and frequently manipulated) regional identities. The various waves of folk music revivals in the twentieth century often privileged British Isles traditions, as young, middle-class enthusiasts embraced mining songs from Kentucky, bluegrass music, shape-note hymnody, and other vernacular musical forms. Today, the immense popularity of various

"**Celtic**" musics, especially Irish music, comes in part from revivalist efforts in U.S. Irish communities, and Irish American communities and musicians are often connected to a transnational set of performers, recording companies, and venues.

In many cases, the musical traditions here reflect very significant cultural change. What was once the music of intimate community life is now often the music of enthusiasts from no particular community. The New England social dances that Nicholas Hawes writes about in this volume are now typically removed from locality. Dance enthusiasts travel from many places to dance together, and they often speak of a "dance community" rooted not in one locality but instead constituted at the dance events. Dancers may still use grange halls and other local venues, and they often valorize the dances as an old New England tradition, but they represent a very different demographic from the people who used to hold kitchen rackets.

Many of the musical traditions have moved away from their earlier functions. Old-time fiddling is primarily a music for concerts, festivals, and **jam sessions** these days, having moved away (although not entirely) from its association with dance. The same is at least generally true of Irish music in the United States, although the very end of the twentieth century saw the development of widespread interest in Irish step dance. There are probably more revivalist shape-note singers than religious congregations that sing the old shape-note hymns. Bluegrass music has a panethnic, international following; Western swing is more a concert music than a dance music. People organize themselves around some of these musical forms, forming old-time fiddlers associations, bluegrass trade organizations, or shape-note singing groups; creating festivals; circulating homemade and locally produced recordings; and publishing newsletters. Although in many cases their local environments have shifted, it is striking that so many of the U.S. musical traditions rooted in the British Isles have flourished so long, proving themselves adaptable to dramatic changes in community, entertainment, and notions of art in American society.

ANGLO-AMERICAN BALLADS AND FOLK SONGS IN VERMONT

Jennifer C. Post

Jennifer C. Post is assistant professor of music and curator of the Helen Hartness Flanders Ballad Collection at Middlebury College. She has conducted fieldwork in both India and New England and has published articles on women and music in India and on traditional music in northern New England.

Ballads and other folk songs played an important role in family and community social life in northern New England from the eighteenth to the twentieth centuries. Anglo-American ballads and folk songs dominated, yet French, Italian, and other European song traditions also played significant roles in the lives of residents during this period. The Anglo-American tradition was maintained at informal gatherings and carefully planned events in household, neighborhood, and occupational communities. The songs, transmitted in oral, written, and recorded form, were popular until the beginning of the twentieth century. By the middle of the century media influence and changing cultural values encouraged individuals and families to discard many songs that were once central to their family and community life. Songs popular today in the region are from different sources, yet provide evidence of continuity from the earlier traditions.

Singing traditions that continued in some families until the mid–twentieth century accompanied work and play, provided entertainment, and established or reinforced relationships in social groups. Singers of traditional songs in New England communities were seldom professionals, nor is there evidence that singers were singled out within a community as consistently as in the neighboring Canadian maritime provinces. Many communities, though, identified specific individuals who were well known as carriers of older song traditions or who could readily provide entertainment for a group of listeners with their knowledge of specific songs or **repertoires**.

Songs were sung in conjunction with communal activities and on occasions when people gathered specifically to sing. Singing also played an important role in daily life, especially to provide relaxation and to ease workloads. Historical information references songs sung during or after a work bee, or **hymns** and other songs sung by women who gathered in the afternoon to socialize after their chores were done. We know that

songs frequently accompanied women's—and sometimes men's—daily work.

In rural families living in Vermont (as well as in other northern states) mothers sang to their children to keep them occupied while the women finished their household chores. A Shrewsbury, Vermont, woman remembers her mother singing songs while doing her kitchen chores:

> During her work she would sing to pass away the time while she was doing her dishes or baking or skimming the milk pans—she had big pans of milk with cream on the top and she would skim the cream from the milk pans—and all that time she would be whistling or singing. And I had an older sister, and we loved to be entertained by our mother. And I remember so well, that in our kitchen we had a big woodbox behind the cookstove. It was painted sort of a cream color with a red trim and a nice wooden red top. And when my mother was mopping, my sister and I would get up on top of the woodbox and then we would plead with our mother, while she was mopping the kitchen floor, to sing to us. And our favorite song was called "Cabbage and Meat," but of course she sang lots of other songs that she'd learned from her father.

In addition to singing while working, women and men sang ballads and songs at small and extended family events and at neighborhood gatherings. It was not unusual for family members to gather in the living room to sing. A Ripton, Vermont, woman talks about her father's music at home:

> Sometimes, you know, when we had company, and sometimes when we was all alone he used to sit there and sing those songs. And he taught us the "Woodmen's Song" there, and that's how we learned our ABC's, I guess. . . . He used to sing "Down By the Old Mill Stream," you know that, and "I Wandered Today to the Hills, Maggie". . . and "Dar-

ling I Am Growing Old." And we used to sit around the table and sing. And then sometimes we'd go in what they called the parlor—the livin' room. And my brother and my sister'd play the organ and we'd sing.

In occupational communities, especially the lumber camps, men entertained one another in the evening with songs, dance tunes, and stories. This became an opportunity to exchange songs from family, regional, and occupational sources. The men who spent winter months in the camps returned to their farms in the spring and shared songs they learned with members of their families at home.

The repertoires of Vermonters included songs brought from the British Isles, regional or local songs learned at home, neighborhood, and occupational community gatherings, and songs learned from newspapers, magazines, recordings, and the radio. Northern New Englanders enjoyed humor, suspense, human tragedy, and moral lessons in the songs that they sang. The old ballads of the seventeenth, eighteenth, and nineteenth centuries, the local songs, and the more recent popular songs all provided this for them. Although we like to think that families in rural New England communities sat around and sang only the old British ballads, in fact they seldom distinguished among the many types of traditional, locally created, and popular songs that comprised their repertoires.

BALLADS AND SONGS

Anglo-American ballads, or **narrative songs**, that were popular in the northern New England states include ballads in classical and **broadside** categories as well as local or regional songs. The classical ballads compiled by Francis James Child in nineteenth-century Scotland and England are frequently characterized musically by their modality and textually by the way the stories are told. Generally the stories are impersonal. The dramatic retelling of a story may contain dialogue and nearly always includes exaggeration; the language is stylized and uses formulaic **phrases** and **stanzas**. Between 1920 and 1965 collectors in the region found examples of many ballads sung in communities in the nineteenth and twentieth centuries. These included the well-known titles "The Outlandish Knight" ("Lady Isabel and the Elf Knight," Child 4), "Lord Bateman" ("Young Beichan," Child 53), "The Farmers' Curst Wife" (Child 20), and "The Golden Vanity" ("The Sweet Trinity," Child 286) but also ballads that were not as well known in the United States, among them "Lizie Wan" (Child 51), "The Keach in the Kreel" (Child 281), and "Johnny Barbour" ("Willie O Winsbury," Child 100).

Johnny Barbour

Fair Mary sat at her father's castle gate
A-watchin' the ships coming in
Her father he came and sat by her side
For he saw she looked pale and thin
For he saw she looked pale and thin.

"Are you sick? Are you sick, dear Mary?"
    he said,
"Are you sick? Are you sick?" quoth he.
"Or are you in love with a jolly sailor lad
Who sails the distant seas?
Who sails the distant seas?"

"I am not sick, dear father?" she says,
"I am not sick?" quoth she.
"But I'm in love with a jolly sailor lad
Johnny Barbour is his name.
Johnny Barbour is his name."

"Is it so? Is it so, dear Mary?" he said,
"Is it so? Is it so?" quoth he,
"If you're in love with a jolly sailor lad,
Then hanged he shall be.
Then hanged he shall be."

Then the old man called up his merry,
    merry men,
By one, by two, by three,
Johnny Barbour had been very last man
But now the first was he.
But now the first was he.

"Will you marry my daughter?" the old
    man said,

"Will you marry my daughter?" quoth he,
"Will you sing and play and dance with
    her,
And be heir to my houses and land?
And be heir to my houses and land?"

"Yes, I'll marry your daughter," the
    young man said
"I'll marry your daughter," quoth he
"I'll sing, and play and dance with her,
But a fig for your houses and lands
But a fig for your houses and lands."

"Although Johnny Barbour is my name,
I'm the Duke of Cumberland,
And for every pound that you give to me,
I'll give her ten thousand pounds.
I'll give her ten thousand pounds."

—May Louise Harvey, Woodstock, Vermont, 1934

Some of the broadside ballads found in northern New England can be traced to songs popular in seventeenth-century England, Ireland, and Scotland. As in other regions, there is sharing of stylistic elements between the classical and broadside ballads. These ballads are descriptive and often show lyrical patterns including a "come-all-ye" opening and a tendency to complete the song with a moralizing stanza. Melodically, singers frequently use popular tunes for the ballads, thereby sharing tunes among metrically related groups of ballads. Broadsides of this type popular in Vermont before the middle of the century include "The Boston Burglar," "The Bold Soldier," "Mary of the Wild Moor," and "The Dark Eyed Sailor."

The Dark Eyed Sailor [Laws N35]

It was of a comely lady fair
Was walking out to take the air;
She met a sailor upon the way
And I paid attention, and I paid attention
To hear what they did say.

He says, "Fair lady, why do you roam
    alone
For the night is come and day's far gone?"
She said, while tears from her eyes did fall,

See glossary for definition of boldfaced terms

"It's my dark eyed sailor, it's my dark
   eyed sailor
That cause me my downfall.

"It's three long years since he left this
   land.
A gold ring he took from off my hand.
He broke the token in half with me
The other is rolling, and the other is
   rolling
In the bottom of the sea."

Says Willie, "Drive him from your mind
As good a sailor as he you'll find.
Love turns aside and cold doth grow
Like a winter's morning, like a winter's
   morning
When the hills are clad with snow."

These words did poor Phoebe's heart in-
   flame.
"Young man, on me you will play no
   game."
She drew a dagger and then did say,
"For my dark-eyed sailor, for my dark-
   eyed sailor
A maid I'll live and die."

Then Willie he did the ring unfold.
She seemed distracted with joy and woe.
"You are welcome, Willie. I have lands
   and gold,
For my dark-eyed sailor, for my dark-
   eyed sailor
So manly, true and bold.

In a cottage down by the riverside
In peace and harmony they do reside.
So girls, be true while your love's away.
Ofttimes a cloudy morning, ofttimes a
   cloudy morning
Brings forth a pleasant day.

—J. E. Shepard, Baltimore, Vermont,
   May 8, 1939

The American ballads in the region are
the product of the influence of both classical and broadside ballads on cultural expression of life in America. Musically and
textually they are patterned after British ballads yet retain a separate identity with local

James Shepard, Vermont
ballad singer, source for
"The Dark Eyed Sailor,"
photographed in
Baltimore, Vermont, c.
1930s

language and melodies used freely. These
ballads were passed both orally and in print
in Vermont and other northern New England states and were popular in labor communities (especially the lumber camps), in
families, and at village gatherings, particularly in the nineteenth and early twentieth
centuries. Locally created ballads also included stories of regional accidents, floods,
and murders and provided narratives of
everyday events. Included in the region are
songs describing accidents, such as a drowning described in "The Calais Disaster," or a
train accident in "The Hartford Wreck," both
from the late nineteenth century. The details
of murders are also described in ballads like
"Josie Langmaid (The Suncook Town
Tragedy)" and "The Murder of Sarah Vail."
The latter describes a murder that actually
took place in New Brunswick but was sung
by families in Maine as well as in Vermont.

The Murder of Sarah Vail

Come all you people lend an ear
A dreadful story you shall hear
This murderous deed was done of late
In eighteen hundred and sixty-eight.

There was a man called John Monroe
Who did Miss Vale a courting go,
This girl was handsome, young, and fair
Few with her that could compare.

Monroe was married it is true,
He had a wife and children, too,
But still Miss Vale he went to see
Not caring what the talk might be.

In course of time an offspring came,
Which brought to light their hidden
*   shame,*
But still together they did go
Until he proved their overthrow.

He led her to that lonely spot,
And there he fired the fatal shot,
A bullet buried in her brain,
She fell in death, there to remain.

Ballad and Folk Song
Origins in Vermont

Then killed the baby with a rush
And covered them with moss and brush,

And hurried off with rapid flight
Not thinking it would come to light.

The jury found it very plain
Miss Vale and baby had been slain,
The jury found it plain, also
That they were killed by John Monroe.

—A. Tolin, Chester, Vermont, 1934

LYRIC SONGS

In northern New England **lyric songs** and ballads were generally performed in the same social contexts. Lyric songs are identified by their expression of an emotional reaction to an experience or idea, rather than their focus on a narrative content (although narration may be implied). Frequently sung in the first person, lyric songs present interpersonal relationships and tend to speak in general terms, while ballads present specific situations. Like ballads, they use formulaic phrases and stanzas. Songs that express a connection to a social group or society (departure from homeland or family, political or economic conditions) are less common than those that express a relationship between individuals, especially between women and men (i.e., love songs). The lyric songs in the region demonstrate their adaptability to the needs of the singer and audience. The songs of northern New England show clear evidence of the sharing of classical and broadside traditions, British and American narrative songs, and also ballad literature and the lyric song. Like some of the broadside ballads, lyric songs can also be characterized by their borrowed and adapted tunes and texts.

"A-Walking and A-Talking" is an example of a lyric song from Vermont that is derived from the narrative tradition. Many songs of this type exhibit a flexible **form** with texts and tunes that grow and shrink with individual and regional tradition and practice. Found in many locations in the United States, Canada, and Great Britain, this version includes lines and stanzas related to "The Cuckoo," "The Unconstant Lover," "Irish Molly-O," and others.

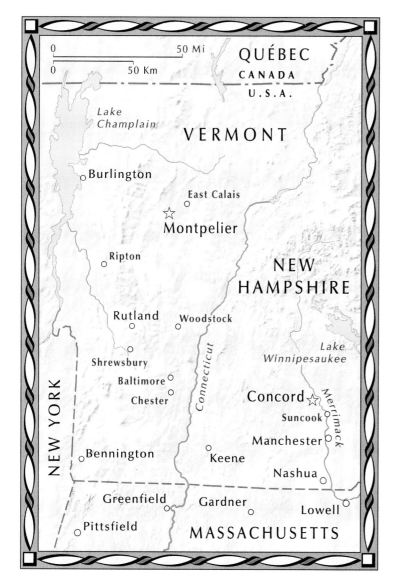

A-Walking and a-Talking

A-walking and a-talking and a-walking
  went I
To meet my sweet William; he's coming
  by'n bye;
To meet him in the meadow, is all my
  delight,
To walk and talk with him, from morning 'til night.
A meeting is a pleasure, but parting is grief,
And an unconstant lover is worse than a
  thief;
For a thief will but rob you and take all
  you have
While an unconstant lover will carry you
  to the grave.

The grave it will mold you, and turn you
  to dust.
There is scarce one in twenty, that a fair
  maid can trust;
They will coax and they'll flatter you, and
  tell as many lies
As the fish in the ocean or stars in the skies.

The cuckoo is a pretty bird; she sings as
  she flies,
She brings us glad tidings and she tells us
  no lies,
She sucks the sweet flowers to make her
  voice clear
And when she sings "Cuckoo" three
  months of the year.
Come all you pretty fair maids take
  warning by me,
Don't place your affections, on the green
  willow tree
For the tree will but wither, and the roots
  they will die.
Oh, if I am forsaken, I know not for why.
If I am forsaken it is only by one
And he's greatly mistaken if he thinks I'm
  undone;
I can court as little by him, as he can
  by me,
So adieu to these young men, who court
  two or three.

*Myra Daniels and Elmer George, East
Calais, Vermont, November 11, 1939*

Myra Daniels, ballad singer, with her cat, photographed in the early 1940s in East Calias, Vermont.

Lyric songs with a religious theme developed during the eighteenth and nineteenth centuries in conjunction with singing schools and the efforts to incorporate group singing into church services. In the camp meetings of the later nineteenth and early twentieth centuries, folk songs and tunes were adopted to supplement the Protestant hymns that were commonly taught. Characterized by their melodic connection to folk tunes, these religious songs were adopted in families and communities and sung along with ballads and **secular** songs popular at the time.

Play-party and other game songs were also popular in northern New England communities. Adults turned to them for entertainment, teenagers used them for courting, and young children sang them on the school playground. Some of the popular titles in Vermont include "Needle's Eye," "Old Cromwell (John Grumlie)," "Water, Water Wild Flowers," and "Go in and out the Window."

The American and British ballads described are not actively sung in Vermont today. Beginning in the 1920s in many northern New England communities, the "old songs" began to be replaced by songs transmitted on the radio and available on commercial recordings or printed on sheet mu-

sic. By the 1970s, 1980s, and 1990s a new generation of "old songs" referred not to the classical and broadside ballads, or even the local or regional ballads and early lyric songs, but to turn-of-the-century popular songs that were sung along with the older ballads. At the same time, though, the narrative tradition and the sentimentalism of the lyric song traditions continued in popular "**hillbilly music**," in Bradley Kincaid's versions of the old ballads, and in contemporary country music traditions. The old songs that were part of individual and family traditions for so long, while seldom sung, remain in the characteristic sentiment of the performances of contemporary popular songs.

BIBLIOGRAPHY

Child, Francis James. (1882–1898). *The English and Scottish Popular Ballads.* 5 vols. Boston and New York: Houghton, Mifflin and Company.

Flanders, Helen Hartness, and Brown, George. (1931). *Vermont Folk Songs and Ballads.* Brattleboro, VT: Stephen Daye Press.

Flanders, Helen Hartness, and Olney, Marguerite. (1953). *Ballads Migrant in New England.* New York: Farrar, Straus, and Young.

Flanders, Helen Hartness, et al. (1939). *The New Green Mountain Songster: Traditional Folksongs of Vermont.* New Haven, CT: Yale University Press.

Flanders, Helen Hartness, et al. (1960–65). *Ancient Ballads Traditionally Sung in New England.* Philadelphia: University of Pennsylvania.

Laws, G. Malcolm, Jr. (1957). *American Balladry from British Broadsides.* Philadelphia: American Folklore Society.

———. (1964). *Native American Balladry: A Descriptive Study and a Bibliographical Syllabus.* Philadelphia: American Folklore Society.

Renwick, Roger. (1996). "Ballad" and "Lyric Song." In *American Folklore: An Encyclopedia,* ed. Jan Harold Brunvand. New York: Garland.

PITTSBURG, NEW HAMPSHIRE: RECONSTRUCTING A COMMUNITY TRADITION

Jennifer C. Post

Please see Chapter 1 in this volume for biographical information on Jennifer C. Post.

If you drive through Pittsburg, New Hampshire, today, you seem to pass quickly through this northernmost New Hampshire town. In fact, Pittsburg is geographically large compared to other towns in the state; its 364 square miles accounts for 4 percent of the land, yet less than 1 percent of the population resides there (867 residents in 2000). Many social, cultural, and economic changes that took place in other parts of New England reached Pittsburg much later partly because of its distance from the urban centers of Concord, New Hampshire; Portland, Maine; Boston, Massachusetts; and Burlington, Vermont. Ultimately, changes did affect Pittsburg, and it began to look like many other small northern New England towns. Many of its unique characteristics are hidden in the memories of people who were young in the earlier years of the twentieth century.

THE TOWN

During the nineteenth and early twentieth centuries the most active social unit in this rural farming community was the neighborhood. As in other farm families throughout the United States at that time, Pittsburg's residents depended on one another for support; the resulting reciprocity turned into a pattern of farm mutuality that was crucial to the well-being of the family and community.

The character of the neighborhoods was affected by relationships to the local geography and by kinship ties. When social and economic changes altered connections to the land and family, the system began to break down. Today neighborhood schoolhouses are gone, replaced by a single regional school; the churches, grange hall, and stores that served as gathering places are weathered, and many are empty. Local businesses

The rolling hills and farms around the small town of Pittsburg, New Hampshire.
Photo © Phil Schermeister/CORBIS.

cater to visitors who travel to Pittsburg to snowmobile in the winter, hunt in the fall, and fish and hike in the summer. The tourist industry plays a huge role in the Pittsburg economy, replacing a lifestyle that once included self-sufficient farmers and lumbermen as well as individuals who contributed to local industry.

The town today combines elements of the old and the new. Some of the long-term residents still recall events of the past and continue their cultural practices in the yearly Old Home Day celebration, occasional **jam sessions**, and senior citizen's gatherings. **Fiddlers** also attend nearby competitions, such as the annual Stark Old Time Fiddlers' Contest.

MUSIC

At one time relatively equal time was given to singing and dance music traditions in the community. Families and neighbors gathered in both organized and casual meetings of friends to share songs and dances. Community residents recall a broad spectrum of songs and dance tunes with little concern for category. Songs include Anglo-American **ballads**, American and British popular songs, **play-party songs**, and **hymns**. Dance tunes demonstrate influence from the British

Isles, but many are part of a larger North American tradition that the media began disseminating in the early years of the twentieth century.

SONGS

When residents talk about musical practices of earlier years, they return again and again to certain songs, each time expressing similar memories about their community. In fact, specific songs seem universally to hold the sentiments of this once tightly-knit community, which is related by family and proximity as well as by common memory.

Among the songs once popular in Pittsburg, "Margery Gray" may be the one members of the older generation refer to most frequently. The ballad—actually a poem written by Julia Dorr in the nineteenth century—tells the story of a woman and her baby who become lost in the woods on their way home from visiting a friend. When Margery's husband returns at the end of the day to an empty house, he alerts his neighbors, and a community-wide search for his wife and child begins. Days later, Margery's baby dies, and she then wanders in the wilderness through the spring, summer, and fall. One day she arrives in Charlestown, New Hampshire:

Wondering glances fell upon her,
women veiled the modest eye,
As they slowly ventured near her,
drawn by pitying surprise.
"'Tis some crazy one," they whispered,
back her tangled hair she tossed.
"Oh, kind friends, take pity on me, for
I am not mad, but lost."

Then she told her pitiful story in a
vague despondent way,
And with cold white lips she mur-
mured, "Take me home to Robert
Gray."
"But the river," said they, pondered,
"how crossed you to its eastern side?
How crossed you those rapid waters,
deep the channel is and wide."

But she said she had not crossed it in
her desolated course.
She had wandered so far northward 'til
she'd reached the fountain source.
Through the dark Canadian forest and
then blindly roaming on,
Down the wild New Hampshire valley
her bewildered feet had gone.

Even today, many Pittsburg residents feel that Margery began her journey in their community. They trace her path from Back Lake (near the Connecticut River) in town up *above* the Connecticut Lakes (Third Lake), where she could cross into New Hampshire without traversing the rapid waters. Residents also make a connection to the story through common life experience. Men who worked in the woods as trappers, guides, and lumbermen know how easy it is to get lost in the woods; those who worked in the lumber camps say that hearing the song drove men to tears as they thought about their wives and children at home.

Residents also refer to other songs that have played an important role in the community. In locally created "Bright-Eyed Etta Lee," one elderly singer helped renew his connections to family, the land, and the community of his youth in Pittsburg. These lines, along with his recollections of Etta

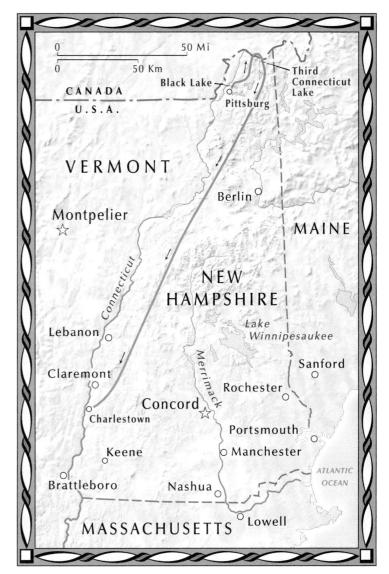

Path of Margery Gray

Lee, include geographical references, personal information, and genuine delight in the memory of an individual with whom his family had contact. His narrative expresses the sentiments of his family and frames his own memory of the world he grew up in:

In the golden vale of Pittsburg
Down by the Connecticut Stream
There dwells a maid that holds my heart
And haunts me like a dream.

At night my rest she does disturb
My mind is never free
All wishing her to be my bride
That bright-eyed Etta Lee.

Contra dancers in "old style" dress (including top hats and eighteenth-century dresses) promenading down the line.
Photographed at the Tunbridge, Vermont, "World's Fair," 1941, by Jack Delano. From the collections of the Library of Congress

Now Etta she is beautiful
Her cheeks are like the rose
The Connecticut River so full of fish
Down by her dwelling flows.

It's not the river, nor the fish
That has my dreams disturbed
I expect some day to make my wife
That bright-eyed Etta Lee.

Songs recounting tragic events and satirical songs commenting on individuals and their behavior were also popular in Pittsburg. "The Four Cousins," found in local manuscripts and still remembered by many in the community, preserves the details of a drowning accident that took place in the nineteenth century. In "The Bare Rock Song" ("The Rocky Road to Diamond") an entire road of families is described and satirized. Memories of these and other local songs play a role in continuing a collective memory of individuals and events in the community as well as expressing a common understanding of their sense of place in the geographic environment.

Recollections of British ballads also hold information on the community before the middle of this century. In earlier times, residents looked to individuals in the community to maintain singing traditions through organized and impromptu events. Evidence

that ballads such as "Lord Banner" ("Little Musgrave and Lady Barnard"), "Lord Lovel," and "The House Carpenter" ("The Daemon Lover") were valued by some members of the community can be heard in narratives of some of the elderly residents. While recalling **verses** of "The House Carpenter," one elderly man sang this stanza choked with emotion by the last line:

Oh its neither for your gold that I weep
Its neither for your store.
Its all for the sake of that darling little
babe
Which I never shall see any more.

His memories were of an older generation of singers, including his parents and family friends. "I used to like to hear them old-timers sing," he said. "Oh, they could sing it so nice. It almost brings tears to my eyes, because I used to like the whole of 'em.

Hymns were also popular and were sung by individuals at home, at neighborhood social occasions, and religious meetings, including camp meetings. Residents remember fewer titles or hymn texts, although references to hymn singing are made frequently. Several elderly residents remembered weekly religious meetings in nearby homes where hymns were accompanied by

Well-known fiddler and dance caller, Ed Larkin plays for the dancers, accompanied by an unidentified man in a top hat playing the melodeon (small pump organ).
Photographed at the Tunbridge, Vermont, "World's Fair," 1941, by Jack Delano. From the collections of the Library of Congress.

fiddle, piano, or organ. "They went a lot, not only just on Sundays, you know, during the week they had meetings," explained one resident. "And the people made a point of going, and that was more or less their social get-togethers, really. And that's where [my mother] learned hymns, I think."

DANCE MUSIC

Early social dance practices in Pittsburg involved neighbors who gathered together on a Saturday night to socialize, share food and drink, and enjoy music and dance. The kitchen dance both entertained and reinforced social bonds formed through mutual help during times of need. At the neighborhood dances, the fiddlers and their accompanists (on piano) came from within the community. This practice, popular in many rural American communities before the mid–twentieth century, went through a gradual transformation during the late nineteenth and mid–twentieth centuries, when residents adopted musical practices from outside the immediate region and an ever-widening group of participants began to attend local events. Ultimately the character of the dances changed, and they were moved out of private homes to locations that could accommodate larger ensembles and bigger crowds.

At neighborhood gatherings guests took part in a variety of dance- and music-related activities. They danced **contras**, **squares**, and **waltzes**, sang songs, and played games, all accompanied by local fiddlers with organ or piano. One resident whose family held weekly dances for many years remembered some of the popular steps:

> We used to have **kitchen junkets**. 'Course then we used to sing old time waltzes: "Alice Blue Gown" and "The Waltz You Save for Me." And then we'd have—they call 'em **square dances** now—we called 'em **quadrilles** then! "Soldier's Joy," "Boston Fancy," but we used to have a lot of galops, a lot of 'em call it **polkas** now—but it's two different dances.
>
> *Left foot, right foot*
> *Any foot at all*
> *Sally lost a bustle*
> *Coming home from the ball.*

Older members of the community also describe play-party games, such as "Go in and out the Window" and "On the Green Carpet." Adults and teenagers took part in these game songs, dancing from room to room of the large farmhouses.

House Dances and Kitchen Rackets

Nicolas Hawes was a freelance folklorist from 1975 until 1989, specializing in field projects and festivals (including the Smithsonian Festival of American Folklife) and producing records and films. He then served for two years as deputy director and the National Council for the Traditional Arts before assuming the post of assistant director of the Acadian Archives/Archives acadiennes at the University of Maine at Fort Kent. The following essay originally appeared in a Smithsonian Festival of American Folklife program guide (c. 1981).

It's Saturday night.

The second-floor ballroom over the town hall in the small Monadnock village of Fitzwilliam, New Hampshire, is filled with dancers. It's a mixed crowd: some old folks, some young, mostly people in their mid-twenties to early fifties. They are standing in couples, chatting restlessly, forming the long, double lines in which traditional New England **contra dances** are done. No one has announced that a contra is coming next, but then no one has to: all of these people have danced to Duke Miller before.

"I don't think Duke's changed his program in thirty years," my partner tells me. "Starts with a contra, three squares, a **polka**, and a break. Then the second set always begins with 'Chorus Jig'." She smiles happily. "He's just great!"

The small bandstand is crowded. Of the nine or ten musicians on the platform, only two have been hired to play—the lead **fiddler** and the piano player. These two sit back to back, the better to hear each other. Directly in front of them is Duke Miller's chair. There is no discussion of upcoming tunes. Like the dancers, the musicians know what's next.

Duke Miller works his way slowly across the bandstand. He is a solid-looking man in his eighties and wears a dark suit and tie and highly polished boots. He is rumored to be in poor health—

in fact, it is said that this might be his last regular dance in Fitzwilliam—but there is no sign of sickness in his voice. It is surprisingly young and strong.

"All right. The first dance is 'Chorus Jig.' First, third, and every other couple is active. You all know how it goes: active couples down the outside and down the middle. Cast off. Turn contra corners. . . ."

Duke nods to the fiddler; the fiddler nods to the piano player. The piano sounds out four chords "for nothing," and the dance begins.

"Chorus Jig" is a classic contra and a great favorite throughout New England. Each active couple dances the complicated figure through with the couple next in line—four movements, one to each eight-measure **phrase** of the music. After thirty-two measures, the tune repeats and so does the dance, but somehow each active couple has moved one place down the **set** and has a new couple with whom to do the figure. And so it goes, repeating again and again, until each couple has danced with every other couple in the set. Depending on the size of the hall, this may take up to fifteen minutes.

Once, twice, three times through the dance, Duke calls out the changes, reminding the dancers of the next move a measure or two ahead. Then, for a while, he just watches. Finally, sure that everyone's all right he settles back comfortably in his chair and closes his eyes.

This is not his first Saturday night in Fitzwilliam.

Each Saturday night, all across New England, in town and grange halls and church basements, people are dancing. There is nothing organized about these dances. They simply happen, a series of independent and very local affairs. Each is unique and is supported by a different community. The Fitzwilliam dance is one of the oldest and most old-fashioned in style. Duke Miller's mixture of contras, **quadrilles**, and singing squares

Fiddlers learned dance tunes from members of their family, from other fiddlers in the community, and also from recordings. One fiddler who began playing for dances in the early 1930s recalled playing "Soldier's Joy," "Boston Fancies," and "Smash the Window," along with tunes such as "Buckwheat Batter," "Rippling Water Jig," and "Black Velvet."

The active fiddlers and other instrumentalists traveled to play at area homes and halls. Fiddlers from the community also began to attend, and later to judge, contests in New Hampshire, Vermont, and Canada, spreading their versions of tunes but also accepting tunes and standards for **old-time** playing from a broader geographical region.

dates from the late 1920s and early 1930s, a period when the rural New England communities were more homogeneous and travel was more difficult than it is today.

Nowadays, most Yankee communities prefer a program of all singing squares like those called by Ralph Higgins of Chesterfield, Massachusetts. In a singing square, the dance directions are sung like lyrics to the **melody** of a popular tune such as "Darling Nellie Gray" or "Redwing." Unlike the contra or quadrille, where the dancers are reminded of the next figure a measure or two ahead, in the singing square the directions are given at the moment when the figure is to be danced. This makes it difficult to dance the figure in time with the appropriate music. Regular dancers solve this problem by memorizing the calls (in fact, many dancers sing along with the **caller**). Newcomers, however, have to stumble through behind the beat until they learn the dance.

One special feature of the square formation is its *exclusivity*—each couple dances only with the other three couples making up their set. Since New Englanders always dance three squares in a row before taking a break, this means that the same eight people dance together for as long as half an hour. And since many of the sets re-form after the break in the same spot on the dance floor and with the same four couples, the "all singing squares" program gives rural New Englanders an opportunity to strengthen and celebrate long-standing family and community relationships now being threatened by the spread of suburbia into the countryside. You may not know your neighbor any more, but you do know whom you're going to dance with on Saturday night.

Interestingly, the "newcomers"—the city people who have moved in large numbers into the small towns and villages now only a short commute from the cities—have adopted as *their* favorite dance the traditional New England con-

tra dance. And they've chosen it because, unlike the square, in a contra it's virtually impossible *not* to dance with every other couple in the hall. A contra dance is a great way for a group of relative strangers to gain a sense of community.

Thirty years ago only a handful of contras like "Chorus Jig" were commonly done, but the contra dance revival has grown to such proportions over the last fifteen years that in some parts of New England it is possible to dance contras five or six nights a week. Major dances, though, are still held on Saturday night. On special occasions, "dawn dances" and contras are danced from 8:30 P.M. until 6:00 or 7:00 A.M. Despite the simple, repetitive nature of contra dances and the small **repertoire** of basic moves (do-si-dos, allemande, swing, etc.) from which they are constructed, the number and variety of contras is apparently unlimited. So, also, is their adaptability. I've seen contras danced at weddings and private parties, in backyards, in hallways, on village greens, in parking lots, and in bars.

One of the most interesting group-dance traditions of the Northeast is the quadrille. Technically, a quadrille is a sequence of short **square dances** performed in sets of four (sometimes eight) couples. It was brought to this country from France and England in the early nineteenth century. Originally, each quadrille consisted of as many as five separate dance figures and, at the height of popularity, there were literally hundreds of different quadrilles. Many of the individual figures linger on as "prompted squares" at old-fashioned programs like the Fitzwilliam dance. But the quadrille as a *sequence* of dances survives today in Franco-American and Canadian maritime communities.

Each Saturday night at the French American Victory Club, in the Boston suburb of Waltham, a three-figure quadrille is still performed. The

(Continued on the next page)

Attending social dances was very important to many Pittsburg residents. As the tradition changed and dances were no longer held in their neighborhoods, many traveled to dances in nearby communities. The dance-music traditions also adapted to the changing interests and tastes of musicians and listeners. Thus, in Pittsburg, ensembles

were expanded to include other **instruments**, including **guitar**, **accordion**, trumpet, trombone, and drums. They also readily accepted influence from the media. Beginning as early as the 1930s some of the musicians organized **hillbilly** bands to accompany dances at the grange hall and other community per-

(Continued from previous page)

house band of **electric guitars**, piano, and drums leaves the stage, and a fiddler and caller take their places. Several dozen people get up to dance. At first glance, the Waltham quadrille appears merely to be a series of rather simple square dances, done in sets of four couples under the direction of the caller. **Repetition**, the secret of the quadrille, becomes apparent only after watching the dance are fully several times. The quadrille is *always* the same—the three figures are danced in the same order every time the quadrille is performed. In Waltham, the quadrille is danced three times a night. In contrast, in the Maritimes, the local version of the quadrille is danced dozens of times in an evening, with breaks only for **step dancing** and an occasional **fox-trot**.

To an outsider, it might seem boring to repeat the same dance so often, but dancing is not all that's going on here. The quadrille to the community of Waltham (like the Fitzwilliam dance to its community and the singing squares and contras to their communities) is more than a dance—it's a statement. It says to the dancers, their families, and friends, "This is who I am and this is where I belong." And that's a very important function of the New England Saturday night dance.

At the center of all traditional dancing in the Northeast is the fiddler. Without him, there is no dance. Only the flute, and earlier, the **fife**, has ever challenged the fiddle's dominance.

Since the earliest days, the roles of fiddler and caller have been intertwined. In some cases, certain dances were done only to specific tunes, and the fiddler, in choosing the tune, also chose the dance. But many fiddlers developed independent reputations as callers. Often the fiddler would just announce the dance and briefly review the figures before beginning to play. Some fiddlers, like the late Ed Larkin of Vermont, would call the changes and simultaneously play the tune.

A fiddler alone was enough to make a band for a small dance. In fact, at the informal house dances, or "**kitchen rackets**," there was rarely enough room for more musicians anyway, and often the fiddler had to perch precariously on a stool in the kitchen sink. In the early twentieth century, the accompaniment (if any) was provided by the parlor pump organ. Today, piano backup is standard, and **guitars**, **mandolins**, **tenor banjos**, and flutes round out the orchestra. Still, no matter what the makeup of the band, it's the fiddler who sets the tempos and chooses the tunes.

Although each of the major traditional northeastern communities (Yankee, French Canadian, Scottish, and Maritime) has developed and maintained its own vigorous and distinctive fiddle

formance spaces. Dance orchestras were also formed to support the increasing interest in dances outside the home environment.

Music in Pittsburg reflects changing interests and needs in this rural farming and lumbering community. Residents' narratives confirm that the dynamic singing tradition in the community was dependent upon shared community values and practices continued by relationships that occurred in household, neighborhood, and occupational spheres. As the geographical and social gaps between families, generations, neighbors, and communities widened, the tradition began to change.

Today the music connected to community traditions of the nineteenth and early twentieth centuries is heard in some homes on cassette, CD, and videotape and at public events where local musicians play fiddle, guitar, accordion, and drums to accompany old-time dances. The local songs, the British ballads, and even the popular songs of the earlier years are offered only as memories. For many, active singing has been replaced by active listening to country songs and other popular **genres**. The memory of the old songs and dances gives residents an opportunity to recall and to celebrate common experiences among relatives, neighbors, friends, and co-workers.

BIBLIOGRAPHY

Pike, Robert. (1935). "Folk Songs from Pittsburg, New Hampshire." *Journal of American Folklore* 48/190: 337–351.

———. (1984). *Tall Trees, Tough Men: An Anecdotal and Pictorial History of Logging and Log-driving in New England.* New York: Norton.

styles, they all share characteristics that distinguish them from other major fiddle regions of North America. Among these characteristics are **unison** (one rarely hears **harmony** or countermelodies), distinct articulation, and absence of **variation**. Additionally, there is a high degree of musical literacy. Many fiddlers learn much of their repertoire from printed sources, and tunes in the "flat keys" (F, B-flat, and even E-flat) are not uncommon.

All of these fiddle styles, all of these traditional dances, are still alive all over New England. Indeed, they thrive at the Saturday night dances.

BIBLIOGRAPHY

Nevell, Richard. (1977). *A Time to Dance*. New York: St. Martin's Press.

Sweet, Ralph. (1966). *Let's Create Old Tyme Square Dancing*. Hazardville, CN: n.p.

Tolman, Beth, and Page, Ralph. (1976). Reprint. *The Country Dance Book*. Original edition, 1937.

Van Cleef, Joy. (1976). "Rural Felicity: Social Dance in 18th-Century Connecticut." *Dance Perspectives* 65, no. 17 (spring).

DISCOGRAPHY

The Dances Down Home. 1977. Joseph Cormier. Rounder 7004. Jacket notes by Mark Wilson; insert booklet by Sam Cormier.

La Famille Beaudoin/The Beaudoin Family. 1976. Louis Beaudoin. Philo 2022. Jacket notes by Paul F. Wells.

John Campbell: Cape Breton Violin Music. 1976. Rounder 7003. Jacket notes by Mary Campbell and Mark Wilson.

Maritime Dance Party. 1978. Gerry Robichaud. Fretless FR 201. Jacket notes and insert sheet by Tony Parkes.

Music from Cape Breton, Vol. 2: Cape Breton Scottish Fiddle. 1978. Various artists. Topic 12TS354. Jacket notes and booklet by John Shaw.

New England Traditional Fiddling: An Anthology of Recordings, 1926–1975. 1978. Various artists. John Edwards Memorial Foundation JEMF-105. Jacket notes and insert booklet by Paul F. Wells.

The Rakish Paddy. 1975. Paddy Cronin. Fiddler FRLP-002. Jacket notes by Frank H. Ferrel.

Vermont Fiddler. 1978. Ron West. Fretless FR 132. Jacket notes by Norma West Mayhew.

Violoneux à l'ancienne mode de Chicoutimi, Québec/Old Time Fiddler of Chicoutimi, Quebec. 1998. Louis Boudreault. Voyager VRCD 322. CD reissue of 1977 LP.

Nicholas Hawes

———. (1987). *Spiked Boots: From New England's North Country, True Stories of Yesteryear, When Men Were Rugged and Rivers Wild*. Dublin: Yankee Publishing.

A BRIEF SOCIAL HISTORY OF FIDDLING IN NEW ENGLAND

Paul F. Wells

Paul F. Wells is director of the Center for Popular Music and associate professor of music at Middle Tennessee State University. His research interests encompass a broad spectrum of American vernacular music, with fiddling and fiddle tunes his primary focus. The following essay is an abridged version of a piece that was originally published in the booklet that accompanies the record album entitled New England Traditional Fiddling: An Anthology of Recordings, 1926–1975, *released in 1978 by the John Edwards Memorial Foundation at the University of California, Los Angeles. Although minor revisions have been made to the original essay, there has been no comprehensive attempt to update it in light of the author's continued research.*

EARLY HISTORY

People in New England have been **fiddling** and dancing to fiddle music since the seventeenth century. Historical evidence relating to fiddling, and dancing in the colonial era is sparse, but sufficient to establish the fact that fiddling and dancing were popular amusements. To give just one example, in 1679 in Salem, Massachusetts, a man named John Wilkeson had to stand before the court to answer charges that he kept "bad order" in his house, including allowing excessive drinking, fiddling, and dancing (Scholes 1934, p. 376).

The music played by people described as fiddlers in colonial times would be unfamiliar today's players. The types of fiddle tunes that are now common, including **jigs**, **reels**, and **hornpipes**, did not become common until the mid-to-late eighteenth century (though some jigs may be somewhat older). However, dance music played on the violin existed before this time. The violin emerged around 1550 and was used almost exclu-

sively as a dance **instrument** in its early years. In all likelihood the instrument merely served as a new medium for the performance of an extant corpus of dance music (Boyden 1961, pp. 110–114). The music found in John Playford's *The English Dancing Master,* originally published in London in 1651, illustrates the type of dances and dance tunes that were popular in seventeenth-century England and that would have been brought to New England by English colonists.

With the Revolutionary era, data on fiddling and fiddle music becomes more plentiful. It is from this time that we have the first concrete information about specific tunes known in early New England and are thus able to establish a link with present-day tradition. The earliest book I have seen containing tunes that are still current in the fiddler's repertoire is a reprint of a manuscript originally owned and compiled in 1777 by Giles Gibbs, Jr., a fifer from Ellington, Connecticut. Contained in Gibbs's book are such popular fiddle tunes as "Flowers of Edin-

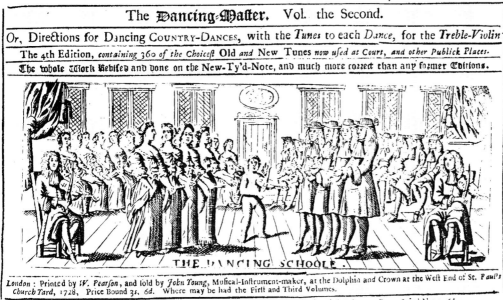

The Dancing-Master. Vol. the Second.

Or, Directions for Dancing COUNTRY-DANCES, with the *Tunes* to each *Dance*, for the *Treble-Violin*

The 4th Edition, *containing 360 of the Choicest* Old and New Tunes *now used at Court, and other Publick Places.*

The whole Work Revised and Done on the New-Ty'd-Note, and much more correct than any former Editions.

THE DANCING SCHOOLE.

London : Printed by *W. Pearson*, and sold by *John Young*, Musical-Instrument-maker, at the Dolphin and Crown at the West End of St. Paul's *Church Yard*, 1728. Price Bound 3s, 6d. Where may be had the First and Third Volumes.

, *Note*, Here is also to be had, the Basses to all the Dances contain'd in the First Volume. Price Stitch'd 1 s. 6d.

Cover of the second volume of John Playford's famous *Dancing Master*. These volumes gave the melodies and instructions for popular dances as performed in seventeenth century England.
From the collections of the Library of Congress.

burgh," "Cuckoo's Nest," "Rakes of Mallow," "White Cockade," and "Saint Patrick's Day," all known in various versions today. The fact that fiddlers and fifers of this time shared, to a certain degree, a common repertoire can easily be seen by comparing the tables of contents of early violin and fife instruction books, as many of the same tunes are given in each type of book. (See Bayard 1944, pp. xii–xiii, and Bayard 1966 for additional comments on the relationship between fiddle and fife music.)

Little is known of the individuals who were active fiddlers at this time. In the late eighteenth century, a man named Hugh Talent, servant of a Colonel Saltonstall of Haverhill, Massachusetts, was said to have been "'an exile of Erin' and a famous fiddler withal" (Chase 1861, p. 309). In her diary of 29 April 1874, Mrs. Mary (Vial) Holyoke of Salem, Massachusetts, stated that she "paid James Noland the fidler for Instructing Children" (Holyoke 1911, p. 110). Lyman Beecher, an important clergyman and educator in the early nineteenth century who lived much of his life in New England, was an enthusiastic, if not proficient, fiddler. His daughter, author Harriet Beecher Stowe, described his interest in music:

Often his old faithful friend the violin was called in requisition, and

he would play a few antiquated **contra dances** and Scotch airs out of a venerable yellow musicbook which had come down the vale of years with him from East Hampton. Auld Lang Syne, Bonnie Doon, and Mary's Dream were among the inevitables; and a contra dance which bore the unclerical title of 'Go to the devil and shake yourself' was a great favorite with the youngsters. He aspired with ardent longings to Money Musk, College Hornpipe, and sundry other tunes arranged in unfavorable keys, although he invariably broke down, and ended the performance with a pshaw! In after years, after his mind began to fail, nothing would so thoroughly electrify him as to hear one of his sons who was proficient on the violin, performing those old tunes he had tried so many times to conquer (Cross 1961, vol. 2, p. 87).

Merrill Ober, a resident of Monkton, Vermont, kept a diary for part of the year 1848, at which time he was sixteen years old. He had begun to play the flute in 1846 and took up the violin in May 1848. His diary reveals that he was an enthusiastic musician who possessed the ability to read and write music and who played at local dances (Ober 1928, pp. 32–40).

One intriguing fact regarding fiddlers from this period is that many of them were black men. Northampton, Massachusetts, had one, or possibly two, black fiddlers in the late eighteenth century. James Russell Trumbull, in his *History of Northampton,* reports that "Before the Revolution, Midah, a negro employed in a tannery of Caleb Strong, Sr., was the principal fiddler in town," (Trumbull 1902, vol. 2, p. 562), while another writer states that "Late in the 18th century Moidore, a negro fiddler, was favorably known in the neighborhood by his playing for dancing" (Hale 1922–23, p. 341). It is possible that both of these writers were referring to the same fiddler, but unfortunately, neither specifies the source of their information.

In the course of what must have been a wild night in Providence, Rhode Island, on 26 January 1780, Dr. Zuriel Waterman, surgeon aboard the privateer *Argo,* notes that as a part of the general revelry in which the ship's company indulged, they "got a Negro Fidler & proceeding up town went in to a house to have a dance" (Waterman 1962, p. 136). In a description of a dance of unspecified date but which presumably took place early in the nineteenth century in New Hampshire, the music was supplied by a fiddler who is referred to as "Black Pelham" (Hatch 1887, p. 25). A man named Joe Brown who was commonly called "Black Joe" and who had served in the Continental Army during the Revolution was a popular fiddler in Marblehead, Massachusetts. He was of mixed blood, "his father having been a Gay Head Indian and his mother a Negress" (Roads 1897, p. 288). His house was a favorite gathering place on festive occasions: "When darkness prevented the enjoyment of outdoor games, the floors of the house were sanded and everybody went in for a reel and a jig. Then Black Joe took up his fiddle and sawing away, played the only tune he knew, until late into the night, keeping a constant accompaniment with his foot" (Roads 1897, p. 288). Sleighing parties from Boston journeyed to taverns in nearby Med-

ford and "brought with them their 'fiddler' or engaged the services of Greenough, a noted colored fiddler of Medford. . . ." (Brooks 1886, pp. 389–390).

The number of reports of black fiddlers in the late eighteenth century and the off-hand manner in which these men are mentioned suggests that at this time the role of "village fiddler" in New England was commonly filled by blacks. However, the phenomenon of black fiddlers playing for white dances in the eighteenth century was not limited to New England. To give just one example, Richard Hunter, a British traveler in the 1780s, journeyed to Baltimore and attended a dance there on 9 November 1785. During the course of the evening, he was obliged to take over the musical duties from the man who had been engaged for the evening when "the poor Negro's fingers were tired of fiddling" (Hunter 1943, p. 181).

Although most of the material that I have seen relating to black fiddlers in New England is from the late eighteenth century, a description of a dance in Deerfield, Massachusetts, in 1892 reveals that the music was provided by "'Old Put' the colored fiddler" (Coleman 1933, p. 98). Black fiddlers who play Anglo-American dance tunes have certainly existed in the south in more recent times. R. P. Christeson, for example, recorded many tunes from Bill Driver, whom he described as "one of two famed colored fiddlers in Missouri" (Christeson 1973, p. xi). At present, I have seen too little material to be able to draw any conclusions about the precise geographical and chronological dimensions of this phenomenon. It is a fascinating topic that should be investigated extensively.

Professional or semiprofessional dancing masters had been plying their trade in New England since the latter part of the seventeenth century, but very little is definitely known about their activities until a century later. Many dancing masters at the turn of the nineteenth century published books of dance instructions, and those that have survived provide an indication of the type of dances that were then being taught. Two collections from this time have been available for examination, and although they contain

See glossary for definition of boldfaced terms

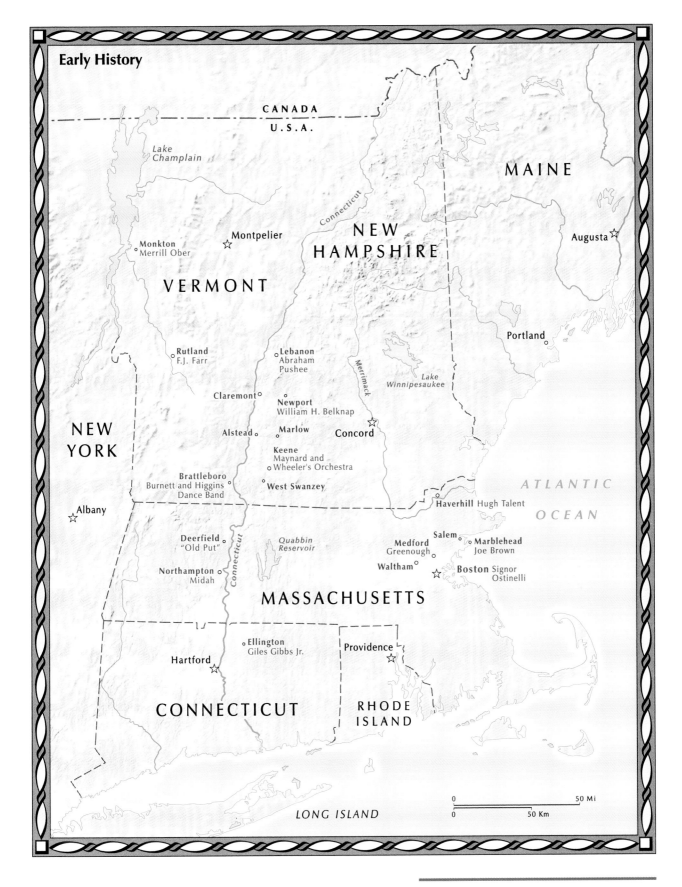

Early History

CANADA
U.S.A.

Lake Champlain

MAINE

Monkton
○ Merrill Ober

☆ Montpelier

Connecticut

NEW
HAMPSHIRE

☆ Augusta

VERMONT

○ Rutland
F.J. Farr

Lebanon
○ Abraham
Pushee

Claremont ○

Newport
○ William H. Belknap

Merrimack

Lake Winnipesaukee

Portland

NEW
YORK

Alstead ○

○ Marlow

☆ Concord

Keene
Maynard and
○ Wheeler's Orchestra

Brattleboro
Burnett and Higgins ○
Dance Band

○ West Swanzey

☆ Albany

Haverhill Hugh Talent
○

ATLANTIC

OCEAN

Deerfield ○
"Old Put"

Connecticut

Quabbin Reservoir

Salem
Medford ○
Greenough ○

○ Marblehead
Joe Brown

Northampton ○
Midah

Waltham ○

☆ Boston Signor
Ostinelli

MASSACHUSETTS

Ellington
○ Giles Gibbs Jr.

Providence
☆

Hartford
☆

CONNECTICUT

RHODE
ISLAND

| 0 | | 50 Mi |
| 0 | | 50 Km |

LONG ISLAND

Eighteenth-Century Fiddlers of New England

25

only dance instructions and no music, the titles of many of the dances, such as "Soldier's Joy," "Fisher's Hornpipe," and "The Cuckoo's Nest," can be linked to perennially popular fiddle tunes and undoubtedly were intended to be danced to the tunes of the same name. (For more information, see John Griffiths's *A Collection of the Newest Cotillions, and Country Dances* and the article "An Eighteenth-Century Collection of Contra Dances.") It is possible that tunes were omitted from dance collections because the dancing masters were primarily concerned with promoting their own choreographic creations and merely assumed that the appropriate tunes would be in the repertoire of any practicing dance musician. Dancing masters may, in fact, have provided their own music, as many of them included instruction on the violin (and other instruments) in their advertisements. (See Pichierri 1960, pp. 215–238, for some New Hampshire examples.)

Another intriguing aspect of fiddling from this time is the existence of a class of professional stage fiddlers, but present knowledge of such musicians is very sketchy. In New York City there was a dwarf fiddler named Mr. Hoffmaster who composed the famous tune "Durang's Hornpipe" for dancer John Durang in the late eighteenth century (Wilson 1976, p. 13). Hoffmaster seems to have had counterparts in New England. A Signor Ostinelli from Boston, described as "the most famous violinist of the day in this country" and who played with musical groups in Claremont, New Hampshire, in the 1830s (Waite 1895, pp. 312–373), may have been the composer of "Ostinelli's Reel" and "Souvenir de Venice Hornpipe," both of which appear in *One Thousand Fiddle Tunes* (p. 41 and p. 109). Abraham Pushee of Lebanon, New Hampshire, was not a stage professional, but was "a noted performer on the violin and teacher of dancing" (Waite 1895, p. 373). Pushee played at an elegant ball at the Eagle Hotel in Newport, New Hampshire, in 1823 and is credited with composing "Pushee's Hornpipe" and "Young America Hornpipe," also in *One Thousand Fiddle Tunes* (p. 88, p. 101). The subsequent

history of stage fiddlers extends through **minstrel** and vaudeville performers and may even include musicians such as Don Richardson and Charles D'Almaine who recorded many fiddle tunes in the early days of the phonograph industry. A thorough study of such fiddlers and their place in the broad scheme of American fiddling is needed.

In the second half of the nineteenth century, fiddling in New England underwent numerous changes. New types of dances and dance music were introduced that did not necessarily eliminate the old types but replaced them in fashionable circles. In addition to such normal evolutionary developments, the influx of large numbers of immigrants from Ireland and Canada brought new styles of fiddling to the area.

By the second half of the century, **quadrilles** and quadrille bands had become popular. The term "quadrille" originally referred to a fixed set of five or six different **cotillions** that were performed from memory rather than with the use of a **caller** or prompter, but its subsequent usage is varied and confusing. It is sometimes used to refer to any set of different figures for a **square dance** (often combining tunes in 2/4 and 6/8 time) whether called or not; sometimes to refer to a single square dance in 6/8 time; and sometimes simply to refer to any square dance. At any rate, quadrilles were originally fashionable dances, and in this capacity they superseded the cotillions and Country Dances of the previous generation.

The new fashion in dances was accompanied by the emergence of quadrille bands, consisting of several musicians and including wind instruments such as clarinet, flute, or cornet in addition to one or two fiddles, string **bass**, and piano or organ (Page 1971, Part 2, p. 13). One such band was Burnett and Higgins's dance band, which was formed in Brattleboro, Vermont, in 1860 (Kull 1961, p. 59). Others were those led by William H. Belknap of Newport, New Hampshire (organized in 1856), and by F. J. Farr of Rutland, Vermont (Wheeler 1879, p. 215). The activities of many southern New Hampshire and Vermont bands can be

See glossary for definition of boldfaced terms

traced through the reprints of articles from local newspapers that are included in the column "It's Fun to Hunt," a regular feature of *Northern Junket,* a dance magazine published by New Hampshire caller Ralph Page. From this source we learn that Burnett and Higgins's band was active into the 1880s. Keene, New Hampshire, had its own popular quadrille band during the 1870s, and a later organization in the same town, described merely as the "Keene Orchestra," was active in the late 1880s, featuring the fiddling and prompting of one George Long, who was known as "one of the best, if not the best." One member of the Keene Quadrille Band, G. B. Wheeler, second violinist, joined forces with T. Maynard, first violinist from Taylor and Long's Band, to form Maynard and Wheeler's Orchestra, which played around the Keene-Alstead area in the mid-1880s.

Sometimes these bands played for dances on special occasions and holidays or for money-raising affairs sponsored by local churches or firefighting organizations, but many dances were organized simply as social events. As reported in *Northern Junket,* a note in the *Cheshire Republican* (published in Keene) for 7 February 1880 states that in nearby West Swanzey, "Quadrille parties are taking the lead among the amusements of the day." Each town seems to have had its own dance promoter or promoters, and A. T. Dinsmore of Alstead and Colonel Petts of Marlow were two individuals who were engaged in this activity.

However, these formal or semiformal dancing parties were not the only occasions for dancing in rural New England at this time. Two venerable social institutions, the husking bee dance and the kitchen dance (also known as the **kitchen junket** or **kitchen racket**) were also popular. Both types of dances may date back to the first part of the century or even earlier, but the earliest documentation that I have seen is from the late nineteenth century.

Husking bees took place in the autumn of the year. After a farmer's corn had been harvested, friends and neighbors would get together to help him husk the ears. Social-izing, singing, and storytelling would accompany the work. The discovery of a red ear was of special significance and in some cases entitled the finder to a kiss from a member (or members) of the opposite sex, but in others obliged him or her to pay a forfeit. Supper and a dance followed the labor. (See Little 1888, p. 470, and Hatch 1887, pp. 188–189, for contemporary descriptions of husking bees.)

Many old New England farmhouses had kitchens that were large enough to contain a group of dancers. In the classic kitchen dance, all furniture was removed from the kitchen, including the stove, and the fiddler played while seated on a stool in the sink.

NEW INFLUENCES

Up to this point it has been feasible to talk of a single fiddle tradition in New England. Differences undoubtedly existed between various localities, and the introduction of new tunes, playing techniques, and performance situations surely made the fiddling of the nineteenth century different from that of the seventeenth and eighteenth centuries. Nevertheless, we have been dealing with what was essentially one continuous line of development. However, the arrival of several groups of immigrants in the second half of the nineteenth century brought new fiddling traditions to the New England states.

Probably the most important, in terms of impact on present-day New England fiddling, were the French Canadians. There were several reasons for their immigration to the United States. First of all, much of rural Quebec, from where most of the immigrants came, was beset by general economic distress in the nineteenth century. Economic prospects were very bleak, especially for young people who were just starting life on their own. The United States Civil War offered an opportunity for young men to escape the conditions at home, and it is estimated that 40,000 French Canadians served in the Union Army (Podea 1950, p. 367). Coincidental with and partially caused by the Civil War was the tremendous growth of industry in New England. With more jobs than workers available, mill owners turned to rural Quebec as a source of cheap manpower, sometimes employing earlier immigrants as recruiting agents. This emigration from Canada continued throughout the second half of the century, and by 1900, there were over half a million French Canadians in New England (Podea, p. 369). The majority of these immigrants found work in the textile mills in cities such as Lawrence, Lowell, Holyoke, and Fall River in Massachusetts; Nashua and Manchester in New Hampshire; Lewiston, Biddeford, and Sanford in Maine; and Providence and Woonsocket in Rhode Island.

The French Canadians experienced problems similar to those of other immigrant groups in this country. Low wages, poor living conditions, unfamiliar working situations, prejudice from other groups, and differences of language and culture often made life unpleasant. However, with the passage of time, many became skilled workers and ultimately were able to rise on the social and economic scale. Also, like other groups, French Canadians formed their own communities within the cities where they worked, creating a situation that fostered the preservation of their native culture.

A strong fiddling tradition had existed in Quebec and was undoubtedly brought to the "Little Canadas" of the New England mill cities. The historical background of French Canadian fiddling is complex and has yet to be thoroughly researched, but a few general points can be made. Many tunes of Anglo-Celtic origin occur in the repertoire of present day French Canadian fiddlers, probably as the result of contact between French and British settlers in Canada. However, a relationship between the dance traditions of France and the British Isles existed prior to the settlement of the New World. In the late seventeenth century, the popularity of the English "Country Dance" spread throughout much of Europe, including France. In 1688, a Parisian dancing master went to England and noted down some Country Dances to teach in his own country (Sachs 1937, p. 420). Such dances apparently became quite

See glossary for definition of boldfaced terms

popular there, and early in the eighteenth century, the French introduced their own modification of the Country Dance, the ***contredanse*** *française* (later anglicized to "contra dance") or *cotillon* (later anglicized to "cotillion") (Sachs, pp. 421–422). Whereas the Country Dance could accept an unlimited number of couples, this was a dance for four couples and was, in fact, the square dance. This new "French Country Dance" in turn became popular in Britain, and thus, the dance traditions of both British and French settlers in North America were probably similar in many ways. In addition to this imported tradition and the influence from other groups in Canada, local changes in repertoire and technique strictly among French fiddlers in Canada have undoubtedly been factors in shaping the development of French Canadian fiddling.

It is difficult to judge how much influence French Canadian fiddling had on the Yankee tradition in the nineteenth century. In addition to the immigrants to the mill cities, numerous French Canadians also moved to rural areas in northern New England, and it seems likely that more avenues of cultural exchange would have existed in these areas than in the cities. French Canadian tunes are currently played by most fiddlers throughout New England, but it is difficult to determine how far back in time this phenomenon extends. Possibly it has occurred only since the advent of radio and the phonograph.

The French Canadians were not, however, the first group of immigrants to make an impact on New England's population. They were preceded by large numbers of people from Ireland who began arriving in the 1840s following the famine in that country. Irish immigrants continued to arrive throughout the second half of the century. By 1875, they constituted one-seventh of the total population of Massachusetts (Knight 1975, p. 76). There had been Irish people in New England prior to this period of mass immigration, and it is estimated that in 1775, 4 percent of the population of Massachusetts was Irish (Knight, p. 74). But, while these earlier arrivals tended to become absorbed into mainstream American culture,

many of the immigrants in the late nineteenth century formed distinct Irish communities in New England cities, primarily Boston. This is an important point in terms of measuring Irish influence on fiddling in New England. Mention has already been made of Hugh Talent, an Irishman who played the fiddle and lived in Massachusetts in the late eighteenth century. Undoubtedly there were others like him, and these fiddlers contributed an Irish influence to the shaping of Yankee fiddling. The fiddling of later arrivals from Ireland, which would have reflected any developments that had occurred in Irish music after the emigration of Hugh Talent and his contemporaries, may or may not have had a direct impact on existing New England fiddling. The degree of influence would have depended on how much social and musical interchange actually occurred between these people and New England natives.

The available evidence relating to Irish fiddling in rural New England is sparse and inconclusive. Francis O'Neill tells of Reverend J. T. Walsh, a priest in East Hampton, Connecticut, who during his youth in County Waterford had become a good fiddler but who had given up music. "Marooned for a quarter of a century among the New England Yankees, he had lost interest in almost everything but the spiritual welfare of his congregation" (O'Neill 1913, pp. 172–173). Father Walsh can scarcely be viewed as a likely source of dissemination of Irish music in New England!

On the other hand, the existence of "Daniel O'Connell's Welcome to Parliament"—a tune named after an Irish political leader of the famine era—in the repertoire of L. O. Weeks, a Vermont fiddler of the early twentieth century who described himself and his family background to collector Alan Lomax as "Yankee," may indicate that some interaction did actually take place. Again, more evidence is needed to assess accurately the musical influence of Irish immigrants in the nineteenth century.

Yet another group of people with a strong, distinctive fiddling tradition came to New England at this time. These were people of Scottish descent from Cape Breton Island, Nova Scotia, who moved to Boston in search of jobs. Their ancestors were Scottish Highlanders who had migrated to the New World in the late eighteenth century. The defeat of the supporters of Bonnie Prince Charlie at the Battle of Culloden in 1746 radically altered the lifestyle of the Highlanders, and throughout the next hundred years, many of them left their native land for a variety of political, economic, and religious reasons. The settlers in Cape Breton retained a strong Highland culture, and the island has become famous for its traditions of music and dance.

By the late nineteenth century, many of the farm families on Cape Breton had grown too large for the land to support, and the young people were forced to look elsewhere for employment. Some went to industrial areas on Cape Breton, primarily to Sydney or to other cities in Canada, but many also settled in Boston. A strong Cape Breton community that still exists today was established in the Boston area. Again, we can only assume that there were fiddlers among the Cape Bretoners in Boston in the nineteenth century, since I have found no concrete evidence to indicate their existence.

If there were Scottish fiddlers in Boston, or elsewhere in New England in the nineteenth century, there is no indication that they had any influence on their contemporaries in rural New England. As was the case with Irish music, a Scottish influence was important in the overall development of Yankee fiddling. "Money Musk," one of the most famous New England contra dance tunes, is a Scottish tune, its composition attributed to Daniel Dow. Numerous tunes of Scottish origin appear early New England fiddle tune manuscripts. However, many of these, such as "Flowers of Edinburgh," "The White Cockade," "East Nuke of Fife," and "Speed the Plough," have long been universally popular throughout the British Isles and have frequently appeared in published collections of tunes. Therefore, their appearance in New England does not necessarily indicate direct influence from Scottish musicians.

Thus, by the end of the nineteenth century, New England had become host to a variety of fiddling styles. At this point, a line

can be drawn between rural and urban traditions. With the possible exception of French Canadians in rural areas in northern New England and perhaps a few isolated Irish and Scottish musicians, the new immigrants tended to settle in cohesive communities in the cities, and their traditions had little recognizable impact on the dance music of the New England countryside.

TWENTIETH CENTURY

In rural New England in the early twentieth century, many aspects of traditional fiddling were little different than they had been in the previous century. Kitchen dances and cornhuskings accompanied by fiddle music were still being held in western Massachusetts in the early twentieth century. Fiddler Wes Dickinson of Whately, Massachusetts, recalled in an interview:

Paul Wells: What was the "kitchen racket"?

Wes Dickinson: I played at two or three of 'em when I was a kid. It's when, say there's a group of people, twenty people, ten or fifteen couples, when one of them has a daughter or son getting married, they go in there with a piano, drums, and a fiddle, and they play in the middle room and they dance in the rooms all around there. And they have coffee and doughnuts and sometimes—they didn't have no whiskey then, unless they made their own—they had a lot of cider.

Doug Goodwin: What about the cornhusking bees you were telling me about?

WD: The cornhusking was more fun than the kitchen racket, because that there, was the same way—Link Barnes played the drums, his wife Edwina played the piano, my father played the fiddle, and I would learn. I used to play with 'em. They used to spread the corn out in the middle of the barn floor, and then they put the baskets on top, and husk, get the farmer's corn husked. When you got a red ear, you'd kiss the girls. I think there was more than kissing going on, but you got the corn husked anyway!

PW: Was the music going on during the husking, or after?

WD: No, they had to get all the corn husked, and then they had to sweep the floor up and put corn meal on the barn floor, and then they'd have cider and doughnuts, or whatever, coffee, whatever they had, and then they'd dance until sometimes two or three o'clock in the morning. And one farmer would get his corn done, next week it would be a different farmer. So every Saturday night there was a corn husking. I went to approximately ten or twelve of them in my life.

PW: About when was this?

WD: Well, I'm fifty-nine years old and I was probably, well, it was about fifty years ago, or maybe forty-five years ago. That's the last of 'em. (Interview with the author, 1 October 1975.)

There were numerous dance fiddlers active in western Massachusetts, and probably elsewhere in New England, at this time. Wes Dickinson's father played the fiddle and some of his contemporaries were Jim LaSalle of Northampton, Charlie Fields of West Whately, and Harry Shippee of Ashfield. In the hill towns of western Hampshire County, the Bates Dance Orchestra, led by Harry Bates of Worthington, was well known. Lou Granger of Chesterfield and Castanus Brown and Oren Gurney of Worthington were other fiddlers in this area. Occasionally at dances in this area prior to World War II, some of the men would engage in solo step-dancing or "jig-dancing" competitions. Bob Sears, a veteran of many dances around Cummington, Windsor, and Hawley, recalls that at the end of a square dance, between sets, or whenever the fiddler could be urged to participate, two or more men would try to "outdance" each other. They would perform motionless from the waist up and would never admit that they grew tired. The one who prevailed would frequently cap his performance with a leap in the air and a click of the heels, simply to further assert his superiority.

The new century brought new interest in folk traditions and customs. Industrialist Henry Ford did much to support traditional American folk arts, including square dance and fiddle music (which he felt was morally superior to the "corrupting influence" of pop-

See glossary for definition of boldfaced terms

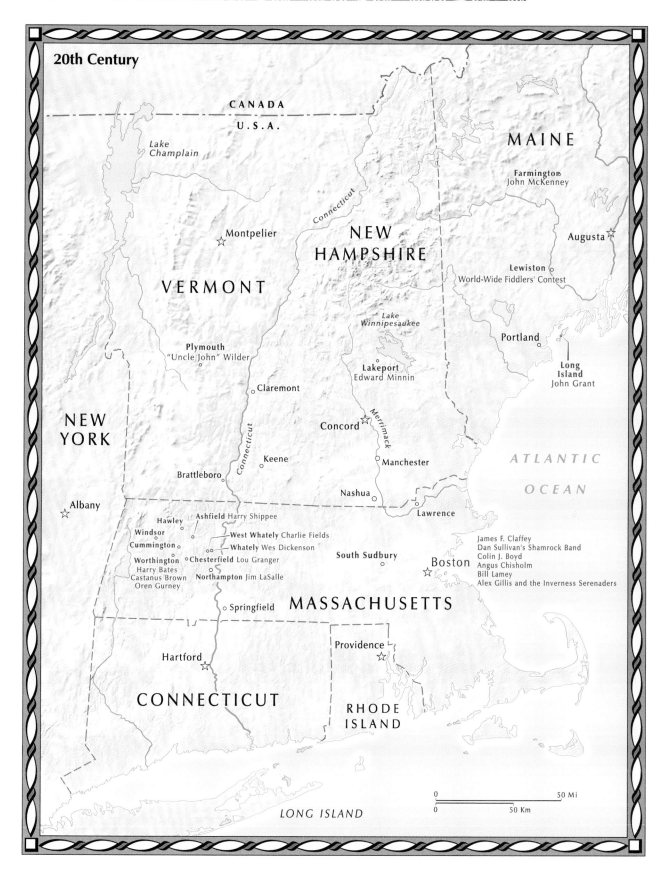

20th Century

CANADA
U.S.A.

MAINE

Lake
Champlain

Connecticut

Farmington
John McKenney

Montpelier

NEW
HAMPSHIRE

Augusta

VERMONT

Lewiston
World-Wide Fiddlers' Contest

Lake
Winnipesaukee

Portland

Plymouth
"Uncle John" Wilder

Lakeport
Edward Minnin

Claremont

Long
Island
John Grant

NEW
YORK

Concord

Merrimack

ATLANTIC

Keene

Manchester

OCEAN

Brattleboro

Albany

Nashua

Lawrence

Hawley   Ashfield Harry Shippee
Windsor   West Whately Charlie Fields   James F. Claffey
Cummington   Whately Wes Dickenson   Dan Sullivan's Shamrock Band
Worthington   Chesterfield Lou Granger   Colin J. Boyd
Harry Bates   South Sudbury   Angus Chisholm
Castanus Brown   Northampton Jim LaSalle   Boston   Bill Lamey
Oren Gurney   Alex Gillis and the Inverness Serenaders

Springfield   MASSACHUSETTS

Providence

Hartford

CONNECTICUT   RHODE
ISLAND

| 0 | | 50 Mi |
| 0 | | 50 Km |

LONG ISLAND

Dance Fiddlers in New England

ular **jazz** dance music). Mellie Dunham, a fiddler from Norway, Maine, earned national fame as a result of the media blitz that accompanied a trip he made to Dearborn, Michigan, to visit and play for Ford in 1925. As a result of this publicity Dunham was signed to a $500-a-week contract on the Keith-Albee vaudeville circuit (Wells 1976, pp. 112–115).

Dunham's fame helped fuel a nationwide interest in fiddling and fiddlers' contests. Fiddlers conventions became common in New England, often sponsored by local Ford dealerships or other businesses, as a means of promoting traditional music. What was undoubtedly the largest contest of this time was the "World-Wide Fiddlers' Contest" held in Lewiston, Maine, during the second week of April 1926. There was a certain amount of validity in this contest's claim to be the world championship, since fiddlers from four nations participated in the event. According to an article published in the *New York Times,* the renowned Scottish fiddler and composer James Scott Skinner sailed to America for the sole purpose of competing in the contest and announced, "I'm going to America to kill jazz" ("Scotch Fiddler"). He was joined on his voyage by John Wiseman, a fiddler from Bantry, County Cork, Ireland. Canada was represented by John Boivin of St. Georges, Quebec, and by pioneer French Canadian recording artist Joseph Allard of Montreal.

Participation by United States fiddlers was not limited to those from the northeast, for two musicians from Indianapolis, Joseph A. Lawson and James O'Donnell, traveled to Lewiston to play in the contest. With the exception of John Boivin, none of these travelers fared very well in the competition. Skinner became impatient with the inability of the contest's pianist to accompany Scottish tunes and walked off the stage in disgust part way through his performance (Junner 1960, p. 97). Wiseman fell ill shortly before the contest began, but he insisted on playing nevertheless, and a nurse stood behind him on stage while he performed.

When the contest was over, James F. Claffey of Boston, aged sixty-seven, was de-

clared the winner, Edward Minnin (or Minion) of Lakeport, New Hampshire, was second, John McKenney of Farmington, Maine, took third, and Boivin finished fourth. Claffey, who had played with the Boston Symphony, was awarded $1,000 and a silver cup for his efforts, and his photograph appeared in the *New York Times* on Sunday, 25 April 1926.

Several New England fiddlers in addition to Mellie Dunham were able to capitalize on the public's interest in fiddling. One of the first to emerge in the wake of Dunham's popularity was "Uncle John" Wilder of Plymouth, Vermont, uncle of then–President Calvin Coolidge. The *New York Times* of 20 December 1925 reported that Wilder sent a challenge to Mellie in the form of the statement: "I can fiddle Mellie Dunham to a standstill" ("Vermonter Enters Fiddling Lists"). There is no evidence of any meeting between the two musicians, but Wilder managed to stay in the public eye for some time. On 7 January 1926, Uncle John went to Boston "prepared to play for the fiddling championship of New England against all comers," but there apparently was no specific event to which he was referring ("President's Uncle in Fiddling Contest"). On 9 January, however, Wilder and seven other fiddlers gathered at the Wayside Inn in South Sudbury, Massachusetts, to play for Henry Ford (Ford owned the inn).

A photograph of Wilder appeared in *Billboard* on 6 February with a caption stating that he was playing vaudeville shows under the direction of the Jacobs Agency of Boston. He was scheduled to open in Boston and additional bookings included Baltimore and Washington. It was also announced that he had a contract to play fairs when the season opened. According to the *New York Times,* Wilder participated in the Lewiston, Maine, contest in April, but failed to qualify for the finals ("President's Uncle Loses").

Uncle John's biggest venture was a tour of Loew's Theaters with the Plymouth Vermont Old Time Dance Orchestra and a group of eight dancers from Plymouth in the fall of 1926. The tour was conceived by Jess Martin and organized by Martin's friend

See glossary for definition of boldfaced terms

William Morris, the well-known booking agent. The orchestra consisted of Wilder and Lewis Carpenter, fiddles; Cassie Cady, piano; Linn Cady, drums; and Clarence Blanchard, clarinet. The dancers included Emma Carpenter, Walter and Jeanetta Lynds, Laura and Aswell Johnson, Julia Messer, and Margaret and Raymond Moore, with calling by Herbert Luther Moore. The dancers were not a formal performing group but were chosen from Plymouth residents who had often danced together at local affairs and who were able to leave their jobs. The orchestra and dancers left home on 24 October 1926 and did not return until early in December. Their tour included performances in New York, St. Louis, Washington, D. C. (where they played at the White House as well as the Palace Theater), Frederick, Maryland, and Carlisle, Lebanon, Harrisburg, Westchester and Johnstown in Pennsylvania.

A few months after the completion of the tour, Uncle John found himself ousted from the orchestra as a result of his refusal to accompany the group on overnight engagements. However, in April 1927, he was hired for a three-day appearance at the State Theater in Pawtucket, Rhode Island, apparently without the rest of the orchestra.

John Grant, of Long Island, Casco Bay, Maine, was booked into a theater in Portland in December 1925 on the strength of the interest in fiddling aroused by Mellie Dunham, but this seems to have been the extent of his public career. A fiddler named "Uncle John" Bernard apparently visited Henry Ford and exploited this fact through appearances at theaters in New York (prologuing the film *The Music Maker*), by playing a few dates on the Keith-Albee circuit, and, according to an article in *Billboard*, through "independent engagements in his native New England" ("Ford's Fiddler"). At least one other New England fiddler, Harry Shippee of Ashfield, Massachusetts, is reputed to have played for Henry Ford.

The most enduring products of this fiddling mania are the phonograph records made by some of the fiddlers who came to prominence at this time. Although fiddlers

outside New England made records as a result of their victories in Ford-related contests (Bunt Stephens of Tennessee) or other association with Henry Ford (Jasper Bisbee of Michigan), the Ford connection was particularly important in regard to fiddlers from rural New England. This is true not because there was a large number of Yankee fiddlers who recorded at this time, but because nearly the only ones who *did* record 78s did so as a result of the Ford-spawned fiddle craze. These include Mellie Dunham, Joe Shippee, and the Plymouth Vermont Old Time Dance Orchestra. Of these fiddlers, Dunham is known to have made nine sides (including one unissued), Shippee four, and the Plymouth Orchestra, two.

It is somewhat surprising that more New England fiddlers were not recorded in an attempt to exploit the fad. Perhaps the companies were insensitive to regional differences in fiddling and merely promoted recordings by southern artists with whom they were already familiar. An article in *Variety* noted that Columbia's "hilly-billy" records which had been "such big sellers throughout the southern mountain territory" were also starting to sell well in urban areas of the north, which lends support to this suggestion ("Hilly-Billy Records Growing").

The only commercial recordings prior to this time that have some relevance to the documentation of New England fiddling are those made by Charles Ross Taggart for various companies in the 1910s and 1920s. Taggart assumed the character of "The Old Country Fiddler" and waxed comic monologues delivered in "Yankee twang" interspersed with occasional bits of fiddle tunes. Researcher Steve Green has established that Taggart grew up in Vermont and had something of a professional career touring on the Chatauqua circuit early in the century. (Personal communication with the author, 25 January 1997.)

Some Yankee fiddlers did appear on square dance records (78s) in later years. New Hampshire caller Ralph Page recorded numerous sides for at least two different companies, Disc and Folk Dancer, backed by bands that included fiddlers. These records were designed to accompany dancing, and the calls, rather than the music, are their main feature. Nevertheless, they are part of the overall picture of documentation of rural New England fiddling.

Commercial recordings were made by fiddlers from the various immigrant traditions in New England, but knowledge of these recordings is presently very incomplete. An Irish fiddler named James Claffy made several recordings for Columbia's 33000-F Irish series in the late 1920s, and he may be the fiddler who won the Lewiston, Maine, contest in 1926 and who was identified at that time as James Claffey from Boston. Dan Sullivan's Shamrock Band of Boston also recorded for Columbia in the 1920s and for Decca's 12000 Irish series. Fiddler Michael C. Hanafin, who played with Sullivan's Band, made some solo recordings as well. In the 1940s, O'Byrne Dewitt of Boston began the Copley label, which released the work of local Irish artists, including fiddler Paddy Cronin.

Hundreds of French Canadian 78s were issued, not only by Canadian companies but also by United States firms such as Columbia and Victor Bluebird, but I am unaware of any French Canadian emigrants to New England recording during this era. Fiddler J. O. LaMadeleine recorded tunes titled "Reel de Holyoke"/"Lanciers Springfield" (Starr 16382) and "New Bedford Reel" (Apex 26312), which makes it tempting to speculate that he lived, for at least a time, in Massachusetts. Local musicians may have been recorded by the La Patrie label of Lawrence, Massachusetts, but little is known about the activities of this company.

Many of the Cape Bretoners who have made fiddle recordings, such as Colin J. Boyd, Angus Chisholm, and Bill Lamey, lived for some time in the Boston area. Alex Gillis and his Inverness Serenaders, a popular Scottish performing group in Boston that played over the radio possibly as early as the 1920s, made some recordings that were issued in the Decca 14000 Scottish series of the 1930s. Copley Records also issued some Scottish material.

See glossary for definition of boldfaced terms

It is regrettable that Columbia, Victor, and the other phonograph companies that recorded extensively in the South did not see fit to pursue similar activities in the Northeast. This is especially unfortunate in regard to Yankee fiddling, because as the twentieth century progressed, many changes took place in the fiddle and dance traditions of rural New England. The extant phonograph records of Yankee fiddling are too few to permit any meaningful general conclusions to be drawn about performance styles in the earlier part of this century. A look at some of the developments in western Massachusetts, the area where I grew up and with which I am, therefore, most familiar, will perhaps be helpful in understanding the changes which occurred throughout New England.

By the time I began attending local square dances in the late 1950s and early 1960s, the dance music consisted entirely of adapted song melodies such as "San Antonio Rose," "Darling Nellie Gray," and "Hot Time in the Old Town Tonight." These were played by a band consisting of **accordion**, piano, and drums, with a singing caller. Between the sets of squares were **polkas**, **waltzes**, and occasionally a **round dance**. Enjoyable as these affairs were, they gave no indication of the heritage of Yankee fiddle music, and contra dances were nowhere in evidence.

Melodies from popular songs were being adapted for use as dance tunes fairly early in the century. Wes Dickinson, who was born in 1917, recalls that "Redwing," "Marching Through Georgia," and "Wait for the Wagon" were among the tunes that his father and his contemporaries played. However, older fiddlers in the area recall that traditional tunes such as "Soldier's Joy," "Devil's Dream," "Rakes of Mallow," and "Miss McLeod's Reel" and contra dances such as "Money Musk," "Pop Goes the Weasel," and "Hull's Victory" were in use at dances until the time of World War II. It may be that the changes in social patterns brought about by the war, coupled with the rise in popularity of country and western music, were responsible for changes in dance practices. Or, as my parents (who are both avid square dancers) have suggested, it may simply be

the case that the old contra dances were too sedate for modern tastes.

The following excerpt from an interview with fiddler Doug Goodwin, who began playing for dances in the Connecticut Valley of Massachusetts in 1946, shows the type of music used in postwar square dances and the way in which new tunes came into usage:

Paul Wells: What kind of stuff were you playing? What kind of tunes?

Doug Goodwin: What do you mean, for square dances? Okay, the eastern square dance, with a singing caller, took in songs like "My Little Girl," which is, I think, an old World War I tune, or "Put on Your Old Gray Bonnet," "Redwing," "Listen to the Mockingbird" with square dance calls put to them. . . . And then, every now and then when a new song would come out, some caller would put words to the song. Like "You Are My Sunshine," came out in the '40s sometime. (Interview with the author, 1 October 1975.)

The situation was much the same in other parts of rural New England. Writing about dance music in southern New Hampshire during the period 1930–1965, Newton F. Tolman, an experienced dance musician, states: "Square dance music, to New England square dance enthusiasts and the world at large, seemed to be irrevocably represented by tunes like 'Darling Nellie Gray,' 'Redwing' and Polish polkas" (Tolman 1972, p. 30). My own discussions with older fiddlers in Vermont have given a similar impression. Thus, although there were undoubtedly areas that retained the older traditional dances and dance music, these areas seem to have constituted quite a small minority.

Meanwhile, in Boston an active fiddling community was developing among the Irish, Scottish (Cape Breton), and French Canadian fiddlers who lived in the area. Music and dancing flourished in halls and clubs, and the recording activity of some of the city's musicians has already been discussed. Irish fiddler Paddy Cronin recalls the music scene in Boston as he knew it in the 1940s and '50s:

At that time, Dudley Street in Roxbury was the big place to play. The Greenville, that was Joe MacPhearson's place. The dance hall was up on the top and we'd go in there because Joe had a bar room. We'd all go in there and drink enough! There was a piano, and every fiddler from Canada, Ireland. . . from everyplace would come. There I first met Tommy Doucet. And in there I met Scotty Fitzgerald. In there I met Johnny Wilmot and Sean Maguire. The Irish dance hall was up over the bar, and you'd come down the stairway and go into MacPhearson's. The ballroom was called the Intercolonial. I played in all those halls . . . the Hibernian, the Rosecry, the Intercolonial, and the Opera House below. (Quoted in Ferrell 1975.)

Although the heyday of fiddling in the city has passed, many traditional musicians still reside there. Further exploration of Boston's role as a center of fiddling activity needs to be done.

LATE CENTURY REVIVAL

Despite the fact that traditional fiddling seems to have languished in rural New England during the mid-part of the twentieth century, there was a considerable revival of interest in fiddling beginning in the mid-1960s. Perhaps the most important factor behind this revival was the formation of the Northeast Fiddlers' Association. Around 1964 or 1965, a group of people in northern Vermont, including Sandy Paton, owner of Folk-Legacy Records, and several people from Goddard College in Plainfield, Vermont, took an interest in Vermont fiddling and organized a fiddlers' convention. Clem Myers, a fiddler from Barre, Vermont, became involved, and this helped earn the cooperation of other musicians. Plans for a fiddlers' organization were made, and in December 1965, the Northeast Fiddlers' Association, Incorporated, was chartered as a nonprofit educational corporation. The Goddard faction eventually withdrew its involvement, however, and the association came under the full control of the fiddlers themselves.

Later in 1965, Clem Myers sent a letter to around 100 people, including 31 fiddlers, asking them to join and support the newly formed association and announcing the first meeting, which was to be held in Hardwick, Vermont, on 28 May 1966. The idea was successful; the association continued to grow, and by the mid-1970s had a membership of approximately 500, of which nearly 200 were fiddlers. The association held monthly meetings at various locations in northern Vermont, and published a monthly newsletter. Myers served as president of the club for the first several years of its existence before being succeeded by Wayne Perry of Stowe, Vermont. (Information on the early history of the Northeast Fiddlers Association was gathered from materials that were kindly lent by Wayne and Evelyn Perry and from conversations with Clem Myers.)

Following the formation of the Northeast Fiddlers' Association, at least three other fiddlers' clubs were organized in New England, including ones in the Champlain Valley, southern Vermont, and Bristol, Connecticut. The desire to get together with other fiddlers on a regular basis without having to travel long distances was a motivating factor in the formation of these other organizations.

Fiddle contests enjoyed a renaissance in the late twentieth century. The most important was the annual National Traditional Old Time Fiddlers' Contest (formerly the Northeast Regional Old Time Fiddlers' Contest), sponsored by the Northeast Fiddlers' Association. This two-day event attracted many fiddlers from Canada as well as from the northeastern United States. The Craftsbury Common Contest in Craftsbury, Vermont, was also a large and popular annual event.

What of fiddling for dancing? In addition to the type of square dance music that was discussed earlier, which may or may not be played on the fiddle, the instrument is widely used in the contradance revival that began around the same time as the formation of the Northeast Fiddlers' Association. This revival had its initial impetus among young people and had strong ties to the

back-to-the-land movement that swept rural New England in the 1970s. Young people moved from the cities to the country and sought to adopt a lifestyle that they conceived to be appropriate to their new environment. Thus, contra dancing, with its long history as part of New England traditional culture, was wholeheartedly embraced. However, at Saturday night dances or fairs in the hill towns, natives of the area still enjoyed themselves square dancing to "San Antonio Rose," "Darling Nellie Gray," and "Spanish Cavalier," quite apart from the contra dance revival.

New Hampshire fiddler and dance caller Dudley Laufman was a key figure in the revival of interest in contra dancing. The area around Keene and Nelson, New Hampshire, has been host to a considerable amount of dance activity and was the center of a square dance revival in the 1930s. (Veteran caller Ralph Page, who has been extremely important in maintaining an interest in traditional New England dancing, is from this area). Newton Tolman described the beginnings of Laufman's involvement with dancing: "Dudley became interested in Nelson's illustrious history as one of the principal centers involved in the earlier revival of square dancing. Soon he began to pick up the old authentic music—such of it as we could remember—and began re-creating the old dance forms, dispensing entirely with the waltzes, polkas, and modern dances which in recent years were generally intermixed with squares at most public dances" (Tolman 1972, p. 37).

In the Boston area there are still several regular dances that feature fine traditional fiddling. The French American Club in Waltham, just outside of Boston, and the Canadian American Club in Watertown remain important venues for dances and concerts for the local Cape Breton and French Canadian communities. Informal sessions of Irish music can be found at pubs in the city nearly every night of the week.

Fiddling has undergone many changes in the more than three centuries that it has been a part of New England life. From a time when fiddlers provided dance music for all

See glossary for definition of boldfaced terms

levels of society, to the addition of the music of various immigrant groups, through decline and subsequent revival of fiddling and dance traditions in rural New England, fiddling has been an enduring form of musical expression in New England. With strong interest in fiddling at the start of the twenty-first century, this music will probably continue to be played for many years to come.

BIBLIOGRAPHY

"American Dance Bibliography to 1820." (1949). *Proceedings of the American Antiquarian Society* 59, part 2 (19 October):216–220.

Bates, Florence. (1976). "The Bates Dance Orchestra." *Stone Walls* 2 (1):30–32.

Bayard, Samuel P. (1944). *Hill Country Tunes: Instrumental Folk Music of Southwestern Pennsylvania.* Vol. 39 of the Memoirs of the American Folklore Society. Philadelphia: Memoirs of the American Folklore Society.

———. "Scales and Ranges in Anglo-American Fiddle Tunes: Report on a Desultory Experiment." (1966). In *Two Penny Ballads and Four Dollar Whiskey: A Pennsylvania Folklore Miscellany,* ed. Kenneth S. Goldstein and Robert H. Byington. Hatboro, PA: Folklore Associates, Inc.

Billboard. 1927. "Ford's Fiddler Leaves New York." 23 April.

Blaustein, Richard. (1977). "The Folks Behind the Fiddlers' Associations; Part I: Clem Myers of the Northeast Fiddlers." *The Devil's Box* 11, no. 2 (1 June):39–44.

Boyden, David D. (1961). "The Violin." In *Musical Instruments Through the Ages,* ed. Anthony Baines. Baltimore: Penguin Books.

Brooks, Charles. (1886). *History of the Town of Medford, Middlesex County, Massachusetts, From Its First Settlement in 1630 to 1855.* Rev. and enlarged ed. brought up to 1885 by James M. Usher. Boston: Rand, Avery&Co., the Franklin Press.

Chase, George Wingate. (1861). *The History of Haverhill, Massachusetts: From Its First Settlement in 1640, to the Year 1860.* Self-published.

Christeson, R. P. (1973). *The Old Time Fiddlers Repertory.* Columbia: University of Missouri Press.

Coleman, Emma L. (1933). "Frary House, Deerfield, Massachusetts." *Old-Time New England* 23, no. 3 (January):88–98.

Coltman, Bob. "Habitantbilly: French-Canadian Old Time Music." *Old Time Music* no. 11 (winter 1973/74):9–13; no. 12 (spring 1974):9–14.

Cross, Barbara M., ed. (1961). *The Autobiography of Lyman Beecher.* 2 vols. Cambridge: Belknap Press.

Damon, S. Foster. (1952). "The History of Square-Dancing." *Proceedings of the American Antiquarian Society* 62, pt. 1 (April):63–98.

Dean-Smith, Margaret, ed. (1957). *Playford's English Dancing Master, 1651.* Facsimile reprint with an introduction, bibliography, and notes by Margaret Dean-Smith. London: Schott&Co., Ltd.

Dickinson, Wes. 1975. Interview by author. 1 October.

Dunn, Charles W. (1953). *Highland Settler: A Portrait of the Scottish Gael in Nova Scotia.* Toronto: University of Toronto Press.

"An Eighteenth-Century Collection of Contra Dances." (1957). *Old Time New England* 47, no. 4 (April–June): 108–111.

Ferrell, Frank H. (1975). Notes to *The Rakish Paddy: Paddy Cronin.* Fiddler Records FRLP-002.

Gibbs, Giles, Jr. (1974). *Giles Gibb, Jr.: His Book for Fife, Ellington, Connecticut, 1777.* Ed. Kate van Winkle Keller. Hartford: Connecticut Historical Society.

Goodwin, Doug. 1975. Interview by author. 1 October.

Green, Steve. 1997. Personal communication with author. 25 January.

Griffiths, John. (1788). *A Collection of the Newest Cotillions, and Country Dances; Principally Composed by John Griffiths, Dancing Master, to which is added Instances of Ill Manners to be carefully avoided by Youth of both sexes.* Northampton, MA: n.p.

Hale, Philip. "Musical and Theatrical Life in a New England Village in the Sixties." *Proceedings of the Massachusetts Historical Society* 56 (October 1922–June 1923):335–343.

Hatch, Mary R. P. (1887). "Early Manners and Customs." *Granite Monthly* 10, no. 1 (January):23–26.

Holyoke, Mary Vial. (1911). *The Holyoke Diaries.* Ed. George Francis Dow. Salem, MA: Essex Institute.

Hunter, Robert, Jr. (1943). *Quebec to Carolina in 1785–1786: Being the Travel Diary and Observations of Robert Hunter, Jr., a Young Merchant of London.* Ed. Louis B. Wright. San Marino, CA: Huntington Library.

Junner, John. (1960). "Scott Skinner: The Strathspey King." *Scots Magazine,* vol. 74:92–99.

Knight, Peter R. (1975). "Ethnic Massachusetts." In *The Commemorative Guide to the Massachusetts Bicenten-*

nial, 1975 Edition. Yankee Press, for the Massachusetts Bicentennial Commission.

Kull, Nell M. (1961). *History of Dover, Vermont: 200 Years in a Hill Town.* Brattleboro, VT: Book Cellar.

Little, William. (1888). *The History of Weare, New Hampshire, 1735–1888.* Lowell, MA: S. W. Huse & Co.

Moogk, Edward B. (1975). *Roll Back the Years: A History of Canadian Recorded Sound and Its Legacy.* Ottawa: National Library of Canada.

New York Times. 1926. "President's Uncle in Fiddling Contest," 8 January; "Scotch Fiddler, 82, Sets Sail 'To Kill Jazz in America,'" 14 March; "Fiddler of 80 in Contest," 4 April; "President's Uncle Loses," 8 April; "Becomes Fiddle Champion," 11 April; "Vermonter Enters Fiddling Lists," 20 December.

Northern Junket. "It's Fun to Hunt" (series of columns). July 1967–January 1974.

Ober, Merrill. (1928). "A Journal of Village Life in Vermont in 1848." Ed. Wilson O. Clough. *New England Quarterly* 1, no. 1 (January):32–40.

One Thousand Fiddle Tunes. (1940). Reprint. Chicago: M.M. Cole, 1940. Originally published in *Ryan's Mammoth Collection,* Boston: Elias Howe, 1883.

O'Neill, Francis. (1913). *Irish Minstrels and Musicians.* Chicago: Regan Printing House. Reprinted with a new introduction by Barry O'Neill. Darby, PA.: Norwood Editions, 1973.

Page, Ralph. (1970). "Those Were the Days." *Northern Junket,* vol. 10, no. 1 (February):2–7; vol. 10, no. 2 (April):16–21.

———. (1971). "Contra Dance Background." *Northern Junket,* vol. 10, no. 10 (October):2–9; vol. 10, no. 11 (December):7–14.

Pichierri, Louis. (1960). *Music in New Hampshire.* New York: Columbia University Press.

Podea, Iris Saunders. (1950). "Quebec to Little Canada: The Coming of the French Canadians to New England in the Nineteenth Century." *New England Quarterly* 23, no. 3 (September):365–380.

Roads, Samuel, Jr. (1897). *The History and Traditions of Marblehead.* Marblehead, MA: N. Allen Lindsey & Co.

Sachs, Curt. (1937). *The World History of the Dance.* New York: W. W. Norton & Co.

Scholes, Percy A. (1934). *The Puritans and Music in England and New England.* London: Oxford University Press.

Tolman, Newton F. (1972). *Quick Tunes and Good Times.* Dublin, NH: William L. Bauhan, Inc.

Trumbull, James Russell. (1902). *History of Northampton, Massachusetts from Its Settlement in 1654.* 2 vols. Northampton, MA: Press of Gazette Printing Co.

Variety. 1926. "'Hilly-Billy' Records Growing." 24 February.

Waite, Otis F. R. (1895). *History of the Town of Claremont, New Hampshire for a Period of One Hundred and Thirty Years from 1764 to 1894.* Manchester, NY: John B. Clarke Co.

Waterman, Zuriel. (1962). "Captains Carousing in Providence." *Rhode Island History* 21, no. 4 (October):136–137.

Wells, Paul F. (1976). "Mellie Dunham: Maine's Champion Fiddler." *JEMF Quarterly* 12, no. 43 (autumn):112–118.

Wheeler, Edmund. (1879). *The History of Newport, New Hampshire, from 1766 to 1878.* Concord, NH: Republican Press Association.

Wilson, Joe. (1976). "A Hornpipe: Durang's Dance and Hoffmaster's Tune." Program for National Folk Festival, 16–18 July:12–13.

CAPE BRETON MUSIC IN BOSTON, MASSACHUSETTS

Burt Feintuch

Please see the Introduction to this volume for biographical information on Burt Feintuch.

The Boston area is home to many immigrants from Cape Breton, an island separated from the mainland of Nova Scotia, Canada, by the Strait of Canso. By road, Cape Breton is about 750 miles from Boston. Thinly populated by aboriginal Mi'kmaq people, the island had become an outpost of French settlers involved in salt cod production and trade by the start of the nineteenth century. During the first half of the nineteenth century, a large influx of displaced Scots who had left their homeland (the Highlands and Western Islands) because of the clearances of agricultural land and the decline in kelp production supplanted the sparse Acadian population. From a population of 3,000 in 1801, the island grew to 55,000 in 1851; by 1871, 50,000 of 75,000 Cape Bretoners were of Scottish ethnicity, and a **Gaelic**-speaking culture grew to larger proportions there than in some of the Gaelic regions of Scotland (Hornsby 1992).

The island's economic base, which has relied on fishing, mining, steel, and agriculture, has never been strong enough to sustain its population. Beginning with a potato famine from 1845–1849 and continuing to the present, many Cape Bretoners—some Acadians and many Scots—left the island seeking better prospects.

Easily accessible by sea and land, Boston is one of the main sites of Cape Breton emigration, along with Detroit, Michigan; Toronto and Windsor, Ontario; and western Canada. Cape Breton out-migration is part of a larger population movement from the Canadian maritime provinces, although the strong Scottish component of Cape Breton identity and the island's isolation allow Cape Bretoners to distinguish themselves from other Maritimers, many of whom also settled around Boston.

Arriving in Boston in the nineteenth and twentieth centuries, Cape Bretoners tended to become carpenters, laborers, factory workers, and domestics, generally settling

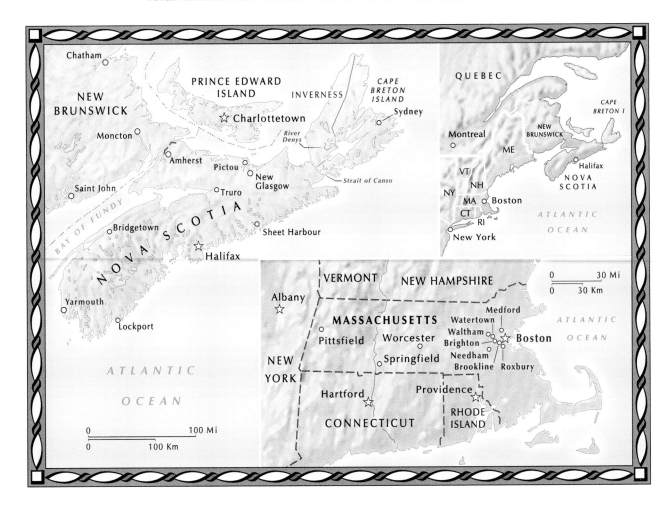

near each other. Demographic data is largely nonexistent; the United States census does not separate Cape Bretoners from other Nova Scotians. But by 1880 the Boston area housed more Nova Scotians than Sydney (Cape Breton's largest city), Yarmouth, and Pictou (both sizable towns on the Nova Scotia mainland) combined (Burrill 1992, pp. 4–5). Today, Watertown and Waltham, cities just west of Boston, are home to many Cape Bretoners, and other parts of the Boston metropolitan area—Brookline and Brighton among them—have had significant Cape Breton populations. In recent years, perhaps because of changing job markets here and in Canada, along with changes in U.S. immigration policies, fewer Cape Bretoners are moving to Boston, tending instead to go to Toronto and western Canada. These emigrants are generally better educated than those of past generations.

THE MUSIC

Cape Breton music is strongly Scottish in derivation, rooted in eighteenth- and nineteenth-century Scottish violin **repertoire** and many of its performance traditions. Because of the ease of communication and travel to Cape Breton and the tight networks linking immigrants and people on the island, the music in the Boston area is nearly indistinguishable from its forms and practices in Cape Breton. It is a violin-based, dance-oriented music, often called "Cape Breton Scottish violin music" or "**fiddle** music." The dance music consists of tunes, most of which have two parts, each part being either eight or sixteen measures. Musicians generally play medleys of tunes organized around the same tonal center. Thus, a medley played "on A" might include tunes in A major and in the corresponding **mixolydian** and **dorian** modes. Some tunes use more than one mode (Dunlay and Greenberg 1996, p. 6).

In accordance with modern practice in Cape Breton, fiddlers tend to repeat a tune once or twice and then move on to another tune of the same **genre**. **Reels**, notated in 4/4 and 2/4, and **jigs**, in 6/8, are most common. **Strathspeys** (4/4, sometimes called "slow reels" but played with every beat emphasized, giving them a propulsive quality), marches (2/4, 4/4, rarely 6/8), **hornpipes** (2/4, 4/4, usually played as reels), **clogs** (2/4, 4/4, played with **tempos** and "lift" associated with hornpipes in Scottish and Irish tradition), and various slower listening pieces—airs and slow strathspeys—are also typical. Musicians enhance melodies with a complex range of bowed and fingered ornamentations. They generally use a flat left-hand, resting their **instruments** in the palm of the hand (wrist toward the violin body), and they usually keep time by tapping their feet strongly and audibly. Bowing involves little slurring. Typically, one fiddler performs, accompanied by a pianist playing in a distinctive, **syncopated**, chordally-based style, and perhaps a rhythm **guitarist**. Unlike other fiddle-based traditions, Cape Breton music has only a minor precedent of fiddlers playing in ensembles. Identified as Scottish, the music actually transcends ethnic distinctions: these days, Cape Breton Scottish and Acadian immigrants play a mostly shared repertoire and style. Indeed, in Cape Breton, a number of native Mi'kmaqs have distinguished themselves as performers of the same music.

Musicians perform for dancing done in **quadrille** formation—"square sets"—for **step dancing** (a percussive **form** of primarily solo dance), and for listening. Square sets require either reels or jigs; for step dancing, a fiddler will generally begin with strathspeys and then increase the tempo by switching to reels. Much of the repertoire may be found in nineteenth-century books of fiddle tunes first published in Scotland. Other tunes, often simply noted as "traditional," include local Cape Breton compositions as well as tunes in aural tradition from Scotland. There is also a vigorous contemporary practice of tune composition as well as a strong presence of tunes from other

sources, especially Irish music and tune books published in the northeastern United States. Musicians learn by ear (including from recordings) and from printed sources. Commercial recordings of Cape Breton violin music began in the 1930s, and many musicians, including some from Boston, make commercial recordings today.

Although Gaelic singing would almost certainly have been part of domestic life, there is virtually no trace of such music in the Boston area these days. With the spoken language, Gaelic singing has declined precipitously in Cape Breton as well, although early collections and recordings document its presence on the island. One Boston-area exception to this general trend is a Gaelic choir associated, at least through the 1980s, with a Presbyterian church in Needham, Massachusetts (Dunlay 1987–88, pp. 6–7). However, the large majority of Cape Bretoners are Catholic, not Presbyterian. Although some Boston residents may speak Gaelic, it is not a living language in Massachusetts.

The exuberant **square dancing**, done in **sets** of four couples, is a localized form of Cape Breton square dancing, sometimes called "Boston sets." On the island, the dance forms tend to be localized as well, but in many Cape Breton communities the old four-couple set has been superseded by sets of various numbers of couples, generally more than four. Many Cape Breton community dances no longer use a **caller** or prompter, whereas in Boston it is more common to have a caller who directs the dancers through the patterned movements. Step dancers will do solo spots during evenings of square sets.

Beginning as early as the 1920s and lasting through the 1960s, musicians played in dance halls, especially in the area around Dudley Square, Roxbury, in Boston, but also elsewhere in the city, including the Orange Hall in Brookline (Burrill 1992, pp. 41–56; Muise 1997). At such dances, and at taverns in the same neighborhoods, the music catered to Cape Bretoners and other Maritimers as well as Scottish, Irish, and French Canadian immigrants. These days, two ethnic clubs, the Canadian American Club in

SQUARE DANCE

Canadian American Club
202 Arlington St. Watertown, MA.

Square Dance to the fine Cape Breton fiddling of:

Raymond Ellis

Piano accompaniment by:

Janine Randall

Prompting by:

Norman MacEachern
Dancing 8p.m.-12p.m.

SAT. MAR 28
Coffee, Tea and Light Lunch Served

For Information:
Bob Steele	978-664-4609
Theresa Avery	617-924-8027

ADMISSION: $8.00

Flyer for a square dance held in Watertown, Massachusetts, sponsored by the Canadian American Club. Note that Raymond Ellis is specifically described as a "Cape Breton" fiddler.

Watertown and the French American Victory Club in Waltham, are primary sites for the music, along with occasional house parties, weddings, and other private events. The clubs feature regular square dances, frequently presenting local musicians. At such dances, the fiddler often alternates with a band that plays country music or sentimental popular Irish music. On occasion, a musician visiting from Cape Breton will play for a special dance, sometimes a benefit. These tend to be especially well attended, and they may not include alternating with a band. The Canadian American Club also is the site of organized Friday-night music sessions, and once a month the Gaelic Club, the Boston branch of the Cape Breton Island Gaelic Foundation (Dunlay 1987–88, p. 8), meets at the Canadian American Club. Meetings feature fiddling, step dancing, and socializ-

ing. In years past, the Gaelic club program included Gaelic singing. With a burgeoning popular interest in music popularly termed "Celtic" and the growing international popularity of a number of fiddlers from Cape Breton, the Boston Cape Breton community is beginning to receive attention from enthusiasts outside the formerly tight ethnic networks. The music has also enjoyed a minor radio presence in Boston; today it may be heard on a weekly program that presents music from maritime Canada.

If anything, the Boston Cape Breton style is more conservative than the music as performed today in Cape Breton. On the island, a number of younger musicians have begun experimenting, embracing influences from contemporary popular music. So far, however, this has not happened in the Boston area, and the Boston sets seem to reflect older dance practices.

As old ethnic networks change and new emigration from Cape Breton slows, there are virtually no young musicians among the Cape Bretoners of Boston. The two leading Cape Breton fiddlers in Boston—John Campbell (born 1929), who comes originally from Glenora Falls and moved to Watertown in 1963 (Campbell 1997), and Joseph Cormier (born 1927), a Waltham resident who came in 1962 from largely Acadian Chéticamp—are both masters of what enthusiasts consider the old style of playing (MacGillivray 1981). Campbell comes from a family with a long musical history in Cape Breton. A number of the several hundred tunes he has composed have become standards in the repertoire both in Boston and "down home," and he has, for more than thirty years, played a key role in organizing dances and other events in the community. His style and repertoire provided a significant number of examples for a 1996 tune book and study of Cape Breton music (Dunlay and Greenberg), and he is well known both in Cape Breton and in the Boston area.

The close ties between the Boston-area community and the island exert a powerful influence on the music. Boston Cape Bretoners frequently travel to Cape Breton, generally in the summer, sometimes maintain-

ing a house on the island and often visiting family. The Inverness Serenaders, one of the first Cape Breton groups to record, were based in Boston. The first modern collection of Cape Breton fiddle music, compiled and arranged by fiddler Gordon F. MacQuarrie of Inverness County, Cape Breton, was published not in Cape Breton but in Medford, Massachusetts, in 1940 (MacQuarrie). The late Bill Lamey, originally from River Denys, Cape Breton, was a major organizer of Boston-area dances after he moved to the area in 1953; his recordings were popular both in Boston and at home. Buddy Mac-Master, perhaps the most active and best-known Cape Breton dance musician, makes annual visits to Boston to play for dances.

Clearly, the community is changing, and those changes are reflected in the music. Earlier in this century, Cape Bretoners brought their music with them when they moved to Boston, and the music flourished, with two or three generations of musicians finding significant community support. Today, on Cape Breton Island, the music is prospering, but in Boston the people who come to the two clubs are aging. Some second-generation sons and daughters of people who arrived a generation ago follow the music, in Boston and on the island, and enthusiasts from outside the community come to the clubs as well. These days, musicians from Cape Breton arrive only occasionally, visiting and perhaps playing for a dance or two. Ironically, despite growing interest and participation from cultural outsiders, it is very unusual for a second-generation Cape Bretoner in Boston to take up the music.

DOCUMENTARY RECORDINGS

John Campbell's *Timeless*, a self-produced compact disc, is his latest recording (1999). *Full Circle: From Cape Breton to Boston and Back* is a recent release (Rounder, 2000) of home recordings of the late influential Boston-area musician Bill Lamey. Joseph Cormier's 1998 *Informal Sessions* is his most recent recording. It features the late Eddie Irwin on piano along with Boston mainstay

guitarist Edmond Boudreau. Jerry Holland reversed the trend: Born in Brocton, near Boston, he moved to Cape Breton, where he has been a very influential musician and composer. His *Crystal Clear* (2000) is his most recent recording. Boston-area fiddler Frank Ferrel's *Boston Fiddle: The Dudley Street Tradition* (1996) is inspired by Ferrel's research into the dance-hall traditions—ranging across Cape Breton, other Maritime, Scottish, and Irish musics—of the Dudley Square area of Roxbury from the 1930s through the 1950s. Ferrel is not a Cape Breton–style fiddler. But while it does not focus exclusively on Cape Breton music, the booklet of notes that accompanies the recording is especially informative. *Traditional Music from Cape Breton* (1993) is a sample of many leading Cape Breton fiddlers from the island, recorded at a festival in Ireland.

BIBLIOGRAPHY

Burrill, Gary. (1992). *Away: Maritimers in Massachusetts, Ontario and Alberta—An Oral History of Leaving Home.* Montreal and Kingston: McGill-Queen's University Press.

Campbell, John. (1997). Interview by the author. Watertown, Mass., 9 February. Dunlay, Kate. (1987–1988). Cape Bretoners in Boston: Maintaining Identity. Unpublished manuscript, available at the Beaton Institute, University College of Cape Breton.

Dunlay, Kate, and Greenberg, David. (1996). *Traditional Celtic Violin Music of Cape Breton.* Toronto: DunGreen Music.

Feintuch, Burt. (2000). "A Week on the Ceilidh Trail." In *Northeast Folklore: Essays in Honor of Edward D. Ives,* ed. Pauleena MacDougall and David Taylor. Orono: University of Maine Press and the Maine Folklife Center.

Hornsby, Stephen J. (1992). *Nineteenth-Century Cape Breton: A Historical Geography.* Montreal and Kingston: McGill-Queen's University Press.

MacGillivray, Allister. (1981). *The Cape Breton Fiddler.* Sydney, NS: College of Cape Breton Press.

MacQuarrie, Gordon F. (1940). *The Cape Breton Collection of Scottish Melodies.* Medford, MA: J. Beaton——.

Muise, Johnny; Muise, Mary; and Randall, Janine. (1997). Interview by Burt Feintuch. Roslindale, Mass., 19 March.

SQUARE DANCE AND SQUARE DANCE MUSIC IN WESTERN NEW YORK STATE

James W. Kimball

James W. Kimball has been on the music faculty at the State University of New York at Geneseo since 1976 as an ethnomusicologist and music historian. During this time he has documented, presented, and frequently written about old-time music and dance traditions in rural New York.

Old-time **square dancing**, as still practiced with considerable vigor in several communities of rural New York State, descends directly from dance and musical traditions that once entertained early pioneers in the area. The details have changed through the years: instrumentation and types of tunes may be newer, many of the older dance figures have been forgotten, new styles of calling have joined the old, dress and etiquette have become thoroughly twentieth century, and some of the refreshments (e.g., pizza, pop, and hot dogs) would have been unknown to those early settlers. The good times and physical energy of an evening of round and square dancing would still be recognized, however, as would at least some of the details.

The makeup of the population has changed as well. In the first half of the nineteenth century, English, Scots, Irish, and Germans became the dominant groups in western New York. Many of them moved west from New England or north out of Maryland and Pennsylvania; others came straight from the old countries. Significant minorities included Native Americans, who were at least partly resettled onto reservation lands, and African Americans, many of whom worked farms or carried on independent trades such as building, barbering, and playing music. By the early twentieth century, the area had welcomed large numbers of Italians and Poles along with local concentrations of Swedes, Danes, and Finns. While the majority of newer immigrants settled in urban areas such as Buffalo, Jamestown, Rochester, and Geneva, many did wind up on farms or in small towns. And many of these took to the local square dances with great enthusiasm as dancers, **callers**, and musicians. For all the changes over the years, old-time square dancing and round and square dance bands are still a lively part of the fabric of rural entertainment in western New York.

HISTORY

The roots of American country dancing, in all its forms (square, circle, and **longways contra set**) lie in the social dance traditions of the British Isles and France going back as far as the seventeenth century. Starting with John Playford's *The English Dancing Master* (London 1651) and continuing through the eighteenth century, we have a steady succession of popular dance methods and collections, many including tunes. American collections start to appear in the 1780s.

The pioneer generation in western New York clearly preferred the longways or contra formation, while more urban society in the east danced French-influenced squares or *cotillons* (or "**cotillion**," as Americans usually chose to write it). Another French term, *quadrille,* came into use in the early nineteenth century to describe some rather formal sets of squares that were published (both music and figures) and carefully taught and memorized in both Europe and America, where they became part of fashionable balls. The cotillions, on the other hand, were more flexible and were featured at more informal cotillion parties. By the 1820s, these parties often featured a caller, generally one of the musicians, who would lead everyone through the figures.

As the Erie Canal and new railroads brought waves of new settlers and goods into western New York, social trends began to change as well. By the mid–nineteenth century only a few of the old **contra dances** were still popular. Taking their place were the new squares from the east, a few dances in the **big circle** format, and a variety of couple or **round dances** of European origin (e.g., **waltzes**, **polkas**, and **schottisches**). The formal quadrilles, along with the similar "Lancers," continued to be part of urban, college, and resort events through most of the nineteenth century but were in time completely replaced by new couple dances as they came into vogue. Squares continued to be popular in the rural countryside, however, though there appears to have been little distinction between the terms cotillion and quadrille; the simple word "set" (or "sett") was often applied to any square dance, and it was always assumed there would be a caller.

Rural calling styles evolved over time, as did the instrumentation and playing styles of the musicians. Most early callers (often termed "prompters") shouted out the figures just before the dancers were to perform them. As early as the 1880s in rural New York and neighboring states, some had taken to singing some of the calls to the tune being played. This was perhaps a natural result of the **fiddler**-caller having to play and call at the same time. With the advent of microphones and public-address systems in the 1930s, the singing caller became the norm throughout the region, as did the widespread appropriation of popular or country songs and instrumentation for square dancing. Square dancing had been declining significantly as younger dancers, even in rural areas, came under the influence of the **jazz** era and Tin Pan Alley. But the new sound attached to the old dances caught on due to various factors, including Henry Ford's outspoken advocacy of old-time dancing, Floyd Woodhull's appearance at the New York World's Fair in 1940, the rise of numerous square dance clubs, demonstration groups and competitions, and the whole feeling in the World War II era that this was a very "American" type of activity. By the late 1940s round and square dances were a regular part of high-school and small-town social life throughout the region.

Although there has been some influence from formal clubs and recreation programs, for the most part the rural dances remain distinctly local. The details of figures and tune preferences are quite different in the Genesee Valley from those of Erie and Chautauqua counties to the west or the eastern Finger Lakes and the Catskills to the east. Whereas modern club dancing is completely standardized around the world (including a network of published figures and recorded music), the old-time rural round and square dance scene is still rooted firmly in local **oral tradition**.

THE DANCES

Square dancing and related forms of country dancing (e.g., contra and circle dances) developed primarily for the purpose of social recreation and entertainment, and this is still true in rural New York. One gets to socialize with friends, meet new people, and benefit from good exercise, all while enjoying the music and being guided through interesting and sometimes amusing figures by a caller. Some individuals also find these dances an outlet for personal expression as they indulge in a bit of showy footwork, extra turns, small pranks, and the like. For the musicians and callers, who generally come from the same rural background, these dances are a fun social time as well as a chance to earn a little part-time income. Dances may also serve as fund-raisers or benefits for a variety of organizations, clubs, or local causes, though the emphasis is still on having a good time. In contrast to modern or western club square dancers, rural dancers seldom "perform" for demonstration or show purposes.

Old-time dances in rural New York generally last about four hours and are billed as "Round and Square Dances." The music is always played by a live band, generally four or five musicians, one of whom may serve as the caller. A few bands have separate non-playing callers. Bands with younger members usually have more of a commercial country sound and will feature **electric guitars**, electric **bass**, drum set, and sometimes fiddle, **steel guitar**, **mandolin**, or five-string. The older generation's less country-oriented bands may include **piano accordion**, stand-up bass, saxophone, tenor **banjo**, and piano or electric keyboard.

The round dances are standard couple dances (e.g., **fox-trots**, waltzes, polkas, schottisches, jitterbugs, and so on) and are generally played in sets of three or more, mixing slower and quicker **tempos**. Two fox-trots or slower country tunes, for example, might be followed by a polka or a jitterbug number. Most of the tunes come from an older popular or country **repertoire**. The vast majority are in **major key** and in steady

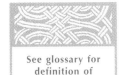

See glossary for definition of boldfaced terms

4/4, 2/4, or 3/4 meter. As is characteristic of much American popular music, many are in AABA or similar forms.

After a few round dances, the caller or a band member will call or signal (e.g., by ringing a **cowbell** or playing a fast fiddle tune) for dancers to form four-couple square sets. When they have formed as many sets as they can, the caller and band simply start the first of what are usually three separate square figures, each to a different tune. There is usually no teaching or walk-through and only occasionally any spoken introduction—a quick joke or greeting to someone on the floor. Only if there is a major breakdown in one or more of the sets will the caller stop the band and explain a figure. The individual square dance figures or calls all fit into two, four, eight, or sixteen bars of 2/4 or 6/8 music. A "do-si-do," for example usually takes up four bars or eight steps. "Grand right and left" takes up sixteen bars, while "two ladies chain and back" takes eight. Some figures have a slower or quicker version: "allemande left" can take two bars or four, depending on the context within the particular dance. "Right and left through and right and left back" can take eight bars or four, and local dancers have developed their own techniques for smoothly rushing these figures. About a dozen figures is all a rural dancer would need to know, and each will be repeated in various combinations through the evening.

The tunes played for these dances must also be based on eight- or sixteen-bar **phrases**. Some of the most successful are in fact only eight bars long (e.g., "It Ain't Gonna Rain No More" or "Pistol Packin' Mamma") and easily fit any figure or **variations** that a caller might come up with. Longer tunes, especially song tunes with distinctive **chorus** sections, require more care so as to match a sequence of figures to the music. In a singing square dance adaptation of "The Beer Barrel Polka," for example, the musicians have to listen carefully for the "allemande left" call as a cue to go to the chorus ("Roll out the barrel. . . ."), which the dancers all sing as they do a grand right and left.

The Pidgeon River Square Dance Team photographed at the Mountain Music Festival, Asheville, North Carolina, c. 1939. They are performing a classic "round" or "big circle" dance, as it would have been performed during this period in New York. *Photograph from the collections of the Library of Congress.*

Callers will often program their squares so as to end each set of three with an especially energetic or favorite figure, one which often involves a good deal of swinging and everyone moving at the same time. Some of the old-timers still call this the "**jig** figure" and expect lively music, a fast fiddle piece, or something with a novelty or fast **swing** character. The square set ends with a "promenade away" call, and all the dancers retire to the sides of the floor, either for refreshments or to wait for the upcoming round dances. A typical evening of round and square dancing will include four to seven sets of square dances (three figures in each) interspersed with round dances. A few bands and callers will add in a novelty dance or two such as the "Hokey Pokey" or the "Chicken Dance" and possibly, among older dancers, a Virginia **Reel**.

Although sheet music or folio editions are easily available for most of the round dance tunes and many of those used for squares, it is unusual to actually see any music at a rural square dance. Many of the musicians cannot read music and very few ever read music while playing a dance. They have learned the tunes by listening to others. Bands that feature mostly commercial country songs for the round dances, however, may have a notebook with song lyrics for a vocalist. There have also been many printed collections of square dance figures and calls, though it is hard to find a rural caller who has ever used one. The market for these published sources has been chiefly more urban or school recreation programs and the network of modern square dance clubs. Printed music and calls also figure prominently in the modern contra dance movement.

Rural callers, on the other hand, have learned their calls from hearing other callers, either live (usually while dancing) or on recordings. Similarly, most rural dancers have learned to dance by watching others and just being pulled into a dance. The most significant recorded sources in central and western New York were the two collections of music and calls performed by Woodhull's Old Tyme Masters, with Floyd Woodhull of Elmira, New York, calling. These were released by RCA in the 1940s and early 1950s. Many of today's callers will say they still have the old Woodhull collections at home and at least some of Woodhull's calls can be heard at any old-time dance in the area. There are no published newsletters or magazines that inform or unify dancers, callers, or musicians in the rural dance scene, only the small ads and occasional commentary in small-town newspapers and pennysavers.

THE MUSIC

Most of the tunes, along with accompanying harmonies, are learned orally from other players or from recordings, although today's players can often remember one or another musician who relied on written notation in the past. An evening of round and square dancing is likely to include a wide variety of tunes, depending largely on the taste, skill, and generation of both the band and the dancers. An older band tends to attract or be hired by older dancers. A younger group will follow a younger band. The older group will generally have a larger repertoire of the older dance forms: fox-trots, waltzes, schottisches, and more of the older square dance favorites. Younger bands rely on more contemporary country or rock music and usually have a smaller repertoire of squares.

The squares themselves come in two main categories: singing and nonsinging. The first of these requires easy song tunes to which the caller sings the calls. This style has been common in parts of New York since the late nineteenth century, and at least a few of the old favorites may still be heard. One good example is the call "First Two Ladies Cross Over," sung to an adaptation of the 1830s Henry Russell song, "A Life on the Ocean Wave." In its original **form** the song takes up thirty-two bars in 6/8 time, AA'BA, plus a **coda** section at the end. All that survives in the square dance setting are the first two A parts followed by a contrasting eight-bar B section for a promen ade. The sung and played A sections are immediately recognizable by the experienced square dance crowd; the instrumental B part, on the other hand, varies from player to player, who may even freely quote some other tune. Younger and less experienced bands will sometimes just play another A part.

Most of the newer singing call tunes—those that became popular from the 1930s into the 1950s—use familiar old standards, folk or popular, or country songs newly popularized in that period. In addition to tunes already named, these include "Little Brown Jug," "Hot Time in the Old Town Tonight," "Alabama Jubilee," "Walking the

Floor Over You," and dozens more of similar character. There was little new in the actual square dance figures, but they were being danced to newer tunes.

Nonsinging calls clearly represent an older and more widespread tradition in New York. Almost any old fiddle tune will do, as long as it is quick and in 2/4 or 6/8 time, though individual callers and musicians will have a few favorites that tend to dominate this part of their repertoire. A few are nameless tunes passed on from earlier players (e.g., "Sanger's Tune" and "C and F," indicating the keys of the two sections). Most are fairly well known fiddle tunes from the Scots-Irish or Anglo-American traditions: "Soldier's Joy," "Arkansas Traveler," "Redwing," "Ragtime Annie," and so on. Musicians may repeat sections or not, AABB, AB or AAAB, depending on the needs of the dance or their own preferences. Three-section tunes are usually reduced to just two, sometimes even one, as less experienced musicians avoid key changes or just don't bother with the whole tune. More complex fiddle patterns become simplified as electric guitars take over the fiddle role.

Rural square dancers demand primarily that the musicians give them familiar tunes played with a steady danceable beat. They appreciate some variety, but don't necessarily make a distinction as to age or source of the music played. Callers need to impart humor and variety into the evening and be able to time the calls with the music. Conversely, the music needs to fit the dance and the call, including being in a comfortable key for the caller's voice and at a suitable tempo for the dancers. Other than this it is a social time. If the company, the hall, the refreshments and, where applicable, the cause is good, the dancers and the musicians will enjoy themselves.

DANCE SPONSORS

Any one of a number of organizations might sponsor round and square dances. Among the best known for many years across rural New York have been the Granges, which

See glossary for definition of boldfaced terms

have long supported education, political advocacy, and entertainment in farming communities. Granges are on the decline, however, and only a few still put on regular dances. Other sponsors in recent years have included rural businesses and arts councils, volunteer fire companies, church and community groups, political parties, schools, and campgrounds. Some dances are held to raise money for individuals who need help relating to illness or fire loss.

The specific nature of the sponsor will determine in part who comes, and many nondancers may attend out of allegiance to the sponsor or the cause. Some of these may be pulled into square dances as extra couples are needed; others will just watch or participate only in the round dances. There is no specific dress code for these events; dancers tend to wear whatever their generation is comfortable with, from jeans and sneakers for the youngest to jackets and ties or dresses for the oldest. A number of experienced square dancers will show up at nearly any advertised dance as they follow favorite bands and callers or groups of friends, sometimes driving an hour or more to get to an event. Most have in common a rural background and a love of square dancing that makes this a Saturday-night priority, especially through the winter months. Many are members of a generation that experienced a wave of popular high school

round and square dances in the late 1940s and 1950s.

DOCUMENTARY RECORDINGS AND FILMS

There is very little commercially available documentation of the traditional round and square dance in rural New York State. One recording that includes a few examples of older-style local square dance tunes, some with calls, is *Mark Hamilton: Songs and Tunes from Wolf Run* (1995). Mark is an old-time caller and fiddler who bridges the older generation from the early twentieth century to the 1940s and 1950s.

BIBLIOGRAPHY

Bonner, Simon. (1987). *Old-Time Music Makers of New York State.* Syracuse: University of Syracuse Press.

———. (1988). "The Anglo-American Fiddle Tradition in New York State." *New York Folklore* 14:23–36.

Kimball, James. (1988). "Country Dancing in Central and Western New York State." *New York Folklore* 14:71–88.

———. (1997). "Old-Time Fiddle Traditions in New York State." *Fiddler Magazine,* 4(4):6–9.

Mark Hamilton: Songs and Tunes from Wolf Run. 1995. Rochester, NY: Sampler Records Ltd. CD recording and booklet with notes by James Kimball.

EARLY SHAKER SPIRITUALS

Daniel W. Patterson

Daniel W. Patterson is Kenan Professor Emeritus of English and Folklore at the University of North Carolina at Chapel Hill. He is the author of numerous books, including The Shaker Spiritual *(2nd edition, Dover Books, 2000). He has also collaborated on several documentary films and recordings. The following essay is adapted from the notes Patterson wrote to accompany a 1976 Rounder Records album entitled* Early Shaker Spirituals Sung by Sister R. Mildred Barker with Sisters Ethel Peacock, Elsie McCool, Della Haskell, Marie Burgess, Frances Carr, and Other Members of the United Society of Shakers, Sabbathday Lake, Maine *(Rounder 0078).*

In 1780 a Baptist preacher from the Berkshires crossed into New York to investigate a "strange work" in the wilderness above Albany, where converts were flocking to an "Elect Lady" from England. He returned home proclaiming the fulfillment of Revelation 14, for his eyes had seen the Lamb and Its virgin company.

"I would as quick speak against the Holy Ghost, as speak against that people," he declared to neighbors gathered in a large barn. "They sing the song of the redeemed, they sing the song of the hundred and forty and four thousand, which were redeemed from the earth . . . they seemed like an innumerable company of Angels, and Church of the first born, singing praises to the Heavenly Host."[1]

He had seen and heard Ann Lee, the daughter of a blacksmith in the slums of Manchester, who six years earlier had fled to America to escape mob violence and harassment from the law. She died in 1784,

but her personality and teachings were the foundations on which American converts founded the United Society of Believers in Christ's Second Appearing, commonly called the Shakers.

In the nineteenth century the group's distinctive beliefs and practices brought it much notice. Rejecting the commonly held doctrines of the Trinity and the atonement, the Shakers conceived the Deity to encompass both the male attribute of *"Power to create"* and the female attribute of *"Wisdom to bring forth into proper order."*[2] They held that the millennial dispensation had already begun, manifested first through Ann Lee and then as a gradual and increasing work in the hearts of the Believers and in the Church. It was the coming of the Christ Spirit, or Divine Love. All could share in it who would cleanse their hearts through confession of their sins and then take up a "full cross" against the World, the Flesh, and the Devil. To further this work the Believers separated themselves from the World, refusing to vote or bear arms,

Shakers service in Lebanon, New York, as portrayed in a nineteenth-century engraving.
© CORBIS

and gathering into self-supporting farming communities where they put "hands to work and hearts to God" and shared all their goods as children of one family. They maintained traditional sexual distinctions in dress and labor but practiced celibacy and at all levels of both the temporal and the spiritual governance of their society gave women an equal role.

Although most of their beliefs and practices had a biblical foundation and parallels in those of other radical Dissenting groups, the Shakers carried them all to their logical limits. What most often caught the eye of travelers and journalists in the course of the century, however, was the Shakers' mode of worship. At a public service they saw lines of Believers in uniform attire file into the meetinghouse, the brethren taking their stand in ranks on the left side of the room and sisters on the right. After singing a **hymn** or anthem, the Believers began a series of religious dances and marches interspersed with shorter songs and with testimonies. Their speaker generally addressed not the Believers but the World's people seated in special sections along the wall. As the service progressed, it often grew emotional and was attended by such Pentecostal manifestations as shaking, turning, speaking in tongues, or "singing in the gift."

In their worship the Believers played no musical **instruments**, which for the Shaker had disturbing associations. Instruments had too often been used "to excite lasciviousness, and to invite and stimulate men to destroy each others lives." But more important, the Shakers believed that the direct result of introducing elaborate instrumental music into a church had always been to "induce a lifeless form."[3] For the same reason they could not countenance part-singing or the use of trained choirs led by a hired professional. They instead wanted "each one for one" to seek "that power of God that alone saves the soul from sin." The Shakers, like others in the Dissenting tradition, were reacting against the exclusion of the common man from full participation in religious worship.

But the Shakers did not sing the psalmody or hymnody of the Presbyterians, Congregationalists, Baptists, or Methodists among whom they were raised. They found the texts of these songs surcharged with erroneous doctrines or sentiments. They felt impelled to make new songs of their own. For melodies they turned, as other groups were then beginning to do, to Anglo-American folk song, itself a tradition that favored unaccompanied solo or **unison** song. Sophisticated observers often recognized—with derision—the source of the Shaker songs. A high-toned Virginian, for example, wrote that he had heard the Kentucky Shakers sing such tunes as "Fire in the Mountains" and others "made use of among the vulgar class at their **frolicks**."[4] And many of the Shakers were well supplied with such melodies. By his own word the early Shaker leader Elder Issachar Bates could in his youth sing "about every song that was going, whether civil, military, sacred, or profane."[5] He was also a **fifer**-boy at the Battle of Bunker Hill.

But there was another and deeper reason why the Shakers drew on **secular** folk song. As the music that they knew and loved best, these tunes met one of the Shakers' major aesthetic criteria, that of helping the members to "unite" in worship. They needed familiar songs that even indifferently gifted members could join in singing, ones "substantial, not given to great extreems, forcible, clear & plain."[6] In services they used them to bring the feelings and thoughts of the Believers into harmony, at times even appointing a specific song to be sung in every village at the same hour, to achieve a more perfect union. They sent songs by travelers or in letters from society to society, finding that they operated "like the magnetic telegraph, to convey love and union from one branch of Zion to another" and "strengthen the bond of relationship already existing with every true Believer."[7] When used with the dances and marches, the songs had a doubly strong effect. The Believer saw these exercises as "beautiful and glorious" because their "unity and harmony" were "emblematical of the *one spirit* by which the people of God are led."[8]

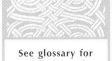

See glossary for definition of boldfaced terms

The Shakers, however, did not simply borrow the World's music. They instead used it freely as a musical language with which to create new melodies. They might convert a **ballad melody** into one for the dance by stripping off two of its **phrases** and adding a strain appropriately higher or lower, singing each half of the new tune twice. Or they might combine the high section of one familiar dance tune with the low part of another, or elaborate a new melody from the opening phrase of an old one.

Shaker musical creativity was encouraged by a second important Shaker aesthetic principle, namely, that only those songs were recommendable that bore the "feeling" of being "given or matured under a heavenly sensation or spiritual impulse"—in other words, ones "received by divine inspiration."[9] We have many accounts of how the inspired received their songs. "I have listened for hours," wrote one sister, "to delightful music, which seemed to flood the air high above my head. And tho' it seemed to be human voices, it sounded like chimes of bells, of different sizes & tones, but in perfect **harmony**." At other times, she said, "I heard no audible voice, but felt my soul filled with music which flowed forth in songs," sitting at twilight singing "one new song after another till they seemingly numbered hundreds, all joined together like links in a chain."[10] Other Shakers received songs from heavenly spirits while having dreams and visions or sang them in possession states as instruments of these spirits.

As a corollary of their openness to inspiration, the Shakers declined even to be bound to any one set of songs or mode of worship. "No gift or order of God," they held, "can be binding on Believers for a longer term of time than it can be profitable to their travel in the gospel."[11] As a consequence, new songs kept crowding old ones from the repertory, and as the decades passed, song type succeeded song type in popularity. In the earliest years their congregational music was the "solemn song," generally a ballad tune sung with **vocables** instead of words. About 1805 these were displaced by long doctrinal hymns, and these in turn gave way about 1820 to shorter hymns of sentiment, both sets of hymns being sung to melodies taken from balladry. Dance, which began as a spontaneous expression of emotional transport, was regularized in the 1780s, and in the eighteenth century the Shakers practiced at least seven different forms, each with its own set of tunes. Two, the "regular step" and the "holy order" dances, continued popular until the Civil War years. Meantime, new dances had been introduced, and beginning in the

1820s, some six forms of marching, all with their special songs. The dances had fallen into disuse by the 1880s, but some marches were still practiced in "young people's meetings" as late as the 1930s. During the pauses between the laboring exercises, the Believers began in 1810 to sing short "extra songs" and about the same time accepted the use of long anthems to open a service. Between 1837 and 1850, during a period of intense revivalism called "Mother's Work," there was an astonishing outpouring of "gift songs," often highly irregular in form—songs with rhapsodic melodic structures and texts wholly or partly in unknown tongues or pidgin English.

Beginning about 1870 the repertory of early songs began largely to pass from use. Shakerism was entering a liberal phase, a change expressed musically in a growing acceptance of nontraditional practices. The Believers now purchased pianos and organs, studied harmony, and, taking late nineteenth-century **gospel** songs and the parlor ballad as their models, created an entirely new repertory of songs, ones they printed in harmonized settings in a dozen hymnals between 1875 and 1908.

These later songs became in many societies the music of the Shaker worship service. Most of the earlier songs would have been lost had Believers not undertaken to write them down. This they facilitated by inventing a simple system of musical notation using the letters of the alphabet as the heads of the notes and dispensing with the notions of fixed **pitch** and key signatures. Between the years 1820 and 1870 most of the villages had scribes who recorded the new songs in this "letteral notation." Nearly eight hundred of their manuscript songbooks survive. They hold a repertory of between eight and ten thousand different tunes, a body of folk songs far outnumbering all the ballads and even all the other **spirituals** known to have originated in America. Yet at their height in the 1840s the Shakers had a membership of only six thousand persons in nineteen villages scattered from Maine across New Hampshire, Massachusetts, Connecticut, and New York to Ohio and Kentucky.

In the nineteenth century several hundred of the Believers could read the music manuscripts. With the change of taste in the 1870s, however, the younger Shakers began to study conventional musical notation and as a consequence to lose all knowledge of the letteral system. To present-day Shakers the early tune **transcriptions** are a closed book, but the sisters at Sabbathday Lake recall a good number of the songs. The Maine communities had always been among the smallest, poorest, and most traditional of the Shaker villages. In the 1870s the ministry in Maine even held out for some time against the urging of the other societies that they purchase instruments and music books from the World. "The *truth* is," wrote one elder there, that instruments "lead to *fashionable* life. The more musical instruments the less *manual labor,* more dress, etc., etc. For us in Maine there is no way or hope, only, to *work* out our salvation."[12]

In Maine many of the early songs are used even yet in services, and when recent members there came among the Believers as children, they heard the older Shakers sing them. The late Sister Elsie McCool learned her repertory at Sabbathday Lake, where she grew up. The late Sisters Ethel Peacock and Della Haskell and Sister R. Mildred Barker were already young women when they came to Sabbathday Lake in 1931 on the closing of the community at Alfred, Maine, and had learned their songs at the latter society. Sisters Marie Burgess and Frances Carr came to Sabbathday Lake in the 1930s and learned from all the older singers there, especially from Sister Mildred. Eldress Harriett Coolbroth at Alfred had been particularly pleased to find Mildred musically gifted and a lover of songs. In the evenings she often invited the child to her room to learn a new one. Sister Mildred taped some 200 early spirituals.

A hundred years have passed, however, since the Shaker folk spiritual began to drop from the active repertory. Present singers therefore cannot offer a sampling of all the song types that once had a place in Shaker worship. No one can sing any of the early wordless dance tunes or solemn songs. Two

or three general favorites, such as "The Rolling Deep" and "I Never Did Believe," originated as early as the 1820s. Sister Mildred sang a number of the "gift songs" of the 1840s, and all the singers know quite a few dating from the 1850s and 1860s. Many of the most beautiful of the early spirituals, however, are preserved only in manuscripts.

Doubtless sheer happenstance played some role in determining which ones would remain in active use, but there are additional reasons. After the uniting of the two Maine societies in 1931, the members tended to sing only the pieces already known to both groups. Sister Mildred's comments show that she also kept some songs like "Mother Has Come with Her Beautiful Song" because they evoke memories of older Shakers whom she loved. The melodies of other songs have intrinsic appeal. Most of all, however, the singers hold to a song because its text moves them. The anthems are usually settings of favorite passages from the Bible. A gift song from "Mother's Work" may still touch the Believer with its words of admonition and comfort from heavenly spirits. But most of the remembered songs are prayers and testimonies, and in present-day worship they are usually sung spontaneously as the spoken testimonies of the various members call them to mind.

"We must remember," wrote Eldress Marguerite Frost of Canterbury, "that these were not just songs, but deep feelings from the soul."[13] They speak vows of renewed dedication. They voice thankfulness and joy in the calling. They are prayers for aid in attaining a more careful walk or a deeper spirituality. Especially in the more modern compositions, these sentiments are often expressed in direct wording.

Older songs at their best draw instead upon symbols once common in Shaker thought and discourse, ones taken from the work-a-day activities of a farming community, from folk tradition, or especially from the Bible. Almost always the symbols that already had currency have been redefined to express a distinctively Shaker view. Thus for the Believers the willow does not stand for weeping but for bending to God's will. The dove is not a symbol of the Holy Ghost but an emblem of the humble soul. The valley is neither a place for penitence nor the valley of the shadow of death, but the low vale of humility. Jordan's banks are not stormy but covered with lilies for the faithful, and its waters roll with cleansing, not mortal, tides. Many of the songs are filled with metaphors for the activity of soul that is the goal of Shaker worship. They call the Believer to rouse from "death," "bondage," or a "scat-

tered sense" and to "wake up" and "shake out all the starch and stiffening." "I feel the need of a deeper baptism," says one thoroughly characteristic song, "into the work of the Lord, The Holy Ghost and fire from heaven, the sharp and quickening word!"

The importance of song to the Shakers grew directly from its relation to this quickened life. In worship the songs helped to lift the Believer from dull spirits into "life and power." They could even be the means by which the seeker passed from the World into the Faith. One early convert said, for example, that when he went to scout out the English Shakers near Albany, he was not affected by the preaching of the elders, though they bore "a faithful and sound testimony against all sin of every name and nature." But when Mother Ann Lee and "her little family" sat down that afternoon and sang in "a solemn and heavenly manner," he said, "I felt as tho I had got among the heavenly hosts, and had no right there; for I had neither part nor lot in it. I cried aloud, in distress of soul; for I believed it to be the worship of the living God, such as my ears had never heard, nor my soul ever felt before."[14] Once quickened, the Believer found his own creative powers and contributed to this tradition of Pentecostal folk song. "And what makes it more striking," wrote one Shaker in 1820, "it is those who had never learned to sing at all—they could scarcely follow after those who were singers. Now they will sing as beautiful as I ever heard anyone; yea beautiful Anthems & Songs, all given when they are under the beautiful operations of the power of God."[15]

ENDNOTES

1. For permission to quote from unpublished manuscripts I wish to thank the following institutions: The Henry Francis du Pont Winterthur Museum (hereafter cited its DWt), the Manuscripts Division of the Library of Congress (WLC), the Shaker Museum of Old Chatham, New York (NYOC), the United Society of Shakers, Sabbathday Lake, Maine (MeSL), and the Western Reserve Historical Society Library (OCWR). Where possible I cite the library's identification number for the item. DWt, SA799.1, pp. 119–120.

2. *A Summary View of the Millennial Church* (Albany, 1823), p. 92.

3. OCWR, SM506, p. [18], and WLC, No. 241, pp. 8–9.

4. "Nourse-Chapline Letters," *Kentucky Historical Society Register* 31 (1933), p. 167.

5. NYOC, Ac. 12.051, vol. 1, p. 19.

6. OCWR, Letter, Lebanon, N.Y., Aug. 6, 1830, Isaac N. Youngs to Andrew, p. [2].

7. OCWR, Letter, Enfield, N.H., June 8, 1854, Ministry to Beloved Ministry, p. [2].

8. Benjamin S. Youngs, *Testimony of Christ's Second Appearing,* 4th ed. (Albany, 1856), p. 588.

9. OCWR, Letter, Lebanon, N.Y., Aug. 6. 1830, Isaac N. Youngs to Andrew, p. [2].

10. OCWR, Alonzo G. Hollister, "Book of Lovely Vineyard," p. 56.

11. *Millennial Praises* (Hancock, 1813), p. iv.

12. MeSL, Letter Book, May 1872–Jan. 1883, p. 65.

13. Letter to author, May 25, 1965, p. 3.

14. *Testimonies Concerning the Character and Ministry of Mother Ann Lee* (Albany, 1827), p. 127.

15. OCWR, Letter, Pleasant Hill, Ky., April 1, 1820, Samuel Turner to Br. Calvin.

BIBLIOGRAPHY

Andrews, Edward D. (1962). *The Gift to Be Simple: Songs, Dances and Rituals of the American Shakers.* Reprint. New York: Dover Publications.

Cook, Harold E. (1973). *Shaker Music: A Manifestation of American Folk Culture.* Lewisburg, PA.: Bucknell University Press.

Early Shaker Spirituals Sung by Sister R. Mildred Barker with Sisters Ethel Peacock, Elsie McCool, Della Haskell, Marie Burgess, Frances Carr, and Other Members of the United Society of Shakers, Sabbathday Lake, Maine, with Notes by Daniel W. Patterson. 1996. Rounder 0078. CD and audiocassette reissue of LP album originally released in 1976.

Let Zion Move: Music of the Shakers. 1999. Roger D. Hall, ed. Rounder CD (2 discs) 0471. Forty songs recorded between 1960 and 1980 at Canterbury, New Hampshire, and Sabbathday Lake, Maine.

Patterson, Daniel W. (1966). "The Influence of Inspiration and Discipline upon the Development of the Shaker Spiritual." *Shaker Quarterly* 6 (fall):77–87.

———. (1968). "'Bearing for the Dead': A Shaker Belief and Its Impress on the Shaker Spiritual." *Shaker*

Quarterly 8 (winter):116–128.

———. (1989–90). "Implications of Late Nineteenth Century Shaker Music," *Shaker Quarterly* 16 (winter):214–235.

———. (1990). "Millennial Praises: Tune Locations and Authorial Attributions of the First Shaker Hymnal," *Shaker Quarterly* 18 (fall):77–84.

———. (1994). "Sister Mildred Barker and the Maine Song Tradition," *Shaker Quarterly* 22 (winter):192–202.

———. (2000). *The Shaker Spiritual.* 2nd edition, corrected, with new preface. Mineola, NY: Dover Publications.

The Shakers. 1972. Tom Davenport. 29 min. Delaplane, VA: Tom Davenport Films. With interviews and song performances by Canterbury and Sabbathday Lake Shakers. Available in color in 16mm film or VHS videocassette format.

MUSIC OF THE OLD REGULAR BAPTISTS OF CENTRAL APPALACHIA

Jeff Todd Titon

Please see the "Introduction to American Musical Traditions" in this volume for biographical information on co-editor Jeff Todd Titon.

A religious denomination descended from the Calvinist wing of the Protestant Reformation, Old Regular Baptists (ORBs) are concentrated in the central portion of the southern Appalachian Mountains, particularly in the counties of southeastern Kentucky and southwestern Virginia (see map). They descend chiefly from English, Scots-Irish, and German (Pennsylvania Dutch) immigrants, most of whom settled in Appalachia in the nineteenth century. Sixteen associations of ORBs comprise approximately 15,000 members and come from all walks of life. In their small region they are the dominant religious group. They preserve an eighteenth-century **hymn** repertory and an even older way of singing that once was common in the American colonies but now is little known or practiced outside this region. (Dorgan 1989 gives an overview of the ORBs' beliefs and practices.)

THE MUSIC

Music serves the primary function of offering praise to the Lord. As in other Protestant hymnody, the whole congregation is invited to sing. The songs are sung in church as part of worship, at memorial meetings and baptisms, and in homes. The singing brings the worshipers closer to God and to each other. The older texts express praise and thanksgiving to God, while more modern texts dwell on the joys of heaven. The singers meditate on the words as they sing.

Songs of the ORBs fall into the musical **genre** of the Anglo-European Christian devotional hymn, with lyrics by eighteenth-century writers such as Isaac Watts, coupled to melodies living in **oral tradition** and taken from the British/Irish folksong stock. The distinctive musical features are:

- melodic elaboration, in which a given vowel of text may carry a sequence of two to five (rarely more) pitches;

- **antiphonal** singing in a manner called "**lining out**";
- slow **tempos** without a regular pulse beat;
- no musical instruments (the music is vocal only);
- a **heterophonic** vocal **texture**.

Like almost all Christian hymns, Old Regular Baptist congregational songs (as they call them) consist of rhymed, metrical **verse** in a series of **stanzas** to which a repeating tune is set. The metrical verse patterns include common meter (alternating lines of 8 and 6 syllables; that is, 8,6,8,6); long meter (8,8,8,8); short meter (6,6,8,6); and various others. The **leader** sings the very first line, and the congregation joins in when they recognize the song. After that the song proceeds line by line: the leader briefly chants a line alone, and then the group repeats the words but to a tune that is much longer and more elaborate than the leader's chant or lining tune.

Listeners or singers who approach this music for the first time have difficulty because there is no steady pulse beat. The rhythmic framework is governed not by metronome time but by breath-time. Yet the singers' sense of time is remarkably consistent from one line and verse to the next, and with experience one learns.

Songbooks are kept at the pulpit and passed around to the song leaders. These books have words without musical notation. The oldest lyrics are the eighteenth-century hymns, written chiefly by familiar English or American devotional poets. These fill their two favorite songbooks, the collections *Sweet Songster* and the *Thomas Hymnal*. Newer song books contain a mix of the older hymns, nineteenth-century **camp-meeting songs** and **spirituals**, **gospel** hymns from the later nineteenth century onwards, and finally a number of contemporary gospel songs—some written by Old Regulars known to have this gift, others popular on

the radio and recordings. The congregation catches the words from the song leader as he lines out the song. They do not have song-books at their seats.

Tunes are passed along orally from one singer to the next and from one generation to the next. Singers learn by following and imitating others, not by reading notes, for there is no musical notation for this music. Melodies are highly elaborated: many sylla-bles have three or more tones, and many have at least two. Their closest parallel in melodic elaboration is to the **Gaelic *sean-nós*** singing tradition in Ireland. Each singer is free to "curve" the tune a little differently, and those who are able to make it more elab-orate are admired. Outsiders are mistaken if they think the intent is singing with unified precision and that the result falls short; on the contrary, the singing is in step and de-liberately just a bit out of phase—one of its most powerful musical aspects.

ORBs believe that their music is a gift from God and should be sung freely to ex-press praise to the Creator. Everyone who can and will, sings. A pretty voice is not im-portant. Singing from the heart brings a per-son closer to God. People who are overcome by emotion during a song shout or weep for joy, but only a small percentage are so demonstrative. Sometimes people cannot clear their hearts and minds to experience music properly and thus they refrain from singing. Music should be unaccompanied, sung "with the voice that God gave us."

ORBs do not preach or sing on radio, television, or other media. Their songs are not for sale. In church, at memorial services, baptisms, and funerals, and among family at home are the usual contexts for singing, but one should sing whenever moved to do so. Stories circulate among the ORBs about men occasionally singing in the coal mines and show that the impulse to sing should not be denied despite ordinary social pro-prieties. Most ORBs oppose changing and modernizing the old songs, many of which date from the nineteenth century or earlier. ORBs consider their music to be one mark of their particular identity, both spiritually and historically.

Gravestones in a family cemetery, Pine Top, Kentucky, 1990. These simple, time-weathered stones reflect the straightforward religious beliefs of the Old Regular Baptists.
Photograph by Jeff Todd Titon.

In church, ORBs sing as a congregation; they do not have choirs, choir directors, re-hearsals, or musical **instruments** to accom-pany the singing. Ministers sometimes will sing a solo or lead a song just before preach-ing, and occasionally members of the con-gregation will request a special song by a small (usually family) group. Most people who become ORBs join as adults. Some wait until middle or old age to join. Youngsters, particularly teenagers, are not expected to be interested. As a result, the membership consists largely of married adults. The formal church organization is patriarchal. Only men are permitted to deliver sermons, lead songs, hold office, and speak in business meetings. Women make their opinions known informally. Men and women church members sit on separate sides of the church by custom; visitors oc-cupy the fourth and largest quadrant of the church sanctuary. While delivering ser-mons, preachers look in all four directions. In some churches, husbands and wives sing duets together upon request. Couples bring babies and young children, who remain during the entire worship service—there is no Sunday school. Children usually are quiet but are free to walk around in the sanctuary, sometimes going to the pulpit to get candy.

HISTORY

Calvinist emphasis on plain, participatory congregational singing is felt in the history of ORB music. More particularly their music is traceable to practices of the sixteenth-century English parish church (Temperley 1981). In 1644 the Westminster Assembly of Divines recommended the practice of lining out, and it was adopted in Massachusetts a few years later. By the end of the seventeenth century lining out had become the "common way of singing" among Anglicans and in other Protestant denominations (Lutherans excepted) throughout Britain and its colonies. African Americans learned it and carry a parallel tradition today, particularly among Baptists in the rural South.

As American settlers moved during the eighteenth and early nineteenth centuries into the frontier South, to the Shenandoah Valley and later across the Cumberland Gap, they carried the "common way" (now called "the old way") of singing with them. Most Appalachian settlers from the English/Scottish borderlands were familiar with this music, for it had lingered there well into the eighteenth century even after it had declined in southern England and the urban parts of the American colonies. The Old Baptists used well-known **secular** tunes and composed other, similar-sounding tunes to carry the sacred texts. Nineteenth-century camp meetings gave rise to newer spiritual songs—usually easily sung, rapid **choruses** with **refrains**. But the more conservative Old Baptist ancestors of the Old Regulars clung to the traditional ways in singing, also resisting musical notation in shaped notes, a reform designed to drive out the "old way of singing."

The greatest challenge to "the old way of singing" among the Old Regulars today comes from the gospel songs on radio and recordings. A few of the churches have succumbed to part-singing, and many include a percentage of gospel hymnody, but usually the gospel hymns are changed to ORB style, lined out and melodically elaborated. Most of the tunes come from the Anglo-American folksong tradition. Some of these, such as the one used for both "Guide Me O Thou Great Jehovah" and "Every Moment Brings Me Nearer" are quite old, while others are more recent compositions in the same folksong style. Some tunes, such as those for "Salvation O the Name I Love" and "The Day Is Past and Gone," are clearly related to tunes that were printed in parts in nineteenth-century **shape-note** hymnals. But this does not mean that the Old Regulars' songs came from those printed versions, for the book tunes were written down from melodies in oral tradition then. More likely, the Old Regulars were already singing the tunes before they were written down by the editors of nineteenth-century shape-note hymnals. Newer tunes are either adaptations of gospel hymn tunes ("Precious Memories," for example, done in a lined-out format) or compositions by local and regional songwriters that draw on the resources of all available melodic traditions.

See glossary for definition of boldfaced terms

BIBLIOGRAPHY

Dorgan, Howard. (1989). *Brothers and Sisters in Hope: The Old Regular Baptists of Central Appalachia.* Knoxville: University of Tennessee Press.

In the Good, Old-Fashioned Way. 1973. Produced by Herb E. Smith et al. Whitesburg, KY: Appalshop. VHS videotape.

Songs of the Old Regular Baptists: Lined-Out Hymnody from Southeastern Kentucky. 1997. Co-produced by Elwood Cornett, John Wallhausser, and Jeff Titon. Smithsonian Folkways SF CD 40106.

Temperley, Nicholas. (1981). "The Old Way of Singing."*Journal of the American Musicological Society* 34:511–44.

While the Ages Roll On. 1992. Co-produced by Kevin Balling and Howard Dorgan. Boone, NC: Appalachian Center, Appalachian State University. VHS videotape.

PRIMITIVE BAPTIST SINGING IN THE SOUTHERN APPALACHIANS

Beverly Bush Patterson

Beverly Bush Patterson is a folklife specialist at the North Carolina Arts Council in Raleigh, North Carolina, where she researches and documents the state's traditional artists and culture, administers a grants program, and consults on a wide variety of folk arts projects, including museum exhibits, publications, films, and heritage tourism. She is the author of The Sound of the Dove: Singing in Appalachian Primitive Baptist Churches *(University of Illinois Press, 1995).*

During the nineteenth century, the Primitive Baptists became a strong presence in Appalachian regions of North Carolina, Virginia, West Virginia, and Kentucky, as they did in other regions such as New England, the middle Atlantic and midwestern states, and parts of the lowland south. Although their numbers have steadily declined, especially in northern states, since the early 1900s, Primitive Baptist churches in the Appalachian region remain active, and some of them continue to attract new members. Their strict adherence to the doctrine of predestination, combined with practices such as foot washing, river baptizing, dinner on the ground, and monthly (instead of weekly) worship services, helps distinguish them from numerous other churches in the region.

Most Primitive Baptists, like Old Regular Baptists, practice some form of unaccompanied, congregational **hymn** singing that is an outgrowth of seventeenth-century psalmody of the British Isles and the American colonies and of early eighteenth-century hymnody. It is one of the oldest traditions of American religious folk song.

The Mountain District Primitive Baptist Association, composed of a group of churches clustered near the North Carolina–Virginia border, was the focus of field research reported in *Pilgrims of Progress* (Peacock and Tyson 1989) and *The Sound of the Dove* (Patterson 1995). Churches in that association not only have contacts with other Primitive Baptists in the region but also with church elders from Ohio, Texas, and Georgia who visit regularly to preach; they also recognize a scattering of like-minded congregations across the nation. Because the Primitive Baptists in other regions have been less studied, this account will draw principally on practices in the Mountain District Association.

HISTORY

Churches in the Mountain District Primitive Baptist Association trace their roots in Amer-

ica to the Welsh Tract Church, which became part of the Philadelphia Baptist Association in 1707. Morgan Edwards, eighteenth-century Baptist historian and preacher, credited the Welsh Tract Church with being "the principal, if not sole, means of introducing singing . . . among the Baptists in the Middle States" (Spencer 1877, p. 41). When the "Old Baptists" split from the main body of Baptists in America in the early 1830s, the dissenting conservatives began calling themselves "Primitive" or "Old School" Baptists to distinguish their churches from Baptists that held Arminian beliefs. Outsiders negatively stereotyped them as "hard-shell" Baptists because of their adherence to the "hard" doctrines of particular election and salvation by grace.

Their rejection of musical **instruments** in church is a position once shared by many American churches, including other Baptists, Presbyterians, Methodists, Campbellites, Shakers, the Amish, and Mennonites. Except for a few "progressive" Primitive Baptists in Georgia who introduced the organ as an aid to singing around 1897, Primitive Baptists have upheld their practice of unaccompanied congregational singing even when their churches have experienced disagreements and divisions. The "conditionalist" churches, for example, applied the doc-

trine of predestination only to salvation. Their interpretation separated them from fellowship with the "absolutist" churches that saw predestination in all things. Both groups distinguished themselves from Primitive Baptist "universalists," also known as "no-hellers." The old style of singing, as practiced by Primitive Baptists in the Appalachian region, has undergone changes as the various congregations themselves have changed over generations. For church members, however, the sound of their own congregational singing remains a powerful expression of their religious identity.

MUSIC

The practice of hymn singing is a significant part of Primitive Baptist meetings: It opens and closes every meeting, sets the tone for worship, and expresses the deep religious beliefs and feelings of church members. A half-hour or more of singing hymns by request precedes every preaching service. An introduction of the preaching service follows the singing and typically includes a hymn as well as an opening prayer and some brief comments. At the close of the service, the congregation sings again during the ritual "hand of fellowship." Over time, individual congregations have developed distinctive musical

Hand of fellowship at the Cross Roads Primitive Baptist Church, Baywood, Virginia.
Photograph courtesy American Folklife Center, Library of Congress.

identities that reveal themselves in such things as their choice of hymnbooks, their preferences for particular hymn texts and tunes, the setting of **tempos**, and even the rhythms and harmonies that develop as they sing together. These differences are especially pronounced in comparisons of African American and Anglo-American Primitive Baptist churches, which Brett Sutton and Peter Hartman have documented in *Primitive Baptist Hymns of the Blue Ridge* (1982).

Lining out hymns, once a standard practice among Primitive Baptists, is no longer common. Occasionally a song leader will lead a hymn in this old **antiphonal** style, chanting one or two lines of text after which the congregation sings those lines in the hymn tune. **Song leaders** have a responsibility to set the **pitch** and start the tune when members of the congregation request hymns. Some stand and face the congregation to do this; many remain seated. Even when tunes are printed in the hymnbook, the song leader may choose yet another tune from memory, knowing from long experience which tunes fit the various texts and which ones the congregation likes to sing.

Although many Primitive Baptist churches now use hymn-and-tune books, one of the most popular hymnbooks in the Mountain District Primitive Baptist Associa-

tion contains only texts. The *Primitive Baptist Hymn Book* is a small, pocket-sized book of eighteenth- and nineteenth-century English and American hymns compiled by D. H. Goble in 1887 and still printed in its original form. "It's got the prettiest songs in it than any book that's ever been [written]," declared one Primitive Baptist woman. Even older is *The Primitive Hymns,* published in 1841 by Benjamin Lloyd and widely used by Primitive Baptists in other regions. Neither book contains tunes or tune suggestions, but both of them include a number of texts by Isaac Watts, John Newton, and other well-known authors whose hymns were widely sung in many Protestant churches in the late eighteenth and early nineteenth centuries. Primitive Baptists have kept these older books in continuous use since they were first issued.

The repertory of hymn tunes draws on a variety of musical sources. Some tunes come from the old English and American **ballad** and **lyric song** traditions of the mountain region. A few tunes have come to their makers through inspiration and have been passed on to the church community orally or in published tune books. Many Primitive Baptist hymn tunes appeared in nineteenth-century **shape-note** tune books (especially those published before 1850) that were widely used in singing schools in

the rural South. The southern tune books that influenced Primitive Baptist tradition are themselves heterogeneous in content, drawing on a diverse range of printed and oral sources. They include European compositions such as the psalm tune "Old Hundred" and American imitations of those models such as "Windham." Intermixed with these are **camp-meeting** and other **spiritual** songs recorded directly from American **oral tradition**, late eighteenth- and early nineteenth-century hymns by Lowell Mason and other composers influenced by German standards of musical composition, and somewhat later **gospel** songs.

A few members occasionally request the "old lonesome tunes," older tunes in minor modes that are not often sung now. All of these types remain in Primitive Baptist repertories, and congregations still sing them from memory. Despite the diversity of historical contexts and musical traditions represented in the songs, Primitive Baptists hear in the actual singing a consistent style that they recognize as their own.

Most Primitive Baptists agree that the voice is the only instrument appropriate for public worship. Among church members are a number of skilled musicians, but they do not bring their musical instruments into the church. They defend the practice of unaccompanied congregational singing by claiming scriptural authority. They find no evidence in the New Testament that musical instruments were used in establishing the early church, and Primitive Baptists do not believe they are necessary now. Neither do they believe in singing any text, or part of a text, that they find inconsistent with their doctrine or religious experience. A much-loved song about heaven such as "A Home in Heav'n! What a Joyful Thought" includes no mention of meeting mothers, fathers, or other family members. Primitive Baptists do not believe that recognition of earthly family and friends will be part of the soul's experience in heaven.

SOCIAL ORGANIZATION

Men and women have well defined roles in these churches. Although men take the public roles as preaching elders and church spokespersons, women exercise great influence in maintaining the fellowship within their local congregation and often among their sister churches as well. Primitive Baptists do not support Sunday Schools, youth groups, missionaries, or missionary societies, nor do they support choirs or special musical pre-

sentations by soloists. On special occasions such as weddings and funerals small groups of singers may perform. Normally, though, the whole congregation participates in the practice of singing, just as it does in all worship services and church business meetings.

BIBLIOGRAPHY

Cauthen, Joyce, ed. (1999). *Benjamin Lloyd's Hymn Book: A Primitive Baptist Song Tradition.* Montgomery: Alabama Folklife Association.

Dorgan, Howard. (1997). *In the Hands of a Happy God: The "No-Hellers" of Central Appalachia.* Knoxville: University of Tennessee Press.

Drummond, Robert Paul. (1989). *A Portion for the Singers.* Atwood, TN: Christian Baptist Library and Publishing Company.

Patterson, Beverly Bush. (1995). *The Sound of the Dove: Singing in Appalachian Primitive Baptist Churches.* Urbana: University of Illinois Press. Includes audiocassette of the same title produced by the author.

Peacock, James L., and Tyson, Ruel W. (1989). *Pilgrims of Paradox: Calvinism and Experience among the Primitive Baptists of the Blue Ridge.* Washington, D.C.: Smithsonian Institution Press.

Spencer, David. (1877). *The Early Baptists of Philadelphia.* Philadelphia: William Syckelmoore.

DOCUMENTARY RECORDINGS

Old Hymns Lined and Led by Elder Walter Evans. [c. 1960] Recorded and produced by elder Lasserre Bradley. Sovereign Grace 6444 and 6057-6058. Two LPs.

Primitive Baptist Hymns of the Blue Ridge. 1982. Recorded by Brett Sutton and Peter Hartman; edited with booklet by Brett Sutton. Chapel Hill: University of North Carolina Press. LP.

BALLAD SINGING IN MADISON COUNTY, NORTH CAROLINA

Beverly Bush Patterson

Please see Chapter 8 in this volume for biographical in-formation on Beverly Bush Patterson.

Madison County, in the mountains of western North Carolina, lies in a region long known for traditional music, song, and dance. The county is dotted with communities where folk song collectors have documented the singing of traditional British and American **ballads** since the early 1900s—Hot Springs, Allanstand, Alleghany, White Rock, Big Laurel, and Sodom (now called Revere). Bascom Lamar Lunsford, who was born there, called it "the last stand of the natural people," and he often featured Madison County musicians and singers in the "Mountain Dance and Folk Festival" he produced in nearby Asheville. Why Madison County is barely represented in the ballads and songs in *The Frank C. Brown Collection of North Carolina Folklore,* the largest single collection of one state's folklore, is an oversight that remains unexplained. In past years, three Madison County ballad singers have won recognition outside the mountain region: The North Carolina Folklore Society recognized Sheila Kay Adams with its Brown-Hudson award, and North Carolina's Folk Heritage Award was presented to the late Dellie Chandler Norton (died 1993) and the late Doug Wallin (died 2000). In 1990, Wallin also received a prestigious National Heritage Fellowship from the National Endowment for the Arts.

HISTORY

Ballads were common in many communities across North Carolina as late as the 1930s, but Madison County's reputation for ballad singing has outlasted that of most other places in the state. Generations of singers have maintained old ballad repertories as they absorbed new musical influences brought in with the county's economic development and social changes. By the late 1800s, the county had a railroad, a flourishing resort hotel, a Presbyterian school for girls, a thriving lumber industry, and a population of over 17,000, including 710

African Americans. Such changes, along with public work and public schools, exposed people to new kinds of music. Doug Wallin and his brother, Jack, for instance, sang songs they had picked up from the outside while keeping old family and community traditions.

Among the first to record Madison County singers were English folksong collector Cecil Sharp and his assistant Maud Karpeles, who visited there in the summers of 1916 and 1917. They made handwritten notations of tunes and texts, mostly ones of British origin, directly from performances by singers they visited. They collected seventy songs from Jane Gentry alone, the most they recorded from any one Appalachian singer. When Sharp's *English Folk Songs from the Southern Appalachians* was published in 1932, it included forty songs given by Jane Gentry and additional songs from Madison County ballad singers whose family names are known today for their songs and tunes: the Wallins, Nortons, Ramseys, Chandlers, and Rays.

The impact of Sharp's visit lives on in stories that continue to circulate more than eighty years later. Introductions to the community provided by John C. and Olive Dame Campbell, Frances Goodrich, and others gave him good access to singers. However, Doug Wallin—who proudly owned a well-worn copy of both volumes of Sharp's book—talked about several in his family who refused to participate in the project.

Doug, born too late (1919) to encounter Sharp, said his mother told him that Sharp and Maud Karpeles often passed by the house in which she and Doug's father had begun to raise their family, but that she never sang for them. "People at first thought they were spies or something—that was during World War I." Doug's grandfather, Tom Wallin, "told his folks that if any of them performed" for Sharp, "he wouldn't fool with them no more." Nevertheless, Sharp published four songs he got from Tom's brother Mitchell and twenty-two from their sister Mary Wallin Sands.

Later researchers produced sound recordings of Madison County ballad singing.

At the Library of Congress, Duncan Emrich recorded Jane Gentry's daughter Maud Gentry Long. A documentary film by John Cohen made in 1963 featured Dillard Chandler and his first cousins, sisters Berzilla Wallin and Dellie Norton. Sound recordings edited by Cohen between 1963 and 1978 highlight these three singers and additional family members, Lee Wallin, Cas Wallin, and Lloyd Chandler. British researcher Mike Yates recorded Evelyn Ramsey, Doug Wallin, Dellie Norton, Inez Chandler, and Cas Wallin. Doug and Jack Wallin are featured on a 1995 CD produced by the **Folklife** Program of the North Carolina Arts Council in collaboration with Smithsonian Folkways. Evelyn Ramsey has taught ballad singing to students at War-

Doug Wallin, Madison, North Carolina, county ballad singer, photographed in 1989. *Photograph © Robnert Amberg, courtesy of the Folklife Program, North Carolina Arts Council, Dept. of Cultural Resources.*

ren Wilson College and Mars Hill College. Sheila Kay Adams (formerly Sheila Adams Barnhill), a seventh-generation ballad singer who learned many songs from her great-aunt and adopted "Granny" Dellie Norton, has produced her own recordings as has her cousin, Lena Jean Ray.

SINGERS AND STYLES

Singers perform ballads in home and community settings for themselves, their families, and friends. They have deep feelings about the songs and bring emotional intensity to their singing, but they do not alter **tempo** or volume to be "expressive," or make gestures for dramatic effect. Their music, like the landscape, is richly storied and carries memories that link generations. Doug Wallin and his brother Jack once recalled a site near their house that was known in the 1930s as "Pretty Polly Gap" in honor of Asbury McDevitt's performances there of "Pretty Polly." Family memory is another powerful feature of balladry. Doug Wallin felt he could no longer sing his mother's favorite song after she died.

In Madison County, as elsewhere in the southern mountains, ballad singing has always been part of a larger musical culture. People loved and sang ballads, but their repertories were broader than that. Jane Gentry sang **hymns** and other religious songs, **lyric songs**, and children's songs. Doug and Jack Wallin remembered their Great-Aunt Mary Sands as a songwriter and singer of hymns and ballads. They also told stories about Great-Uncle "Mitch," who loved to play the **fiddle** as well as sing. Their father, Lee, played fiddle and **banjo**, sometimes in the early morning while their mother made breakfast, and the family made music and told tales by the fireside at night. Their own repertories include **gospel** songs, sentimental and popular songs, and dance tunes, sometimes accompanied by Doug's fiddle and Jack's banjo or **guitar**. When Doug Wallin began to sing at the age of five or six, the music he heard was family and local music, and he developed a preference for playing **old-time** dance tunes on the fiddle and for playing and singing the older love songs and ballads. In this older tradition, most singing was performed solo and without instrumental accompaniment, a style brought by early settlers from the British Isles such as the Wallins' Shelton and Chandler ancestors.

The stories in the ballads are about elemental themes such as love and death. The words are simple and poetic. Plots are pared to the essentials, each **stanza** generally a crucial speech or action. The texts, however, are not fixed, and the wording of a song commonly varies slightly from one singing to the next and from one singer to the next. Song preferences vary also. Doug Wallin's mother, Berzilla, and her first cousin, Dillard Chandler, both liked love songs. John Cohen and Peter Gott wrote that Berzilla Wallin "sings songs connected with the feminine aspects of love while Dillard Chandler seems preoccupied with the amorous side—yet his approach is colored with a personal sorrow that is revealed in all his songs." Doug Wallin impressed a visitor as having a serious, reflective personality, a temperament that seemed to carry over into his song choices. He was drawn to stories of tragic love and faithful love. He sang songs of dalliance, but took a delicate, poetic, even instructive approach.

The ballad melodies are short, memorable, and moving. Many of them have a minor cast or are in old five-tone **scales**. Most have four **phrases**, but even a repetitive two-phrase tune becomes interesting when the singer incorporates subtle irregularities and embellishments. The stanzas are easy to understand because the grammatical units exactly match the musical phrase. Singers may have a favorite tune for a given text, but most will know additional tunes for at least some of the ballads they sing. Doug Wallin loved to perform songs as his father did, playing the tune on the fiddle before singing it and sometimes again between stanzas.

Ballad singing, Doug Wallin once said, has to "come from the heart," and some singers are better than others. He described William Riley Shelton, who sang for Sharp, as a "brag ballad singer," the man regarded as the best, and named two cousins and his mother as others who deserved the title. Ballad texts, tunes, and performance styles are open to interpretation, and variations naturally develop, even within families. Jack Wallin reported that he and Doug sang differing versions of the same songs and that his mother and father did that also.

Although women are often identified as the primary keepers of the ballads, men have also been very visible in these ballad-singing communities. All developed individual styles of singing. John Cohen and Peter Gott pointed out the contrast between Cas Wallin's "exaggerated and vigorous singing" and Lisha Shelton's "more 'even' approach." Dillard Chandler combined a high **pitch** and vocal intensity with vocal "flourishes" and a tendency to make subtle melodic variations from stanza to stanza and performance to performance. Doug Wallin's style was marked by unusual clarity of diction, great elegance of phrasing, and subtle ornamentation.

BIBLIOGRAPHY

Brown, Frank C. (1952). *The Frank C. Brown Collection of North Carolina Folklore.* Vol. 2, *Ballads,* and Vol. 4, *Music of the Ballads.* Ed. Newman I. White, et al. Durham: Duke University Press.

Cohen, John. (1977). "A Visitor's Recollections." *Southern Exposure* 5 (summer–fall):115–118.

Dirlam, Hilary. (1989). "An Interview with Sheila Adams Barnhill," *Old-Time Herald* 1 (Feb.–April):6–9, 31.

Hollifield, Adrienne. (1995). "Family Tradition, Orality, and Cultural Intervention in Sodom Laurel Ballad Singing," *North Carolina Folklore Journal,* vol. 42, no. 1 (winter–spring):1–34.

Sharp, Cecil. (1932). *English Folk Songs from the Southern Appalachians.* 2 vols. London: Oxford University Press.

Smith, Betty N. (1998). *Jane Hicks Gentry: A Singer Among Singers.* Lexington: University Press of Kentucky.

DOCUMENTARY RECORDINGS

Anglo-American Songs and Ballads. (1947?). Library of Congress Archive of Folk Culture. Ed. Duncan Emrich. AFS-L 14 and AFS-L 21. Ballads and songs sung by Maude Gentry Long and others recorded in various states by Artus Moser, Vance Randolph, Duncan Emrich and other collectors from 1938 to 1947.

A Spring in the Burton Cove. 1990. Sheila Kay Adams. Granny Dell Records, PO Box 750, Mars Hill, NC 28754.

Crazy about a Song: Old-Time Ballad Singers and Musicians from Virginia and North Carolina. 1992. Vaughan Williams Memorial Library 007. Recorded by Mike Yates from 1979 to 1983. Two cassettes with booklet published by the English Folk Dance and Song Society.

Dillard Chandler: The End of An Old Song. 1975. Ed. John Cohen. Folkways 2418.

Doug and Jack Wallin: Family Songs and Stories from the North Carolina Mountains. 1995. Ed. Wayne Martin and Beverly Patterson. Smithsonian Folkways Records SF 40013.

High Atmosphere: Ballads and Banjo Tunes from Virginia and North Carolina. 1974. Ed. John Cohen. Rounder Records 0028.

Loving Forward, Loving Back. 1987. Sheila Kay Adams. Granny Dell Records, PO Box 750, Mars Hill, NC 28754.

My Dearest Dear. 2000. Sheila Kay Adams. Granny Dell Records, PO Box 750, Mars Hill, NC 28754.

Old Love Songs and Ballads from the Big Laurel, North Carolina. 1964. Ed. John Cohen and Peter Gott. Folkways 2309.

FILM

The End of an Old Song. 1970. John Cohen. 28 mins. New York: Cinema Guild. Black and white 16 mm film and VHS videocassette.

NEW STRINGS ON THE "OLD HARP": THE 1991 REVISION OF *THE SACRED HARP*

John Bealle

John Bealle earned his Ph.D. in folklore at Indiana University and has taught at Indiana University, Miami University, and the University of Alabama. He has written on the folksong revival, bluegrass performance, and printed folktale collections. Bealle is also the author of a book on the revival of Sacred Harp singing entitled Public Worship, Private Faith: Sacred Harp and American Folksong *(University of Georgia Press, 1997). The following essay originally appeared in the summer 1994 issue of* Tributaries: Journal of the Alabama Folklife Association *and was revised by the author, who also added a preface that furnishes some historical context.*

reface: **Sacred Harp** singing is a type of religious folk music that had its origins in the singing school movement of eighteenth-century America. This movement was given sharper definition after 1800, when resourceful music teachers began notating music in **shape notes** to facilitate instruction in note reading. One of these shape-note books, *The Sacred Harp* (originating in Hamilton, Georgia, in 1844), proved unusually resilient and has maintained an active following throughout the turbulent history of American music.

The decade of the 1980s was a particularly exciting time for Sacred Harp singing. Many singers of the post–World War II generation were still active in the singing tradition. A boundless optimism prevailed as new singers from outside the South discovered what seemed a dauntless energy extending deep into the past, and as traditional singers saw Sacred Harp reach a geographical expanse that only a few years before had seemed unimaginable. Much of that optimism was reflected in the publication of a new edition of the book in 1991.

The following essay, originally published in 1994, the sesquicentennial year for Sacred Harp tradition, concerns the publication of that revision of the book and bears the stamp of the accumulated excitement of that time. It appeared in *Tributaries,* the journal of the Alabama Folklife Association, and directly addressed readers invested in the folk traditions of that state.

A decade later, Sacred Harp singing thrives in traditional and new areas. Singers scarcely remember the previous edition of the book; already, several photocopy editions of new songs have been assembled. Travel to and from traditional areas has become routine, and the new conventions that appeared with such excitement during the time of the new revision are entering their second decade. Most prominently, many of the great singers who gave that era its unmistakable character have now passed on.

In a sense, this essay reports a particular historical moment—a moment that once seemed invincible. But it is also about how traditions manage their own discovery, and in this regard it maps a process crucial to American musical traditions that come into the view of an admiring public.

A DAY TO REMEMBER

On December 15, 1990, a group of several hundred singers met at Samford University in Birmingham, Alabama, to perform and record sacred vocal music. Most had never seen the music they were to sing. Indeed, the music unveiled that day consisted of new songs to be added to a book now in its 150th year in active publication and use—*The Sacred Harp*. Honored among those in attendance were twenty-one contemporary composers and authors of the new songs. Over the course of only four hours, the singers—trained in the "shape-note" system of Sacred Harp singing—recorded the complete catalog of sixty new songs!

In keeping with traditional practice, the audience was small and the **chorus** large. The singers sat in the customary "hollow square," with tenors, trebles, altos, and basses facing one another as on the four sides of a square. Each song was recorded by first singing the tune using the names of the shapes (fa, sol, la, and mi) and then proceeding to the lyrics. Although ordinarily an "arranging committee" would see that all singers present had a chance to lead the song of his or her choice, this occasion featured the invited composers, called upon one by one to lead the new songs from the center of the square. From this vantage, amidst the unrestrained, emotionally vivid, and sometimes austere sound produced by the best of the tradition's singers, **leaders** experienced the highest aesthetic and spiritual quality the music had to offer.

The significance of this music in Alabama is difficult to overstate. First published in 1844, *The Sacred Harp* was one of several hundred nineteenth-century songbooks to feature shape-notes, a notation system in which note heads were given different geometrical shapes according to their degree of the musical **scale**. Compilers such as *The Sacred Harp*'s B. F. White (1800–1879), a newspaper publisher and later mayor of Hamilton, Georgia, adopted shape-note systems for their ease of learning. Some designed and patented their own unique notation systems and then vigorously promoted them as singing teachers. White worked primarily from his home, printing his arrangements in his newspaper so that the public could enjoy them.

Largely through community singing schools, shape-note books became the mainstay of a vibrant popular American vocal music movement that spread throughout regions populated by Europeans. Early singing schools, sometimes taught by itinerant music teachers promoting their own books, were at one time important community events and social affairs.

B. F. White himself was a tireless music teacher; consequently *The Sacred Harp* achieved immediate success in his region of Georgia. Although compilers such as White were talented composers, their books relied as heavily on a stock **repertoire** of popular colonial American and English songs as they did on original material. By the close of the nineteenth century, however, "better music" crusaders advocating European styles and pedagogical methods as well as the familiar "round-note" system of notation successfully displaced shape-note music from the American musical mainstream. Indeed, the absence of Sacred Harp music or shape-note pedagogy in Alabama school and college curricula is likely the result of this "better music" movement. It is a tragic irony that music for which Alabama is internationally esteemed is given so little attention by our public institutions of learning.

The significance for Alabama lies in the fact that this round-note campaign was least successful in the South. Shape-note books, with the spiritual candor of their songs, followed the spread of evangelical religion in the South. Consequently Alabama and Georgia, especially their rural independent churches, have played pivotal roles in a

See glossary for definition of boldfaced terms

somewhat systematic disregard of the "better music" boosters, serving ultimately as primary custodians of this once-national tradition. Through the work of a series of energetic and culturally astute innovators, along with numerous devoted followers of the tradition, *The Sacred Harp* has remained in continuous use here while elsewhere in America the vast majority of other books have long since dropped out of use and out of print. In fact, of only a handful of books nationwide that enjoy active popularity today, three are published and regularly used in Alabama.

REVISION AND "RE-VISION": *THE SACRED HARP* IN TRANSITION

The story of this tradition has been eloquently chronicled in George Pullen Jackson's *White Spirituals in the Southern Uplands* (1933) and, more recently, in Buell Cobb's *The Sacred Harp: A Tradition and Its Music* (1978). Both are indispensable references for any study of this music. As these works have shown, pivotal moments in the development of the tradition have occurred when the design and contents of the books were changed. These "revisions" provided the opportunity for a resolute and enduring stance regarding competing styles, the inclusion of groups of participating singers, and the character of previous revisions and other books of sacred music.

As the centerpiece of the tradition, the book was always intended to focus the most profound spiritual feelings of its users. As 1911 reviser Joe S. James said, "when sung to the honor and praise of God, [the book] will open the door to the soul." Because of this enduring relationship between singers and the book, a revision ran the risk of alienating those most invested in its particular character. Well aware of this danger, B. F. White warned that future custodians of the tradition could "scarcely . . . do better than abide by the advice—'Ask for the old paths, and walk therein.'"

Consequently, these highly charged

moments have been infrequent; only two major (and six minor) revisions have preceded the current one. It is no accident, then, that histories of the tradition are treated largely as histories of the revisions of its texts. Previous major revisions were completed in 1911 and 1936, when in both cases the book changed legal ownership. Each had its particular significance and purpose.

For the 1911 edition, a music committee chaired by Georgia lawyer Joe S. James (died 1931) took a staunchly conservative approach to the music. Disdaining popular **gospel** styles that had infused other books, the "James Revision" reclaimed the austere character of the 1844 B. F. White book. The committee added *Original* to the title *Sacred Harp*, intending to declare the book heir to the purest strain of the tradition. James himself wrote a "Brief History of the Sacred Harp" in 1904 as well as footnotes in the revision containing biographies of the composers and indicating, where known, the sources of each tune. New compositions by Southerners claimed a more important role; an effort was made to include those representing the growing popularity of the book in Alabama.

The 1936 edition was largely the result of the tireless work of members of the Denson family of Winston County, Alabama. In fact, their contributions, which span nearly the entire history of the book (James M. Denson composed "Christmas Anthem" for the 1844 edition), surely earn them recognition as Alabama's most influential Sacred Harp family. Brothers Seaborn M. (1854–1936) and Thomas J. Denson (1863–1935), who initiated the work on the 1936 revision, are said to have taught over 10,000 pupils in singing schools, many in Winston, Fayette, Walker, Cullman, and Cleburne counties; they are to be credited with the strength of singing that remains there today. Their stature in the tradition surely ranks them among Alabama's most accomplished musicians. Both died before the revision was finished, and it was left to Thomas's son, Paine Denson of Birmingham, to finish the work. Editors of the "Denson Revision" removed 176 of the less popular tunes to make room for new

Southern composers and to reduce the physical dimensions of the book, which had reached a size some deemed unmanageable.

It should not go without saying that the tradition that includes these books has been deliberately nurtured as a tradition. In retrospect, the revisions appear self-evident and self-assured. Yet, in truth, they can be moments of precarious exposure. When the James Revision was published in 1911, two other books vied for singers' attention. A 1902 edition by W. M. Cooper of Dothan (the "Cooper Revision," which is still the book of choice in southern Alabama), and a 1909 edition by J. L. White of Atlanta both laid claim as true successors to the 1844 book. The Cooper committee even filed a lawsuit (which was ultimately unsuccessful) claiming that the James edition's added alto lines were plagiarized. In 1913, in an attempt to win support from singers, *both* James and J. L. White were recorded as having donated books to the singing convention

of the Alabama Sacred Harp Musical Association in Birmingham. Despite this generosity, one singer spoke in praise of the "old-time Sacred Harp" of 1869. In 1936, because of a single song among the 176 removed, an influential Georgia leader led a boycott of the new book that lasted for several decades.

It has been the particular good fortune of the Denson/James lineage, however, to have extended its popularity by protecting the traditional character of the work. In naming the work *Original,* in preserving much of the content and style of the earlier editions, and in claiming the Denson Revision as "the true successor of the James Revision of 1911," the revisers of *The Sacred Harp* held fast to the vision that some eternal quality, infused into the original work, should be protected. Thus they also established for the tradition as a whole a discernibly anti-modernist place in the cultural landscape. At the same time, the revisions

have been able to incorporate scores of new composers, lyricists, teachers, and singers into the visible center of the tradition. This has been the genius of the tradition's leaders and the legacy that the current revisers have sought to duplicate.

THE 1991 REVISION

In keeping with these previous revisions, editors of the new edition have sought that delicate balance between tradition and innovation. For the past several years, the 1991 revision has been an ongoing concern of a music committee consisting of Alabama and Georgia singers and chaired by Hugh McGraw of Bremen, Georgia. To make room for the new songs, forty-five of the less popular songs (as determined by their frequency of appearance in the published minutes of singings) have been removed from the old book. All pages have been reset so that they can be more easily read, and the biographical footnotes that formerly appeared below many songs have been removed and replaced by a companion volume of more complete biographies.

On the surface, the collection of new songs has that customary conservative appearance that affiliates it with the "old paths" of the B. F. White tradition. Nearly half of the sixty lyrics were borrowed from the poetry of Issac Watts (1647–1748), the prolific English **hymnist** whose texts dominated many of the nineteenth-century shape-note books. The editors added or restored from earlier editions of *The Sacred Harp* selections by popular colonial American composers such as William Billings (1746–1800) of Boston ("Africa" and "Jordan"), Daniel Read (1757–1836) of New Haven, Connecticut ("Amity" and "Mortality"), and Timothy Swan (1758–1842) of Northfield, Massachusetts ("China," "Rainbow," "Poland," and "Bristol").

Yet, as with the previous revisions, this edition was designed to breathe new life into the music. "If you leave anything alone," says Hugh McGraw, "it will die—I don't care how good it is." Well within the realm of the "old

paths," the practice of routinely revising the book to introduce the work of living authors has been instrumental in preserving the active practice of Sacred Harp singing. Thus by including twenty-one contemporary composers and lyricists, the editors of the 1991 edition have sought to draw from those to whom the mantle of the tradition will ultimately pass. It is the interest and energy of these authors, of their friends and families, and of those with whom they sing that will keep the tradition alive.

Although this revision, like others, has a subtle style of its own, it is most striking in the degree to which contemporary writers have adhered to the salient traditional components of Sacred Harp music. The six lyrics by contemporary authors employ the same poetic style and express much the same humility and devotion to God as hymns from earlier editions. The thirty-six new musical compositions were carefully selected for their allegiance to "true dispersed **harmony**"—that quality of Sacred Harp music that draws upon the wide dispersal of voice parts (at or beyond two **octaves**), the crossing of voices, the frequent appearance of open chords (lacking the **third**), and the sense of melodic autonomy of the four parts. In most every aspect, the new songs draw upon the best features of the old ones.

Again, Alabama (six authors, six songs) and Georgia (eight authors, sixteen songs) writers predominate. Alabamians include John Hocutt, a retired Jasper farmer/carpenter and veteran singing-school teacher who had three songs in the previous *Sacred Harp* edition, contributing "A Thankful Heart." Jim Carnes, a writer and editor living in Montgomery, composed "Rockport." Retired barber Toney Smith of Tuscaloosa, who has sung on a number of Sacred Harp recordings and has taught singing schools and performed nationwide, authored "Love Shall Never Die." Terry Wootten of Ider, DeKalb County, who operates a farm-supply business, contributed "Shining Star." Also among the new compositions by Alabamians are "Easter Morn," by mathematician David Ivey of Huntsville, and "Heav-

Alabama's Four Shape-Note Books

The following essay originally appeared in the summer 1994 issue of Tributaries: Journal of the Alabama Folklife Association, *in which it accompanied John Bealle's article on the Sacred Harp tradition. Please see Chapter 10 for that essay as well as for biographical information on the author.*

Compiled by William Walker of Spartanburg, South Carolina, and published in 1866, *Christian Harmony* adopted the seven-shape notation system introduced in 1832. For Walker, the book was intended as an improvement of the earlier *Southern Harmony,* which used a four-shape system. Undoubtedly bolstered by Walker's prior popularity, the *Christian Harmony* was immediately successful, attaining sales of 750,000 throughout the South in its first decade. Though earlier use is certain, the first Alabama convention to adopt the book was the Warrior River Christian Harmony Musical Association in 1885. Nowadays, the book has a dedicated following in central Alabama and other areas of the Southeast; the 1991 minutes of the Alabama Christian Harmony Music Association lists eighteen scheduled singings.

The B. F. White **Sacred Harp**—commonly called the "Cooper Book"—was compiled by W. M. Cooper of Dothan and first published in 1902, some thirty-three years after the previous new edition of *The Sacred Harp.* Cooper is credited with introducing into the tradition the conventional inclusion of the alto part, a practice adopted in subsequent revisions of the book. The Cooper revision did not enjoy universal acceptance, particularly among pupils and followers of B. F. White; nor was Cooper's legal claim to exclusive right to titles and songs supported by the courts. The book's influence was strongest in southern Alabama, where it is still predominant today; it is also used by singers in Texas. A new edition adding recent compositions was issued in 1992 under the editorial leadership of Stanley Smith of Ozark, Alabama.

In the southeastern "Wiregrass Region" of Alabama and neighboring areas of Florida, a vibrant four-shape tradition among African American singers has existed since the late nineteenth century. As did other singers in this region of the state, they adopted the "Cooper Revision" of *The Sa-*

enly Land," by Jeff Sheppard, who lives in Anniston and operates a moving and storage business.

The most striking change in the book is the inclusion of authors from elsewhere in the country. Seven authors from Illinois, Connecticut, Massachusetts, and New York contributed songs. Included are Middletown, Connecticut, resident and Wesleyan University music professor Neely Bruce, author of "Heavenly Union." Bruce had discovered *The Sacred Harp* while researching early American music at the University of Illinois and founded a performing ensemble that sang and recorded from the book. Dan Brittain, formerly of Cazenovia, New York, and now a choir director in Berryville, Arkansas, composed "Cobb," "McGraw," "Akin," and "Novakoski." He first encountered Sacred Harp while stationed in the Army in Georgia. Three Chicagoans are represented: Textbook editor Ted Johnson wrote "New Agatite," real-estate broker Ted Mercer composed "O'Leary" and "Sheppard," and Judy Hauff contributed "Granville," "Wood Street,"

"Ainslie," and "Stony Point." From Massachusetts, Bruce Randall of Boston submitted "Mount Desert," and Glen Wright wrote "Natick."

To grasp the significance of this geographical range, consider that in the 1911 and 1936 editions, *no* added songs were written by contemporary authors from states other than Alabama and Georgia. In 1960 and 1966, when a number of songs were added as appendices, only Florida and Tennessee joined the list of states represented. Thus the 1991 edition both reflects and facilitates a change in the role of southern singers as sole custodians of the tradition. To some extent, this change is an inevitable response to a growing interest in Sacred Harp elsewhere in the country over the past two decades. But, much as in the widespread expansion into Alabama from Georgia earlier, this enthusiasm has been nurtured and enjoyed by southern singers in a way that is in keeping with the most basic sentiments singers hold for the tradition. This affirming posture is the heart and soul of the new *Sacred Harp* revision.

cred Harp. In order to publish a collection of African American compositions, however, delegates of the Dale County Colored Musical Institute and the Alabama and Florida Union State Convention convened during the 1930s to plan a publication of their own. The book was to be written in four shapes, titled *The Colored Sacred Harp,* and authored by Judge Jackson of Dale County. It was published in 1934 with seventy-seven songs, all but one of which were new compositions by the singers. A revised edition appeared in 1973 with support from the Alabama State Council on the Arts and Humanities.

In 1970, the visibility of the black tradition was boosted with the formation of a performing group called the "Wiregrass Sacred Harp Singers." Led by veteran singer Dewey Williams, the group has appeared at concerts and festivals internationally, including the Smithsonian **Folklife** Festival in Washington, D.C. Williams also supervised the 1973 reprinting of *The Colored Sacred Harp* and has produced recordings of the group as well as organized regional television and radio programs featuring singers from the tradi-

tion. In 1983, he was awarded a prestigious National Heritage Fellowship, becoming the first Alabamian to receive that honor. (Hugh McGraw was a 1982 recipient.)

At one time, singers' affiliation with each book—based on geography, family loyalty, or race—was more exclusive than now. Today's singers are far more cosmopolitan (except for their loyalty to the nineteenth-century **shapenote** tradition as a whole), and they enjoy the vitality of the different books used in Alabama and neighboring states. Sacred Harp newsletters, published by local groups throughout the country, often list dates and locations of singings from these and other books based on the nineteenth-century tradition. Largely the work of Christian Harmony singer Art Deason, an annual "Capital City Sing" featuring the four Alabama books is held in Montgomery each third Thursday in July. The event takes place on a weekday so as not to compete with an established singing from any of the four books.

John Bealle

THE *SACRED HARP* AS FOLK MUSIC

In her 1987 thesis on "The Sacred Harp Revival in New England," Wesleyan University music student Susan Garber submitted questionnaires to various New England singers to determine, among other things, their introduction to the music. A New York singer responded that she ". . . first heard 'Wondrous Love' in Israel, soon after reading George Pullen Jackson's book in a U.S.I.S. library in India." This response was not as uncharacteristic as it might seem, for singers across the country who were not exposed to the tradition directly will attest repeatedly to having discovered it through recordings, folk festivals, and written works that address the tradition as American religious folk music.

The Sacred Harp singing tradition, of course, long preceded its own label as folk music. Although this identification was probably inevitable, two individuals whose work reflected the emerging regionalist mindset of the 1920s and 1930s had considerable influence on the character of the discovery.

One of these was Carl Carmer (1893–1976), the seemingly inveterate New Yorker who taught English at the University of Alabama during the 1920s. Fascinated by the South, Carmer made copious although sometimes unflattering notes on its culture. In 1926, Carmer spoke on the campus on "'Harp' Songs as Folk Music" nearly a decade before his portrait of Alabama culture, *Stars Fell on Alabama* (1934), included a chapter on the subject. As faculty sponsor of the Glee Club, he noted that "it is not an unusual occurrence at the University of Alabama for an aspirant to membership in the Glee Club to announce that he can sing only by shaped notes."

It was Vanderbilt German professor George Pullen Jackson (1874–1953), however, who devoted his life to the study of the music. His family moved from Maine to Birmingham most likely during the 1880s and for some time operated a bakery business there. Apparently unaware of traditional music during his youth, Jackson earned school and college expenses playing in concert bands. His 1895 Birmingham

High School graduation oration—"Imaginary Address to the Board of Education Upon the Value of Vocal Music in the Public Schools"—undoubtedly charted much of his life's course. Thus it was somewhat in spite of his Birmingham upbringing and musical interests that Jackson discovered the shape-note tradition in 1920 on the recommendation of a teaching colleague. Jackson's urban musical affiliations led him throughout his career to write of the "strange notation . . . and music theory, singing schools, teachers, and songs books"—as culture alien to his own.

Jackson published numerous books and articles on the subject, endeavoring to advance the neglected "white spirituals" within the canon of American national music. His most genuine interest was in that species of tunebook songs that were religious song texts set to orally transmitted secular melodies and then rendered in shape-notes by book compilers. His performing troupe of "Old Harp Singers" toured from 1932 to 1938 and performed at the first National Folk Festival in St. Louis. Jackson worked closely with singers to promote the music in the South. He helped organize a week-long centennial celebration attended by 1,295 singers in Double Springs in 1944 and served on the committee to honor the Denson brothers by erecting a granite monument that still stands on the courthouse lawn there. Observations in his centennial treatise, "The Story of the Sacred Harp, 1844–1944," have become a part of the historical record of the tradition, particularly through the writings of singer Ruth Denson Edwards (1893–1978). His work has been decisive in establishing the significance of nineteenth-century shape-note songbooks and of contemporary practitioners of the tradition within the context of American musical culture.

Although such published material has been available for some time now (Jackson's book was first published in 1933), its impact on singing has been most strongly felt in the past two decades. At least until recently, those outside the tradition commonly have "discovered" the music through concert or festival performances, workshops, or, like the questionnaire respondent above, through written and recorded material. Some have attended "folk camps" where Sacred Harp is featured among courses in a variety of canonized traditional genres. The difference in recent decades is that many have taken up singing—and this has led to a network of energetic groups centered in New England, the Midwest, and the West Coast that meet regularly to sing. Although there is some use of other books such as the *Christian Harmony* or the recently published *Northern Harmony,* the most commonly used book nationwide is *The Sacred Harp.* So vigorous has this singing become, that National Public Radio's *All Things Considered* and ABC News have done feature stories on the Midwest Sacred Harp Convention that meets in Chicago. In 1990, the prestigious United Sacred Harp Musical Association held its eighty-seventh annual convention in Chicago—the first time it had been held outside the South.

Perhaps in spite of this, as Buell Cobb notes, the idea that Sacred Harp is folk music receives mixed reviews by singers. Revisers of the book, after all, had acquired some measure of cultural savvy in locating the "old paths" within the treacherous maze of evolving American musical taxonomy. As the demise of other books indicated, this came at no small risk. Furthermore, Joe S. James's 1904 history had established an historical consciousness that cited spiritual authority mediated by the movement's venerable leaders, not cultural authority, as the source of power for the music. Thus the attention brought to the music after the 1930s by regional writers, folklorists, and music collectors came well after an entrenched identity had already been established.

Some aspects of the tradition that gave rise to the label "religious folk music" were indeed in congruence with that identity. Its self-proclaimed ties to antiquity, its affinity for anonymous tunes and texts, its antimodernism, its association with independent churches, even its perennially reputed decline—these were features of the tradition captured in the popular sense of that term. Other aspects suggested, however,

See glossary for definition of boldfaced terms

were not so popular. Folk-oriented writers at times focused so exclusively on the antique, unfamiliar, or rural appearance of the tradition (even Jackson referred to singers as a "lost tonal tribe") as to neglect the spiritual foundation, the prestige and astuteness of its leaders, and the hard work by which it was established.

When, in 1954, a *Birmingham News* feature writer predicted that Alabama's "disappearing singers" would be gone within a decade, an annoyed singer took exception, describing in a letter the complex organization of singings, the sometimes extraordinary distances traveled, the intensity of the music, and the depth of commitment of singers. Even so recently as 1986 the Georgia-based *National Sacred Harp Newsletter* reported a request to assemble a group of Sacred Harp singers for a "hootenanny" and admonished its readers to distinguish when you should and when you shouldn't.

"Many people," the writer continued, "insist that the mountain should come to Mahomet, but in the natural order of things the reverse is true and Mahomet should come to the mountain—he'll be welcomed gladly."

THE NORTHWARD SPREAD

Mahomet, it seems, has come to the mountain. This example—apparently alluding to the secular orientation of some folk music presentations—is in numerous other cases replaced by not only a sincere deference to traditional practice but also a high regard for the potential spiritual fulfillment provided by the Southern tradition. In a society where packaged cultural experiences situate consumers as detached observers, Sacred Harp singing is energetic, emotionally engaging, democratic, and fully participatory. Those who discover Sacred Harp as religious folk music, in fact, find that as a tradition it has much to offer on its own terms.

Chicago composer Ted Johnson reasons that singers in his area turned "toward Southern tradition because that seemed to offer so much satisfaction in so many ways that we didn't predict—it's just changed our

lives in many ways." Indeed, "going South" has become a rite of passage for singers outside the tradition, an event recounted in lengthy testimonials in New England and Midwest regional Sacred Harp newsletters. For example, Stephen O'Leary wrote of his 1988 trip to Sand Mountain in the *Chicago Sacred Harp Newsletter*:

> When we arrived at Antioch Baptist Church, I slid into a back pew in the bass section, only to have Mr. Hugh McGraw invite me up to sit next to him in the front row. . . . Behind and around me were more than twenty barrel-chested deep-voiced patriarchs (Oh for a bass section of that power here in Chicago!). All told, there were somewhere over a hundred, at times perhaps a hundred and fifty, singers. Now, I've been singing this music for a year now, and we've had some fine singings in that time. But *nothing* that I'd ever heard before could have prepared me for what happened when the books were opened and we began to sing.

Unlike earlier regionalist writing, accounts such as these have as their object not the literary product, but the experience of singing.

Much of the spirited quality attained at singings in Chicago and elsewhere is due to increasing interaction with southern singers. Outsiders have provided a talented and enthusiastic population; traditional singers have provided proven models of how to conduct singings efficiently in such a way that extracts the deepest sentiments from the music. Undoubtedly Stephen O'Leary left Sand Mountain with expectations raised. This dialogue with an energetic new singing population has at times been movingly ironic, as if something were really being "discovered," and at times self-evident, a union of those whose spiritual interests coincide. Through this dialogue, the tradition as a whole has moved into new cultural territory—at times uncertain—but with exciting results. This is the territory mapped by the 1991 revision.

There have been numerous moments when the synthesis of these two forces has been profoundly felt. Certainly the revelation of the new compositions in December 1990 was one of those. But one event is said to have been more pivotal than others in foreshadowing what has emerged—when the Word of Mouth Chorus from Vermont toured the South by bus and attended the Georgia State Sacred Harp Convention in 1976. Under the direction of Larry Gordon, the Word of Mouth Chorus was founded in 1972 as a madrigal group based at a Vermont commune. Before long, Sacred Harp music (initially included experimentally on the recommendation of a friend) became increasingly important in the group's repertoire. But, as Gordon reports in the notes to the recording the group made in 1978 (*Rivers of Delight,* Nonesuch H-71360), they were unprepared for what they experienced in the South:

> We were moved by the deep fellowship among the participants, a fellowship that reached out to include us, bridging vast boundaries of age, culture, politics, and religion. Moreover, the singing itself— the rhythmic drive, the unrestrained quality of the voices, the sheer power of the sound—permanently altered our approach to Sacred Harp music.

Returning to Vermont, Gordon's group made its influential recording, which, largely because of its wide distribution, inexpensive price, and accommodation of mainstream musical tastes, set the tone of the stylistic presentation of the music outside the South for years to come.

Yet the most significant development was not just that the groups had come together in the same place. Gordon mentioned to Hugh McGraw that the New England singers were planning a performance at Wesleyan University in Middletown, Connecticut, co-organized by Neely Bruce. As Susan Garber reports, "He [McGraw] in turn announced that the singing in Middletown would be a first annual *convention,* and on the spot, according to Neely Bruce, some forty Southerners agreed to travel to Connecticut to attend it." As would happen repeatedly during the ensuing years, Southern singers *did* travel to the "convention," and they provided considerable direction and focus regarding the manner by which this and other singings would be conducted. Singers nationwide who attended or heard of this singing remember it as an event of great significance.

What time has proved incorrect is the idea that the cultural differences were that vast. Whereas the back-to-the-land Vermont commune dwellers were apprehensive about the religious character of the music, in truth, it turns out, the music was always meant as pandenominational.

Other underlying similarities central to the traditions include the extraordinary effort singers make in traveling to singings. Recorded "minutes" taken at singings as far back as they go report singers coming from great distances. Nor was travel always easy: The Fourth of July convention at Helicon, Winston County, Alabama, established in 1891, was twenty-five miles from the nearest railroad. For singings near Villa Rica, Georgia, railroads would put on an extra train from Birmingham and Heflin. Today, the low-airfare "Sacred Harp Shuttle," as the *Chicago Sacred Harp Newsletter* has called it, transports singers both directions between Birmingham and Chicago. Bus tours organized by Oxford resident Ruth Brown have carried Alabama singers to places such as Denver and Chicago and to various New England conventions. The Sixth Annual Midwest Convention in Chicago drew singers from twenty-three states, with the largest number coming from the host state of Illinois. The second largest number came from Alabama.

The sharing of food is much the same in the traditional "dinner-on-the-grounds" as in the contemporary "potluck dinner." In both cases, prepared food is not only an individual creative expression but also a stunning visual display of the communal fruits of labor. Furthermore, in scheduling the **old-time** conventions, leaders had what George Pullen Jackson called "a fraternal considera-

See glossary for definition of boldfaced terms

tion for the calendar rights of their neighboring singing groups," indicating a kind of cosmopolitan sensibility necessary in any context where competing interests might intrude upon one another. Singers from all regions seek and enjoy social institutions that are democratic, as singings are, in that all participants are invited to lead and each musical part is of relatively equal melodic interest. Perhaps most important, many singers hold the view that spiritual and social experiences are to be sought as a direct consequence of music.

THE VISION OF HUGH MCGRAW

There is little doubt, singers will confirm, that in the manner of B. F. White, Joe James, and the Denson brothers before him, Hugh McGraw has been at the center of much of this extraordinary change. Manager of a clothing manufacturing plant in Temple, Georgia, McGraw comes from a family with deep roots in Sacred Harp music. Exposed to Sacred Harp as a small child, he did not take up singing himself until 1954, after he had married. One night during that year, he happened to hear some singing while out walking, and it "just petrified him." Later, when the 1960 book was being revised, the committee held meetings in McGraw's house. This, he says, is where he got his training.

His exposure to singing outside the South came partly in his capacity as executive secretary of the Sacred Harp Publishing Company. Over the course of the 1960s and 1970s, McGraw began to receive correspondence and book orders from faraway places:

> For instance, I would get a letter from a girl, say, in Seattle, Washington. And she says, "I studied Sacred Harp under Neely Bruce in Champaign, Illinois, years ago and I've been living out here singing from sheet music. And I think I deserve my own book. And I'm getting a group started—I want ten books." Then another group would order twenty books. Eventually, I would go out to some of these

places and teach singing schools. . . . . . Then I really started expanding, going out to colleges and speaking, demonstrating the book, doing concerts, taking groups to Washington.

It was during these trips—including important appearances at the Smithsonian **Folklife** Festival in Washington, D.C., and the Canadian Festival of Music in Montreal—that McGraw observed directly the magnitude and degree of sincerity of interest in singing outside the South. Bringing this to bear on his experiences within the creative core of the tradition, he has been uniquely positioned to direct the energies of so diverse a population as has recently come to Sacred Harp singing.

Yet more was involved than merely promoting the music. With little tradition to draw upon, new groups customarily met in one another's homes. Crafting social practices out of prior experience in recreational group singing and vocal performing ensembles, new groups would endeavor to balance the competing aesthetic ambitions of various members with values favoring democratic participation and fellowship. Often, eight or so singers might struggle through no more than two dozen songs before dismissing. Gradually, by venturing South or studying with McGraw or others, new groups would learn that at a traditional "all-day singing," more than a hundred songs might be sung! At larger singings, even the more difficult pieces—anthems such as "Heavenly Vision" or "Easter Anthem"—would be managed without the kind of fussiness that attends new groups. Later, when locales such as Chicago, San Diego, and several New England cities hosted conventions attended by southern singers, much of the splendor of traditional singings could be experienced at home.

Under such circumstances, southern tradition served both as a prestigious heritage and a model for spiritual fulfillment. As the primary point of contact, McGraw's role in linking the old and the new was pivotal. His enduring leadership during the decades leading up to this revision is widely recognized as important both in the ad-

vancement of Sacred Harp singing nationwide and in the steadfast attention to its southern heritage. Recognizing these contributions, singers at the "new songs" singing in 1990 unanimously approved a motion that the new book bear the subtitle "McGraw Revision," but he declined the honor.

Singers undoubtedly experience the revision (as well as the changing tradition it represents) in diverse ways. The excitement of a collection of new songs and new authors is rightfully balanced by an intensified devotion to those reliable old songs that comprise the bulk of the book. This devotion points not only to the proven excellence of these old songs, but also to their capacity to bear the accumulated sentiments of repeated singing—memories of cherished friends and relations who have held them as favorites. It is because of these profound attachments that the music committee has taken extraordinary and perhaps unprecedented care to assure that all changes to the book have the endorsement of the widest span of active singers. Thus, of the book's 551 songs, 386 will have been included continuously since 1911, and 171 will have appeared on the same page of each edition since 1844!

Overall, however, the sesquicentennial of *The Sacred Harp* marks a time of heightened confidence for the tradition. Little evidence is apparent of the contentious atmosphere that the community has experienced in previous years. The excitement of singings that draw participants from new and distant states affirms the importance of the music and, perhaps, recalls the excitement of the grand conventions of yesteryear. Yet the 1991 revision looks for its grounding beyond these circumstances to what is truly eternal about the music. The book's revisers have intuitively grasped that newcomers to the music are discovering what has been discovered by others repeatedly over the course of the book's history— that even where other means fail, music is a bridge by which singers can share com-

mon spiritual sentiments. Though this seems uniquely relevant today, for Sacred Harp singers, it is another walk within those hallowed "old paths."

See glossary for definition of boldfaced terms

BIBLIOGRAPHY

Bealle, John. (1997). *Public Worship, Private Faith: Sacred Harp and American Folksong.* Athens: University of Georgia Press.

Britton, Allen P. (1961). "The Singing School Movement in the U.S." *International Musicological Society* 1(1961):89–99. Report of the Eighth Congress, New York.

Carnes, Jim. (1989). "White Sacred Harp Singing." In *Alabama Folklife: Collected Essays,* ed. Stephen H. Martin. Birmingham: Alabama Folklife Association.

Cobb, Buell E., Jr. (1978). *The Sacred Harp: A Tradition and Its Music.* Athens: University of Georgia Press.

Dyen, Doris J. (1977). "The Role of Shape-Note Singing in the Musical Culture of Black Communities in Southeast Alabama." Ph.D. thesis. University of Illinois, Urbana.

Ellington, Charles Linwood. (1960). "The Sacred Harp Tradition of the South: Its Origins and Evolution." Ph.D. diss. Florida State University.

The Fasola Homepage. Available at http://fasola.org.

Garber, Susan L. (1987). "The Sacred Harp Revival in New England: Its Singers and Its Singings." M.A. thesis. Wesleyan University, Middletown, Connecticut.

Jackson, George Pullen. [1933] (1965). *White Spirituals in the Southern Uplands.* Reprint, New York: Dover Press.

Kelton, Mai Hogan. (1986). "Living Teacher-Composers of the Sacred Harp." *Tennessee Folklore Society Bulletin* 51 (1986):137–43.

1991 Sacred Harp Revisions. 1991. Bremen, GA: Sacred Harp Publishing Co. Audiocassettes, 2 vols.

Willett, Henry. (1989). "Wiregrass Notes: Black Sacred Harp Singing from Southeast Alabama." In *Alabama Folklife: Collected Essays,* ed. Stephen H. Martin. Birmingham: Alabama Folklife Association.

Willett, Henry, ed. (1999). *In the Spirit: Alabama's Sacred Music Traditions.* Montgomery: Alabama Folklife Association.

MUSIC TRADITIONS OF THE OKEFENOKEE REGION OF SOUTHEAST GEORGIA AND NORTHWEST FLORIDA

Laurie Kay Sommers

Folklorist and ethnomusicologist Laurie Kay Sommers is founding director of the South Georgia Folklife Project at Valdosta State University and research associate with Michigan State University Museum. She specializes in regional music traditions in the United States.

The Okefenokee Swamp occupies more than 600 square miles of southeast Georgia and northwest Florida. Indian peoples occupied the "Land of the Trembling Earth" through the early 1800s, when most were driven out or forcibly removed by Europeans. Until 1937, the swamp housed an independent, self-sufficient community of "Crackers," most of Scotch and Scotch-Irish origin via North Carolina, who scratched out a living through cattle grazing, subsistence agriculture, and turpentining. This distinctive folk region was shaped by Celtic ethnicity, geographic isolation, and Primitive Baptist religion. The establishment of the Okefenokee National Wildlife Refuge in 1937 marked the end of the historic period of music and **folklore** in the Okefenokee itself, although certain longstanding traditions have adapted and persisted in nearby communities. The present-day economy is based on forest products and agriculture.

Cornell biologist and amateur folklorist Francis Harper documented this folk com-munity from 1912 to 1951. Georgia South-ern professor Delma E. Presley published a sampling of Harper's work in 1981. Harper's work documents historic folk culture *of* the swamp, but a rich musical culture still ex-ists in the surrounding region. The major musical **genres** include a distinctive regional variant of **sacred harp**, Primitive Baptist **hymnody**, the remnants of the **secular fid-dle** tunes, hollering, and **balladry** docu-mented by Harper, plus **bluegrass** and **gospel** sings. This entry focuses on British American traditions and the Harper legacy, to the exclusion of other **repertoires** and cultural groups found in the region.

REPERTOIRES OF MUSIC

The music of the Okefenokee Scotch-Irish and their descendants includes both sacred and secular repertoires. The sacred music is dominated by two intertwined musical styles: unaccompanied Primitive Baptist hymns and

sacred harp. The most distinctive hymnody traditions are associated with the Crawfordite sub-sect of the Alabaha River Association of Primitive Baptists in southeast Georgia and northwest Florida. Hymn texts are drawn from *Primitive Hymns* by Benjamin Lloyd, an 1841 compilation of preexisting hymn texts, organized according to topic, which reflect Primitive Baptist belief and discipline. Crawfordites use the "700" hymn version as opposed to the more widely adopted "705" in deference to the old ways. The Lloyd hymnal contains no tunes; instead, the texts are sung to memorized sacred harp tunes in the appropriate meter. If the singers remember all four parts to the sacred harp tunes, then hymns are sung in **harmony**; otherwise, worshippers take the tenor (**melody**) line. The influence of sacred harp melodies among Crawfordites has shaped a rich, fervent, full-throated singing style that is much less ornamented and **heterophonic** than performance practices

found among other old-line Baptist groups in the United States. Crawfordite **ornaments** are composed of upper and lower neighbors and passing tones. Congregational hymns occur more informally at the beginning and end of worship and during foot washing. By contrast, lined hymns are part of the formal worship procedure, and may be "given out" only by a licensed minister. **Tempos** in general are quite slow, allowing the singers time to meditate on the text.

Sacred harp sings date to at least the 1860s in the Okefenokee. Although historically part of the larger sacred harp movement in the South, the cultural isolation of southeast Georgia fostered a distinctive stylistic variant characterized by the same slow tempos and ornamentation found in the Primitive Baptist meeting house, walking time in a counterclockwise fashion according to the meter of the tune, and occasional use of the "**drone**" or human **bagpipe**. The drone involves a core of six to eight singers

standing in the center of the room who sing all three parts of the sacred harp harmonization. Three circles of singers, composed respectively of bass, treble, and tenor, drone the **tonic**, **dominant**, and **octave** of the **scale**, while walking in opposing directions. Alto singers are not used in the drone technique and are a recent addition to the local singing style. Singers use the B. F. White revised Cooper edition; other books have been used in the past but always with four-shape rather than seven-shape versions of sacred harp notation.

Contexts for sings include monthly singing schools, rites of passage, family reunions, and individual homes. Sacred harp, or "notebook singing," once was so widespread that different families each had their own sound. Francis Harper documented sacred harp among the Chesser family of the Okefenokee in 1944, for example, a tradition perpetuated today, although in altered form, by descendants of Harry Chesser at the annual Chesser Homestead Open House in the Okefenokee National Wildlife refuge outside Folkston. Few families maintain their own singing style today.

Historically, sings were nondenominational; however, factionalism among Primitive Baptists gradually eroded the social and community base of sacred harp until, by the early 1990s, the tradition was in severe decline. Many Crawfordite Primitive Baptists did not realize that other people sang sacred harp until the mid-1990s. In 1995, cousins David and Clarke Lee began to revive the monthly sings at the Hoboken School in Brantley County, Georgia, a tradition initiated by David's great-uncle Silas Lee around 1950. The national sacred harp community since has taken tremendous interest in the Okefenokee style, resulting in a growing cross-fertilization of musical styles. The Georgia-Alabama-Florida Sacred Harp Convention, held in Hoboken for the first time in the fall of 1997, included singers from at least eight states. Regular monthly sings currently take place at Hoboken School and at Nathalene, a Crawfordite meeting house in Nassau County, Florida.

Collector Francis Harper provides the best documentation of swamper secular music. His field notes and sound recordings include locally composed songs and variants of widely disseminated ballads such as "Barbara Allen" and "The Little Mohee" (or "Lassie Mohee"). The annual Chesser Homestead Open House and the Harper field recordings provide incentive for a few swamp families to perform several of the old tunes. Harper also documented hollering, a distinctive, yodel-like alternation of head and chest tones, sometimes interspersed with song fragments, which was used to call hogs and cattle, to signal that an individual was returning home, or simply for the sheer joy of it. This tradition is no longer widespread, although a few more traditional families maintain the practice.

The old-fashioned **frolic**, with its fiddling and **square dancing**, was once a common form of community entertainment. Frolics peaked during the fall harvest season as part of cane grindings, hog killings, fodder pullings, and candy pullings. Holidays such as Christmas and the Fourth of July, as well as impromptu house parties, were also settings for music and dance. Harper reports that local tune favorites included "Sally Goodin," "Molly Put the Kettle On," "Cotton-Eyed Joe," and "One-Eyed Gopher." The swamp's cultural isolation also fostered distinctive local repertoire among families of fiddlers. Fiddle performance practice included the southern tradition of using a straw or piece of cane to beat rhythmic accompaniment to the tune. **Banjos**, some of them homemade, were almost as popular as fiddles. Little of this older musical repertoire survives today. Bluegrass and **old-time** country are now widely popular in the region.

IDEAS ABOUT MUSIC

Primitive Baptist beliefs about music, especially those of the conservative Crawfordite faction, have had a powerful influence in the Okefenokee. Religious prohibitions against radio and television and against prayer led by non–Crawfordites reinforced the region's cultural isolation and encouraged the preser-

vation of regional musical styles. The strongly predestinarian Crawfordites model their worship on the early or "primitive" church, eschewing evangelism, Sunday schools, musical **instruments** in church, or a professional paid clergy. In their prohibitions against instruments they follow the practices of early frontier Baptists and Methodists as well as Scottish Calvinists. The lay preachers or elders deliver "inspired" sermons in a heightened speech or chant. The Lloyd hymnal, as well as the sacred harp notebook, are viewed as sacred texts by the more conservative Crawfordites, and any change is viewed as disrespectful if not sacrilegious.

Primitive Baptists also prohibit dancing and drinking among members. These beliefs conflict with many secular music traditions. If the children are not yet formal members of the church, they are sometimes allowed to attend dances. In the past, some Primitive Baptists allowed their children to attend **play-parties** but forbade frolics.

SOCIAL ORGANIZATION OF MUSIC

See glossary for definition of boldfaced terms

Primitive Baptists sing as a congregation; there are no choirs or formal musical organizations. To preserve the same-sex decorum of foot washing, men and women sit on opposite sides of the meetinghouse. Visitors generally sit in a separate section, although they are not required to do so. In keeping with the Apostle Paul's views of women's role in the church, only men are allowed to lead songs, serve as elders and deacons, and speak in church. Sacred harp leadership is also confined to men, although all are welcome and encouraged to sing. Singers now sit in the "hollow square" formation common to the larger sacred harp tradition, although in earlier years a circle formation was used.

DOCUMENTARY RECORDINGS AND FILMS

Francis Harper's field recordings from August 1944 are available from the Archive of Folk Culture, American Folklife Center, Library of Congress (AFS 7721-7737). Included are stories, ballads and songs, and sacred harp. A CD of the all-day sacred harp sing in Hoboken, Georgia, recorded by Keith Willard in December 1996, was released in 1999. It is available from Willard, who can be contacted via e-mail at: kwillard@abaton. com; 486 Mt. Curve Blvd., St. Paul, MN 55116; telephone 612-699-2040.

BIBLIOGRAPHY

Cauthen, Joyce. (1999). *Benjamin Lloyd's Hymn Book: A Primitive Baptist Song Tradition.* Montgomery: Alabama Folklife Association. Includes CD featuring four a cappella hymns sung by the Lee Family of Hoboken, Georgia. Alabama Traditions 108.

Crowley, John G. (1998). *Primitive Baptists of the Wiregrass South.* Gainesville: University Press of Florida.

Harper, Francis, and Presley, Delma E. (1981). *Okefinokee Album.* Athens and London: University of Georgia Press.

Morgan, Nancy Fouraker. (1997). *Out of the Pocket: My Life on the Florida/Georgia Frontier.* Self published. Tallahassee, FL: Rose Printing Co. Available at Stephen Foster State Park Gift Shop, White Springs, Florida.

Puckett, Martha Mizell. (1975). *Snow White Sands.* Douglas: South Georgia College.

ADAM MANLY REECE: AN EARLY BANJO PLAYER OF GRAYSON COUNTY, VIRGINIA

Andy Cahan

Andy Cahan has done extensive fieldwork throughout the Blue Ridge and has produced and appeared on many albums of traditional music. He toured and recorded two albums with Tommy Jarrell and served as the banjo picker with Earnest East's Pine Ridge Boys from 1979 until East retired. During the 1980s, he also played and recorded with Carlie Marion of Elkin, North Carolina. The following essay originally appeared in the Galax Gazette *newspaper of Galax, Virginia, in the weekend edition of August 11–13, 2000.*

The evolution of the **string band** of the Blue Ridge has been the focus of many enthusiasts and scholars of mountain music. Most of the oldest players contended that the idea of a "band" originated when the **guitar** began to circulate and become intertwined with the older tradition of the **banjo/fiddle** combination. To this day, most fiddlers' conventions in the southern mountains require a bare minimum of a fiddle, a banjo, and a guitar as the instrumental requirement for bands competing in contests.

The historical circumstances surrounding the integration of the guitar into the mountain ensemble are relatively well understood. Industrialization and modernization in the early 1900s made factory-made and other non-local goods more accessible to people in the mountains. The way the guitar made it into the musical world of the Parishes of Coal Creek, for example, was not atypical. In the early 1980s, Leona Parish recollected:

Daddy was the first person in the whole country around to order from Sears and Roebuck, and he began ordering in early 1900. In the fall we would make out a freight order for the things we would need that winter, and two guitars were among the first things. The guitars were some of the first in the area that I know of.

Our understanding of the marriage of the banjo to the earlier fiddle tradition is less cut and dry. There has been a lot of speculation on just when the banjo arrived in the mountains, and under what circumstances. It is an accepted fact that the banjo, in its original form, came to America with the African slaves. It has been suggested that it arrived in the mountains due to direct contact between African Americans in the Piedmont South, and whites in the Piedmont and the mountains. The presence of black railroad laborers in the mountains after 1870 could have been a source of black/white musical exchange. It has also been suggested that the banjo and the clawhammer playing style came into the mountains with traveling blackface **minstrel** groups and tent and medicine-show entertainers. There are many potential answers to the question of how the banjo came to be paired up with the fiddle in mountain music, as the complex scenario of musical migration and interchange in the nineteenth century encompassed varied circumstances and individual experiences.

The facts surrounding at least one very early mountain banjo player, Adam Manly Reece (1830–1864), of the Grayson and Carrol counties area of Virginia, have surfaced. Information about Manly (the name he went by) had been retained and passed down through his family and was imparted to the author through Reece's great-nephew, Kahle Brewer (b.1903) of Galax, Virginia. Hailing from a family that virtually overflowed with musicians, Kahle himself was an **old-time** fiddler of the highest caliber. He had a strong and serious regard for the intricacies of both the music and its history. Kahle had a brief recording career in the 1920s, when he participated in the commercial recordings of Ernest Stoneman. His musical mentors were older fiddlers such as Emmett Lundy, Joe Hampton, Eck Dunford, Charlie Higgins, and others whose music was linked to that of the legendary fiddler Greenberry Leonard (1810–ca.1892).

Kahle Brewer was also a participant in an ongoing inter-family musical circle that spanned several generations. This community of musicians was loosely composed of members of the Leonard, Brewer, Reece, and Frost families, all of which were based in and around the Oldtown section near present-day Galax. The earliest musical partnership in this circle was banjoist Manly Reece and fiddler Greenberry Leonard. Their playing days date back to the 1850s, making them the earliest known specific banjo/fiddle combination traceable in the area. Manly Reece was Kahle Brewer's maternal great-uncle, and it seems he is the earliest nameable banjo player within the region. Most of what we know about Manly is due to the care that

the Brewer family took to preserve the family history from generation to generation, as well as an exceptional collection of photographs and letters that were lovingly cared for. Perhaps the highlight of what was saved is the actual banjo that Manly built some time before 1849, when his family came to Virginia from North Carolina.

Most of what Kahle Brewer knew about Manly Reece was learned from his grandparents, Julia Reece Green (1842–1911) and her husband, Bill Green. Julia, Manly's sister, was herself an accomplished banjo-picker, and also played the **accordion**. Bill played the banjo too. While growing up, Kahle had many occasions to hear about the old music and old ways from Julia and Bill.

The Reece family of Manly's generation was native to Randolph County, North Carolina, and had migrated to Virginia. Manly's father, George, was a blacksmith, the trade that Manly assumed. Sometime just after 1845 the Reeces left Randolph County for reasons unexplained and headed northwest. The 1850 census shows that they had by then settled in Hillsville, Virginia, after stays in Christiansburg, Virginia, and Princeton, West Virginia. The Brewers offered a possible explanation for the Reece family's move to the Grayson/Carroll counties area: Manly's older sister Larthena had become the fiancée of one Garland Anderson, a substantial landowner there. Shortly after arriving in Hillsville, the family settled in the Oldtown section.

It is difficult to clearly understand the origin and character of Manly Reece's music so many years after his death, although some of the picture can be assembled. Kahle Brewer clearly remembered his grandmother Julia telling him that her brother Manly began learning to play while he was still a boy. From all accounts it seems that Manly had been playing long enough to have become proficient by the time the family left North Carolina, at which time he was sixteen to eighteen years old. Judging from his legendary high musical caliber he was likely to have become an accomplished player before the Reeces arrived in Virginia. Supporting this is the fact that the arduous traveling, set-

See glossary for definition of boldfaced terms

tling, and resettling that the family undertook in the late 1840s would have provided less than ideal circumstances for sustained contact with other musicians. And there is no evidence that another banjo player was along for the trip. It is safe to assume, then, that Manly began playing the banjo while he was still living in North Carolina.

But from whom did he learn? In speculating on this we must consider the banjo's historical position in the 1840s. It was during this time that the minstrel show was beginning to emerge—the caricaturizing of blacks by whites was becoming an institution of performance entertainment. Banjo playing was integral to the minstrel show. Although the minstrel show eventually became a popular, mainstream entertainment form in itself, the early minstrel theater of this time still had substantial connections with the music that originally inspired it—that of the slaves. But both deliberate and subconscious musical alterations would eventually render these connections insignificant. The music was played primarily by whites who, by and large, had little concern for playing true to the forms of the blacks whose music inspired it. Most were more concerned with putting on a marketable show. The eventual drift from traditional forms, however, was only in its earliest stages during the time Manly would have been learning to play.

The possibility that Manly Reece learned to play the banjo from black musicians can only be speculated upon. The 1840 census shows no Reeces in Randolph County who were slaveowners, yet the overall number of slaves there was substantial.

While Manly Reece's specific early musical mentors are no longer known, there is a smattering of information about his family's musical interests, activities, and contacts. Kahle remembered his grandmother Julia

Photograph of Manly Reece playing the banjo. c. 1850s

Photograph courtesy Andy Cahan

mentioning that her (and Manly's) father, George, played the fiddle. She herself learned to play the banjo from Manly, and as noted earlier, played the accordion as well. Family letters from the 1860s reflect the family's active involvement with rural religious singing schools that used both **shape-note** and round-note songbooks. The letters also reflect an interest in **secular** songs. Among the Reece letters are verses of songs of the era that were written down by Manly's younger siblings and friends from Christiansburg. Notable among these are the words to Stephen Foster's "Hard Times Come Again No More," there titled "Hard Times."

When asked to recall the older family member's descriptions of Manly Reece and his music, Kahle and his wife, Edna, offered some fascinating images. These images suggest both the possibility that Manly had been exposed to popular musical forms of the time as well as a compatibility with the traditional music of his adopted home in Oldtown. Kahle noted that:

> Grandma said he could play anything he ever heard. . . . [He was] a natural banjo picker. . . . He was a genius.

Manly was known to have been a great entertainer as well as a fine musician. A blacksmith by profession, he was also an accomplished ventriloquist and a natural

showman. When asked what he knew about the specifics of Manly's music, Kahle allowed that he played "nearly all of the old tunes" and that he also played Stephen Foster songs. Kahle had been told that Manly played the banjo in the clawhammer style, as was common among both blacks and blackface minstrels of the time, and which later became the dominant style among whites in the mountains. Manly had apparently also learned to fingerpick, and Kahle specifically noted that he learned clawhammer style first.

We can speculate further on the nature of Manly's banjo music through the situations in which he seems to have done much of his playing. Kahle Brewer remembers hearing from the old people that Manly did indeed play with several fiddlers in and around Oldtown. The one fiddler in particular that Kahle could specify was Greenberry ("Green") Leonard. The combination of the two is the earliest specifically known example of a banjo/fiddle partnership in the region.

Nowadays, there is no one left who can relate firsthand information about the state of the region's music in the nineteenth century. It is generally still acknowledged, however, that the most renowned fiddler of the period was Green Leonard. Even more than a century after his death, he has remained a legendary figure to whom much of the area's fiddle style and repertory can be traced. By all accounts, it seems that in the days of Leonard's youth (the 1820s and 1830s), the fiddle was not played with the banjo, which almost certainly had not arrived in the area by that time. Thus, the changes in tune repertory, rhythm, and tuning that came about through the integration with the banjo had not yet evolved.

The recordings of Galax-area fiddler Emmett Lundy (1864–1953) are the best available examples of music learned directly from Green Leonard. The sound of the music and the tunes is strongly "old world" in nature. There is a stately, almost elegant feel to the fiddling, and it seems to stand as complete on its own as it does with accompaniment. It is, truly, music from another era. Looking into the origins of Green Leonard's

music, almost no information remains as to who his teachers and early contacts were. It has been discovered, though, that Leonard's great-grandfather, Thomas Blair, had a fiddle listed among the items in his estate. Blair was a native of Scotland who settled in Grayson County.

The musical combination of Green Leonard and Manly Reece was probably experimental in a way. It may have taken more adjustment on the part of Leonard, as he was most likely at least forty years old when he met twenty-year-old Reece and was steeped in the oldest solo-fiddle tradition in the region. In contrast, Reece was from an area over one hundred miles away and played an **instrument** that presumably was new to Grayson County and not yet firmly established as a white person's instrument. Despite the contrasts, information that has been passed down suggests not only that Leonard accepted but admired Reece's music.

Otie Leonard (1901–1985) of Oldtown was Green Leonard's great-grandson, and he had heard a great deal about his locally famous ancestor. To Otie, the musical combination of Green and Manly Reece was a solidly remembered milestone within his very musical family. During my visits with Otie in 1983 and 1984, he spoke of the two musicians and recounted that Green was said to have held Manly's music in great esteem.

Several letters written to Manly Reece during his period of service in the Confederate Army underscore the legendary reverence bestowed upon his music. The following is an excerpt from a letter dated August 13, 1863, and was written by Louisa Leonard (1826–?), Green Leonard's younger sister:

> Amos Ballard wrote you had been to see them and said to tell me you was well and could pick the banjo yet. I wish you would pick my favorite tune for me and just imagine I was listening, for I think you could almost see my spirit hovering around. I have not heard the banjo for so long. When you see Lee, Amos, and Ellis give them my love and tell them their folks is all well. . . .

Louisa's letter reveals much more than her delight in Manly's music. The Amos Ballard she cites was remembered by fiddler Luther Davis (1887–1986) as one of the early fiddlers of the area. Kahle Brewer recalled his grandfather speaking of him as well. The "Ellis" Louisa refers to was Green Leonard's son (1840–?), Otie Leonard's grandfather, who was also a fiddler. Ellis served in the war at the same time as Manly. These references to Manly's social contact with other fiddlers provide the possibility of his musical involvement with them as well.

Another significant point in Louisa's letter is when she mentions, "I have not heard the banjo for so long." This suggests the scarcity of the instrument in the area at the time, possibly intensified by the potential number of banjo players called off to war. An earlier letter to Manly dates from August 9, 1861, and was written by Elizabeth Kegley, also of Grayson County:

> . . . whichever side is a'goin to win I wish they would hurry and do it for I am getting tired of it. I used to see pleasure but I don't see no pleasure. No, I didn't know how much pleasure I was a'seeing when I used to go to singing school. I hope the time is not far. Listen, when you can, come home and sing and pick the banjo. I have often thought of past times, and wish that times was like they once was.

The heartache and destruction that accompanied the Civil War occasionally gave way to at least some relief through music. Generals Jeb Stuart and Robert E. Lee were particularly noted for their interest in music, for their own enjoyment and that of the troops. In her book *Robert E. Lee: The Complete Man (1861–1870),* Margaret Sanborn writes:

> Evenings at the camp were often made lively by the company of ladies and the fun-loving Jeb Stuart, who always brought with him his court minstrels—Sam Sweeney, the banjo player; Taliaferro, the fiddler;

Bob, a mulatto boy who worked the bones; a guitarist; and several staff members who, like Stuart, had excellent voices.

Sam Sweeney was, in fact, a professional minstrel who became a rebel soldier in the Civil War. He was a brother of Joel Walker Sweeney, one of the most celebrated of the early backface minstrels. In *War Years with Jeb Stuart,* W. W. Blackford notes:

> Stuart would have an eye, not only to the reliability of the man and horse, but sometimes to the man's accomplishments in the line of enlivening a march, or beguiling the time around a campfire. . . . In this way he collected around him a number of experts. . . . Sweeney and his banjo and his negroe melodies were the favorites; and Sweeney always carried his instrument slung at his back on marches. The life of the men was restored by its tinkle.

Kahle Brewer's descriptions of Manly Reece's experiences during the Civil War are in ways similar to the descriptions of Sweeney. While his service in the Confederate Army deprived Grayson County of a significant musician, it provided the troops with some relief from the hardships of war. This is the other of Manly's main musical contexts of which we are aware. A provost guard in Pickett's division, Manly is said to have been given special treatment on account of his musical talents. Indeed, a letter written in 1863 by Manly's sister Larthena to her mother and sister attests to this:

> I have heard from Manly and he was well . . .has escaped once more unharmed. Manly is one of the Provost guard . . . does not have to go into battle. He has quite an easy time if there is anything he has it and has choice of clothing.

Family information from the Brewers asserts that Manly had also been recognized by Lee and Stuart, who on several occasions personally invited him to entertain the troops. Kahle specifically noted that Manly brought with him to war a four-string banjo

that he had previously converted to a five-string. Kahle also recollected a letter within the family collection that mentioned Lee and Stuart's intentions of introducing Manly to one of the Sweeney boys. The meeting, however, was destined never to take place.

Manly's musical activity during the war, and Lee and Stuart's enthrallment with him, would seem to imply that his music had an accessible, popular character. The idea of bringing him together with Sweeney also points to the possibility that Manly's music was oriented toward the minstrel music of the period, as well as being compatible with the age-old fiddle tunes he had accompanied Green Leonard on back home.

The recognition Manly gained for his music during his military years certainly must have earned him a more bearable existence. It could not, however, completely insulate him from the perils of war. His untimely death came in March 1864—not in battle, but while traveling with a group of soldiers atop a troop train near Petersburg, Virginia. Smoke from the locomotive blinded them as the train approached a tunnel. On March 10, 1864, Larthena wrote:

> Dear Mother and Sister
>
> I received your letter by to days mail. I had heard the sad news before your letter came. . . . Let's bare [sic] it as well as we can. All our grief will do no good . . . we can change nothing that has happened. If so it would not be as it is tonight. Dear Mother I know you are troubling yourself very much. Please think of it, it will not bring him back.

Manly Reece lived and played music in the Grayson/Carroll counties area for barely over a decade. But considering the status he held among a small circle of distinguished local musicians, it seems that he may have ended up becoming a strongly influential player had he lived to return from the war. The extent of the influence he already wielded is hard to measure and makes one wonder again about the characteristics of other banjo players in the area at that time. There are hints as to the answers: Manly had

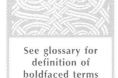

See glossary for definition of boldfaced terms

taught his sister Julia to play, and Kahle Brewer remembered her as having been a fine clawhammer banjo player. Julia taught her husband, Bill Green, to play, and the couple had several children who themselves became noteworthy old-time musicians.

Kahle also recollected his grandfather, Bill Green, telling him about the music of local slaves, who played tunes such as "'Sheep Shell Corn,' 'Sourwood Mountain,' all them tunes like that" on the banjo, in the clawhammer style, and that there was at least one black fiddler among them.

And finally, we know without doubt that Manly was not the only banjo player from the area that went into the Confederate Army. Among the letters saved by Julia Reece was one written by a soldier named A. R. Frashure. Other information about Frashure is unknown at this time, and there are no clues as to why the letter was among the others that the Brewers saved. Its purpose, however, is unmistakable:

Dear Sir,

I take the pleasure this morning of dropping you a small note to inform you that the boys are well in camp. . . . My intention of sending this note to you is to inform you that I am very much in need of some music. I wish you would be so kind as to send me my banjo by the next opportunity by someone who is coming down this way or unless send it by express to which I will pay the carriage. . . .

And you will oblige your friend
A. R. Frashure

UNCLE WADE: A MEMORIAL TO UNCLE WADE WARD, OLD-TIME VIRGINIA BANJO PICKER

Eric Davidson and Jane Rigg

During the 1960s and 1970s, Eric Davidson, Jane Rigg, Caleb Finch, and others produced a series of recordings of musicians from southwestern Virginia and adjacent regions of North Carolina for Folkways, all of which are still available from the Smithsonian Institution. Their revival old-time band, the Iron Mountain String Band (consisting of Eric Davidson, Caleb Finch, and Brooke Moyer) has remained active since the 1960s. The following essay is derived from the liner notes that accompany the memorial album assembled by Davidson and Rigg entitled Uncle Wade, *released as Folkways 2380 in 1973 following the banjo player's death.*

Wade Ward was seventy-nine when he died "just settin'" early in the evening of May 29, 1971, on his familiar porch overlooking the Peachbottom Creek meadows. He had spent most of his life in that house, outlived two wives, operated a small farm, and became famous as perhaps the greatest living exponent of the old time clawhammer **banjo** style. Wade began playing the traditional **fiddle** and banjo tunes of his country as a lad. Like most of the traditional mountain musicians he was born into a family of musicians, and for the first years his musical performances consisted of playing with his brother Crockett at nearby home dances. By the end of his life, his music had been distributed by major record companies, and interested people had come from all over the United States and England to see and hear him play.

All his life Uncle Wade stayed home and played music at local affairs, with local people. In a time when great highways and new populations and the events of history were uprooting the customs of his youth, Uncle Wade remained near Independence, Virginia, always living in more or less the old-time rural way. His **repertoire** contained few, if any, "new" tunes, and his musical style was never overlain with **bluegrass** harmonies and rhythms, as was so generally the case for old-time musicians who originated in his area over these same years. His was a rich and humorous outlook, and the comings and goings of local people were a source of pleasure and amusement to him. Everyone who knew him loved his gracious, easy ways. For whatever deeper reason, Wade was spared the frequently bitter and destructive restlessness which led so many mountain men off to wars and violent troubles and distant adventures. If ever there was a man who liked where he was, it was Wade.

So, for the love of playing, all his life Wade preserved his country's most intricate and memorable local traditions in music. Banjo-fiddle **string band** music was the first music Wade learned, and was always the

music he played best, and by his own words the music he loved best.

ORIGINS

Benjamin Wade Ward was born October 15, 1892, one of five sons and four daughters of Enoch Ward and Rosamond Carico Ward. Both his father's and mother's people came from the mountains and valleys above Independence, Virginia. As far back as legend goes the Wards had lived near Saddle Creek, where Wade was born. Enoch Ward had been raised in Saddle Creek, and he died near there in 1922, at the age of seventy-five, which would set the year of his birth around 1847. Tradition has it that the first Wards to come to Virginia were three brothers, all confirmed bachelors. One morning one of the brothers, who did all the cooking, set a fourth place at the table, and each time he took something he placed the same on the fourth plate. When breakfast was over he pointed to the fourth plate and said, "It would take too much food to keep a woman here." But eventually one of the brothers, the Ward family ancestor, married, and when this happened the other two brothers left, never to be heard from again.

When Wade was nine, the family moved to the nearby Rock Creek Community, and in the next year, 1902, Enoch Ward purchased the Peachbottom Creek farm a few miles above Independence where Wade lived ever since. One of Wade's earliest memories dated from this period. He once told me that he had gone into Independence town one summer day when he was nine or ten and saw a great crowd around the County Courthouse, which still stands. Peeking through the fence, he watched a Negro being hanged by the sheriff there, a sight which he said he always remembered and never wanted to see again.

Wade began learning to pick the banjo when he was eleven, and began fiddling when he was sixteen. His main teacher in both **instruments** was his brother, David Crockett Ward, who was twenty years older than Wade. Eventually Wade became an even more proficient banjo picker than Crockett though Wade's aunt Katy Hill states that there were certain tunes Wade never did learn "just right." Although Wade was mainly to become famous as a brilliant clawhammer banjo picker, he was also a first-rate fiddler. Katy feels that Crockett and Wade were about equally good on the fiddle, though she felt Crockett's performance was a little more "old timey."

There was much **old time** music in the Ward family background. Enoch Ward had played the fiddle, though by this time he had quit, and Rosamund Ward was the source for many of the **ballads** and songs which Crockett knew and later performed. There was also another older brother, Joe Ward, who picked the banjo as well. Wade once explained to me that he never sang with the banjo himself because he had a physical disability with his voice stemming from a bout with whooping cough when he was fourteen, but this could not be confirmed. A contributory reason was probably that there were always good singers around, first Crockett, and then Crockett's son, Fields. Whatever the reason, Wade's later musical activities were almost exclusively instrumental.

Wade played intensively during his teens. During this period he was out making music with Crockett almost every night. By this time the duo had become well known in the area and were playing at a variety of local events, including Christmas and other festivities at school houses in the Independence and Sparta, North Carolina, area, and weekly dances at a local Independence hotel. The main activity of all rural family string bands such as Crockett and his young brother Wade, however, was playing at home dances associated with important events, both social (weddings, celebrations) and economic (corn shuckings, house raisings, etc.).

The traditional banjo repertoire and the traditional fiddle repertoire in general overlap; i.e., a given banjo tune normally has a matching fiddle counterpart, and vice versa. The extent of overlap is not symmetrical for the two instruments, however, for although

all banjo pieces may have possessed matching fiddle counterparts, the converse was clearly not true. The traditional fiddle repertoire was thus more complex, even though the major part of this repertoire was indeed banjo-fiddle string band music.

Both the clawhammer banjo and the old-time fiddle music are characterized by the prevalence of **drones**, usually in fourths and **fifths**. This is accomplished by the use of almost continuous double stops on the fiddle, and on the banjo by the use of the monotonic fifth string. This string is never noted on the fingerboard of the instrument, and is plucked continuously with the thumb. On both instruments, the strings are tuned differently for different songs. Five or six tunings exist on the banjo as played in Grayson and Carroll counties, and at least three or four on the fiddle.

The exciting harmonic character of the early banjo-fiddle music is due basically to the extensive use of **bagpipe**-like drones, and to the prevalence of unusual **scales** or modes. These are the factors which give this music an archaic, unique flavor. Most of the tunes and songs collected elsewhere in the United States are couched either in the common seven-note major (ionian) or minor (aeolian) scales, but the traditional southern Appalachian songs utilize a variety of **pentatonic** and **hexatonic** scales as well as some uncommon seven-note modes such as the **mixolydian**. In the Grayson and Carroll counties area almost all the early rural band style dance tunes are pentatonic or hexatonic, and the instruments tend to be tuned directly to the main notes of the scale. Chording and noting with the left hand on the fingerboard are kept to a minimum in this style, and the one or two chords used in a given piece always include open strings acting as drones. This open-stringed harmonic structure, based on **intervals** of fourths and fifths, tends to be harmonically incompatible with conventional "major" or "minor" chords such as are played on **guitar**, **accordion**, piano, and so on.

The old-time dance music is characterized by a driving, accented rhythm, in which

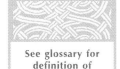

See glossary for definition of boldfaced terms

upbeats and offbeats are often stressed. Intricate offbeat notes picked on the banjo are interlocked with equally intricate fiddle rhythms; the two instruments are integrated perfectly in the old-time versions of the band dance tunes. One of the most fascinating aspects of this music, in fact, is the ease with which the traditionally learned fiddle part to a given tune can be fit to the traditional banjo part of the same tune by musicians who are both from the same general area, but who may never have played together before.

WADE THE MUSICIAN: MANHOOD

On August 6, 1913, Wade married Lelia Mathews, who was then nineteen years old. He was twenty. Lelia came from the community of Spring Valley, Virginia, a few miles north of Wade's farm. Wade met Lelia through one of his sisters, who with her husband was working on the farm of a neighbor. There Lelia was staying also, and Wade's sister induced Wade to visit specifically so that Lelia and Wade would meet. Often Lelia would travel about over the countryside with Wade and whoever was playing with him. She is remembered as a woman who enjoyed such travels but who was jealous of Wade's time, and particularly when she stayed home, of the days and nights he was off picking the banjo and fiddling. She was not a musician, and according to some informants she never really became closely familiar with his music. Wade and Lelia lost two children in childbirth and raised one son, who, like so many others, left the mountains when he was grown to return only for occasional family visits.

Nineteen-nineteen, when Wade was twenty-six, was an important year for his musical activities. This was the year the Buck Mountain Band was formed, including Wade, the banjo picker, a well-known local fiddler called Van Edwards, and the latter's son, Earl Edwards. Earl played guitar, and the Buck Mountain Band was one of many new string bands forming in this area in which the guitar was for the first

time incorporated. This instrument had been unknown in these mountains until after the turn of the century. The advent of the guitar in the local music would result eventually in many changes. Along with other influences it can be said to have been partly responsible for destroying much of the unique harmonic structure of old-time music, leading in the end to its replacement with bluegrass music. In the less distant future, however, lay one of the great periods of traditional southwest Virginia band music, in which guitar, an increased use of vocals, and the old banjo-fiddle tradition were blended excitingly together, sometimes with the addition of **autoharp** as well. The band music of this period, which we referred to in earlier essays as the "Old Galax Band Style," still relied mainly on the older repertoire and harmonics.

Some years later, Wade was to become a key figure in what was one of the greatest of all the string bands of this **genre**, the Grayson County Bog Trotters. His early musical experience with the Buck Mountain Band must have served to prepare his ear and his repertoire for later participation in the Bog Trotters Band. Wade began to pick the banjo Charlie Poole style, with his fingers and picks, in order to fit with the guitar and fiddle on tunes with which the archaic clawhammer harmonies and rhythms were not completely compatible.

The Buck Mountain Band played for the Parson's Auction Company, at public land sales. The day he died Wade had played for a Parson's sale—for fifty-one years Wade and his partners made music for the Parson's auctions. After Van Edwards died, Wade played with Crockett and Fields Ward, the guitar player and singer who was Crockett's son. Then for many years Uncle Charlie Higgins was his fiddler, and later Charlie and Wade played with Dale Poe, a local guitar player. Wade also played with men of the Lundy family, and with other local musicians. According to Joe Parsons, the band was dubbed "Buck Mountain" in the early days by a man whose forced sale of property was accompanied by the music of Wade and Van Edwards, and the name stuck.

Besides dances and land sales Wade and the band also played at local Republican party meetings. "Born a Republican," Wade played at campaign stops all over the country, particularly in association with John Parsons and the latter's son, Joe Parsons, who was county clerk from 1928 to 1960 and was Wade's lifelong friend. Bud Ward, Wade's brother, was a local Republican sheriff for many years, and Wade was well known as a campaign adjunct, providing music between the speeches, for many other Republican candidates as well. On election day he would drive around and help "get out the vote." Playing for political events and for the Parson's Auction Company were both considered exceedingly lucrative, particularly in relation to the scarcity of cash on the farms.

After his father's death in 1922, Crockett moved in to Galax, where he earned a living as a carpenter. Wade would come in to play with Fields and Crockett, and up the road a little ways Uncle Eck Dunford, another old-time fiddler, heard them playing. Eck got a neighbor who knew the Wards to introduce him, and thus the Bog Trotters were born. The fifth regular member of the band, Doc Davis (autoharp), was brought in by Eck Dunford. During the Bog Trotters' era Wade and Fields and sometimes Crockett roamed widely about the countryside, playing music at land sales and other events. Sometimes they were gone for three or four days at a time. The Bog Trotters convened to play at the famous fiddle conventions at White Top Mountain and at Galax and were frequently heard under the auspices of the Galax Moose Lodge.

With the Bog Trotters Wade played in relatively distant places in Virginia, including Roanoke, and locations in North Carolina, Tennessee, Kentucky, and even Arkansas. At one contest held at Mt. Vernon, Kentucky, the top prize of which was the honor of being recorded for commercial records (the day was won by the famous Coon Creek Girls), the Virginia band was offered $200 a week to stay on, but were unable to accept. This was a far cry from the days of a boyhood trip to Tennessee, when,

97

according to his recollection, Wade and his group had agreed to play a dance for fifteen cents a piece. Later the Bog Trotters played for the campaigning governor of the state down the Shenandoah Valley at Blacksburg, Virginia, and on another occasion they provided the "official" music at the state dedication of a bridge at Hillsville, Virginia. Wade was competing in the widely attended Old Fiddler's Conventions at Galax in the meantime, and was regularly walking off with the first place year after year.

Nineteen-forty was the high-water mark. Three years previously John Lomax had recorded Wade and the Bog Trotters for the Library of Congress and now, through Alan Lomax, it was arranged for the Bog Trotters to appear on a nationwide CBS radio program, *American School of the Air,* originating in Roanoke, Virginia (January 9, 1940). When the time came for the program to go on the air, everyone in Grayson County near a radio stopped work to listen; in Independence itself the county courthouse was the scene of a trial that day, and as the program hour approached the judge temporarily halted the proceedings and called for a radio to be brought into the courtroom. By this time, Wade (1940) was a deep and seasoned performer. He had been playing banjo for thirty-seven years and fiddle for thirty-two, and he was still playing with the man he had first learned from, his brother Crockett Ward.

The music played by the Bog Trotters differed from the older banjo-fiddle music of the country. Some basic changes have occurred, and the way the old Galax string bands turned a tune differs from the mode in which the same tune would have been played by the earlier banjo-fiddle string bands. Often the **tempo** is slowed down and squared off, with accents relatively confined to downbeats. This is a consequence of the fact that the dominant rhythmic role has been taken over by the guitar instead of remaining with the clawhammer banjo, as in the old rural band music. Despite all the innovations and changes, there is retained an amazingly strong flavor of the ancient rural traditional music, and the main component in the stylistic and repertorial background of the old Galax band music is, in fact, the music of the old rural bands. It is the fiddler who is mainly responsible for this retention of older elements, or the fiddler and the clawhammer banjo player when they play an old tune together, for their parts are least changed.

From about 1930 on, Wade was the sole owner of his Peachbottom Creek farm, and it was this farm which for the rest of his life provided him and his family with a basic living. Income derived from music was always extra, a welcome assistance, but not the source of his livelihood. Wade, like the old-time musicians before him, was not economically dependent on professional music performances.

During the period I knew Wade the main income from his farm accrued from the sale of heifers that he had raised and milked. Vegetables were grown, and in his house the whole range of traditional pre-electricity preparations of food for winter storage was practiced: curing of hams and pickling or "canning" of beans, squash, tomatoes, peaches, and virtually all other fruits and vegetables. Potatoes, apples, and cabbages were buried deep in the earth, beneath the frost level. Wade himself had no enormous appetite for farm labor, and apparently never had. Wade "never cut himself too much at hard work," as one informant told me: "What did he like to do besides hard work? Pick the banjo and carry on, laugh and tell jokes, run around. That was his main thing all his life." And he did a lot of fox hunting. Fox hunting was a passion with Wade. This sport consisted mainly of letting the dogs go up on a ridge, and with a large fire and some cronies to keep one company, listening to those wonderful dogs bay the whole night long.

During the war the Bog Trotters stayed home and played around Galax, occasionally appearing on local radio or at Moose Lodge functions. Then, in the early 1950s, disaster struck. Fields left the mountains for Maryland, where he had found a job. That meant the end of the Bog Trotters, for Fields had always been the vocalist and no one else could sing. Though, as Katy Hill put it, "We all hated for him to go, we couldn't tell him

See glossary for definition of boldfaced terms

not to go," for Fields had got a good job and that was a serious concern. About the same time Crockett Ward, then in his seventies, suffered a debilitating stroke, and though he remained alive until he was over ninety, he never played the fiddle again.

On May 10, 1951, Lelia died at the age of sixty-three. Wade and Lelia had been married for thirty-eight years. Wade began courting again and about three years later, in 1954, he married Mrs. Mollie Yates.

UNCLE WADE : THE LAST FIFTEEN YEARS

In 1956 and 1957, Wade was visited by Michael Seeger and myself, respectively, and this began a phase of widening contacts and ever-increasing fame that lasted until his death. In contrast to the old days of the pre-war Lomax visits, electricity was now available in the mountains, and it was now possible to make a thorough study of the whole of Wade's repertoire. Comparison with the earlier recordings shows that at this time he had lost none of his famous precision and speed. Later this was no longer routinely true, though on occasion, particularly in the excitement of playing with others, he could still summon his old brilliance.

In 1962, Wade was featured on two records assembled by the writer and others: *Traditional Music from Grayson and Carroll Counties* (1992 audiocassette reissue, Smithsonian Folkways 03811) and *The Music of Roscoe Holcomb and Wade Ward* (Folkways Records FA 2363). Half of the latter album was devoted exclusively to his music. From 1963 to 1966 we made an attempt, in which Wade enthusiastically cooperated, to put Wade together with Glen Smith, a very excellent old-time fiddler from Hillsville, Virginia. For some of these sessions Fields Ward, who happened to be in his home country at the time, was also present. Released in 1967, *Band Music of Grayson and Carroll Counties, Virginia* (Folkways 2832) includes some of the pieces then recorded. Wade exulted in the pleasure of playing the old-time banjo-fiddle music, and his per-formances were often as good as in the best of his younger days, though he was already well over seventy.

Wade's years with Mollie, a sweet and generous woman, were happy ones, and he was devastated by her death from cancer on August 4, 1961. While Mollie was alive, and for several years thereafter, her mother, Granny Porter, then in her eighties, also lived in the Peachbottom Creek house. Granny was as pithy, sharp, and humorous as Uncle Wade, and together they made a memorable pair. Once a banjo picker herself, Granny Porter too had deep roots in old-time music, having come of the family of a legendary old-time fiddler, Van Sage. Occasionally Granny and Wade made music together. Wade accompanies Granny on a striking rendition of "Barbr'y Allen" in *Songs and Ballads of the Blue Ridge Mountains* (Folkways 3831, 1968).

As the 1960s wore on Wade was invited to visit the great urban centers of the Northeast to perform there. This he was reluctant to do, finally being persuaded to come to the Smithsonian Festival at Washington in 1967. On the way he stopped in Richmond and performed for the governor, Mills Goodwin. He was seventy-five, and it was virtually the first time Wade had taken his music out of his native hill country.

Thereafter he made several other trips to Washington, and on one trip, in 1969, he performed with Fields in Maryland. Recognition was his finally, and as a recent article by John Cohen put it, "the trip to Wade's house was part of the homage to old-time music that one paid." (*Sing Out* 20 (5), 1971).

But it was very late in his life. By now Wade had outlived not only his two wives and all his brothers, and the two generations of old-time musicians he had played with during his long career, but also the isolated mountain culture from which he and his music grew. He died on a chilly, late May day, a day on which he had done just what he always did, picked the banjo at the land sale, stopped in to see Katy Hill, and gone home to sit on his porch and look out over Peach-bottom Creek.

BIBLIOGRAPHY

Band Music of Grayson and Carroll Counties, Virginia. 1967. Folkways 2832.

Cohen, John. (1971). *Sing Out!* 20(5).

The Music of Roscoe Holcomb and Wade Ward. 1962. Folkways Records FA 2363.

Songs and Ballads of the Blue Ridge Mountains. 1968. Folkways 3831.

Traditional Music from Grayson and Carroll Counties. 1992. Smithsonian Folkways 03811. Audiocassette reissue of 1962 recording.

Uncle Wade: A Memorial to Uncle Wade Ward, Old-Time Virginia Banjo Picker. 1973. Folkways 2380.

COUNTRY MUSIC IN TENNESSEE: FROM HOLLOW TO HONKY-TONK

Joe Wilson

Joseph T. Wilson, a native Tennessean, has served since 1976 as executive director of the National Council for the Traditional Arts, for which he has produced numerous festivals and national and international tours by folk artists as well as recordings and radio programs. He is also coauthor with Lee Udall of Folk Festivals: A Handbook for Organization and Management. *The following essay originally appeared in a Smithsonian Festival of American Folklife program guide.*

Among the less jarring opinions of Tennessee's fire-breathing Parson Brownlow, editor, governor, and Rebel "ventilator," was that the state would "ever be plagued with fleas and **fiddlers**, singers of morose songs, and the depredations of Old Scratch." Though he clearly disapproved of it, the sour parson was right: Tennessee's favorite music is tenacious. It came in folk form with the first settlers and continues to the present in a variety of styles and contexts from country taverns to Nashville recording studios. An historical example illustrates the linkage from the earliest folk styles to the country music of today.

George Dotson and Henry Skaggs were among the first eighteenth-century "long hunters" to view the sunny glades and hazy ridges of what is now east Tennessee. Today, a community called "Meat Camp" in Watauga County, North Carolina, takes its name from the spot in the Blue Ridge where each fall these far-ranging hunters salted and stored meat before it was carried to settlements east of the mountains. One of the lowest gaps in the Alleghanies, the one they called the "Trade Gap," is five miles from Meat Camp.

Henry Skaggs sought furs beyond the Trade Gap, and his explorations reached 150 miles west into Kentucky. Daniel Boone was a later traveler here and was assisted by Skaggs and his brothers. George Dotson remained near the Trade Gap and made a farm on the Bulldog Branch of Roan's Creek. Some of his descendants still live in Trade, Tennessee, the easternmost community in the state.

George's son Reuben was born in Trade in 1765 and lived there for 104 years. Among remembrances carried by descendants is his comment, "I've lived in four states but have never moved and live in the house I was born in." (Ill-defined boundaries led the first settlers to believe they were in colonial Virginia while they were actually in North Carolina, which in turn became the short-lived State of Franklin and ultimately

Uncle Dave Macon (right) photographed with his son Dorris, c. 1938; this photograph appeared in the magazine *Rural Radio* to promote the duo. Notice the WSM microphone, indicating that this photo was taken in the famous radio station's studios, which were the home of the Grand Ole Opry.

Photograph courtesy of the Folklife Program, North Carolina Arts Council, Dept. of Cultural Resources.

Tennessee.) Reuben loved "the singing of **hymns**, the old ballit [**ballad**] songs, and the playing of the fiddle." How well he loved fiddling and dancing is documented in the minutes of the Cove Creek Baptist Church. Reuben and his wife, Sarah Green, so offended the stern brothers and sisters that they were "sited to meeting" five times between 1811 and 1820. Their promises to sin no more were accepted, but in 1823, "a report taken up against Brother Reuben Dotson and Sister Dotson his wife that they both went to a **frolic** and stayed all night" resulted in their exclusion from the church. This conviction, that the fiddle is the devil's box, continues among some Tennesseans, but others have resolved the ancient dispute. Among them is prominent Nashville country musician Ricky Skaggs, a devout Christian and descendant of Henry Skaggs.

The Anglicizing of names has masked the ethnicity of Tennessee's first carriers of country music. In contrast to the widely held view that the early settlers were all of "the purest English stock," George Dotson was of Ulster Irish extraction, and Henry Skaggs was descended from an English mariner. Many who crossed the mountains with the Scotch-Irish and English were of German or French Huguenot descent. The latter included Ten-

nessee's first governor, John Sevier, who, like Reuben, was a devotee of balls and frolics.

The Appalachian **dulcimer**, derived from the German *Scheitholt* and now almost an emblem of Tennessee mountain culture, was actually rare until the craft revivals of the present century. It was the fiddle that remained the favorite Tennessee **instrument** until recent times, but highly skilled fiddlers who could play classics like "Rack Back Davy," "Arkansas Traveller," and "Forked Deer" have always been uncommon. On the other hand, the "ballit book" and religious songbook were open to all. Huge outdoor camp-meeting revivals that began in 1801 sent a knowledge of hymnody and songbook throughout the Volunteer State in a wave of religious fervor. Within five years these songs and a new way of singing spread throughout the nation and even to Ireland and England—Tennessee's first musical influence beyond its borders.

Tennessee fiddling was modified by popular influences during the second half of the nineteenth century, principally through traveling circuses and stage shows that featured musical performers. Improved communication brought popular sheet music to the state. But the most important of these influences was the wave of **minstrel** performance that began in the 1840s and contin-

Uncle Dave Macon

The following essay is derived from liner notes that accompanied the 1963 Folkways recording Uncle Dave Macon *(F-RF 51).*

Back in 1939 Republic Studios in Hollywood, California, after sending a representative to visit the Grand Ole Opry of Radio Station WSM in Nashville, Tennessee, decided to make a motion picture of the show. Since it was impossible to get all the stars of the Grand Ole Opry of that time into one movie, the choice was narrowed down to and included Uncle Dave Macon and his son, Dorris, Roy Acuff and his Smoky Mountain Boys, with Little Rachel, and George D. Hay, "The Solemn Old Judge" from whose dream the Grand Ole Opry got its start and who for many a year thereafter controlled its destiny.

The motion picture was made in 1940 and was an immediate success. If you've missed it, watch your television programs. It's still being primarily shown on "Late Shows."

Uncle Dave Macon was the star of the picture. Not because he wanted to be or even tried to be. It just worked out that way. Kindliness, human understanding, humor, combined with dignity, have a way of making themselves felt. This is a description of Uncle Dave Macon.

But this is not all the story. The man and his music must be cultivated, studied, and understood, and the intense enjoyment thereafter cannot be entirely explained in words.

We started talking about Uncle Dave's motion picture first instead of giving his birth date, etc., because we wanted to tell a story as it was related to us. Biographical details can come later.

In 1940 Uncle Dave Macon was a young man of seventy years. Behind him was an eminently successful career. He was one of America's greatest folk singers. He was known and loved by millions and did not need to worry about money if the "house needed a new roof." Still he was a man of nature, of the soil upon which he was raised. He did not make a motion picture because of a need or desire for money, but because he was a folksinger—and such people must sing. But on to our story.

Uncle Dave traveled from Tennessee to California in Roy Acuff's station wagon. Before leaving home he packed one of his own home-smoked Tennessee hams in a wooden box to take along for the trip. By the time they all got to Hollywood the ham was all eaten up. So, Uncle Dave, who was about to make a picture that would net him enough to buy quite a few lumber yards, took the empty box to Roy Acuff and asked that it be carefully stowed in the wagon and taken back home because it would make a good hen's nest.

We tell this little story as an introduction to [his music], for the philosophy herein is part and parcel of his songs and his style of rendition. He had a song for everyone who has been broke, or hungry, or happy, or drunk, or in love. He touched each of these with a tender humor that never judges but only understands.

David Macon was born at Smart Station in Cannon County, Tennessee, on October 7, 1870. He sang a song about the Cannon County Hills, which was never recorded.

The words went like this:

In the Cannon County Mountains
They have bright and growing fountains,
In every hill they have a still;
But just you remember
One hundred and forty-nine days from
*   next November,*
There'll be moonshine in the Cannon
*   County Hills*

Chorus:
On those hills; those beautiful hills
(Continued on the next page)

ued into the present century. Handmade **banjos** fashioned after slave prototypes were in Tennessee before the minstrels, but blackface performers improved on the instrument and developed new ways of playing in ensembles that featured several instruments. The **old-time string band** and even its modern manifestation, the **bluegrass** band, is heir to minstrel instrumentation and **repertoire**. In this way Tennessee country folk have long been in contact with commercial forces that have modified the old ballads, fiddle tunes, and sacred music.

Tennesseans and other Americans were "busking" for coins and selling song "ballits" generations before technology made possible

(Continued from previous page)

There'll be moonshine in the Cannon
County Hills
Bright lights on Broadway—
The sun shines bright in Dixie
But there's moonshine in the Cannon
County Hills

If you want to sing this song, although Uncle Dave deviated somewhat, the music to the state song of West Virginia, "Oh! Those Beautiful Hills," fits.

He was one of a large family, which was customary in those days. The Macons were prosperous farmers admired by and a credit to their community. Still today the name of Macon is highly respected locally. The name is also known intimately throughout the South and by lovers of folk music throughout the world. World fame was the doing of "Uncle Dave," but more about this later. Suffice it to say that the Macon family remain the kind of people who make this country great.

When David was still a little boy the family moved from the farm to Nashville, Tennessee, when they had purchased and intended to operate a hotel on Brood Street. Nashville was a cultural center in those days, as it still is in the folk/country music fields as well as others. Most of the leading musical, or, for that matter, dramatic shows of the country passed through the city. Many of these entertainers often stayed at the Macons' hotel. Young David Macon was enchanted by his surroundings, the people, their stories, and their music. He acquired a five-string **banjo**. His friends in show business taught him how to play. Very soon he was going very well indeed although his avocation was somewhat limited by chores and school. Dave Macon attended what is now known as the Hume-Fogg High School.

All of this happened seventy-six years ago as of this writing [c. 1963]. Uncle Dave died in March 1952, at the age of eighty-two. He never retired. Just a couple weeks prior to his death he made his regular appearances at the Grand Ole Opry, Radio Station WSM, Nashville, Tennessee, and brought down the house as always.

For over sixty-six years Uncle Dave Macon, also fondly known as the "Dixie Dew Drop" or "King of the Banjo Pickers" or "King of the Hillbillies" or "The Squire of Readyville," entertained many millions of Americans by playing his three banjos (he always carried three, each tuned to a different key), and singing the old, a few of the new southern folk songs and **ballads**, as only he could. Over the years he lightened the burdens of these millions. He brought cheer into sickrooms, taught children to respect their parents, taught parents to love their children and each other. During the Great Depression he brought sunshine into every home that could afford a five-dollar used radio or knew someone who could. During World War II, as an old man far past normal retirement age, he not only kept up the pace but added to it by entertaining service people whenever he had a chance.

Although Uncle Dave has been purported to have enjoyed "corn liquor" throughout most of his life, he gave it up for religious convictions as brought out in his song "From Earth to Heaven," recorded on Burnswick record number 329. Be this as it may, Uncle Dave knew the Bible from front to back and back to front, as evidenced by his many religious recordings and his inimitable quotes. During his extensive travels through the length and breadth of this land, he never hesitated to lay down the banjo to preach a sermon in some little out-of-the-way community. But Uncle Dave was not only a musician, a folk artist, and a preacher; he was above all a man, an American, and an individualist. He knew both sides of the old King's English. He "shore" could cuss. But his cuss words were always appropriate and never off-color.

a country music industry. That technology was first applied to the music of rural Americans in the 1920s and soon created audiences for recordings, radio broadcasts, and stage appearances. At first, Nashville was less important than Atlanta and Chicago as a country music center and largely ignored in the field-recording forays of commercial record companies when rural musicians first found their way onto major labels in the 1920s. A single institution, the Grand Ole Opry, made the Tennessee capital a music center. Begun in 1925 and broadcast on the static-free, clear-channel, 50,000-watt signal of WSM, it reached much of the United States. Opry founder George D. Hay, with a

Above all, Uncle Dave was a man who never grew old. He was as young as eighty as most of us were or are at twenty, or thirty, or even forty or more.

At this point, we would like to quote, with permission for which we are very grateful, from a book written by George D. Hay, the Solemn Old Judge of the Grand Ole Opry, and entitled "A Story of the Grand Ole Opry":

Back in about 1939, our station, WSM, received a tentative offer from Republic Studios, in Hollywood, to make a picture of the Grand Ole Opry. They dispatched a representative to Nashville to 'catch' the show and look over the situation. We asked Uncle Dave if he would mind entertaining our friend at his farm in the Cannon County Hills, knowing that the producer would get the right background and become acquainted with a true representative of the Opry. Uncle Dave was delighted. He asked his cook to prepare a real, sho' 'nuf Tennessee dinner with all of the trimmings and we drove down from Nashville on a beautiful day.

Friends, we hope some day that some of you will be fortunate enough to be Uncle Dave's guests at dinner. Until that day arrives, we fear that you will have missed a great deal in the realm of culinary art and true Southern hospitality. Uncle Dave asked the blessing and we were served a dinner which is not for sale anywhere in these United States, more is the pity. We were forced to satisfied with rich country ham, fried chicken, six or seven vegetables, done to a Tennessee turn, jelly preserves, pickles, hot corn bread and white bread. Then came the cake. Oh, well, why carry this any further. . . .

After dinner Uncle Dave invited us to be seated under a large tree in his front yard, where we discussed the possibility of the Grand Ole Opry picture. As the producer and your reporter drove back to Nashville, that experienced executive said, "I have never met a more natural man in my life. He prays at the right time and he cusses at the right time and his jokes are as cute as the dickens." Needless to say, Uncle Dave was chosen to be one of the stars of the Opry picture. Roy Acuff and his boys and Little Rachel and the Solemn Old Judge were the other representatives of the Opry in the picture which was produced in 1940 in Republic Studios by Armand Schaefer, and directed by Frank McDonald. Uncle Dave was the most popular man in the picture. Everybody loved him.

In 1932 about twenty of us, including Uncle Dave, played a large picnic in the woods of West Tennessee, promoted by a Mr. Dowland. We got there early in the morning and, on a crude bandstand, played to eight or ten thousand people throughout the day, putting on about five one-hour shows. Uncle Dave was our star and he shined forth in all of his glory that day. The next year we repeated it and for three or four years we played two picnics a year for Mr. Dowland in Tennessee and Kentucky. It was on one of these occasions that we saw Uncle Dave without a word to say—no comeback when the boys played the celebrated "badger game" on him. Usually, he thinks very quickly on his feet, but on that occasion all he could do was to say, "Shucks"!

(Continued on the next page)

concern for variety, chose his acts carefully. The first was Uncle Jimmy Thompson, a fiddler with a nineteenth-century style and repertoire. Hays soon added Dr. Humphrey Bate's "hell-for-leather" string band, the minstrel-influenced banjoist Uncle Dave Macon, **barbershop quartets**, and, beginning in the 1930s with the addition of "western" to country music, a variety of pseudo–cowboy-style bands. Although the Opry in the early years paid virtually nothing to its artists, performers could sell stage appearances and recordings throughout the South, the Mid-Atlantic states, and much of the Midwest, as it became the apex of country music success to be a Grand Ole Opry performer.

(Continued from previous page)

We ran across a picture of Uncle Dave, taken when he was eighteen. He was very carefully dressed with his little coat buttoned closely beneath his white collar and tie, topped off by a hat of soft felt, turned up in front. His banjo was in his lap. He was a city dude—no mistake about it. However, it was not until thirty years later, at the age of forty-eight, that Uncle Dave left his farm with his boys and started on his professional career as "King of the Banjo Pickers." That was twenty-seven years ago. What a career, started at an age that many of us are hunting a soft place to light for the later years.

Asked how he finally made up his mind to turn professional entertainer, Uncle Dave told us:

All of my life I had played and sung for fun. My neighbors always asked me to play at picnics and special occasions. Finally one very self-important farmer approached me and asked me to play at a party he was planning. I was very busy and a bit tired, so I thought I would stop him. I told him I would play at his party for fifteen dollars. He said, "Okay, it's a deal." It was a large affair and in the crowd was a talent scout for Loew's Theatres.

My act seemed to go over very well. When I had finished, the theatre man offered to book me at a leading theatre in Birmingham, Alabama, at several hundred dollars a week. They held me over many weeks and booked me throughout the country. I was in the show business and I have been in it ever since.

Uncle Dave has been ably assisted by his son, Dorris, who plays the **guitar** and sings with him occasionally. Dorris is a fine, upstanding farmer who looks after his dad under all circumstances.

Besides his son, Dorris (incidentally, Uncle Dave had seven sons, Dorris being the fifth), Uncle Dave was often joined on records, radio, and personal appearances by his close associates Sam and Kirk McGee (the McGee Brothers) and Sid Harkreader (**fiddle** or guitar). There was also a Mitzi Todd (fiddle) on some of the Fruit Jar Drinkers sides recorded by the Vacalion Record Corporation.

As a matter of interest to real died-in-the-wool folk collectors, Uncle Dave plays the guitar on one Vacalion record of "The Girl I Left Behind Me" with Fiddlin' Sid Harreader on the fiddle. Real "old timers" will also recall that Uncle Dave Macon could play piano as on some occasions, for variety, the Solemn Old Judge would ask Uncle Dave to sit down at the "old three-legged piano" and play "The Girl I Left Behind Me" or "Eli Green's Cake Walk," just for example.

Besides being one of America's greatest banjo players, rendering our heritage of **old-time folk music** in any appropriate style, Uncle Dave was also a great showman and a trick banjo artist. Many have tried to imitate his style but none have succeeded.

This is a kinda' mixed up thumbnail sketch of the Grand Old Man. This is Uncle Dave "with his gates-a-jar collar, gold teeth, three banjos, great big Tennessee smile and NO MAN'S COLLAR DOES HE WEAR!" How many times have us old timers heard him introduced this way!

Norman Tinsle

Because so many musicians "worked out of Nashville," the first recording studios were built there. Country music with its folk roots was viewed as a specialty item for major companies, worth doing but not significant in the overall business. The best that could happen to a country music "hit" was a "cover" by a popular artist that would increase song publishing royalties. Increases in the expendable income of rural and urban blue-collar workers encouraged an annual growth of country music as an industry throughout much of the late 1940s and early 1950s.

Part of what came to be called "the Nashville sound" was much influenced by the success of a small group of musicians in Memphis in the mid-1950s. The best known were Elvis Presley, Jerry Lee Lewis, John R. Cash, and Carl Perkins. Their "**rockabilly**" recordings merged rural Black **blues** and white "**hillbilly**" style with an electric studio sound. They, and Black artists such as Howlin' Wolf, B. B. King, and Rufus Thomas were recorded by Sam Phillips and his associates at Sun Records. The immediate popularity of the rockabillies and the later emer-

gence of commercial rock and roll showed recordings produced in Tennessee to be far more than specialty items.

As country music in general moved further from its folk roots, the production of a Nashville record became formulaic. Sharp edges were eliminated, while the goal became a recording that could "crossover" to pop and youth markets. String sections and "doo-wah" **choruses** were used along with session musicians whose motto was, "Play as little as you can as well as you can."

This synthesis of blues, balladry, and string band music is still largely the music of working-class whites. Its development continues, but the past is recalled especially by well-known traditionalists such as Ricky Skaggs and Bill Monroe. Perhaps more important, much of Tennessee's country music is still for the consumption of local folk—distant from the recording industry—in fiddle contests, church meetings, house parties, and **honky-tonks**.

BIBLIOGRAPHY

Malone, Bill C. (1968). *Country Music, U.S.A.* Austin: University of Texas Press.

Toches, Nick. (1977). *Country: The Biggest Music in America.* New York: Dell Publishing Co., Inc.

Wolfe, Charles K. (1977). *Tennessee Strings: The Story of Country Music in Tennessee,* Knoxville: University of Tennessee Press.

———. (1999). *A Good-Natured Riot: The Birth of the Grand Ole Opry.* Nashville: Country Music Foundation Press and Vanderbilt University Press.

RECORDINGS

Fiddlin' Arthur Smith and His Dixieliners. 1978. 2 vols. County Records 546, 547.

Early Classics. 1984. G. B. Grayson and Henry Whittier. 2 vols. Old Homestead Records OHCS 157, 165.

Old-Time Music in Nashville: The 1920s (title on container: *Nashville: The Early String Bands*). 1976. 2 vols. County Records 541, 542.

Uncle Dave Macon: Early Recordings. 1987. County Records 521.

DOWN YONDER: OLD-TIME STRING BAND MUSIC FROM GEORGIA

Art Rosenbaum

*Art Rosenbaum teaches art at the University of Georgia. A renowned **banjo** player and collector of traditional music, he has recorded dozens of albums documenting the traditional musical styles of Georgia, Iowa, and Indiana, among other places. He is the author, along with his wife Margo, of two books on traditional music—Folk Visions and Voices: Traditional Music and Song in North Georgia (1983) and Shout Because You Are Free: The African American Ring Shout Tradition in Coastal Georgia. The following essay is derived from the liner notes Rosenbaum wrote to accompany the 1982 Folkways recording Down Yonder: Old-Time String Band Music from Georgia (FTS 31089) and subsequently updated for publication in American Musical Traditions.*

Gordon Tanner welcomed his old friend, Smokey Joe Miller, and Uncle John Patterson, the "Banjo King" from Carrollton, into the "oblong concern of a chicken coop" back behind his home on the outskirts of Dacula, Georgia. He had converted it into a music room and explained, "We run the chickens off, brought some half-stumps in."

"I'm a country boy and feel right at home," said Uncle John.

Actually the now-famous building is well fitted-out, with a carpeted area at one end for the musicians, old photos and more recent trophies lining the wall, and an assortment of upholstered chairs and two wood stoves provided for the comfort of the folks who gather on Friday evenings to hear Gordon **fiddle** the pieces he recorded with his father's renowned **string band**, Gid Tanner and the Skillet Lickers. He is usually joined by his son Phil and the Jr. Skillet Lickers who lean toward more of a **bluegrass** approach.

Gordon has continued to work on the earlier sound however, and this warm October Saturday in 1979 he had the typical **old-time** string band, with "one on the fiddle, one on the banjo, and one on the **guitar**," as Uncle John declared. "This is the first time I played with Gordon Tanner, but I played a thousand times with his dad." John was explaining why he had no trouble falling in with the familiar old numbers. He was in typical form, his bare feet patting out a beat, his bare fingers picking and strumming his old S.S. Stewart, the banjo muted but not dulled by a towel behind the head. Gordon's fiddle began to wail out, then whispered, then chopped out a breakdown rhythm, and he smiled and cocked his head back in a pose reminiscent of his father's old photographs. Joe Miller's guitar line was well salted with runs learned firsthand from Riley Puckett, the guitar picker of the original Skillet Lickers. The three men were putting their lifetimes' experience into some of the finest string band music to come out of Georgia in years.

Gid Tanner and his Skillet Lickers; left to right: Tanner, Clayton McMichen, Riley Puckett, and Land Norris. This was the original band that recorded for Columbia Records; at different sessions, the lineup was augmented with other musicians.
Photograph courtesy of the Folklife Program, North Carolina Arts Council, Dept. of Cultural Resources.

Born in 1916, Gordon Tanner has lived most of his life in Gwinnett County, where his father was a chicken farmer, Saturday night fiddler, and frequent participant in the fiddlers' conventions in nearby Atlanta. Gordon remembers the time in 1924 when he heard his parents discussing the offer by Frank Walker of Columbia Records that Gid go up to New York to make recordings; Gid said he would go if he could get a certain "blind boy" to go with him. A few weeks later Gordon was listening to the Tanner-Puckett duo on the "little grindin' Victrola" his father brought back from New York.

Gid Tanner expanded his recording group into the famous Skillet Lickers, which included Clayton McMichen, Lowe Stokes, Fate Norris, and others. Gid was a warm and exuberant entertainer and was much sought after for live shows. As Gordon tells it, "he'd be full-time (in music) till things got shallow, then he'd bounce back on the farm. He always kept two mules at home, and a milk cow, and raisin' two hogs a year, but he never hesitated to unhitch the mules and get his fiddle and go, whenever there was a request for him."

It was difficult to assemble the Skillet Lickers for live performances, and Gid Tanner often recruited other musician friends and members of his family for shows close to home. Of Gid's children Gordon was "strongest with the musical talent," and Gid fitted out his shy little red-headed son with thimbles to play rhythm on a **washboard**; Gordon would also be asked to sing songs like "It Ain't Gonna Rain No More" and "Letter Edged in Black," dance a buck and wing, and play straight man to his dad's jokes.

Gordon remembers going to Atlanta with his father on a wagon and seeing Gid attract a huge crowd in front of some merchant friend's store with his fiddle, only to be moved on by the police. As Gordon told it,

> The law has to come in, the streetcar is blocked—and made him put his fiddle up. Of course, me, small as I was, it scared me. Of course, it didn't scare my daddy. . . . He'd scramble around and put his fiddle up, we'd walk around the corner, do the same thing, and I was scared to death the law was coming again. . . . But that's the way it was. They was hungry for that kind of music.

Gordon recalls other occasions when he had to provide an impromptu "second" on his dad's banjo when Gid had to play at a courthouse square or similar setting.

> He'd give me the banjo, and had a clamp on it. . . by the thumb string,

109

and right below there were two fingers, and that was G chord, and he said, 'Hold that right there!' He knowed I could beat time on anything. I would play that, you know. . . . He didn't have time to be teaching me. Had to get goin'! 'Course, a lot of his songs, you had to be quick to get in another chord anyway! So . . . I learned that I wasn't wigglin' my fingers up and down there too much, and somebody might find out I wasn't playin'! So I begin to feel bad about that, and then the fiddle created a lot of interest, and I wound up bein' a fiddler.

Gordon's first modest goal on the fiddle was to play a recognizable tune. At fourteen he was playing "Georgia Wagoner" with his father and Riley over the radio in Covington, Kentucky. During his high school years Gordon played in occasional contests and joined his dad playing for Gene Talmadge's 1932 gubernatorial campaign. His fiddle playing progressed quickly; though Gid was still his chief influence, he learned much from the Skillet Lickers' lead fiddlers, Clayton McMichen and Lowe Stokes, both through occasional personal contact and through the records which were at the Tanner house.

In 1934 Stokes and McMichen had left the band, and Gid was asked by RCA to reassemble the Skillet Lickers to cut some sides in San Antonio, Texas. Riley went along, and Ted Hawkins was added on **mandolin**. Gordon, a seventeen-year-old student in Dacula High, was told by his dad, "'You gonna be out of school for a week—talk to your teacher.'" Gordon presumed that he was being asked along to help drive, as Riley was blind, and Hawkins, as old as Gid, didn't drive. Gordon recalls the trip vividly:

> We didn't drive at night, so it took us three days. We'd get up early and drive as long as daylight'd last, then (we'd lodge) in a boardin' house or tavern. We'd have to take whatever we could. . . . One place we stopped, the sidewalks were made of boards, like a Western town. . . . We was drivin' an old '30 Chevrolet. It was already four years old, and my daddy had done a lot of travelin', and it was wore out, the front end was out of line, and I'd be give out in four hours, and he'd take over. . . . Every long hill, he'd say, "Son, cut the motor off, save all the gas you can." . . . We went into this San Antonio Hotel, the oldest hotel in San Antonio, and this here recording setup was in, looked to me like it was big enough for a basketball court. And no furnishing in it . . . and we was out almost in the middle of it, settin' around one mike. We didn't rehearse, and so this man got us spaced around it. . . . Course I was at the mike, my daddy in back, and Riley on the left, Ted on the right. So he begin to name out things he wanted us to play.

When asked if he really didn't know he would be playing until the session, he replied, "Well, I sensed that I might be privileged to play one or two numbers . . . but I did play lead fiddle on everything that was played." Among the twenty-four sides cut in that historic session, the Skillet Lickers' last, were some of their most popular numbers, "Back Up and Push," "Soldier's Joy," "Tanner's Hornpipe," and, of course, "Down Yonder."

Gordon's name was not on the labels, though his picture appeared in an RCA publicity booklet. For years he respectfully deferred to the assumption of many that his dad was playing lead fiddle. Though Gid never did claim to have played "Down Yonder," Gordon remembers that he "coached my daddy in learnin' to play it after I saw that it was selling. I said, 'People's gonna ask you to play it wherever you go.' But I never could get him to get the double stops. He would 'single-out' strings. And people would say, 'Nobody plays "Down Yonder" like your daddy!' I said, 'That's right.' I never did have no reason to try to steal the credit, because I was lucky to be on."

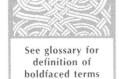

See glossary for definition of boldfaced terms

Three generations of Tanners: Gordon and grandson, Russ, and son Phil, guitar, photographed in Dracula, Georgia, 1978
Photograph © Margo Rosenbaum

Gordon graduated high school in 1936. Though he was offered a basketball scholarship to North Georgia College, he didn't want to go into debt to buy the uniforms and stayed at home. He married later that year, and he and his bride, Electra, worked at chopping cotton for seventy-five cents a day to pay the rent on the house they rented, later bought, and still live in. Gordon also sharecropped with his father, drove a school bus, and later went to work for General Shoe Company in the county seat of Lawrenceville.

Even at $9.45 a week such jobs were hard to find in the midst of the Depression, and Gordon was reluctant to leave for the uncertain life of a professional musician, particularly after the couple's first child was born. He worked his way up to being a foreman at General Shoe, and later worked at Georgia Boot in Flowery Branch until his retirement in 1981.

Gordon did continue playing with his father in the area and at church on Sundays. In 1956 he began to make violins and has mastered this difficult art.

Gid Tanner died in 1960, and in 1968 Gordon and his son Phil organized the Jr. Skillet Lickers to keep the name and the music going. They have played at the Georgia Grassroots Festival in Atlanta and the Georgia Mountain Fair in Hiawassee, where Gor-

don won the "King of the Mountain Fiddlers" crown, just one of his many recent honors. In 1980 Gordon and Phil performed at the Smithsonian Festival of American **Folklife** in Washington.

Norm Cohen has pointed out that Gid Tanner, forty at the time he started to record, was older than Puckett or McMichen, and unlike these musicians who absorbed popular and **jazz** influences into their music, "his orientation was toward traditional music." ("The Skillet Lickers: A Study of a Hillbilly String Band and Its Repertoire," *Journal of American Folklore* 78, 1965.) Gordon has inherited this love of the older material from his father and knows a good portion of the traditional songs and tunes played by Gid and others in the Skillet Lickers' circle. Like his father, Gordon can sing along with the fiddle, and, though he does not have Gid's gift for extroverted comedy, he is a warm and communicative performer and has surpassed his father's technical ability on the fiddle. The good response to his music at recent festivals has convinced Gordon that it still can speak to contemporary audiences: "It's genuine, not a fad . . . something that blooms up and goes away, and you talk about it years ago, that come up like a storm, and went on."

Joe Miller is a longtime friend of the Tanner family and played guitar with Gid Tanner and Riley Puckett in many shows in the forties. He can evoke a vivid contrast between the generous, outgoing, and comical "Mr. Gid" and the introverted and moody Puckett. He was born in Walton County in 1918, and his family wanted to instill an interest in music in him at an early age: His mother made him a gourd fiddle fitted with strings unwound from a sieve, and a cornstalk bow. When Joe was four or five his uncle bought him a twenty-five-cent Marine Band **harmonica**, and, Joe says, "Next time he came to visit, I was playing that thing, and it just thrilled him to death! So that fall he gathered his crop and bought me several more, different keys. I though I was really uptown! I'd tote three of them in my pocket. People would give me nickels and dimes to play. . . . I was so little, you know, the curiosity."

It was the guitar that most attracted him, and, as he tells it, his parents "ordered a 'leven-dollar-ninety-five-cent Bradley Kincaid Hound-Dog guitar, and that was my start. Mother's brothers would come by and tune it up for me, and sing a few songs, show us a few chords. . . . And on those long winter nights we'd parch peanuts and I'd thump on that old guitar."

Joe first heard Riley Puckett play when he was about six or seven, and he took every opportunity to go to Skillet Licker shows. "I was always hanging around the side of the stage . . . to catch what I could. Riley just took my fancy as a guitar player, and it never changed." Joe adapted Riley's unique way of playing runs with index and middle fingers to the flat pick. His first professional experience was with fiddler Charlie Bowman playing for the WSG Barn Dance at the old Erlanger Theater in Atlanta. Having extremely poor eyesight, Joe felt he could make a living as a musician, and in 1939 went up to Chattanooga, Tennessee, to play over WDOD with Chester Anderson and Kentucky Evelyn. He was guaranteed five dollars a week, which "didn't leave much to play on" after spending two dollars for groceries and three dollars for a one-room apartment with a bed, two-burner stove, a little table and chair. After "a few months . . . my shoes would get to ramblin', I'd get to thinking

See glossary for definition of boldfaced terms

about things back home. . . . I'd get homesick and was ready to give it up."

In the early forties he went on the road again, this time with Fisher Hendley and the Rhythm Aristocrats out of Columbia, South Carolina. Hendley gave him the nickname "Smokey Joe" for his ability to play lightning-fast runs and note-for-note fiddle tunes.

Back in Georgia Joe worked with Gid Tanner, whom he considers "the most honest, the most congenial man I ever worked with in show business. . . . I played with him up to the time I got married, and some for good old brotherly love after that." His marriage was in 1943, and shortly thereafter he went to work at the Carwood overall plant, a job he held until his retirement in 1981. He got the calling to preach in 1951 and was ordained by the North Georgia Conference of the Congregational Holiness Church. For the last twenty-six years he has had a radio ministry, first out of WIMO, Winder, then WMRE, and currently WKUN, both in Monroe.

His wife died in 1981, and Joe lives alone in a big house in the Walton County village of Campton; he gives music lessons in the tiny music store he keeps in the side room. Music is the cement for his friendship with Gordon Tanner, whom he considers dear as a brother. "There's a bond like that between most musicians. . . . It's the best recreation I have. (Some) go to their football games . . . hoot and holler their head off—just give me my old guitar and two or three of my good friends, brother, I'm in heaven!"

Though he is a religious man and often sings and plays **gospel music**, he continues to love the **secular** folk songs and parlor songs of an earlier day. For him,

> it expresses the early pioneer life of people in America, their heartaches and sorrows. . . . Back in those days when a tune came out, it usually had an authentic background. . . . They sang about things that were tragic, and some love songs. But I remember as a young child sitting

around the fireside, and hear musicians sing these songs on phonograph and radio, it just seeded in my soul. And at a tender age I could just weep when they'd sing those beautiful songs with that pretty **harmony**, telling those sad stories. I guess I'm living in a changing age, and it breaks my heart to see those old songs put back on the shelf, and the younger generation doesn't know about it. And I'm persuaded to believe that if it's introduced to them . . . it would touch their heart. It made a better person out of me. I'm sure of that.

John Patterson died in the spring of 1980. He was a warm and outgoing southern gentleman of the old school, and a master stylist and technician on the five-string banjo. He will be missed by his many friends and the growing number of people who are coming to appreciate his importance to the story of southern old-time music.

He learned to pick "Shout Lulu" on his mother's lap when he was three years old. If his first tune was typical for southern banjo pickers, his very early start and subsequent spectacular career certainly were not. Bessie Patterson was a champion banjo player, and when she died in 1924 she had already schooled her fourteen-year-old son in the basics of his extraordinary style, a combination of **two-finger or up-picking style** with chordal brushes and **three-finger style melody** playing; on her deathbed she had him promise never to let anyone beat him playing a banjo.

John got his first chance to defend his mother's title a month later at the Fiddlers' Convention at Atlanta's City Auditorium. He found himself up against Rosa Lee, the daughter of Fiddling John Carson, later to be known as "Moonshine Kate." The full story of this epic contest has been told by Uncle John in his own words in the notes for his banjo LP (*Plains Georgia Rock*, Arhoolie 5018), and by Dr. Gene Wiggins in both prose and poetry ("Uncle John Patterson, Banjo King," *Devil's Box* 13, no. 3).

Rosa Lee had already played John's best piece, "Spanish Fandango", so the sixty-seven-pound boy, wearing a shirt made out of a flour sack and a pair of his "granddaddy's pistol pants," picked "Hen Cackle" so spiritedly that "old Gid Tanner, and even John Carson . . . got to cackling and got to crowing." In the finals John was allowed to play "Spanish Fandango" and won. "And from that time till now I've managed to take care of myself," he said in recent years. He has been national champion and never lost a contest.

Uncle John—he has worn the "Uncle" since boyhood—had been playing at dances with the famous fiddler Ahaz Gray, like the Pattersons a resident of Carroll County on Georgia's western edge. He later teamed up with John Carson, as well as many other noted Georgia string musicians, in the 1932 Talmadge campaign; he met Gordon on some occasions when Gid Tanner was along, but Gordon was usually helping with the driving rather than playing.

After Gene's election, John, who had been a sharecropper, became the governor's bodyguard. John Carson was made elevator operator in the statehouse, and the two musicians often played together in the statehouse and at Talmadge parties. Following Talmadge's defeat in the early forties, John went to work at Lockheed Aircraft as a hydraulics engineer. Music was not neglected during the following years: John toured with Smiley Burnett in 1952, and in 1962 he played his banjo composition, "John Glenn Special," in a five-hour marathon, exceeding his goal to play it as long as the astronaut was in orbit! John had politics as well as music in his blood, and he served from 1968 to 1974 as state representative from Carrollton.

John was an all-around musician, adept on the fiddle, piano, and musical saw as well as banjo. After losing his picking index finger in an accident in the fifties he simply shifted the lead to his second finger. Before his Arhoolie record, on which he was

backed by his son James on guitar, he recorded little—one disc in 1931 and another in 1947 with his Carroll County Ramblers. In his last years John performed at the Georgia Grass Roots Festival in Atlanta. In addition to his other achievements, Uncle John Patterson will be remembered for his work with two other veterans of Georgia's great age of old-time music.

Afterword: Gordon Tanner died in 1982 after having played at the National Folk Festival at Wolf Trap Farm in Virginia, but before he could make a scheduled appearance at the Brandywine Festival at a reunion of musicians from the early Skillet Licker band. Smokey Joe Miller is still an active musician at this writing (2001). The Skillet Lickers' early 78-rpm recordings (dating from 1923–1934) have been reissued by both County Records (release numbers 506, 526, and 3509) and Old Homestead (release numbers 192 and 193).

The author subsequently expanded this essay into a chapter on Gordon Tanner and his circle of musicians that was published in the book *Folk Visions and Voices: Traditional Music and Song in North Georgia* (University of Georgia Press, 1983). Currently the Tanner legacy is being carried on by Gordon's son Phil and his grandson Russ, a fourth-generation Tanner family fiddler, in a band that still bears the name Skillet Lickers or Skillet Lickers II.

BIBLIOGRAPHY

BOOKS AND ARTICLES

Cohen, Norm. (1965). "The Skillet Lickers: A Study of a Hillbilly String Band and Its Repertoire." *Journal of American Folklore* 78.

Daniel, Wayne W. *Pickin' on Peachtree: A History of Country Music in Atlanta, Georgia.* (1990). Urbana: University of Illinois Press.

Rosenbaum, Art. (1983). *Folk Visions and Voices: Traditional Music and Song in North Georgia.* Athens: University of Georgia Press.

Wiggins, Gene. "Uncle John Patterson, Banjo King." *Devil's Box* 13, no. 3.

Wiggins, Gene. (1987). *Fiddlin' Georgia Crazy: Fiddlin' John Carson—His Real World and the World of His Songs.* Urbana: University of Illinois Press. 1987.

RECORDINGS AND VIDEOS

Down Yonder. 1982. Produced by Clate Sanders with Art Rosenbaum. 28 min. Georgia Public Television documentary featuring Gordon Tanner, Phil Tanner, and Smokey Joe Miller. Available from Media: Georgia Center for Continuing Education, University of Georgia, Athens, GA 30602.

Phil Tanner's Skillet Lickers: The Tanner Legacy Now! Produced and annotated by Art Rosenbaum. Global Village CD 311.

Plains Georgia Rock. 1977. Uncle John Patterson. Arhoolie 5018.

Skillet Licker Music, 1955–1991: The Tanner Legacy, with Gid Tanner's Last Recordings. 1992. Produced and annotated by Art Rosenbaum. Global Village CD 310.

Smokey Joe Miller and His Georgia Pals Newman Young and Lawrence Humphries Sing Old American Heartthrobs. 1982. Folkways FTS 31093.

"A PECULIAR WIGGLING OF THE BOW": OLD-TIME FIDDLING IN ALABAMA

Joyce Cauthen

Joyce Cauthen is the author of With Fiddle and Well-Rosined Bow: Old-Time Fiddling in Alabama, *published by the University of Alabama Press, and is director of the Alabama Folklife Association. She received her B.A. from Texas Christian University and her M.A. from Purdue University. The following essay, which Cauthen revised for publication in* American Musical Traditions, *originally appeared in* Alabama Folklife: Collected Essays, *edited by Stephen H. Martin (Alabama Folklife Association, 1989).*

Prior to a fiddlers' convention at the Fayette County Courthouse in 1930, an announcement in the *Fayette Banner* read:

> These Conventions have always been a source of amusement to the large number of people who attend, the music being different from the ordinary music of the day as most of it has been transmitted from one generation to the other without being in the form of written music, and learned and played entirely by ear, and as "variety is the spice of life," everybody seems to enjoy the peculiar wiggling of the bow passing across the **fiddle**.

The usual number of prizes will be awarded to the best fiddlers playing the **old-time** pieces such as "Turkey in the Straw," "Billie in the Low Grounds," "Lazy Kate" or any of the other gals. As fiddlers have about 100 pieces to select from, any tune they may choose to play will be acceptable.

It is an apt description, addressing many elements of a musical **form** that has been an important part of life in Alabama since black and white settlers first came to the territory. It first explains that fiddle tunes are transmitted from generation to generation orally (or "aurally"), without the aid of the written note. While some scholars consider the idea that most fiddlers do not read music to be a myth, it is certain that few Alabama fiddlers of the past relied upon the printed note. There were those who could read music and play the semiclassical tunes required by dance masters for soirees and balls; even more could read **hymns** and parlor tunes. When it was time to play a good southern breakdown for a **square dance** or fiddlers' convention, however, they turned to tunes that have never or only recently been captured in musical notation. Had they played "Turkey in the Straw," "Billie in the Low

FIDDLERS' CONVENTION!
$500 In Cash Prizes!!

FIRST PRIZE--$100 in Gold   SECOND PRIZE--$75 in Gold

THIRD PRIZE--$50 in Gold

4th, 5th, 6th, 7th and 8th Prizes---$25

9th, 10th, 11th, 12th, 13th, 14th, 15th, 16th, 17th and 18th Prizes---$10

ONE $25 PRIZE---Best Buck and Wing Dancer   ONE $25 PRIZE---Best Comical Singer

Kindly Mail Me Particulars in Regard to Rules of Your "Fiddlers' Convention"

NAME ....

ADDRESS ....

If you draw a mean bow or shake a wicked hoof and are interested---clip this coupon and mail it to---

"P. O. BOX 103, WOODLAWN"
BIRMINGHAM, ALA.

Municipal Auditorium, February 25th
AUSPICES OF
NATHAN BEDFORD FORREST KLAN No. 60
BIRMINGHAM, ALABAMA

Fiddlers Convention announcement, *Birmingham Age Herald,* January 25, 1925.

Grounds," "Lazy Kate" or "any of the other gals" as written in a tune book, they would have been dissatisfied with the result, as musical **transcriptions** seldom convey the nuances by which a fiddler turns a piece of music into a zesty, southern-style fiddle tune.

Such nuances are described in the *Fayette Banner* as "the peculiar wiggling of the bow passing across the fiddle." Here "peculiar" is used in its oldest sense, meaning "particular," "unique," or "private property" and refers to the fiddlers' tendency to make personal variations in a tune while retaining its basic structure and **melody**. Barney Dickerson of Dothan recently explained the process:

Every bit I got—and it's not much, but I learned it by listening. . . . You pick up a lot of good turns and a lot of good things in a tune by listening at the other fellow. Of course, there is tunes that I play that I make up little bypasses in, because it'd be easier for me to play it like

that than it would to play it like the other fellow played it all the way through. Like I told my brother. He told me, says, "You don't play 'Billy in the Low Ground.'" And I says, "Listen, let me tell you something. You didn't hear the fellow that wrote 'Billy in the Low Ground.'" I said that was before mine and your day. And said it passed right on down, right on down, right on down. I said my daddy played it. You don't play it like my daddy does. I don't play it like my daddy does. I just picked it up and played it, and I put parts in that you won't never know weren't originally put in there.

Even if a fiddler wished to play a tune exactly as another fiddler played it, he would have trouble doing so unless he had learned to play from that fiddler. Some fiddlers hold their **instruments** down on their chests and others under their chins. Some use four fin-

gers, placing them precisely where they are wanted, and others use two fingers that they **slide** from note to note. Some grasp their bows near the middle, leaving room only for short, choppy strokes, and others hold them close to the end, allowing space for long swooping strokes. So there is little likelihood that a group of old-time fiddlers could play in true **unison**. A University of Alabama student in 1925 described in her master's thesis the effect at fiddlers' conventions whenever the contestants assembled on stage for a "grand overture":

> . . . although this invariably brings the audience to its feet with yells, I must confess that it is the greatest conglomeration of tones, and the furtherest from ensemble music that ever came to my ears. For this fiddler is no sodden conformist; he has his own individual conception of how "Turkey in the Straw," "Arkansas Traveler," and "Dixie" should be played—and he plays it that way—although each interpretation is pleasing because of its rhythm and queer **harmony**, when played individually, no word in the English language can describe the sound when they play together.

The Fayette announcement concludes with a brief discussion of the old-time fiddlers' **repertoire**. The statement that "fiddlers have about 100 pieces to select from" refers to the individual fiddler's stock of tunes rather than the entire body of fiddle tunes—of which there are thousands. A fiddler who had grown up listening to his family and neighbors playing fiddles could easily know 100 tunes. One of the traits most often attributed to good fiddlers of the past was that they "could play all night and never repeat a tune."

Thus, from the organizers of the Fayette fiddlers' convention we learn what makes old-time fiddling "different from the ordinary music of the day." We shall now have to turn to historians to learn the origin of fiddle tunes and the evolution of styles in which they have been played in Alabama.

The American colonies were populated by settlers from the British Isles at a time when fiddling and dancing were at their height of popularity at home. Immigrants brought fiddles and tunes like "Billie in the Low Grounds" (variously called "Billy in the Low Ground," "Billie in the Low Land," etc.), and the music thrived on American soil. Some tunes survived in fairly unaltered states, while others merely endured name changes from titles like "Miss McLeod's Reel" to "Hop Light, Ladies." Portions of old tunes were fused into new tunes; for instance, "Turkey in the Straw," also known as "Old Zip Coon," came from two Irish **hornpipes**. Many more tunes were composed in this country bearing the structure of those that came with the settlers, that generally being thirty-two measures in 2/4 or 6/8 time, the first eight measures played twice and the second eight, with a different but related melody, repeated also.

In the southern United States, fiddling took on distinctive regional characteristics due to the interaction of two predominant ethnic groups, Scotch-Irish and African. Africans had been in the American colonies since the early 1600s, and there is evidence of their involvement with fiddles as early as 1700. Some played as free men; many more were slaves who had been provided fiddles by slave owners desiring music for their families and communities. Slave fiddlers provided music appropriate for the **cotillions** of their masters, but in the slave quarters they added bow shuffles and **syncopations** to the same tunes to power the intensely rhythmic, athletic dances done there. The terms "**hoedown**" and "breakdown" were used to describe this vigorous dancing and showy footwork, and soon those words were applied to the type of tunes that inspired such dancing.

Slave narratives and memoirs written by whites who grew up on plantations provide ample evidence of black and white fiddlers playing together, admiring each others' tunes and skills and learning from each other. One result of this interaction was the development of **minstrel** shows. By the mid-1840s, white fiddlers were touring the coun-

John McDougal, strawbeater, and Charles Sellers, fiddler, photographed near McCalla, Alabama, in the 1890s

Photo courtesy of Frances and Howard Colburn.

After the Civil War, black fiddlers continued to play for dances and also formed minstrel troupes, but by the beginning of World War II, the fiddle had fallen out of favor among African Americans. Since then old-time fiddling has largely been the domain of white musicians who continued playing in an African-influenced "hoedown" style, distinctive from that of New England, the Midwest, and the British Isles.

Over the years that followed, other factors caused changes in the way fiddlers played. One was the growing availability of accompanying instruments. Prior to 1900, most of the old-time fiddling done in Alabama was unaccompanied. Descriptions of rural dances in Madison, Talladega, and Lamar counties in the 1880s mention only fiddlers, and many older fiddlers interviewed across the state recalled that their elders always played alone.

Unaccompanied fiddlers tuned their instruments to whatever pitches pleased them and, as one fiddler observed, they "cut corners in some places and added them in others to suit themselves." Such fiddlers were prone to "cross-key" tunings. Rather than tune the strings in the classical E-A-D-G configuration, they would lower and raise the pitches of various strings in configurations that allowed them to play the melody on two strings, leaving two strings open to resonate or **drone** in **bagpipe** fashion. Some were minor tunings that gave a lonesome quality to the pieces. Besides affecting the character of the music, such tunings gave added volume and sometimes placed the notes within easier reach than the classical tuning did.

Open strings also left a place for the **strawbeater**'s art. "That was a band back in those days," said Northport fiddler A. D. Hamner, "a fiddle and someone beating straws." While the fiddler played, another person would stand close by and strike the open strings with thin stalks of broom sedge or with knitting needles. A pleasing percussive sound, in tune with the fiddle, would result.

try in minstrel troupes, "delineating the character of the southern Negro" and popularizing his fiddle styles. During the Civil War, African-influenced fiddling was spread among southern soldiers by those who brought fiddles when they reported for duty. One fiddler, Ben Smith, a Georgian in an Alabama regiment, was described as playing distinctive southern music, "some of which I have heard our slaves often play with exquisite taste and great gusto on our Georgia plantations." The popularity of soldier-fiddlers like Ben Smith and of minstrel-show fiddlers insured that the southern, hoedown-style of fiddling would spread throughout the South, even into areas with no black population.

At this time, the only stringed instrument likely to accompany the fiddle was the **banjo**, an instrument of African origin that has been played in this country since the mid-1700s. Like the cross-tuned fiddle, the banjo was retuned each time the musicians wanted to play in a different key. Though other instruments such as pianos, **guitars**, **accordions**, and flutes were available at music stores in Mobile and Montgomery, few country people had the means to purchase them. Around the turn of the century, however, mail-order catalogs began to offer mass-produced instruments at affordable prices, and by the 1920s Alabamians were acquiring them in great numbers. Across the state, musicians began forming **string bands** consisting of fiddles, guitars, banjos, **mandolins**, mouth harps, and, occasionally, cellos and bass violins. During the 1920s and 1930s, fiddlers' conventions, which had once been the domain of fiddlers (and, at times, banjoists), began to hold competitions among a variety of instruments, and string band competitions became highly popular.

As a result of the fiddler's involvement with other musicians, he began to use the classical or standard tuning, which enabled him to play in any key without the nuisance of retuning. With accompanying instruments, he no longer needed the increased volume provided by the resonating strings, and open strings were no longer needed by strawbeaters, who had been replaced by guitarists. Thus cross-key tunings became a thing of the past and today are used mainly by those making conscious efforts to play in older styles.

Another development in the 1920s had important consequences for fiddling. The phonograph, which had been around for decades with little relevance to old-time fiddlers, suddenly became interesting to them when commercial recording companies realized that there was a market for country music. Agents began to scout fiddlers' conventions and other rural entertainments for talented country musicians. As quickly as records by the Skillet Lickers (a popular Georgia fiddle band) and others came out, fiddlers across the country bought them or traveled to the homes of those who had and learned new tunes. Thus, fiddlers began to hear and adopt fiddles styles different from those they had grown up hearing. In the 1920s, fiddlers whose elders may have played in short, choppy bow strokes were attracted to the smoother, "long-bow" style of Georgia fiddler Clayton McMichen; in the 1930s many attempted to emulate the rapid, "rolling bow" of Tennessee fiddler Arthur Smith and the swing fiddling of Texan Bob Wills.

Each decade has seen fiddlers who influenced large numbers of fiddlers across the nation: Tommy Jackson, a Nashville square dance fiddler; Kenny Baker, a Kentucky **bluegrass** fiddler; Benny Thomasson, a Texas-style contest fiddler; and Tommy Jarrell, a traditional fiddler of North Carolina. As a result of nationally distributed phonograph and tape recordings, regional and local fiddle styles and repertoires became less identifiable, less "peculiar." Though this was a regrettable consequence, the recording industry did produce some good results. Rather than put the fiddler out of business, as some predicted it would, commercial recordings made fiddling accessible to the general public and created a wider audience for the music. It also preserved great numbers of tunes that would have been otherwise forgotten.

Until preserved on wax and vinyl, old fiddle tunes had been kept young by use. They stayed fresh and energetic as long as they remained the dance tunes of choice. When "Alabama fever" hit the nation in the early 1800s and the territory was rapidly settled, pioneers brought ancient figures with them that they danced at house raisings, log rollings, weddings, and other community gatherings.

"Fiddle dances" remained popular throughout Alabama for more than a century. Most often they were held in homes from which most of the furniture had been removed. A fiddler and a strawbeater or banjoist, later an entire string band, would set themselves up in a corner or in the doorway between two rooms, and as many couples as could fit in the space would form a circle. When the music began, one couple would begin a series of visits to every other couple, with whom they danced old figures like "Cage

the Bird" and the "Ocean Wave." The dances were long and spirited and required the fiddler to apply elbow grease profusely. Especially good hoedown tunes stayed in demand; dancers would not let the fiddlers forget them.

In the mid-1940s, as electric amplification became available in rural Alabama, dances began to move from homes to large dance halls. There dancers began to request fox-trots and **waltzes** between old dances, which were now being called "square dances" even though they were done in a circle. Fewer fiddlers and fewer hoedown pieces were in demand. After World War II, the call for such music further decreased, especially when rock and roll began to take over the dance halls. At that time, an attractive alternative to rock and roll was western-style square dancing done in clubs. However, square dance organizations became interested in developing an international network in which one could do the same dances at any club in the world in exactly the same way to the same music. Obviously, there was no place for the "peculiar wiggling of the bow" in that scheme.

Thus, the fiddler was gradually displaced from his most important role as a provider of music for community dances. At such dances, young fiddlers had served their

apprenticeship, first observing the master dance fiddlers, then taking over for them when they tired for the evening or stopped playing for dances entirely. The dancers' need for vigorous music had kept fiddlers and their music vigorous.

Today fiddlers play mostly for seated audiences—those at the many weekly musical "jamborees" or "opries" held across the state and at fiddlers' conventions. This, of course, affects the way they play. There is more emphasis on singing and showy instrumental work. Thus "bluegrass," a newer and more complex playing and singing style that grew out of old-time music, is popular. Fiddlers also like to play swing tunes from the big-band era and country-western tunes at such functions.

At fiddlers' conventions, old-time tunes like those mentioned in the 1930 Fayette announcement are still played. However, there is more emphasis on smoothness, creativity, and technical skill than on the energetic bowing of earlier years. A style of playing that developed at fiddlers' conventions in Texas has become so successful in competition across the nation that Texas-style players have won at many Alabama conventions in recent years.

In response, the organizers of the 1988 Tennessee Valley Old-Time Fiddlers' Convention (Alabama's largest convention, held annually in Athens on the first Friday and Saturday of October) stated that Texas-style fiddling would not be eligible for prizes. This rule was made in an effort to help preserve the "flavor of old-time music in our region." The ruling was unworkable, however, as Texas-style fiddling was already too deeply entrenched at the Tennessee Valley Old-Time Fiddlers' Convention and there was little regional flavor left to preserve. Later, contest officials initiated a separate "Classic Old-Time Fiddler" category that has been successful in encouraging those who play in older, more "peculiar," styles to get up on the stage and be heard.

Old-time fiddling is an ever-changing art. Most fiddlers still play by ear—though

today that ear may be turned to a recording of another fiddler more often than to one seated beside him. Fiddlers continue to make "little bypasses" and other changes in tunes to please themselves and their listeners while still keeping the tune recognizable and compatible with other renditions. Each change admits into their playing the influences of their fellow musicians and admired recording artists, the types of other instruments they perform with, the popular music they listen to, and the types of audiences and events at which they play. Fiddling, while "different from the ordinary music of the day," is affected by it, for fiddlers and audiences in Alabama have kept it very much alive and part of their culture.

BIBLIOGRAPHY

Cauthen, Joyce. (1989). *With Fiddle and Well-Rosined Bow: Old-Time Fiddling in Alabama.* Tuscaloosa: University of Alabama Press.

Delmore, Alton. (1977). *Truth Is Stranger Than Publicity.* Nashville: Country Music Foundation Press.

Epstein, Dena J. (1977). *Sinful Tunes and Spirituals.* Urbana: University of Illinois Press.

Owsley, Frank Lawrence. (1949). *Plain Folk of the Old South.* Baton Rouge: Louisiana State University Press.

Possum Up a Gum Stump: Home, Field and Commercial Recordings of Alabama Fiddlers, Past and Present. Brierfield, AL: Brierfield Ironworks Park. Album and 24-page booklet featuring Alabama's legendary fiddlers of the past and living fiddlers who play in older styles.

Southern, Eileen. (1971). *The Music of Black Americans: A History.* New York: W. W. Norton.

THE AUTOHARP IN OLD-TIME SOUTHERN MUSIC

Mike Seeger

Mike Seeger is a well-known folklorist and performer who has been active in recording and performing southern music since the mid-1950s. He has recorded dozens of albums for Folkways Records, many of which have become classics of traditional music. The following essay is based on the liner notes Seeger wrote to accompany the 1962 album Mountain Music Played on the Autoharp *(Folkways 2365), which was reissued on CD in 1998 (Folkways F-02365).*

A BRIEF HISTORY OF THE AUTOHARP

The **autoharp** was most likely invented in Germany in the 1870s and first produced in this country by Charles F. Zimmerman, a German musical **instrument** dealer, repairman, and innovator who had come to the United States in 1865. Its design was based on the **zither**, a well-known German instrument. Zimmerman was hoping to use the autoharp as a vehicle to establish his own system of musical notation. He patented it in 1881 and first produced it in Philadelphia in 1885. During the first three years of production, 50,000 autoharps were sold, their main attraction in that invention-happy era being an easy, novel way to make music at home.

In 1892, the C. F. Zimmerman Company was bought by piano maker Alfred Dolge and moved to Dolgeville, New York. Dolge launched an advertising campaign, and the autoharp soon became popular amongst parlor music makers. Autoharp clubs sprang up,

a minor composer wrote a minuet for it, and "the world's greatest autoharp performer," Aldis Gery, who also worked for Dolge designing autoharps, toured with Victor Herbert's band from 1895 to 1897. By 1897 Dolge had produced nearly 300,000 autoharps in models ranging from the most basic three-chord-bar model to the concert grand model with forty-nine strings, six sliding bars, and ten shifters, capable of sixty chords.

By about 1900 the demand for autoharps had decreased, probably due to a variety of factors: the slackening of a fad, the advent of the talking machine, unwise management, and certainly, the inherent limitations of the instrument, including consumer discovery of the need for frequent, skilled tuning. In 1910 the production of autoharps was taken over by the Phonoharp Company of Boston, which produced a much more limited number of models. Around the turn of the century the instrument was introduced to rural southerners through mail-order houses and by door-to-door salesmen/teachers. It also

came into use for music training in elementary schools and for music therapy in hospitals. In 1926 Phonoharp merged with Oscar Schmidt International, the present makers. The instrument was also manufactured over a long period of time in Germany.

Autoharp manufacture remained essentially the same until the late 1960s, when the instrument was totally redesigned to make it easier to produce with automated machinery and to hopefully make it more stable, requiring less frequent tuning.

In the mid-1990s, the instrument is being manufactured by Oscar Schmidt International at factories in the Far East. Another manufacturer that markets its instruments under the name "Chromaharp" also uses production facilities in the Orient to produce an instrument similar in general design to the pre-1960s autoharps. There are also a few makers that hand-build the high quality instruments that are used by most contemporary performers.

MY INVOLVEMENT WITH THE AUTOHARP

My mother, Ruth Crawford Seeger, used the autoharp in her music education work and encouraged me to play it, which I did in the simplest strumming fashion from about age ten. I had pretty much laid it aside when I started playing fretted and bowed instruments in the early 1950s. I first saw "Pop" Stoneman play autoharp in a **bluegrass/ old-time** band with his children at a spirited Gambrills, Maryland, music contest. He sat playing amplified autoharp on its case while some of his children exuberantly played music around him and others were out in the audience cheering. I was recording the event and asked him if I could come and visit him, as I had heard some of his early recordings.

At this time, in the early days of rock and roll, few people remembered or cared for the old-time music recordings, and "Pop" (as he was known around the Washington, D.C., area) was receptive. This began a series of many visits to his self-built home in the Washington suburbs with my recording machine, a heavy, primitive Magnecord, and one omnidirectional microphone. I proposed a Folkways recording, which we recorded in late 1956 and early 1957, which was issued as Folkways 2315. This was his first LP, and it included the first recording of an autoharp instrumental, "Stoney's Waltz." We recorded in the main room of his house, with his wife and some of his thirteen children circulating around. It was difficult to get things done. Pop joked later that he hadn't thought that I'd really put the record out, that he would have taken more care with it. He had made all of his previous recordings in studios under professional conditions, and I can now understand his mystification at the new Folkways recording method.

We played music together and talked of the old times and of the autoharp. And he told me of Kilby Snow, something like: "If you really want to hear someone play the autoharp, you should find Kilby Snow. . . . He lives down near Fries [pronounced "freeze"], Virginia—freeze or fries, depending on the time of year." So in the summer of 1957, with almost no money and no job, while I was going to electronics school, I took off to visit Wade Ward, an outstanding Galax area banjo and **fiddle** player, and to try to find Kilby Snow.

He wasn't in Fries but "over near Galax" somewhere. After going to the post office and power company office and asking quite a few people, I found his house, and he was away at a construction job, over near Wade Ward's home. I asked Wade if it would be OK for Kilby to visit. They were acquainted and it was. I eventually found Kilby way out in the country where he was putting up a block outbuilding, and during our first conversation I especially remember his bemused wonderment at having to build from a drawing. It wasn't difficult to talk him into visiting awhile, talking very soon of autoharps, and pretty soon he had his worn old autoharp out of the back of his Henry J (an early 1950s economy car) with his knee propped up on the bumper playing a few tunes. After a few tunes more, he had to get back to work and agreed to come over to Wade's for

Some Pioneering Autoharp Virtuosi

Please see Chapter 18 in this volume for biographical information on Mike Seeger. The following essay is based on the liner notes he wrote to accompany the 1962 album Mountain Music Played on the Autoharp *(Folkways 2365), which was reissued on CD in 1998 (Folkways F-02365).*

Ernest V. Stoneman

Ernest V. Stoneman was born in 1893 near Galax, Virginia. He started playing **autoharp** at about age eight and remembered his first tune as being "Molly Hare." He learned to tune the autoharp from a nearby school teacher. Several members of his family played or sang **old-time** songs, and he remembered his grandmother Bowers picking tunes on the autoharp in a very different fashion from his own style. When Mr. Stoneman demonstrated his grandmother's style, he picked a melody note and then strummed a chord after it without a regular rhythm. A couple of other autoharp players, one from southern Ohio and another from western North Carolina, also played in a similar manner, especially on religious songs.

Up to about the age of thirty-one, Mr. Stoneman worked mostly in the carpentry trade and played occasionally for dances and other gatherings, sometimes just playing mouth harp and autoharp by himself. In 1923 he heard the first recording of a country (then called **hillbilly**) singer and **guitar** player, Henry Whitter, and like many others, believed he could do better. He contacted the Okeh Company and went to New York City to record the first two country songs to be recorded with the autoharp, "The Titanic" and "The Face That Never Returned," on September 6, 1924. The Okeh recording director, Ralph Peer, was especially interested in the novelty of the autoharp but later favored the guitar as he said it was not so limited.

For about five years, Mr. Stoneman continued to record a great variety of old-time music for

Ernest Stoneman (lower left) playing the autoharp and harmonica in an advertisement for Okeh Records from the late 1920s.
Courtesy of the Folklife Program, North Carolina Arts Council, Dept. of Cultural Resources.

nearly every phonograph company of that period, both solo and with other Galax-area musicians. He was accompanied on some of those discs by his wife, Hattie, who sang and played **fiddle**, **banjo**, and parlor organ, and who was still playing music with him occasionally in the 1960s. In the early 1930s the Stonemans moved to the Washington, D.C., area where they lived until they moved to Nashville in the 1960s. They had thirteen children, all of whom played music and most of whom joined their father at one time or another at Washington, D.C., area music contests, dances, theater shows (including Constitution Hall!), and occasional night clubs during the

a little while later in the day. Wade's house was full of music and appreciation for it. Wade's mother-in-law, Granny Porter, especially loved Kilby's music, and he had a good time playing to his audience. There was no thought of LP production, and I set the recording aside for a while.

In 1961 I was recording the Union Grove Fiddler's Convention for a Folkways

recording, and Annie Bird, a singer and old-time music enthusiast, mentioned that she had spent some time listening to a really good autoharp player on the steps outside. That was Kenneth Benfield. After hearing him, I realized there was a lot of good music here that no one was aware of, and I knew there was a growing interest in the autoharp. So between music gigs and taking care of my

1940s and 1950s. In 1957 I recorded a number of songs by "Pop" (as he came to be called) and his family, which were included on Folkways 2315, his first LP. In the 1960s he had a second career in music when the Stonemans had their own syndicated TV show, toured out of Nashville, Tennessee, and made LP recordings. They appeared on the Grand Ole Opry, country music shows, a number of folk festivals, concerts, and coffeehouses, some as far away as California, always presenting a lively mix of acoustic music combining Pop's old-time style with the **bluegrass/**country style of his children.

Ernest Stoneman was the first person to record with an autoharp, the first to record an autoharp instrumental, and the only country music artist whose career included making recordings on acoustic disc and cylinder recordings, electric discs (including LPs), and videotape. Many of his early recordings are highly valued and remain in print for both their musical and historical value.

Ernest "Pop" Stoneman passed away in June 1968.

Stoneman's Music

Mr. Stoneman's style of melody playing consisted primarily of picking the melody string, usually in the top two **octaves** with the index finger (in a motion towards **bass** strings), and occasionally at the same time picking bass strings with the thumb (in a motion toward treble strings). This is a kind of "pinching motion" with thumb and first finger moving towards one another. Between most "pinch motion" melody notes the back (nail side) of his first finger and **finger pick** strummed a light "backlick" in the opposite direction, or upwards towards the higher pitched strings. This reverse motion with index finger was possible because of the special pick that Mr. Stoneman fashioned from a coil steel spring with an oval loop which fit very

tightly on the flesh side of his finger and which protruded only a slight distance, like a fingernail.

Most of the sound you hear during his melody picking comes from the forward (towards bass) movement of his index finger followed quickly by a quieter "backlick" movement of his first finger (towards treble strings) with the thumb in the bass or middle strings on the first beat, and then with his index finger, a sweep downwards towards bass strings and quickly upwards, on the third and fourth beats. Like all traditional "lap" players, he picked between the bars and string anchors, on the wide end of the harp.

Mr. Stoneman's autoharp was a late 1950s Oscar Schmidt model with several of the seventh chords changed to straight major chords, enabling him to play in more keys. He also moved the chord bars to the left (towards the tuning pegs) to get more room to pick, and to allow him to pick closer to the middle of the strings, where the sound is more mellow. He also put some sound-deadening felt under the bar retainers to quiet bar action.

When playing Mr. Stoneman put the autoharp on top of a wooden case that he built for it, which gives it additional resonance. It was made of solid, good-sounding wood, not plywood. Since he sat down to play and couldn't move to a microphone, at shows he sometimes also used an electric contact pickup mounted on top of his autoharp.

Neriah and Kenneth Benfield

Neriah McCubbins Benfield, affectionately called "Mr. Cub" by his family, was born in 1893 in Catawba County, North Carolina. When he married he moved to Rowan County, North Carolina. He was a veteran of World War I and farmed much of his life. He passed away in February 1983. His son, Kenneth, wrote in 1961:

I was talking to dad the other day about

(Continued on the next page)

family, I again tracked down Kilby, who was now living along Rt. 1 in southeastern Pennsylvania, to record a few more pieces by him and to record the rest of the music heard on the original *Mountain Music Played on the Autoharp* album.

Mr. Stoneman's and Neriah Benfield's styles were developed by the early twentieth century and were among the earliest south-

ern rural **melody** playing on an instrument that had been invented just a few decades before. Kilby Snow's style was certainly a later development, as he was still evolving it into the early 1960s. This style was initiated and virtually disappeared during the lifetime of two of these players. Partly due to this recording but more to the efforts of a few urban players, the music played here had

(Continued from previous page) the autoharp and he said the first one he remembered was when he was five years old. His seventy-seven-year-old brother who is living had it. Back then it didn't have a cover over the [right end of the] strings and you were always tearing up your fingers when you played it. When he was around twenty years old he said he could play pretty well. By that he meant pick like we did only without missing notes. He has always played by note [by ear] and always played lead. He knew people who played but mostly by chords. Forty-five years ago they had a real **string band**.

Hubbert Mayes, his brother-in-law, picked the five-string banjo. Dad's seventy-seven-year-old brother Robert "Bob" picked the five-string also. Dad played the autoharp. Hubbert said Dad's playing then beat anything he ever heard and I think he is about right. I can remember how he played thirty years ago and I thought the same. He would sit with his back to a wall [with his autoharp] flat on the floor and play under his right leg. That is the way Hubbert said it sounded so good. Can't you just picture that in your mind forty-five years ago?

As for the music they played then it is pieces like he still plays today. "Coming Around the Mountain," "Nelly Grey," "Wildwood Flower," "Katy Cline," "Weeping Willow," "Eller's Grave," "Idaho Girl" and tunes like we played when you were here. . . .

Kenneth Lee Benfield was born in 1923 and has been playing the autoharp since he was about thirteen years old. He adds that he couldn't tune

one until he was twenty-six. He first learned from his dad from whom he learned most of his older tunes. He learned a great number of songs after about 1950 from radio and records. He and his dad rarely sang with the autoharp, reserving it for instrumental music. In fact they shared one autoharp and one guitar, and the latter, in a reversal of roles, was used primarily for accompaniment of autoharp pieces.

My second visit to the Benfields was two days after the Snows had recorded with double autoharps, which was the first time I had heard two traditional autoharpists play together. The Benfields tried it on my suggestion and played autoharp duets a good part of that night. When my Ampex recorder broke down, we probably heard "Weeping Willow Tree" for a half hour while I was trying to fix the machine. Each time they picked it better and more lively, each of them alternately picking in the upper and lower ranges, and none of us could tire of it.

Kenneth Benfield and his wife and daughter made their home near Mt. Ulla in central North Carolina. He has worked in nearby mills, raised cattle, and is now retired. He hasn't played the autoharp since the late 1980s and plays banjo for enjoyment.

Both Kenneth and Neriah Benfield played mostly around home for family and friends. In 1964, they appeared at the Newport Folk Festival, their only performance away from their home community.

The Benfields' Music

Both Neriah and Kenneth Benfield held the autoharp on their lap and picked in a similar manner, with a thumb pick and usually no pick on the first finger. In the late 1950s, Neriah had started using a pick on the back or nail side of his first finger. Most melody notes were played with the back of the first fingernail in a motion upwards towards

found new life and will continue to influence autoharp players everywhere.

AUTOHARP PLAYING IN THE SOUTH

Both Neriah Benfield and Pop Stoneman recall the autoharp being played in their com-

munities during their childhood, around the turn of the century. The styles that Stoneman and Benfield's generation first heard surely varied as their elders began adapting their **repertoire** and current musical sounds to the new instrument. Early techniques included simple rhythmic or non-rhythmic strumming of chords; the picking of simple melodies on single strings, alternating with the treble string similar to **frailing** a banjo. Additional notes were picked with the front or flesh side of the first fingernail in a "back and forward" motion similar to flatpicking, and occasional chords were strummed with the thumb. They used a standard Oscar Schmidt instrument.

Kilby Snow

John Kilby Snow was born May 28, 1906, in hilly Grayson County in southwestern Virginia. By about the age of four he had started playing autoharp (his first tune, like Pop Stoneman's, was "Molly Hare") and at the age of five he beat his brother-in-law (from whom he had first learned) in a Winston Salem, North Carolina, contest. Although he played other instruments, the autoharp was his first love. For a few years in the 1920s he traveled around playing wherever he could. He told me of spending a couple of days with the Carter Family and playing some music with them around Bristol, Virginia, probably in the late twenties. He worked mostly as a builder and carpenter and later for the highway department until his retirement and raised four children, two of whom play autoharp and other instruments.

Kilby Snow's Instrument and Music

Kilby Snow's autoharp, a forties or fifties Oscar Schmidt model, had ten considerably modified bars, and he was left-handed. He fashioned his thumb and finger picks out of brass sheet metal, usually from the headlamp reflectors of a Ford Model T. He wore the finger pick approximately parallel to his fingernail, on the front, flesh side of his index finger. He slanted the last one quarter of an inch of the tip slightly so that it struck exactly perpendicular to the strings despite the fact that the motion of his finger was not at an angle of ninety degrees to the strings.

Autoharp master Kilby Snow photographed in the late 1960s.
Photograph © David Gahr

Most of Mr. Snow's melody and chord fills came from an upward (in pitch) movement of his first finger. In watching and listening to him, I could never quite figure out how or how much he was using his thumb. It is possible that he picked both up and down with his finger as I heard and saw some evidence of this; he said several times that he only pulled upward (in pitch) with his finger, down with his thumb. He usually sat while playing, and like Stoneman, occasionally attached an electric pickup to his harp in the 1950s. Like Stoneman and the Benfields, he picked at the wide end of the harp.

The distinctive sound of Mr. Snow's style is due largely to his innovation of what he called "drag notes," which roughly approximate the slur of sliding from fret to fret or "hammering on" on

(Continued from previous page)

chords, which Pop Stoneman demonstrated for me as being his grandmother Bowers' style; or some very early rhythmic melody picking that would precede the styles heard on this recording. These techniques basically follow the suggestions of early 1890s autoharp self-teaching manuals: accompaniment with thumb and first finger, and simple melody picking with the first finger

with occasional chord strums with thumb and first finger.

Based on my conversations with older musicians, I believe that most of the first generation of country autoharpists took a few tips either from a door-to-door salesman, or, less often for most play-by-ear rural musicians, from written instructions. Then they adapted those tips to their own way of

(Continued from previous page)

a banjo or guitar string. The most usually slurred note is the third note of the **scale**, which the key of D, for instance, would be E-F-F-sharp. He would effect this **slide** by "dragging" his finger pick upwards (towards the higher pitched strings) on the E, F, and F-sharp strings. While playing the E and F strings he left the chord bar up, and then, when his pick reached the F-sharp string, he pressed down on the D-chord bar.

The "drag note" effect is easiest and most natural when the autoharp is played left-handed and the picking hand can be rested on the string anchor cover. Furthermore, to get this sound one must be very accurate, have a strong hand, and play on the wide end of the harp, between the bars and the string anchors. Mr. Snow did most of his playing with his index finger, even for the occasional chord strums between melody notes, and did not usually play plain chords behind his singing. Instead, he played the melody while singing, just as many solo old-time banjo pickers and guitar players did.

By the early 1960s, Kilby Snow had started playing melodies with a flatted seventh note. By 1961 he had added "Muleskinner Blues" and "Ain't Going to Work Tomorrow" to his **repertoire**, both of which use a flatted seventh. His style moved more towards bluegrass in his choice of material, rhythmic drive, strong touch, and melodic sense. His use of drag notes certainly has been at the center of his adapting **blues** and modern country songs to his autoharp repertoire. He first drew his repertoire from family and community and later from commercial recordings by early

country artists such as Blind Alfred Reed and the Carter Family. In the late fifties and sixties he picked up songs from Bill Monroe, Earl Scruggs, and country singers like Carl Smith and Merle Haggard. He also composed several country-style songs of his own.

During the 1960s, Kilby began performing at concerts, on folk festivals, and in coffeehouses, helped a good deal by the efforts of Mike and Ellen Hudak. He was great fun to play music with and accompaniment seemed to spur him on. I especially remember a time in the early 1960s at Sunset Park near Oxford, Pennsylvania, where Bill Monroe was putting on a show. Kilby played autoharp while I backed him on guitar in one of the parking meadows, and a crowd gathered around to hear old favorites like "Budded Roses" as well as some of the more recent Bill Monroe songs like "Close By" or the Monroe classic, "Muleskinner Blues." It was exciting to feel the spark that came from his music at those times. Later in the decade I helped him record a solo Folkways recording (released in 1969 as Folkways 3902), and I arranged a concert tour for us on the West Coast where we recorded a few of his songs on videotape. Up to the late 1970s he played a few contests and festivals, most notably the Brandywine Mountain Music Convention, where he was a regular. At the time of his passing in March 1980, he was rarely playing any programs.

In the mid-1990s, Kilby's son Jim started working on his autoharp playing, encouraged by the autoharp community and especially by Joe Riggs and Mary Lou Orthey. His sound is remarkably close to Kilby's yet possess its own identity.

Mike Seeger

playing, sometimes influenced by playing styles of instruments already in traditional use. There was certainly a fair amount of **improvisation** and experimentation, especially amongst those who had no models or instructions to follow. I believe that country musicians, especially in the South, brought a stronger rhythmic feel to the instrument than that which existed in parlor playing practice, probably due to the influence of fiddle, banjo, and dance traditions. In my estimation, Stoneman and Benfield are exemplary of the second generation of southern autoharp players. Kilby Snow's innovations were certainly a later development.

Around the turn of the century, the songs played or accompanied with autoharp included almost every type to be found in the southern mountain areas: old **hymns**, recently composed religious songs, **waltzes**, sentimental songs, folksongs, and instrumental tunes. The autoharp also brought with it some of the current urban popular songs of the day.

Blues were not generally suited to either accompaniment or melody-picking on the autoharp, which was a detriment to the popularity of the instrument in the blues-happy twenties and beyond. The limitations of the instrument, its quietness, frequent tuning,

lack of expression due to fixed strings, and the usual seated position while playing kept the instrument in the home with a small repertoire, and it didn't venture forth very much with the louder, brasher banjo, expressive fiddle, and more versatile **guitar**. The primary attractions of the autoharp were its novelty, initial ease for playing, and its playing of chords, then a new idea to musicians familiar mostly with banjo or the lap **dulcimer**. In some ways it paralleled and sometimes took over the role of the lap dulcimer, also a quiet instrument with northern European roots. The dulcimer played only melody and **drone** and lent its sparse sound to the older songs and tunes, especially the "modal" ones, but the harmonically rich sound of the autoharp could accompany the newer popular songs and mix with the equally new sounds of the guitar. Contrary to its brief life as a fad up North, it took hold in the South and established a modest, home-based place for itself in early twentieth-century old-time music tradition.

As far as I can tell, there were a fair number of men and women playing the autoharp until homemade music traditions started winding down in the late thirties, due to the influence of radio and records. One man of about seventy, living in western North Carolina, played a dozen tunes for me, mostly waltzes, on his amplified autoharp in the early 1960s. He had a clean, clear style and told me of a couple of other players nearby. Another man of about the same age that I met in the early sixties in Chicago played tunes such as "Red Wing" and "Little Brown Jug." When he was a teenager in Ohio, an autoharp teacher/salesman had sold him and his sister autoharps, taught them how to play, hired a local school auditorium for them to perform in, and then took orders for more autoharps at their performance.

Mrs. Elizabeth White, of Greenville, South Carolina (mother of Josh White, the blues singer), sang me several religious songs to the accompaniment of the autoharp, which she strummed with a clothespin. Her grandson, age about eighteen, sang some of Josh White's more modern songs which he accompanied with autoharp. A Mr. Peaslee and Mrs. Waterman, both of Pittsfield, Massachusetts, played autoharp duets, one picking, the other chording, from about 1895 until Mr. Peaslee's death in 1963. Their repertoire consisted primarily of hymns and popular songs current in the Northeast around 1900, and they played at home and in churches and hospitals. Tex Isley, who played and recorded with early country singers Tom Ashley and Charlie Monroe, was a good autoharp player.

Home craftsmen also made a variety of their own versions of the instrument, some of them quite elaborate, similar to **hammer dulcimers**. I visited one such man in Goshen, Indiana, and heard of another in southwestern North Carolina.

Until the 1950s, the autoharp's role on phonograph recordings was almost always as accompaniment. The first recording of autoharp was by Ernest V. Stoneman in 1924. On that recording he used the autoharp for accompaniment while he sings or plays the melody on the **harmonica**. He soon laid the autoharp aside for the more versatile and tunable guitar. (He once told me, "People were lost when [their autoharps] went out of tune. I bet there are thousands of them up in garrets for that reason.")

A few groups that performed old-time music on early 78 rpm records used autoharp for accompaniment as well, most notably the Carter Family of southwestern Virginia. Collectors of recorded folk music were rarely interest in the instrument. Exceptions were recordings of the Bog Trotters Band of Galax, Virginia, which used it only as accompaniment, and some exceptional autoharp melody picking by J. B. Easter, recorded by E. C. Kirkland in 1937. One song of Mr. Easter's is on "The Kirkland Recordings" released by the Tennessee Folklore Society on LP # TFS-106 in 1984.

The first appearances on record of anything approaching melody picking on the autoharp were by several different old-time music groups about 1930. The Yellow Jackets (also known as the Shady Grove Wood Choppers) recorded an autoharp instrumental medley for the Gennett labels. About halfway through the recording a mouth-harp joins in playing the melody, and towards the end of the disc a slide whistle appears, also playing melody. This could best be described as a rural novelty recording. The Thrasher Family and the Blue Ridge Mountain Singers were vocal groups that used guitar and autoharp for accompaniment and occasional melodic lead. The autoharp playing on their recordings was similar and complemented the rather stiff singing. These were groups with which Frank Walker, A&R man for Columbia, was trying to compete against the Victor Company's Carter Family.

A couple of recordings by the Lee Brothers for the Brunswick label were much looser and more driving. It is possible that these last three groups, all from the same area in northern Georgia, used the same autoharp player. Charles Wolfe writes that Archer Lee Chumbler definitely recorded with the Chumbler Family (another old-time singing group similar to the Thrashers) and the Lee Brothers Trio. Wolfe says Chumbler was from around Gainesville, Georgia, that he learned from his mother, and that his family believes he recorded with the Thrasher Family. Except for some of the Carter Family discs, use of the autoharp in recording diminished in the 1930s and 1940s.

The most important popularizer of autoharp melody picking in the 1950s was Maybelle Carter, the guitar picker and **harmony** singer of the original Carter Family. She took a few clear autoharp breaks on at least two early 1950s recordings with her daughters, the Carter Sisters, "Fair and Tender Ladies" and "I Never Will Marry" (Columbia 4-20920 and 4-20974). The autoharp remained relatively obscure until a 1956 recording by the Wilburn Brothers, "Go 'Way with Me" (Decca 9-30087), featuring Maybelle Carter's autoharp playing. This recording did very well on the country music charts and brought considerable attention to the autoharp as a melody instrument. Maybelle Carter's influence was felt among her fellow country music professionals of Nashville, Tennessee; one of the Wilburn Brothers learned to play autoharp, and another performer, Cecil Null, played and built a few. And away from Nashville,

Maybelle Carter's autoharp playing influenced many to take up the instrument who had never heard it before, as well as some like myself, who had just strummed it and had never thought of playing melody on it. Maybelle had played the instrument as a child and had usually tuned the instrument used by Sara in Carter Family programs, but didn't start playing melody until the late 1930s. I asked her how and why she took up playing melody on the instrument and she said something like, "I just started." One of the first tunes she played was "San Antonio Rose," which remained a favorite of hers on her Grand Ole Opry performances.

Maybelle Carter is also the person who evolved the style of holding the autoharp vertically against her chest so that she could stand and work a microphone just like other instrumentalists and vocalists. Until this time autoharp players had always played the instrument on their lap. In the 1950s, many performing autoharp players, including Ernest Stoneman, were experimenting with contact pickups and amplifiers for their instruments in an effort to stay seated with the instrument on their lap in the usual way, yet still be heard on public address systems, which, at the time, usually used only one microphone. Maybelle Carter's innovation changed all that. Now her style of holding the instrument is used by nearly everyone.

The folk revival of the 1960s inspired many more musicians to play the autoharp, usually influenced by the styles of Maybelle Carter, Ernest Stoneman, or those influenced by them, like myself. A few makers experimented with building better instruments, with mixed success. In the 1970s and 1980s, however, playing of the autoharp increased exponentially due to a new style evolved by Bryan Bowers in the early 1970s. His is a virtuoso style, built less on the driving 2/4 rhythms heard in traditional performances and more on slower **phrase** patterns or rapidly picked melody notes, played on an instrument tuned to one diatonically tuned key. Repertoire amongst the new players has broadened to include classical, **jazz**, and show tunes with all their harmonic complexities. At present most performance players' styles are

See glossary for definition of boldfaced terms

based in this general area, and many evolve their own tunings to get the effects they desire. The number of autoharp makers has also increased though not in proportion to the number of players. There are autoharp mini-festivals around the country, two autoharp magazines, autoharp classes one may attend at a variety of levels, and a great number of recordings by the dozen or two top players.

BIBLIOGRAPHY

Autoharp. 1986. Mike Seeger. Woodstock, NY: Homespun Tapes. Audio teaching tape.

Beginning the Appalachian Autoharp with Evo Bluestein. 1986. Lark in the Morning Instructional Video LAR 001. Distributed by Mel Bay.

Blackley, Becky. *The Autoharp Book.* (1983). I.A.D. Publications.

The Kirkland Recordings. 1984. Tennessee Folklore Society TFS-106.

Moore, A. Doyle. (1963). "The Autoharp: Its Origin and Development from a Popular to a Folk Instrument." *New York Folklore Quarterly* 19, no. 4 (December).

Stiles, Ivan. (1991). "The True History of the Autoharp," *Autoharp Quarterly* 3, no. 3 (April).

BLUEGRASS

Jeff Todd Titon

Please see Chapter 7 if this volume for complete biographical information on Jeff Todd Titon.

Named for Kentucky, the "Bluegrass State," **bluegrass music** was invented by Bill Monroe shortly after World War II. Drawing on the high and close harmonies of brother duets in early country music, but with elements of **blues** and **swing jazz**, bluegrass began as a high-powered, peak-experience, acoustic, stringed **instrument**-based sound associated with Monroe and his band, the Bluegrass Boys, that appealed to an audience in the upland South. Soon copied by other regional bands such as the Stanley Brothers, by the early 1950s bluegrass had become a regional style of country music that could be heard on recordings, radio programs, and in concerts.

After the rise of rock and roll in the mid-1950s, and concurrent changes in country music that moved it toward a more easy-listening mode, bluegrass fell out of favor with the music industry. It underwent a revival beginning in the late 1950s when it found a new audience among northern and western college youth who flocked to blue-grass concerts and the newly founded bluegrass festivals that showcased several bands at once. Jim & Jesse and the Virginia Boys, Mac Wiseman, The Country Gentlemen, Jimmy Martin, Joe Val and the New England Bluegrass Boys, and several other groups, along with Monroe and the Stanleys, kept their music alive among the hardcore audience of their own generation in the Appalachian South while appealing to this new audience that found in the music a representation of the older, more natural world of rural America at a time when corporate America seemed to be turning out buttoned-down urban conformists.

Bluegrass, no longer the latest version of popular music in the upland South, became a specialty music, gradually increasing its appeal to fans throughout North America and eventually, in the 1960s, to Europe and Japan. Today, subgenres such as classic bluegrass, newgrass, and bluegrass fusion testify to the strength of the music and its hold on musicians and audiences alike. Whereas only a decade ago the country music industry ignored bluegrass, today the Nashville Network and other industry image makers portray bluegrass as a roots music, and they acknowledge young bluegrass stars like Alison Krauss while at the same time established country music celebrities like Dolly Parton make roots albums that put them in bluegrass settings.

The bluegrass sound is a unique mixture of musical elements. Many were old, some were new when, in 1946, Monroe and his Bluegrass Boys recorded "Will You Be Lovin' Another Man," regarded as the moment when bluegrass coalesced into the particular sound that is its own. High vocal harmonies, with the **melody** ("lead") harmonized from a third above ("tenor part") in a duet, and harmonized with a tenor part and from below ("baritone") in a vocal trio, sometimes rested at cadence points on **intervals** of the perfect fourth or **fifth**, offering a sound that was quite distinct from the conventional SATB (soprano, alto, tenor, bass) choral **harmony**. This way of harmonizing goes back to nineteenth-century southern **shape-note** singing, still practiced in **Sacred Harp** singing throughout the United States, but it was combined with more modern **barbershop-style close harmony** singing.

Singers **pitch** the songs at the very top of their vocal **range**. Sometimes the tenors must sing a portion **falsetto**. The vocal inflections of bluegrass, the twists and turns that elaborate the melodies (so apparent in the much-admired singing of Ralph Stanley, usually considered the best singer in the **genre**), derive from Old Baptist (Old Regular, United, and Primitive) singing in central Appalachia. Bluegrass lyrics take up the same general subjects of commercial country music, love and love lost, contrasts between city and country life, and nostalgia for childhood, love of parents, and the old country home; but the bluegrass repertory also features folksongs and **old-time gospel** songs as well as instrumentals—none of which can be found in contemporary country music.

Instrumentally, bluegrass is a peak-experience, virtuoso music, requiring great skill to execute the sometimes breakneck tempos and intricate melodies. The **repertoire** consists of songs, and of instrumental pieces usually based on **fiddle** tunes that were used for dance music. Monroe wrote a number of instrumentals derived from the sounds the old fiddle tunes, particularly the Scots Irish ones, and these have become classics of the genre. But bluegrass today is a concert and jam-session music; it is not a dance music. Although bluegrass standards can be found in musical notation, and bluegrass method books (also containing notation) are available for various instruments, musicians use the notation as a reference and guide for learning and recalling tunes. When

Bill Monroe, the "father of bluegrass music," shown in a photograph taken in the late 1940s/early 1950s. *Photograph courtesy Bob Carlin collection*

The Mother of Blue-grass Gospel

Erin Kellen's folklife research in Alabama's Piney Woods has focused on bluegrass gospel performer Margie Sullivan and the role of women in early bluegrass music. In the past, Kellen has worked at the Alabama Center for Traditional Culture (where she was director of the Sacred Harp Video Project) and the Southern Folklife Collection at the University of North Carolina at Chapel Hill. She is currently a librarian for the 11th Circuit Court of Appeals. The following essay originally appeared in In the Spirit: Alabama's Sacred Music Traditions, edited by Henry Willett, published in 1995 by Black Belt Press.

Twelve-year-old Margie Brewster worked hard in the cotton fields that her family sharecropped. After her daddy sold his portion of the season's crop, he used the money he got for the cotton seeds to buy her a **guitar** and taught her to play. Her father's death later that year grieved Margie so deeply that her mother gave her permission to leave home to go on the road with a lady evangelist named Hazel Chain. So she left Winnsboro, Louisiana, and began traveling the Pentecostal revival circuit that stretched from east Texas through Louisiana and Mississippi to Alabama. The pair traveled by Greyhound bus and scheduled their engagements by mail.

It was dark and deserted at the crossroads where the Greyhound left them in Sunflower, Alabama, where they were supposed to conduct a revival. The loss of their luggage had delayed them for hours at the bus station in Mobile. Soon, a little boy came riding up on a bicycle and said, "You must be Sister Margie and Sister Chain."

They said, "Yes."

And he said, "Well, follow me," and guided them to the little church. Margie was tired, but she sang because, she says, "Wild horses couldn't keep me from singing back in those days!" That was the night she met a young man named Enoch, who played the **fiddle** and sang gospel music with his father, the Reverend Arthur Sullivan.

Three years later, in 1949, Margie and Enoch were married. That same month, the family's **string band** had its first radio performance on WRJW out of Picayune, Mississippi. They hadn't thought about what to call themselves, so they just told the radio announcer to say they were "The Sullivan Family."

For forty-five years Enoch and Margie Sullivan have been the core of the Sullivan Family—especially since **banjo** player Emmett, Enoch's brother, passed away in the spring of 1993. They called their music "Bluegrass Gospel," and they have journeyed far and wide to play it at country and urban churches, at civic events and political rallies, at prisons, and at festivals across the United States and in Europe. In 1993, they were inducted into Bill Monroe's Bluegrass Hall of Fame at his Bean Blossom Festival in Bean Blossom, Indiana. These days they travel in their own bus, emblazoned with the words "The Legendary Sullivan Family" on its sides.

On the home front, in St. Stephens, Alabama, there were five children to raise. From the beginning, the Sullivans kept a small farm, raising and putting by much of their own food. Now that the kids are all grown and gone, Enoch still likes to keep a few cows, and Margie still cans and freezes produce from the garden. They like to stay grounded in the unpretentious rural dailiness of their lives in little St. Stephens, the oldest town in the oldest county in Alabama.

Enoch and Margie have enough working years behind them that you'd think they might consider settling down into a comfortable retirement. Instead, they keep up a pace that would wear out most people half their age.

In the early days, there were few women traveling the back roads playing **bluegrass** music, and most of them stayed in the background. But Margie has stayed right up front with Enoch—accompanying him on guitar, singing lead and **har-**

singing and playing with others bluegrass musicians do not read notation, and the music is still transmitted orally, for there is no substitute for hearing it played.

Although in the rock and roll era some bluegrass musicians such as The Osborne Brothers experimented with electric instruments and a drum set, today's bluegrass bands avoid electronically amplified instruments and drums entirely. The usual bluegrass band consists of acoustic **guitar**, five-string **banjo**, fiddle, **mandolin**, and string **bass**, although in practice the fiddle and/or mandolin sometimes are omitted. Any of the musicians may sing, but traditionally the lead vocalist is also the guitarist. Each in-

mony in her husky alto, writing songs, and preaching the gospel. It was through **gospel music** that many women entered the field of bluegrass music, most frequently through family bands like the Sullivans. Margie's prominent place in the band may reflect the family's Pentecostal background; it is not out of the ordinary for women to preach or assume leadership positions in Pentecostal churches. And the Sullivans see themselves first and foremost as spreaders of the gospel—their role as bluegrass pioneers comes second.

An examination of "string band gospel" groups like the Sullivan Family, and gospel music in general, is crucial to any investigation of the origins of bluegrass. Before anyone even called their music "bluegrass gospel," the Sullivans' performances incorporated the harmony singing, banjo **syncopation**, instrumental breaks between singing, and faster **tempos** that define the music as a separate **genre**. Though the southern Appalachians are stereotypically associated with bluegrass music, the phenomenon of the Sullivan Family, and other groups from the coastal plain, reminds us to recognize the significance of other regions' contributions to the style.

Now that women performers are so commonplace in bluegrass, it is time to take a closer look at the experiences of one of the pioneers. In the course of four decades, Margie Sullivan has transported the music from backwoods brush arbors to urban areas. She has felt the loneliness of being the sole woman traveling with men who "only wanted to talk about coon hunting and such," in the days when most male musicians had some familiarity with that pursuit. Today's women of bluegrass, like their male counterparts, are increasingly urban, middle-class, and non-southern. Their sensibilities are shaped by circumstances radically different from those that shaped Margie Sullivan.

Margie herself never fails to marvel at the path her life has taken. She likes to tell about the time the Sullivan Family performed seven songs at a Sunday morning service in a Catholic Church in Belgium when they traveled to Europe in 1984. An interpreter introduced each song, explaining the meaning to those who could not understand English. When they finished playing, people in the audience presented fresh flowers to Margie, as was customary. Then she, in turn, presented fresh flowers to the priest:

> When I handed him the flowers, he reached over and kissed me on the cheek. And then he kissed me on the other cheek—that's a blessing of acceptance. And when he did that, the crowd was amazed. So they wanted me to say something. And I was not prepared to say anything. And for just a minute I was shocked beyond words. And then I thought, well, I'll just tell them what I really feel in my heart. And I thanked them for so graciously receiving us. And I said I hope that we have represented the Sullivan Family well here today, performed in a way that was a credit to our group and our name. And I really do hope and trust that we really represented our country, the United States, real well. But more than all of that, I hope that we have really represented the Lord Jesus Christ. And I don't know why I said that. It was spontaneous. And when I said it, they stood. They went to clapping. Some of them were crying; some of them were laughing. I never saw such an acceptance. I just stood there and cried. In a big Catholic Church as long as from here to that road almost. Oh, honey, it's beyond my fondest dreams to think that I would ever get to do anything like

(Continued on the next page)

strument is played in both a lead (melodic) and backup (harmonic and rhythmic) style. Sung **verses** alternate with instrumental breaks in which the various instruments are showcased in turn while the others back up, in a setting reminiscent of jazz. Some outstanding musicians **improvise** lead breaks on the spot, creating melodies from a store-house of patterns. The banjo, in particular, has a distinct bluegrass style, a rapid and elaborate **three-finger** (thumb and first two finger) method that encases the melody. This bluegrass banjo style, invented by Earl Scruggs and imitated by every bluegrass banjo player since, usually is considered a marker of the music, and was the most ob-

(Continued from previous page)

that. I mean, when I was singing in that cotton field, pulling that sack up and down those rows and singing with all of my heart praise to the Lord, not knowing if anybody else even heard me or not, I wasn't doing it for anybody else. But I never, you could have never made me believe I'd have the chance to do the things that I've had the chance to do.

Bibliography

Alabama Bluegrass Music Association website. Information on The Sullivan Family and their recordings. Available at http://www.alabamabluegrass.org.

Alabama Center for Traditional Culture website. Information on The Sullivan Family and their recordings. Available at http://www.arts.state.al.us/actc/compilation/sullivan.html.

Sullivan, Enoch, and Sullivan, Margie. (1999). *The Sullivan Family: Fifty Years in Bluegrass Gospel Music.* Many, LA: Sweet Dreams Publications.

The Sullivan Family Homepage. Available at http://www.1fx.net/popup.shtml.

Willett, Henry. (1995). *In the Spirit: Alabama's Sacred Music Traditions.* Montgomery, AL: Black Belt Press.

Erin Kellen

vious new element in it. Bluegrass fiddle owes a great deal to the innovations of **Western swing** jazz, but combines these with techniques and a sound based in the fiddling traditions of the Upland South. Kenny Baker, who fiddled in Bill Monroe's band, is a much-admired contemporary bluegrass fiddler.

Although many regard bluegrass as a quintessentially Anglo-American music, it contains several African American elements, including **polyrhythm**. The Scruggs banjo style is based on 3-3-2 accent patterns that cross polyrhythmically with the duple meter of the other instruments. Monroe's music was strongly influenced by jazz and by the singing and repertoire of Jimmie Rodgers, a country music star of the late 1920s and early 1930s who featured blues songs that he had learned from black musicians in Mississippi. Monroe always credited Arnold Schultz, a black guitarist and neighbor, with helping to form his conception of rhythm and what was possible on the guitar.

Monroe exercised a great deal of control over his band's arrangements, and he fused the bluegrass style from British-American, Irish, and African American elements. Thus although Irish music lurks in the background of bluegrass, the contemporary claim that bluegrass is an extension of Celtic music will not stand up to the historical record.

Bluegrass today is a specialty genre sung and played all over the world. It has both commercial and folk sides. A few bluegrass groups always have been able to make a living from recordings and tours, but most commercial groups, even those with a string of recordings to their credit, consider bluegrass no more than a part-time job. Still, the music is presented to its fans through the usual industry outlets, including radio, television, recordings, and concerts. The International Bluegrass Musicians Association (IBMA) promotes bluegrass worldwide. At the same time, bluegrass has a core contingent of many fans who also are amateur musicians—some of whom are very good indeed—and who gather in homes and at festivals to make music for their own enjoyment. A bluegrass museum was established a few years ago in Owensboro, Kentucky. Bluegrass clubs that promote concerts, and semipublic **jam sessions** held in stores after hours, can be found in many towns and cities, while festivals take place in every part of North America.

Bluegrass festivals, some of which last for several days at a time during the summer months, are ritual experiences. Fans, musicians, and their families arrive in their

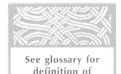

See glossary for definition of boldfaced terms

campers a day or two early if possible and settle into festival campgrounds. Informal bluegrass singing and "picking" sessions begin almost at once in outdoor parking lots in an atmosphere of picnic food and good humor. While many listen to the acts from the main stage, many others move in and out of various jam sessions, searching for peak experiences with other musicians, some known, some new. As this music has well-understood rules and a repertoire of favorite songs and instrumental pieces, it is possible for musicians who have never met to play well together without rehearsal.

Geographically, bluegrass's strongest identity today is bound up with the central region of the southern Appalachian Mountains, and it is epitomized by the sound of Ralph Stanley, with its strong and obvious links to the Anglo-American folk music of the mountains. The late Bill Monroe, on the other hand, was from western Kentucky, outside the Appalachian region, and his music em-

bodied the mix of Anglo- and African American strains that was more characteristic of the bluegrass region of that state. Today, bluegrass in New England and the maritime provinces of Canada is sung with New England, rather than Appalachian, accents; and West Coast bluegrass sounds comparatively smooth and relaxed, reflecting the sophisticated musical aesthetics of that region. Like blues, jazz, and country music, bluegrass has its roots in regional American folk musics; but it has transcended those roots, spread geographically, and become a commercially disseminated music available to everyone.

BIBLIOGRAPHY

Cantwell, Robert. (1984). *Bluegrass Breakdown: The Making of the Old Southern Sound*. Urbana: University of Illinois Press.

Rosenberg, Neil V. (1985). *Bluegrass: A History*. Urbana: University of Illinois Press.

Legends of Bluegrass

MUSIC AT BILL'S PICKIN' PARLOR IN THE SOUTH CAROLINA MIDLANDS

Pat Ahrens and Jane Przybysz

Pat Ahrens is a freelance writer and the author of Union Grove: The First Fifty Years. *A rhythm guitarist, she is past president of the South Carolina Bluegrass and Traditional Music Association and has served on its board of directors for more than a decade. In 1996, she received the South Carolina Heritage Award. Jane Przybysz is executive director of the San Jose Museum of Quilts & Textiles and former curator of research and folklife at McKissick Museum, University of South Carolina. She earned her Ph.D. in the Department of Performance Studies at New York University.*

A short distance from the heart of South Carolina's capital city, Columbia, Bill's Music Shop and Pickin' Parlor is the center of gravity for an emergent community of **bluegrass** musicians. While Columbia's own WIS radio station once broadcast the "**hillbilly**" music that became known as bluegrass, and the Piedmont region of the state was the training ground for people like Don Reno and Carl Story who were active in the post–World War II regional bluegrass music scene, bluegrass did not enjoy a post–rock-and-roll revival in South Carolina as it did elsewhere in the country. Not until Bill Wells—a retired Navy man and musician raised in the coal-mining region of southwestern Virginia—moved from Chicago to his wife's home state did a community of bluegrass musicians begin to take root in South Carolina at the Pickin' Parlor he opened in December 1985.

Why choose West Columbia as a site? Because in his experience, wherever there was a major university, an appreciative au-

dience for bluegrass lay waiting. In Columbia, however, this was not the case. Newspaper ads for bluegrass **jam sessions** were answered by musicians playing mostly **old-time** country tunes. Pappy Sherrill and the Hired Hands and the Lucas-Harmon Brothers, presently among the state's most expert bluegrass musicians, were exceptions rather than the rule.

Over ten years later, Wells still works to cultivate in local audiences and musicians an ear for bluegrass. But now, on any given Friday night, anywhere from 50 to 150 women and men, young and old, carpenters and teachers, machinists and dentists, travel from all across the state and neighboring Georgia and North Carolina to jam with other musicians or simply listen to music at Bill's. While men with last names suggesting an Irish, Scottish, English, German, or Dutch heritage predominate among the players, the Parlor's proximity to the University of South Carolina, the Fort Jackson military base, and I-77, I-26, I-20, and I-95 ensures that in ad-

dition to the audience of mostly wives, children, and girlfriends, there is often a sprinkling of international business school students, Asian and African American wives of Army servicemen, and vacationers who regularly stop by on their way to and from Florida.

In South Carolina, bluegrass brings together musicians who value an acoustic sound and virtuosity in most all musical **forms**—be it **jazz** or opera—but who want their music making to occur in environments conducive to social interaction. As Pickin' Parlor founder Bill Wells puts it, "Every bluegrass gathering is a social event of some kind. It might be a potluck or something. The musicians go off in one little group, and the wives and girlfriends go off in another little group."

While bluegrass is the only kind of country music Wells features in concert, improvised groups of musicians scattered throughout the space at Friday night jam sessions will variously take up **Western swing**, big-band tunes, jazz, old-time and modern country. Some even play popular oldies like *Under the Boardwalk* bluegrass-style, meaning with traditional bluegrass instrumentation such as **guitar**, **banjo**, **mandolin**, **bass**, and **fiddle**. By accommodating diverse musical styles, the Pickin' Parlor attracts players at different skill levels who can, if they choose, jam with increasingly better musicians and eventually develop the technical virtuosity bluegrass demands. Bill Wells is among these better musicians. His band, the Blue Ridge Mountain Grass, regularly practices together at Friday-night jam sessions, effortlessly producing the "high lonesome" sound prototypical of bluegrass in the vocals and fiddle playing.

While people who play an **instrument** say "it's the love of the music" that brings them out to Bill's, older folks who come just to listen appreciate the informal, family-like atmosphere in which drinking alcohol and smoking are not allowed. Particularly for widows and widowers, the Pickin' Parlor is a haven in a heartless world where, for the cost of a one-dollar donation, they can spend an evening sampling some of the region's best musicians singing songs they grew up listening to on the radio.

TEXTS AND TUNES

Among the musicians who play bluegrass at Friday night jam sessions, songs written and performed by the Stanley Brothers; Bill Monroe and the Bluegrass Boys; and Lester Flatt, Earl Scruggs, and the Foggy Mountain Boys are popular with their themes of home, family, and religion. But you are just as likely to hear a song by Alison Krauss, whose bluegrass-inflected songs have successfully crossed over into the popular music market. The older songs are common knowledge and are learned mostly from other musicians but increasingly off of records, tapes, CDs, and sometimes from books as well.

As for where the older bluegrass songs come from, popular wisdom at Bill's has it that they are partly rooted in church music, especially **shape-note** and **gospel** singing. As one older regular put it, "If you don't start there [in church], you can't make it [in bluegrass]." The other readily acknowledged source is Irish fiddle music, to which people traditionally danced **square dances** and **waltzes**. This explains the 4/4 and 3/4 time in which the majority of songs you will hear at the Parlor are performed. Aware that much of what has become traditional bluegrass **repertoire** was made up more than handed down, Wells especially credits A. P. Carter with "finding songs" and then arranging them in what he calls "the circle of **fifths** tune structure" that characterizes so many bluegrass tunes.

IDEAS ABOUT MUSIC

The son of a Primitive Baptist, and later a Free Will preacher, Bill Wells brings a missionary sensibility to the Pickin' Parlor. He has dedicated himself to keeping traditional bluegrass music alive. It is not a sound "natural" to South Carolina, he says, in the way it seems to be in North Carolina, and he is

not sure why. "Playing bluegrass is a lot harder" than playing country music, he observes. Asked to explain what else distinguishes bluegrass from other forms of country music, he says it is the "emphasis you give to a word to give it feeling"—that and an audience-oriented performance aesthetic. "You can watch a band and tell whether they're working for the people or working for themselves," Bill says, himself clearly committed to working for the people.

SOCIAL ORGANIZATION

The emergent musical community that has formed around Bill's Pickin' Parlor includes people like Bill who grew up in the musical culture that gave rise to bluegrass as well as musicians who have adopted this musical culture as their own. Some aim to earn their living as musicians by teaching and playing. But most have taken up music as an avocation or simply enjoy listening to country music. Most are over forty, although several younger men can usually be found at any given event. Younger women—daughters of musicians who frequent Bill's—work the snack bar or seem content to be an audience for the mostly male players. It should be noted, however, that Bill Wells is looking to a teenage granddaughter with unusual musical talent to carry on his work.

The Pickin' Parlor provides four overlapping musical contexts and experiences. On weekdays, a group of regulars often straggle in after Bill opens the place at 10:00 A.M. just to chat, while throughout the day people drop by to purchase instruments, songbooks, and CDs and take music lessons. Except for the lessons, which take place in a room towards the back of the building, these activities occur in the 40 x 40-foot space that functions largely as the store at the front of the 6,000-square-foot building.

Come weekend evenings, however, the Parlor becomes a performance setting. At Friday night jam sessions, diverse kinds of acoustic music are performed simultaneously by improvised groups of two to ten musicians who stand in huddles in the various performance pockets created by room dividers strategically placed in the 40 x 60-foot space just beyond the less hectic front room, where older musicians sit singing slower-paced, old-time country tunes. Children roam throughout with small bags of popcorn or moonpies in hand. Young, middle-aged, and older couples park themselves at the fast-food booths or the old theater seats arranged around the rooms, drinking a hot cup of coffee, a can of RC Cola, or a bottle of locally produced Blenheim's ginger ale. The music starts around 7:30 P.M. and generally goes on till midnight, when "Mr. Bill" flicks the lights to signal it is time for everyone to go home. At that point, each group usually tries to squeeze in one or two more songs.

Though the repertoire of the different groups varies considerably, the way a song is taken up tends to be the same. Typically, the most accomplished singer of what operates as the "core" of any given group of musicians—a person each on guitar, banjo, mandolin, bass, and fiddle—will suggest a song and look for nodding heads as a sign of group consensus. He or she then strikes up the song. Others join in with their instruments and vocally as well, if the song traditionally includes a **chorus** performed with tight vocal harmonies. According to Wells, bluegrass songs usually will have three different **verses** with a chorus that repeats after each verse. It is not unusual, however, for a practiced group of regulars to take turns featuring individual instruments as well during a song. Often another ring of musicians, usually less experienced, will form around this core group to inconspicuously jam along. Listeners only generally stand or sit quietly at the very fringe of the group.

Saturday nights are reserved for concerts featuring professional bluegrass musicians performing on the Parlor's proscenium stage located at the rear of the 40 x 60-foot room just beyond the front sales room. Framed by the rural autumn mountain scene serving as the stage's backdrop, these musicians model the aural and performance aesthetic Bill Wells aims to promote. The charge for concerts ranges from four dollars to fourteen dollars, depending on the group's size and drawing power.

See glossary for definition of boldfaced terms

Finally, the third Friday of each month is when the Parlor sponsors an open mike, giving local musicians a chance to perform on a proscenium stage with microphones. Serving as a training ground and impetus for innovation, these evenings showcase aspiring professional musicians who—playing solo or with a group—can try out a traditional tune, a new arrangement of a traditional tune, or even an original song. Open-mike night thus bridges the experience of the informal jam sessions with that of the formal professional bluegrass performance setting.

As much as Wells is a purist when it comes to preserving an acoustic bluegrass sound and performance aesthetic, developing an audience for this music has meant embracing the variety of musical styles performed at jam sessions as well as the more active role women musicians are playing in the musical culture that has grown up around the Parlor, particularly in the South Carolina Blue Grass and Traditional Music Association Wells helped found in 1991. When the Lucas and Harmon Brothers band performed at Bill's seventieth birthday party, Randy Lucas—a national award-winning professional mandolin and banjo player once featured in the *State* newspaper as a stay-at-home-Dad—had his five-year-old daughter Bailee join the group on a small fiddle. It was a sign of the Parlor's vital role in ensuring that younger bluegrass musicians in South Carolina will have a context within which to grow their art.

DOCUMENTARY RECORDINGS AND FILMS

McKissick Museum is home to both the South Carolina Broadcast Association's Archive and the state's Folklife Resource Center. Television footage of Pappy Sherrill and the Hired Hands, as well as of the Lucas and Harmon Brothers, has been transferred to VHS format for researchers interested in South Carolina musical traditions. Documentary audio recordings of these musicians, of jam sessions at Bill's Pickin' Parlor, and of banjo and fiddle contests held at the South Carolina State Fair also are available to researchers and the general public by appointment at the McKissick Museum Folklife Resource Center, University of South Carolina, Columbia, SC 29208, 803-777-7251, (fax) 803-777-2829.

A video library at Bill's Music Shop and Pickin' Parlor containing approximately 200 VHS tapes of concerts by local, regional, and national bluegrass bands is open to researchers by appointment. Approximately 25 percent of these tapes feature South Carolina–based musicians. Contact Bill Wells, Bill's Music Shop and Pickin' Parlor, 710 Meeting Street, West Columbia, SC 29169, 803-796-6477.

BIBLIOGRAPHY

Ahrens, Pat J. (1970). *A History of the Musical Careers of Dewitt "Snuffy" Jenkins, Banjoist and Homer "Pappy" Sherrill, Fiddler.* West Columbia, SC: Wentworth Corporation.

———. (1970). "The Role of the Crazy Water Crystals Co. in Promoting Hillbilly Music," *JEMF Quarterly* 4, no. 19 (autumn):107–109.

Hope, Harry. (1979). "Train Songs, Hill Songs and One Sweet Waltz or Two." *Sandlapper* 12, no. 10 (October):8–14.

Libby, Steve. (1949). "South Carolinians in the Entertainment World." *South Carolina Magazine* 12, no. 1 (January).

Tice, J. Olin. (1968). "They Stole That Nashville Sound from Carolina." *Living in South Carolina* 18, no. 7 (June/July).

BLUEGRASS MUSIC IN MINNESOTA

Philip Nusbaum

Philip Nusbaum is a music professional who conducts research from his position at the Minnesota State Arts Board and also plays in bluegrass and country bands. For over three decades, he has hosted folk music programs on radio and has conducted extensive field recordings of many types of traditional music. His work has appeared on commercial recordings and on local and national public radio. His writing about traditional music has appeared in liner notes and in scholarly and popular articles.

Originating in the American South, **bluegrass** is one of several music styles that, in the late twentieth century, are supported by adherents throughout the world, including Minnesota. First emerging in the 1940s as a substyle of southern country music, the type of **string band** known as a bluegrass band combined several Anglo-American southern folk music traditions and reorchestrated them with influence from African American **blues** and **jazz** and other popular music styles. Those who perform and listen to bluegrass in Minnesota are not necessarily Anglo-American but are generally of European American background.

THE MUSIC

The players whose post–World War II recordings serve as performance models for bluegrass players worldwide were from the American South and considered their work as a part of commercial country music. However, because Minnesotans do not usually speak idiomatic southern English, many say that their typical sung inflections make Minnesota bluegrass sound "northern."

Many Minnesota players were inspired to play bluegrass after hearing the style within the context of the United States folk music revival that began in the 1950s. As a result, some Minnesota observers note that the taste of the Minnesota bluegrass community relates strongly to the folk revival and not to traditional playing. It takes a practiced ear to tell the difference between traditional and folk revival-inspired playing, because each type of bluegrass employs the same standard **instruments** and typically uses the AABB song and tune **form**. However, insiders say that folk-inspired players evidence restraint, while players following the performance model set by the original southern players display a more aggressive approach to their singing and playing.

By the end of the twentieth century, Minnesota bluegrass continued to develop with reference to both its own stylistic antecedents and to adjacent folk, folk revival, and popular styles. Progressive substyles borrowing from rock music and jazz have also evolved. The ratio of stylistic ingredients present in performance differs from musical group to musical group and among individual players. Experienced listeners understand such distinctions, and the bluegrass community is familiar with terminology such as "traditional bluegrass," "contemporary bluegrass," and "progressive acoustic music," among other reference points. In other words, Minnesota bluegrass musicians make aesthetic choices among a wide palette of options and are encouraged to create individualistic interpretations of songs and tunes that seem to fall within, or at least make reference to, bluegrass tradition.

HISTORY

Country music influenced the playing of Minnesota's European immigrants and their descendants. Old-timers recall the 1940s and 1950s live radio broadcasts of Slim Jim and the Vagabond Kid, which combined elements of country and Scandinavian music. There have been instances of Minnesota Norwegian language-singing set in bluegrass-like musical settings, and Minnesota **polka** bands have long included country songs in their **repertoires**. Minnesota musicians played commercial country music as well, and when bluegrass evolved, some of them were attracted to the style. By the late 1950s, there were bluegrass bands whose members lived in Minnesota, and nationally known bluegrass figures performed in the state.

However, unlike most ethnic-based folk music styles in Minnesota, bluegrass participation has not usually been a consequence of either ethnic group membership or neighborhood connections. Most Minnesotans who have enjoyed bluegrass music have been people who choose to perform the music or become part of the audience for it. This development mirrored culture changes in the United States, especially since the end of World War II. Good roads and access to automobiles allowed adults to travel to socialize, and they socialized more and more on the basis of sharing an interest rather than local or family connections as a basis.

By the early 1960s, many people had begun to perceive bluegrass music as distinctly different from the pop music–influenced country music of the period. Folk revival interests saw bluegrass' traditionality, and embraced the idiom. Its new popularity reflected a changing demographic for bluegrass. Unlike bluegrass music's original supporters in the South, Minnesota bluegrass adherents were largely urban, well educated, and of college age. As in many other states and Canadian provinces, an organization to further bluegrass was formed, the Minnesota Bluegrass and Old Time Music Association (MBOTMA). Established in 1975, the group promotes formal concerts as well as events at which informal musical performances occur, such as instrument swap meets, **jam sessions** for members, and bluegrass festivals.

The model for MBOTMA activities became the multi-activity bluegrass community occasion or celebration rather than the private party or promoted musical show. While enjoying bluegrass music had always been a reason for like-minded individuals to engage in sociability, at many MBOTMA events enjoying bluegrass seemed to many participants to resemble a type of total immersion experience in the culture of bluegrass.

Bluegrass's social and musical malleability account for bluegrass taking root in regions remote from its birthplace. In Minnesota, bluegrass contains several musical stylistic niches that can be experienced through a variety of social occasions in which fans choose to participate.

DOCUMENTARY RECORDINGS AND OTHER MATERIALS

The CDs *The Minnesota Album* and *Hand Stitched: Minnesota Mountain Music* document a great number of Minnesota bluegrass bands. They were both produced by the Minnesota Bluegrass and Old Time Music Association

(MBOTMA), which can be contacted at P.O. Box 11419, St. Paul, MN 55111-0419; www.mtn.org/~mbotma/.

Also of interest from MBOTMA is a monthly magazine entitled *Inside Bluegrass,* formerly known as the *Minnesota Bluegrass and Old Time Music Association Newsletter.* It has been a source of primary materials and articles relating to Minnesota bluegrass music since 1975.

BIBLIOGRAPHY

Cantwell, Robert. (1984). *Bluegrass Breakdown: The Making of the Old Southern Sound.* Urbana: University of Illinois Press.

Hand Stitched: Minnesota Mountain Music. 1998. St. Paul: Minnesota Bluegrass and Old Time Music Association. MBOTMA CD 9801. CD recording.

Kisliuk, Michele. (1988). "A Special Kind of Courtesy: Action at a Bluegrass Jam Session." *Drama Review* 32 (3):141–57.

The Minnesota Album. 1992. St. Paul: Minnesota Bluegrass and Old Time Music Association. MBOTMA CD 101. CD recording.

Rosenberg, Neil V. (1985). *Bluegrass: A History.* Urbana: University of Illinois Press.

———. (1967). "From Sound to Style: The Emergence of Bluegrass." *Journal of American Folklore* 80 (2):143–50.

BLUEGRASS AND OLD-TIME ON THE FRONT RANGE

Brenda M. Romero

*Brenda M. Romero is an associate professor on the musicology faculty at the University of Colorado in Boulder. She received a Ph.D. in **ethnomusicology** at the University of California, Los Angeles (focusing on indigenous and Hispano traditions of New Mexico) and B.Mus. and M.Mus. degrees in music theory and composition at the University of New Mexico. She frequently gives lecture/recitals on the older folk music of New Mexico and southern Colorado and networks with old-time, bluegrass, and various other musicians along the Front Range of the Rocky Mountains in Colorado and Wyoming.*

Bluegrass is very popular on the Front Range of the Rocky Mountains in Colorado and Wyoming, with a strong presence in the Denver/Boulder area. **Old-time**, which is regularly mistaken for bluegrass by those who are not familiar with the traditions, is also popular in that region; it, too, is described in this essay. Bluegrass musicians far outnumber the old-time musicians on the Front Range, but bluegrass fans tend to include many old-time fans as well. The KGNU bluegrass radio program "Old Grass/New Grass" will occasionally play old-time music. A Boulder bluegrass **disc jockey** (DJ) of twenty years, Joan Leonard Wernick, emphasizes that people of all walks of life are involved in bluegrass music making, and the same is true for old-time. The mostly white bluegrass community is comprised of many good players with a high level of self-motivation that can find its reward in the region's big audiences for this music. The old-time musicians fulfill quieter functions, playing primarily for community gatherings.

MUSIC

OLD-TIME

Old-time music uses the clawhammer style of **banjo** playing, without **finger picks**, holding the hand in a claw shape, and playing the **instrument** percussively. Singing occurs mostly in non-dance contexts and features **ballads**. The **fiddle** is the center of the old-time band, which also includes the banjo, **guitar**, **mandolin**, and bass; everyone plays together as one unit. There are approximately 100 old-time musicians in the area. Among the better-known fiddlers are Dave Brown, Anita Dolan, and Tim Rogers (Boulder); Larry Edelman (Denver); and Eric Levine (Fort Collins). Jeff Haemer is one of the few excellent old-time mandolin players, since most mandolin players play bluegrass. Vinny Varsetta, recently moved from the Nashville area, is the most prominent clawhammer banjo player on the Front Range. Mike "Woody" Woods is another sought-after clawhammer player but does not appear in public as often.

BLUEGRASS

In bluegrass music, the banjo is played using picks on all fingers and plays melodically in very fast **tempos**. Singing is a common feature of bluegrass. The band features the mandolin, largely a result of Bill Monroe's influence as both the founder of bluegrass and a mandolin player. Bluegrass instrumentation is the same as old-time, but bluegrass has used instruments of all types. All instruments take accompanying lines while others take a solo lead. In between are **verses** and **chorus**. This reflects an influence from lined **hymns** and **spirituals** and classic **jazz**. The Live Five, a contemporary band led by local bluegrass celebrity Pete Wernick, features bluegrass tunes played on jazz instruments. It is also not unusual for bluegrass players to play on many different instruments. The familiar **repertoires** of festival jams offer opportunities to hone skills on unfamiliar instruments.

SOCIAL ORGANIZATION
OLD-TIME

Old-time jams take place on Wednesday nights in North Denver at the Common Ground Coffee House and in Boulder at alternating households. These groups play for dances, weddings, funerals, benefits, parties, festivals, and fairs, especially in the summertime. There are enough people who enjoy old-time in the area that the Mid-Winter Bluegrass Festival recently featured the Freighthoppers, a famous old-time band from North Carolina. It is common for the regional bluegrass festivals to share the stage with old-time music, including the traditional fiddler's contest. The Boulder chapter of the Colorado Friends of Old-Time Music and Dance, a national nonprofit organization, organizes old-time events.

See glossary for definition of boldfaced terms

BLUEGRASS

Weekly bluegrass jams are held in restaurants, churches, and other venues all along the Front Range. The Millsite, in Ward, holds its jam on Saturday nights; in Nederland the Acoustic Coffee House and the Sundowner Cafe jam on Sundays. A Boulder group meets on Tuesday nights and there is a weekly jam in Louisville, east of Boulder. Denver has hosted a number of jams since the late 1970s, including ones at the Old Town Pickin' Parlor and Ralph's Top Shop. Bluegrass groups play in restaurants and bars as well as at concerts, festivals, and fairs. Summer bluegrass festivals are held in Telluride, Pagosa Springs, Durango, and Lyons, Colorado, and in Cheyenne, Wyoming. The Telluride Bluegrass Festival is considered to be somewhat eclectic, featuring popular local groups like Leftover Salmon, a slamgrass, rock-oriented bluegrass band, and many other innovative groups. The Rocky Mountain Bluegrass Festival originated in Brighton, moved to Loveland, and is now held in Lyons. Once sold to Planet Bluegrass, an organization that produces bluegrass concerts, the festival changed names and is now known as Rocky Grass. Missouri native Ken Seaman of the Bluegrass Patriots founded the Mid-Winter Bluegrass Festival, which has now moved from Ft. Collins to Northglen in the Denver metropolitan area. This festival attracts people from as far north as Casper, Wyoming.

Societies dedicated to the preservation and dissemination of bluegrass include the Black Rose Society, which includes the Black Rose Band in Monument, Colorado. The Colorado Bluegrass Music Society (CBMS) was founded in 1972 and regularly publishes a newsletter. Pete Wernick of Longmont, Colorado, is the president of the International Bluegrass Organization, which is headquartered in Owensboro, Kentucky. Various radio stations across the Front Range have ongoing bluegrass programming and announce upcoming events. The CBMS has a telephone hotline that also announces events.

HISTORY
OLD-TIME

Old-time music dates back to the early music introduced by the French and English and includes many old tunes suitable for **clog-**

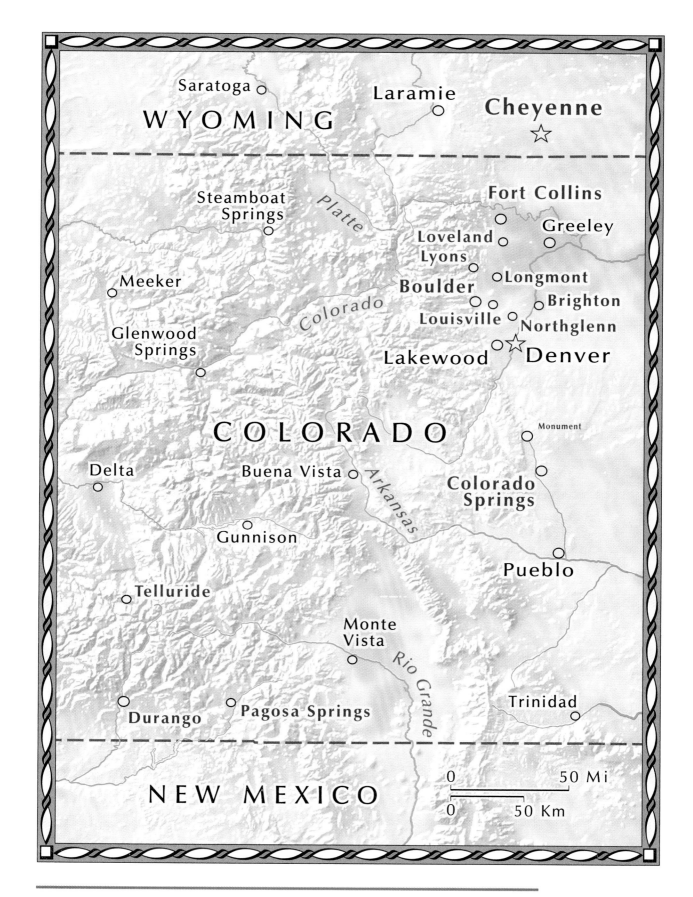

Bluegrass and Old Time Music in Colorado

Legendary Colorado bluegrass band Hot Rize, featuring Pete Wernick, Nick Forster, Tim O'Brien, and Charles Sawtelle, in its heyday.
Photo by Russ Arensman

ging and **contra dancing**. Old-time is a preserved tradition, and, on the Front Range, it attracts aficionados who develop a scholarly knowledge of the tradition. There are a few teachers of the old-time music, some of whom occasionally travel to give workshops.

BLUEGRASS

The strong presence of bluegrass along the Front Range dates back to 1973, when Bill Monroe put up seed money for the first regional festival, the Rocky Mountain Bluegrass Festival. Monroe was motivated in part by the desire to find a place for his traveling Bluegrass Festival bands to perform that was located between the east and west coasts. He approached the CBMS with his offer and supported the festival for three years. Bluegrass is an innovative music that was always a very fluid **genre**, beginning with Monroe's use of the electric organ and other instruments. On the Front Range, there are many bluegrass teachers at various local music stores and twenty or more bluegrass groups. The band called Front Range is now getting national attention but no longer works out of this area. Tom Wilhelm hosts a bluegrass radio program in Laramie, Wyoming, and also plays guitar in his group, the Big Hollow Bluegrass Band.

Of legendary status on the Front Range, the band Hot Rize started the bluegrass craze in this area and performed for large audiences in the 1980s. During the last five of those years, they became one of the top three bluegrass groups worldwide, appearing in Australia, Japan, France, Holland, Scandinavia, Ireland, England, Belgium, and Canada.

Hot Rize made their last recording in 1990 but still do up to ten reunion shows around the country every year. The group featured founder Pete Wernick on banjo, Nick Forster on mandolin and **bass**, Tim O'Brien on mandolin, fiddle, and vocals, and the late Charles Sawtelle (who died in 1999) on guitar. All of these artists became producers. Wernick (called Dr. Banjo in deference to his doctorate degree in sociology as well as his virtuosic banjo playing) conducts banjo workshops locally and nationally, including once a year between Christmas and New Year's. Nick Forster plays regularly as host of the nationally syndicated *E-Town* radio show, which is recorded in Boulder. Grammy nominee Tim O'Brien plays various instruments well and is a remarkable songwriter in various styles, as his many albums demonstrate. He helped shape the bluegrass scene in Boulder for many years but recently moved to Nashville.

The Telluride Bluegrass Festival, owned by Planet Bluegrass, has influenced bluegrass nationally by launching innovative trends. For many years, Telluride featured the New Grass Revival, a Kentucky group that developed different rhythms and styles and attracted younger, more modern, hippie-oriented audiences. The festival also has featured top names (such as Bill Monroe) and well-known artists of music of different kinds.

DOCUMENTARY RECORDINGS, FILMS, AND OTHER MATERIALS

Recordings representative of the Front Range groups in the 1990s include the Bluegrass Patriots' *E Pluribus Bluegrass* and Hot Rize's *Take It Home. Old Grass/New Grass* is

a Saturday-morning bluegrass program on KGNU, a Front Range listener-supported station on which the bluegrass program brings in the most revenue and reaches a worldwide audience via the Internet at www.banjo.com/CBMS.

Also of interest is *Pow'r Pickin'*, the newsletter of the Colorado Bluegrass Music Society. Information is available on the Internet at www.banjo.com/CBMS or by call-ing the group's telephone hotline at (303) 364-GRAS.

BIBLIOGRAPHY

E Pluribus Bluegrass. 1996. Bluegrass Patriots. RF CD 1776.

Take It Home. 1990. Hot Rize. Sugar Hill Recordings SH CD 3784.

Willis, Barry. (1997). *America's Music: Bluegrass.* Frank-town, CO: Pine Valley Music.

MUSIC OF THE ARK-LA-TEX

Michael Luster

Michael Luster is director of the Louisiana Folklife Festival and host of two weekly public radio programs in Monroe, Louisiana. He studied at the University of Arkansas before earning a Ph.D. in folklore and folklife from the University of Pennsylvania. He is former folklife specialist with the North Carolina Maritime Museum and was cultural consultant to the BET feature film When We Were Colored. *He is married to photographer Deborah Luster.*

The musical traditions of the Ark-La-Tex represent a mingling of those of African American and Anglo-Scots-Irish-American residents in the adjacent portions of Arkansas, Louisiana, and Texas—the westernmost extension of the American South. Settled by a combination of people from upland and lowland southern areas in the years following the Louisiana Purchase, the Ark-La-Tex is centered on the middle section of the Red River. Musically, the region's principal city is Shreveport, Louisiana, with important additional contributions from Texarkana (which straddles the border between Arkansas and Texas) and Tyler, Texas.

Shreveport's early involvement in radio broadcasting and especially the staging and broadcast of the *Louisiana Hayride* there between 1948 and 1960 made it an important center for the creation and dissemination of **hybridized** forms of American vernacular music such as **Western swing**, **honky-tonk**, and **rockabilly**, as well as distinct forms of African American **blues** and **gospel**.

MUSIC

The social music of the region can be divided into two broad categories, music for **secular** entertainments and music primarily intended for worship. Social dance music among African Americans and Anglo-Scots-Irish-Americans has existed in rural house party, tavern, and media-created settings. **Instruments** used have included the **fiddle**, **mandolin**, **guitar**, **electric guitar**, piano, drums, and a variety of other instruments. In African American tradition, the **repertoire** of Hudie "Lead Belly" Ledbetter (1888–1949) is particularly instructive as it combines **work songs**, dance pieces, parlor songs, **ballads**, and blues. Former Louisiana governor Jimmie Davis (1899–2000) performed and recorded a repertoire that ranges from double entendre blues to cowboy songs to sentimental songs of mother and home to sacred numbers, all of which reflect his time, his place, his culture, and his character.

While Lead Belly remains the best known of the region's blues performers,

other artists working in the area and the **form** include Henry "Ragtime Texas" Thomas (born 1874 in Big Sandy, Texas), one of the oldest of the recorded blues performers; his twenty-three issued recordings contain pre-blues forms that include the archaic **panpipe** or **quills**. Among the others working in blues were a number of artists active in the Blue Goose district of Shreveport during the 1920s and 1930s, including Jesse "Baby Face" Thomas and his older brother, Willard "Ramblin'" Thomas.

The rural **string band** music of the area included several groups who performed in late nineteenth- and early twentieth-century ensemble styles combining fiddles, mandolin, guitars, and, distinctively, the bowed string **bass**. While the recorded repertoire of groups such as the Pelican Wildcats, the Taylor-Griggs Louisiana Melody Makers, and the East Texas Serenaders include many sentimental parlor songs, they also prefigured the development of Western swing, the

syncopated, **improvisational**, fiddle-lead music that emerged in the 1930s. The region was the spawning ground of honky-tonk, a form of amplified ensemble country dance music that appeared with the move from the house party to the professional tavern. Rockabilly, a faster-paced, more blues-based, and instrumentally more restricted form that first emerged in the Mississippi Delta, received its national prominence through the agency of the *Louisiana Hayride.*

Sacred forms include a variety of cross-fertilized Pentecostal musics—many of which share features, instrumentation, and influence with the secular forms—as well as Baptist, Methodist, and other Protestant denominations. In the African American church, a distinctive musical form and setting are the networks of amplified, instrumentally accompanied **gospel quartets** and other ensembles that regularly perform throughout the region in an ongoing exchange of anniversary programs in which a

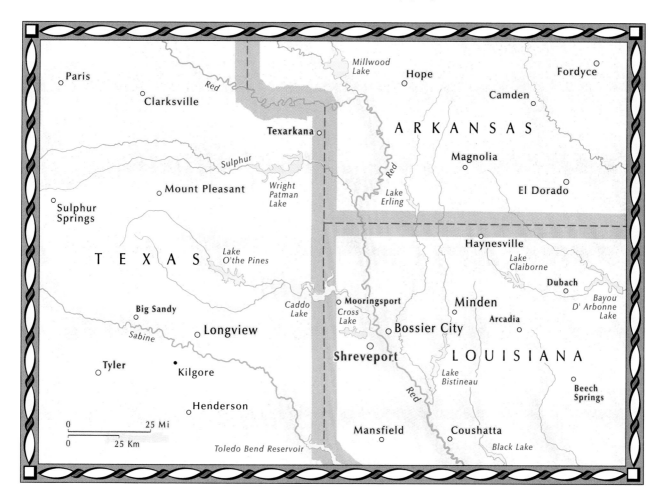

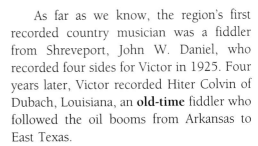

given group is honored by their peers in a special program of spoken tributes, musical selections, and financial offerings.

HISTORY

We have little direct or documented knowledge of music in the Ark-La-Tex before 1900. Scott Joplin, "the King of the **Ragtime** Writers," was born in 1868 near what would soon be named Texarkana. His father played the fiddle and his mother played the **banjo**; his siblings played the violin and sang. Joplin took to the piano and had developed a regional reputation at churches and socials by the early 1880s and soon began to explore the improvisational music associated with area clubs and honky-tonks. While still a teenager, he began performing with a vocal group called the Texas Medley Quartet before heading north to St. Louis around 1885. There he continued to work as a vocalist and a pianist.

Meanwhile, other significant figures in the Ark-La-Tex tradition were also emerging on the scene. At Mooringsport, Louisiana, in 1895, the young Hudie Ledbetter received a small **button accordion** from his uncle, a guitar-playing songster. "Ragtime Texas" seems to have been performing as an itinerant songster as early as 1890 and may have appeared at the Columbian Exposition in Chicago in 1893. Jimmie Davis was born in 1899 (1902 by some accounts) to a fiddling father and a **harmonica**-playing mother near Beech Springs, Louisiana.

Lead Belly got his first twelve-string guitar in 1912, the year he met another itinerant guitarist and singer, Blind Lemon Jefferson. A fixture on the streets of Dallas, Jefferson would ultimately work with and influence a number of Ark-La-Tex musicians before his death in 1929, including Aaron "T-Bone" Walker, a native of Linden, Texas. Lead Belly's impact did not make itself known until much later, however, since he ended up spending many of the next twenty-two years in prison before being released to the custody of Texas folklorist John Lomax.

As far as we know, the region's first recorded country musician was a fiddler from Shreveport, John W. Daniel, who recorded four sides for Victor in 1925. Four years later, Victor recorded Hiter Colvin of Dubach, Louisiana, an **old-time** fiddler who followed the oil booms from Arkansas to East Texas.

Nineteen-twenty-eight saw the first radio broadcasts of Jimmie Davis as well as his first tentative recordings. That same year, Shreveport blues artist Ramblin' Thomas and the Taylor-Griggs Louisiana Melody Makers, a string band from Arcadia, Louisiana, each made professional recordings, and the Pelican Wildcats, another Louisiana string band featuring Bill Nettles, Norman Nettles, and Buddy Jones, began broadcasting from Shreveport. Jimmie Davis began recording in earnest for Victor the following year, the same year that Ramblin' Thomas's younger brother, Jesse "Baby Face" Thomas, recorded the regionally significant "Blue Goose Blues," a tribute to Shreveport's most celebrated blues district. Two of that area's denizens were a pair of blues guitarists, Ed Shaffer and Oscar Woods, who began recording both on their own and as backup for Jimmie Davis in 1930 for a series of bawdy blues outings in what may have been one of the first integrated recording sessions.

Radio station KWKH had gone on the air in Shreveport back in 1925, and for the next few years it gave listeners a chance to hear the music of Jimmie Davis and other singers. But it was not until 1933, when Leon Chappell and the Shelton Brothers left Tyler, Texas, and joined KWKH as the Lone Star Cowboys, that the station began its reign as an important beacon for country music. Their recording of "Just Because," remade twenty-one years later by Elvis Presley, was a regional sensation and proved instrumental in launching KWKH's *Saturday Night Round Up,* a weekly stage show and broadcast from Shreveport's Municipal Auditorium featuring artists such as Jimmie Davis, the Rice Brothers, the Blackwood Brothers, the Sunshine Boys, and the Shelton Brothers.

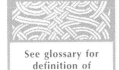

See glossary for definition of boldfaced terms

The show debuted in 1936 and continued until the outbreak of World War II, encompassing the years between the death of Western **swing** founder Milton Brown, the emergence of the East Texas honky-tonk sound with musicians such as Moon Mullican, and the sweet, if borrowed, success of Jimmie Davis's "You Are My Sunshine."

During the war years, Mullican teamed up with the Shelton Brothers and Western swing fiddler Johnny Gimble of Tyler, Texas, to back Jimmie Davis and his successful bid for the Louisiana governorship. A Kentucky native, Harmie Smith, relocated to Shreveport and billed himself as the Ozark Mountaineer, broadcasting over KWKH and recording a session for Victor backed by Owen Perry, a Western swing fiddler turned hot guitarist, and the solid rhythm guitar of future honky-tonk star Webb Pierce. All three performers were fixtures on early morning radio in Shreveport.

On April 3, 1948, the void left by the old *Saturday Night Round Up* was filled when KWKH launched a new program called the *Louisiana Hayride*. Like its predecessor, it was a Saturday-night stage show and broadcast originating from the Municipal Auditorium. With KWKH's new clear-channel, 50,000-watt signal, the station and the program quickly became a powerful voice in country music, a suitable rival to the established success of Nashville's Grand Ole Opry.

Both regional performers and those from further away flocked to the station to vie for a slot on the program. One of the first was Alabama singer and songwriter Hank Williams, who used his *Hayride* appearances as a springboard to wider fame and an eventual spot on the Grand Ole Opry, setting a pattern that would be followed by some of the biggest stars of country music in the 1950s. Among them were Louisiana natives Webb Pierce, Faron Young, and Floyd Cramer; Arkansans Jim Ed Brown and the Wilburn Brothers; and Texans George Jones and Jim Reeves. Of the major stars, only Slim Whitman and Johnny Horton refused to leave the *Hayride*.

With the 1950s came a new strain of country music, one brewed not in the honky-tonks but by the bedroom radios and snatched window glimpses of white artists enamored of the new jump blues some were calling "rock and roll." Elvis Presley went into a Memphis recording studio in July 1954, and by October he had secured a place on the *Louisiana Hayride* playing what had been dubbed "rockabilly," a hybrid of rock and roll and the **hillbilly** music that was the *Hayride*'s usual fare.

By the end of the following year, Presley too was gone, taking with him the *Hayride* drummer D. J. Fontana, but in his wake came a host of new rockabillies, again mixing homegrown talent with those drawn to the *Hayride*'s reputation for making reputations. Among them were Johnny Cash, Carl Perkins, Sleepy LaBeef, Bob Luman, and Shreveport's own Dale Hawkins. Hawkins and guitarist James Burton used the KWKH studios after hours to record "Suzi Q," which featured a tough guitar lick, a clanging **cowbell**, and a vocal that got them placed on the otherwise all-black Chess record label out of Chicago. Hawkins would go on to successes in record production and as a bandleader with a reputation for identifying outstanding guitarists from James Burton to Kenny Bill Stinson. Burton would find further fame in California, first with Bob Luman, then as a featured television performer with Ricky Nelson, as a studio session ace, and as a long-time guitarist with Elvis Presley.

Not so the *Louisiana Hayride*. It ceased to be a weekly program in 1960, the year Johnny Horton was killed in a Texas car wreck. Shreveport saw additional successes with such British-influenced rock bands as the Uniques and John Fred and the Playboys on the local label Paula Records. Another local label, Ram Records, enjoyed some regional hits but is primarily important for the pioneering role of its founder Mira Smith and her partner and protégée, Margaret Lewis. The two women gained some notoriety as songwriters and performers, and Smith became the first inductee in the Women in the Music Industry Hall of Fame. Margaret Lewis Warwick is the leading force, along with contemporary artists the Blue-

birds, Kenny Wayne Shepherd, and Dr. Cookie and Louisiana Dan, in carrying the musical legacy of Shreveport—and by extension the Ark-La-Tex—into the twenty-first century.

BIBLIOGRAPHY

Boyd, J. A. (1998). *The Jazz of the Southwest.* Austin: University of Texas Press.

Brown, M. (1988). "The Grigg Family and the Taylor-Griggs Louisiana Melody Makers: The History of a North Louisiana String Band." *Louisiana Folklife* 12 (September):16–24.

Escott, C.; Merritt, George; and MacEwen, William. (1994). *Hank Williams: The Biography.* Boston: Little, Brown&Company.

Guralnick, P. (1994). *Last Train to Memphis: The Rise of Elvis Presley.* Boston: Little, Brown&Company.

Logan, H., and Sloan, Bill. (1998). *Elvis, Hank, and Me: Making Musical History on the* Louisiana Hayride. New York: St. Martin's Press.

Reed, A. W. (1985). "Scott Joplin: Pioneer." In *Ragtime: Its History, Composers, and Music,* J. E. Hasse. New York: Schirmer Books.

Weill, G. (1977). *You Are My Sunshine: The Jimmie Davis Story, an Affectionate Biography.* Gretna, LA: Pelican Publishing Company.

Wolfe, C., and Lornell, Kip. (1994). *The Life and Legend of Leadbelly.* New York: HarperPerennial.

WESTERN SWING

Guy Logsdon

A cowboy singer and musician, Guy Logsdon was for many years the director of libraries at the University of Tulsa. He has lectured extensively on cowboy music and poetry and collects and publishes Western songs. Logsdon was one of the organizers of the Cowboy Poetry Gathering in Elko, Nevada, and also serves as the director of the annual Oklahoma Cowboy Poetry Gathering held at the National Cowboy and Western Heritage Museum in Oklahoma City. The following essay originally appeared in the 1982 Smithsonian Festival of American Folklife program guide and was updated for publication in American Musical Traditions.

Western swing has become the traditional music of Oklahoma. While it was "born in Texas," it was in Tulsa where it matured. One of the major figures in its development, Johnnie Lee Wills, lived in Tulsa for fifty years and continued to play at dances there until his death in 1984. And Hank Thompson, the man who took Western swing from the Southwest to national and then international audiences, lived near and worked out of Tulsa for nearly forty years before moving to Texas, where he still performs.

A cultural blend of musical styles, Western swing has one primary characteristic—a danceable beat. While country and **bluegrass music** primarily emerged as listening traditions, the principal audience for Western swing is a dancing crowd. If the listeners on a Saturday night outnumber the dancers, the band has failed at playing good Western swing.

Cowboys loved to dance; if women were not available, they danced with each other,

calling it a "stag dance." In the late nineteenth century, as the range cattle industry moved northward and the cotton industry moved westward, the cowboys' music and passion for dancing began to blend with the black **blues** brought from the cotton fields. The blend effected a change in **fiddle** styles, the fiddler adopting a slower "**long bow**" technique and adding blues **improvisations**. Also, the fiddler became sufficiently versatile to accompany any popular style of dancing.

Bob Wills—the "Daddy of Western Swing"—was born into a Texas fiddling tradition. Although he grew up hearing and playing ranch house dances (his father was a cotton farmer), he was also exposed to the work music and blues of the black workers in the cotton fields. In 1929, after holding a variety of jobs as a young man, Bob played as a "blackface" fiddler in a medicine show in Ft. Worth, where he met a young **guitarist**, Herman Arnspiger. As a team they started playing house dances in Ft. Worth

The Original Light Crust Doughboys c. 1931: Milton Brown, vocalist; Durwood Brown, guitarist; Truit Kinzey, announcer; Bob Wills, fiddler; and Herman Arnspiger, guitar.
Courtesy of the Folklife Program, North Carolina Arts Council, Dept. of Cultural Resources.

and were soon joined by a singer, Milton Brown.

In 1931 they took the name "The Original Light Crust Doughboys" and advertised the Burrus-Milling Elevator Company products over the radio and through personal appearances. Because the company's general manager, W. Lee O'Daniel, did not want them to play dances, Milton left the group and, soon afterwards, Bob organized his own

band. O'Daniel disliked Bob and through financial influence with radio stations forced Wills out of Texas as well as Oklahoma City. As a last desperate try, Bob and his manager, O.W. Mayo, convinced KVOO Radio management in Tulsa to give them a chance to perform on February 9, 1934. They were an immediate success, and when O'Daniel tried to interfere, it was he, not Wills, who had to leave. As a result, Tulsa soon became the

Johnny Gimble (right) with his son Dick Gimble (guitar), photographed in the late 1980s.
Photograph © Nick Spitzer, courtesy the Smithsonian Institution, Folk Masters

The Texas Playboys and Johnny Gimble

Nick Spitzer is a folklorist widely known for his work on Creole cultures and cultural policy and as a public radio broadcaster. Artistic director and host of the "Folk Masters" concert series from 1990–1997 at Carnegie Hall and Wolf Trap, he also served as senior folklife specialist for the Smithsonian Institution and as the first Louisiana State Folklorist. In addition, Spitzer hosts American Routes, *the nationally broadcast weekly public radio music series. He is professor of cultural conservation and urban studies at the University of New Orleans. The following essay is a combination of two previously published essays. The first piece on the Texas Playboys is reprinted from the program guide for the Folk Masters 1992 concert series, held April 1–May 8 at the Barns of Wolf Trap in Vienna, Virginia; the second piece on Johnny Gimble is reprinted from the program guide for the Folk Masters 1993 concert series, held March 5–April 10 at the Barns of Wolf Trap.*

Country music has long been referred to as the "White man's **blues**." Jimmie Rodgers is the best-known early country music star with significant influence from blues, but black influence on Anglo-American folk styles and their commercial transformation neither began nor ended with him. Country **fiddlers** were long influenced by local blues musicians or by hearing **jazz** on 78s. Likewise, contemporary **honky-tonk** country music and rock and roll have their sources partly in **rockabilly**—the blending of country music with **rhythm and blues**. Two major figures popularized the blending of Anglo- and African American styles in the southwest and southeast: Bob Wills and Elvis Presley.

Bob Wills's Texas Playboys were the most influential **Western swing** band in the history of country music. With his roots in **old-time** Texas fiddling, and with a keen sense of showmanship,

Wills helped fuse country music and jazz in a manner that touches artists today from Merle Haggard to Ricky Skaggs. His early 1930s work with "The Original Light Crust Doughboys" band selling flour in radio and personal appearances in the Ft. Worth–Dallas area recalls the fusion of tradition and the marketplace that is at the heart of much American popular folk-derived music.

Wills's tenure as fiddler and leader of the Texas Playboys spanned four decades. The Western swing sound brought together breakdown fiddling, **string band** style, cowboy songs, Dixieland jazz, **big band**, and **minstrelsy**. During the Depression and afterwards, the music defined the cultural transition rural Anglo-Americans were making as new patterns of migration and industrialization affected their lives. The house and barn dance became the roadside honky-tonk and city ballroom. The fiddles started working in sections and **improvising** like horns a la big-band jazz. With his Texas Playboys, Bob Wills was able to leave his Texas and Oklahoma bases and become a national figure. As a result, songs like "San Antonio Rose," "Faded Love," and "Take Me Back to Tulsa" are permanently imprinted in our consciousness.

Several outstanding musicians have been associated with the Wills bands at various times. Many of them have gone on to have influential careers as session players, soloists, and members of various "Texas Playboys" reunion bands.

Johnny Gimble is widely regarded as the greatest Western swing fiddler alive. Also a master **mandolin** player, Gimble grew up on a farm in Tyler, Texas, with four brothers who also played music. Their musical education came at the house dances and family farm gatherings where they were called on to play **reels**, breakdowns, **waltzes**, and **schottisches**. At thirteen he and his brothers played on local radio. Later he

(Continued on the next page)

"Capital of Western Swing"; ultimately the four most popular Western swing bands called Tulsa their home.

Within six years Bob and His Texas Playboys were favorites throughout the Southwest, and musical legends were beginning to emerge from Cain's Ballroom, their headquarters. Their popularity was

based on their ability to play any kind of danceable music: **waltzes**, **polkas**, and **two-steps** as well as **ballads** and **fox-trots**. Furthermore, they never priced themselves beyond the pocketbook of the working man.

In 1940, Bob successfully worked in California and, with the outbreak of the war, found great demand for his music on the West

(Continued from previous page)
joined the Shelton Brothers on the influential KWKH in Shreveport, home of the *Louisiana Hayride* [program]. Gimble also played in the campaign band for the singing governor of Louisiana, Jimmie Davis of "You Are My Sunshine" fame.

In 1949, after serving in World War II, he joined Bob Wills's Texas Playboys. More radio and then television work followed on the *Big D Jamboree* in Dallas, and, more recently, *Hee-Haw* and *Nashville Now*. As the premier Western swing session man in Nashville and elsewhere, Gimble recorded with Lefty Frizzell, Marty Robbins, Ray Price, Chet Atkins, Willie Nelson, George Strait, and many others. Johnny stimulated the Western swing revival of the 1970s, and he was named the Country Music Association's instrumentalist of the year in 1978 and four more times since. Gimble now resides near Austin in Dripping Springs. Despite his wide success and recognition as a fiddler, Johnny keeps to a Texas country gentleman demeanor—not forgetting the house parties and family gatherings in Tyler that shape his musical direction to this day.

Herb Remington of South Bend, Indiana, has been a definitive stylist on a definitive **instrument** of Western swing, the **steel guitar**. Wills hired Remington on the spot just out of the service in 1946 on the strength of an audition. He played with the band for the next four years before going on to work with Hank Penny and T. Texas Tyler. Remington is especially remembered for his tune "Remington Ride," which is still played in jazz and swing circles. He has lived in Houston since the 1950s, and his shop, Remington Steel, is a gathering place for players seeking his handmade instruments or just some good advice. Herb has been responsible for putting members of the old Texas Playboys back together for festivals and programs.

Eldon Shamblin of Wetherford, Oklahoma, was Bob Wills's **guitarist** from 1937 until the bandleader's death in 1975. He was absent only during World War II service. Shamblin first played guitar in bands around Oklahoma City. He refers to his pre-war days with Wills as musical "basic training." Shamblin's single-string **electric guitar** lines were highly influential on an entire generation of country players.

Nick Spitzer

Coast. He encouraged his brother, Johnnie Lee Wills, who had been a Texas Playboy when they arrived in Tulsa, to organize his own band and helped him in doing so. When World War II forced the Texas Playboys to dissolve and Bob moved to California in 1942, Johnnie Lee Wills and All His Boys continued the daily radio shows and the dances at Cain's Ballroom. In fact, many southwesterners who with fondness recall listening to Bob actually had been listening to Johnnie Lee.

By the late 1950s, rock and roll and television had changed the dancing habits in the Southwest. In 1964, Johnnie Lee disbanded his group after thirty years of playing for a radio show and one dance six days and nights each week. He remained in demand for dances and personal appearances, but not at the grueling pace of the past. As he neared seventy, Johnnie Lee Wills had provided dancing entertainment in Tulsa and the Southwest for forty-nine years. No other Western swing leader can lay claim to having played as many dances.

Leon McAuliffe joined the Texas Playboys in Tulsa in 1935 and became the first full-time steel guitarist in country-western music. He was influential in making the **steel guitar** the popular **instrument** it is today. Following the war, Leon organized his Cimarron Boys, and the Cimarron Ballroom in Tulsa became their headquarters. He continues to be a popular attraction with the Original Texas Playboys, but he disbanded the Cimarron Boys in 1968.

Hank Thompson and His Brazos Valley Boys moved to Tulsa in the late 1950s, but his career started in Texas in 1945. Hank is the leading second-generation bandleader. His accomplishments are legion, one of which was to be the first to take Western swing to northern and eastern states as well as abroad. Another very important but now nearly forgotten swing band moved to Tulsa in 1942—Al Clauser and the Oklahoma Outlaws. They played at the Crystal City dance hall in southwestern Tulsa and over KTUL radio station. As a young girl in the mid-1940s, Clara Ann

Fowler became their featured singer and produced her first record with them; she later became nationally famous as Patti Page. Al continued to make appearances until 1968.

The Western swing band requires fiddles, drums, a **bass** fiddle, horns, a steel guitar, and a rhythm guitar performing in a strong, heavy rhythmic style. The voicing of the fiddles provides the distinctive sound for each band. Bob Wills voiced his fiddles to play **harmony** above the lead fiddle, Leon McAuliffe voiced his below the lead to simulate a saxophone-trombone effect, and Spade Cooley, an Oklahoman who had a popular California band, used arrangements that voiced the fiddles above the lead, punctuating the music with a strong staccato sound.

The sound and the quality of Western swing music was determined by the leader. Musicians "play better" behind an outstanding leader, and the greatest of the leaders have made Tulsa their home.

BIBLIOGRAPHY

The Bob Wills Anthology. 1993. Sony Music Special Products WK 75055. CD reissue of 1973 Columbia Records LP.

Malone, Bill C. (1968). *Country Music U.S.A.* Austin: University of Texas Press.

Townsend, Charles R. (1976). *San Antonio Rose: The Life and Music of Bob Wills.* Urbana: University of Illinois Press.

Bob Wills and his Texas Playboys at the height of their popularity in 1935. L to r: C. W. Mayo (band manager), Art Haines (trumpet), Robert "Zeb" McNally (saxophone), Leon McAuliffe (slide guitar), Herman Arnspiger (guitar), Sleepy Johnson (guitar), Bob Wills (fiddle), Willim F. "Smokey" Dacus (drums), Jesse Ashlock (fiddle), Johnnie Lee Wills (tenor banjo), Tommy Duncan (vocals), Son Lansford (bass). *Photograph Courtesy of the Folklife Program, North Carolina Arts Council, Dept. of Cultural Resources.*

OLD-TIME DANCE FIDDLING IN THE NORTHWEST

Vivian Williams

Vivian Williams of Seattle, Washington, has been playing fiddle since 1960. Over the years she has played for old-time dancing, contra dancing, and bluegrass and has judged and competed successfully in fiddle contests in the United States and Canada. She is owner of Voyager Recordings and Publications, which specializes in fiddle music (particularly from the Northwest), and helped found the Seattle Folklore Society and Northwest Folklife, an organization that produces festivals, arranges for traditional artists to perform in schools, and otherwise promotes folk traditions of the Northwest.

Beginning with the French and Scottish Canadian fur trappers in the early nineteenth century, traditional dance fiddling, or what we now call "**old-time** fiddling," has been an important part of the northwestern cultural fabric. Later waves of immigration brought a wide variety of fiddlers to the region. Most prominent in terms of **fiddle** styles were settlers from Canadian, northern Plains midwestern, and Scandinavian communities (first-generation as well as via Minnesota and North Dakota). In addition, Irish, Scottish, German, Métis, and Mexican music were also important. While some communities maintained distinct ethnic identities, there was also a mixing of dance and fiddle traditions at logging and mining camps as well as schoolhouse, grange, and house dances through the nineteenth and up to the mid–twentieth centuries. An evening's dance most typically included **waltzes**, **schottisches**, **two-steps**, and **quadrilles** (**square dances**). Depending on the community, one might also dance hambos, hop waltzes, **polkas**, or the newer pattern dances such as the varsouvienne, tuxedo, butterfly or three-, five- or seven-steps. A good fiddler could play unaccompanied or was "seconded" by another fiddler. Portable parlor organs or pianos were also common as accompaniment. **Guitars, button accordions**, **banjos**, and **mandolins** became more prevalent in the early twentieth century. Later, fiddle-led dance bands also included saxophones, lap steels, flutes, and other **instruments**.

Old-time fiddlers raised in rural northwestern communities before the 1940s, while steeped in the **hoedowns**, waltzes, and two-steps popular throughout the ranch and farming country of the West, also reflect a strong Canadian and Scandinavian influence. There isn't a single "northwestern style," but rather several clusters of styles that reflect the fiddlers' family backgrounds and early influences. Over several generations, these styles have tended to blend together, yet still retain many essential ele-

Please see Chapter 25 in this volume for biographical information on Vivian Williams.

In the mid–nineteenth century, the site of Weiser (pronounced "Wee-zer"), Idaho, on the Snake River close to the Oregon border, was a way station for Oregon Trail emigrants. **Fiddle** contests were held there for a few years before World War I. In 1953, Blaine Stubblefield, Chamber of Commerce secretary, started the Northwest Mountain Fiddlers' Contest, which became the National Old-time Fiddlers' Contest in 1963 in conjunction with Idaho's Territorial Centennial. It has become one of the largest and most prestigious contests in the country, attracting over 360 contestants in 1998.

The contest takes place in the Weiser high school gymnasium during the third full week in June, from Monday morning through Saturday evening. There are eight divisions: the Championship division, which is open to anyone; the Small Fry division (for contestants under the age of nine); the Junior-Junior division (ages nine to twelve); the Junior division (ages thirteen to seventeen); the Young Adult division (ages eighteen to thirty-six); the Adult division (ages thirty-seven to fifty-nine); the Senior division (ages sixty to sixty-nine); and the Senior-Senior division (ages seventy and over). For each round, the contestant plays a **hoedown**, a **waltz**, and another dance tune that is neither a hoedown nor a waltz, with a total time limit of four minutes. Depending on the division, successful contestants play three to six elimination rounds.

Judging is done by six-member panel, only five of whom work at a time so that each judge gets a break from the long days of listening. The judges are themselves top fiddlers from many regions of the United States and Canada. They sit in a separate room where they can hear the contestants' playing but cannot see them or hear their names. Without consulting with the other judges, each judge fills out a score sheet that has categories for **old-time** fiddling style, danceability, rhythm and timing, and tone quality. In each round the highest score and the lowest score given to each fiddler are thrown out. The total of the scores from all the rounds determines the winner.

Contestants come from all over the country, with the majority coming from the western United States. In the early years, the local fiddling styles of Idaho and Montana prevailed. Over the years more and more of the competition has been dominated by fiddlers who play in the Texas-derived "contest style" pioneered by Benny Thomasson. In this style, creative **variations** on the original melody are valued, and it requires clever editing to fit these elaborations into the time limit and still maintain the recognizability of the tunes.

In addition to the contest itself, hundreds of musicians show up to camp, socialize, and play informally in **jam sessions**. Here can be found players of many styles of music, including Texas-style fiddling, swing, southern old-time, **bluegrass**, **jazz**, Canadian, Irish, midwest **accordion** music, and local dance styles. During contest week, the population of Weiser, normally a little over 4,000, doubles as contestants and non–contestants alike gather at this huge and exciting annual reunion of musicians and their families, friends, and fiddle fans.

Vivian Williams

ments of rhythm and phrasing of earlier generations of fiddlers. Rooted in one or another of three broad styles—Scandinavian and northern European, Canadian and Celtic, or midwestern and western—they also typically incorporate tunes and stylistic elements heard from other fiddlers in their community when they were young.

Clair Lundin (now of Spokane, Washington), for example, learned Swedish tunes and style from his family in the Idaho panhandle in the twenties. These form the basic framework for his phrasing and bowing even as he plays other types of tunes such as **jigs** and **reels** from Canada or hoedowns from the "Missouri homesteaders" who also settled in the community. Many of the northwestern fiddlers of Swedish or Norwegian background have a decidedly Scandinavian "accent," as they incorporate a pulsing Scandinavian bow stroke or apply the "long-short-short" schottische bowing to hoedowns and reels (similar to what American fiddlers call the "bluegrass" or "Nashville" shuffle).

Similarly, another cluster of fiddlers draws on a crisp and bouncy western Cana-

dian sense of phrasing, rife with two- and three-note slurs across the beat. Another subgroup, particularly in Oregon, draws much more on Missouri and midwestern saw stroke and shuffle bowing as a rhythmic framework that they also apply to waltzes, jigs, or polkas of northern European, Canadian, or Mexican origin.

Partly due to this mix of influences as well as to waltzes being a common thread with immigrant communities in the Northwest, the region's fiddlers are particularly known for their lyrical, very danceable waltzes. Most are also as at home with "six-eighters" (jigs) as they are with a Missouri-style hoedown. At a **jam session** today, an old-time Norwegian schottische easily follows a rag from Texas. Though the "old-time" community dances are less a part of rural community life today, Montana, Idaho, Washington, and Oregon have all had active old-time fiddle associations since the 1960s that have served to bring fiddlers together at camp-outs, fiddle shows, and contests. Older fiddlers continue to share the dance tunes of their youth, and younger fiddlers learning in that context hear much the same mix of styles heard a generation ago.

As is true across the country, recorded music and modern trends in fiddling have had a great impact. **Swing** and **Western** swing have been very popular since 1930s. Square dance clubs continued to include live fiddlers until the switch to recorded music in the 1950s. The 1950s and 1960s brought the beginnings of the urban folk revival movement with a particular interest in southern Appalachian fiddling and square dancing, **bluegrass**, and Irish music. In Seattle, the "Skandia" society was at the forefront of an international revival of Scandinavian music and dance. With the national fiddle contest in Weiser, Idaho, and Benny Thomasson and Dick Barrett moving to the area, Texas-style contest fiddling has swept through the region.

Mark O'Connor is the best known of many great "Texas" or progressive fiddlers to emerge from the Northwest since the 1970s. By the 1980s, the New England **contra dance** movement was well established in the cities of the Northwest. The music at these dances ranges from a traditional New England style to the modern, rock-influenced, contra dance band sound. Though these are largely separate communities of musicians, there is a great deal of overlap in **repertoire**, and some of the traditional northwestern fiddlers also play for the contra dances.

IRISH TRADITIONAL AND POPULAR MUSICS IN THE UNITED STATES

Rebecca S. Miller

An ethnomusicologist and public-sector folklorist, Rebecca S. Miller has documented and presented the traditional arts of a number of immigrant and refugee communities throughout the United States since 1982. Her work has culminated in publications, recordings, festivals, and radio and video documentaries. Miller spent 1996–1997 doing dissertation research on traditional music and cultural representation in Carriacou, Grenada, on a Fulbright fellowship. She received her doctorate in music (ethnomusicology) from Brown University in 2000.

One of the largest ethnic groups in the United States, Irish Americans number an estimated 38,736,000 (according to the 1990 census). Twenty-four percent of those claiming Irish ancestry live in the Northeast; 25 percent in the Midwest; 33 percent in the South; and 17 percent in the West, with particularly large immigrant and second- and third-generation communities in New York City, Boston, Philadelphia, Chicago, and other cities. Irish immigration to the United States began in the eighteenth century and continues to this day, with new immigrants replenishing a rich legacy of folk and popular culture, including a variety of musical **genres**. This transnational exchange of Irish music is also accomplished through international media and the commercial recording industry as well as via the migration patterns of young Irish between Ireland and the United States.

Significant musical expressions of Irish Americans span the generations and include a variety of traditional and popular musical genres. Among them are Irish instrumental dance music and ***sean-nós*** ("old-style") song, contemporary Irish folk song, high art Irish American song (popularized by singers such as John McCormack in the 1920s and 1930s), **hybridized** Irish American popular song, showband music, and **Celtic** rock.

HISTORY

The mid-1800s saw the arrival of massive numbers of Irish who came to America to escape the devastating effects of the Irish potato blight. Unlike the earlier Scots-Irish immigrants who settled in rural areas throughout the east coast, the newly arrived Irish moved to America's cities—New York, Chicago, Boston, Philadelphia, and New Orleans. In general, the Irish language and other aspects of traditional Irish culture did not survive the transition from a rural, agrarian-based life to an urban American lifestyle. Irish traditional music, however, proved surpris-

ingly resilient, and master **fiddlers**, pipers, accordionists, flutists, and others found work on the vaudeville circuit and in dance halls, pubs, and other venues. Similarly, Irish American popular music such as vaudeville numbers, Irish nostalgic songs, and **ballads**, for example, were easily integrated into popular American culture.

By the early 1900s, New York City had become a focal point for Irish music when record companies reacted to the market potential of the "Golden Age of Irish Music" and began producing hundreds of 78 rpm recordings (McCullough 1974). During the first three decades of the twentieth century, the "Golden Age" was fueled by the arrival of hundreds of thousands of immigrants who hailed primarily from the northern and western regions of Ireland. By the early 1930s, Irish immigration dramatically decreased due to the Depression and, later, World War II. These considerations, along with a wartime shellac ban, curtailed the recording industry's interest in ethnic music in general.

Shortages of consumer goods and rising unemployment marked the years in Ireland just after World War II. Small farms and large families forced the young Irish to seek work elsewhere, but with little industry in Ireland, jobs were scarce, leaving many with little choice but to emigrate. Thus, the increase in Irish immigration to the United States during the latter half of the 1940s was notable; between 1941 and 1945, only 1,059 Irish came to the U.S., whereas 26,444 arrived between 1946 and 1950. The numbers increased even more after Congress passed the Immigration and Nationality Act of 1952 (also known as the McCarran-Walter Act), which allowed, among other things, unrestricted immigration from the Western Hemisphere and a stated preferences for those with relatives who were American citizens. Thus favoring Irish immigrants, this bill opened the doors wide to a surge of new arrivals.

By the 1950s, the traditional Irish music scene in the United States had waned to the point that there was little, if any, op-

See glossary for definition of boldfaced terms

portunity for public performance. The exceptions were monthly *ceilis* (group folk dances) sponsored in some East Coast cities by the **Gaelic** League and an annual *feis* (Irish music festival/competition) in New York City sponsored by the United Irish Counties Association. In general, however, the new Irish immigrants were eager to assimilate into American society and leave behind the vestiges of folk culture. Many Irish traditional musicians who came to the United States during this era were thus forced to set aside their **instruments** as a professional endeavor or learn a more contemporary style of music such as showband music or country-western, for example (Miller 1996). The rare opportunity to play traditional music was at the occasional house music *seisun* (session).

A resurgence of interest in Irish traditional music had its beginnings in the mid-1960s as a result of a number of cultural and social developments both in the United States and in Ireland. Most influential was the international attention brought to Irish music by the Clancy Brothers and Tommy Makem with their gutsy renditions of Irish folk songs. Many who play Irish traditional music today initially became interested in the older styles from listening to these performers and eventually turned their attention to the older masters of instrumental music.

Simultaneously, the revival of interest in traditional music in Ireland was sparked under the aegis of *Comhaltas Ceolteoiri Eireann* (Irish Musicians' Association) and soon extended to America. As a result, music seisuns began anew in pubs and Irish social halls in New York, Boston, Philadelphia, Chicago, and elsewhere, and concerts of traditional bands from Ireland—Planxty, the Bothy Band, the Boys of the Lough, and the Chieftains, for example—were presented in both general and Irish American venues. Eventually, many of the older traditional players who had immigrated in the 1940s and 1950s were invited to perform as well.

The 1960s also saw the physical dissolution of many Irish neighborhoods in major American cities. As the demographics of

these neighborhoods changed, Irish families increasingly moved to the suburbs, and for a number of Irish and Irish Americans, the loss of immediate physical community, combined with the outside recognition of Irish traditional culture, encouraged a reevaluation of heritage and community. Unlike earlier generations, Irish immigrants from the 1940s and 1950s were able to retain closer ties with Ireland via affordable transatlantic flights. Irish-born parents could renew an interest in their heritage and inspire the same in their children.

The sense of importance of ethnicity thus rekindled, the 1970s and 1980s saw an unprecedented number of Irish American youngsters flocking to schools for Irish traditional music and **step dance** in major American cities. Two of New York's most popular Irish music schools—John Glynn's in Brooklyn (taken over after his death in 1971 by his daughter, the late Maureen Glynn Connolly) and the late County Limerick fiddler Martin Mulvihill's in the Bronx—taught literally thousands of students music on a variety of instruments. In addition, the late 1970s saw the creation of several annual Irish traditional music festivals, including the Philadelphia Ceili Group's Irish Music Festival; the Irish Arts Center's Irish Traditional Music Festival at Snug Harbor, Staten Island, New York; the Milwaukee Irish Music Festival; and the Annual Washington Irish Folk Festival at Wolf Trap, Virginia.

IRISH TRADITIONAL DANCE MUSIC

Traditional Irish instrumental music originated centuries ago primarily as accompaniment for dancing. Today, in both Ireland and the United States, the music is played most often in concert settings, at Irish traditional music festivals, and at informal seísuns as well as at ceilis in community and familial contexts. Like most folk arts, the music has historically been passed down from the elder to the younger generation as an **oral tradition**. In the United States, in-

creasing numbers of players—those who are Irish or Irish American, as well as non–Irish—learn the music from recordings, radio airplay, and from each other at Irish music seísuns and festivals. Playing styles and **repertoire** are generally learned through listening and imitation, tunes are composed more or less anonymously, and the music is, on the whole, crafted through a communal process.

Among the most commonly found instruments in traditional Irish music today are the fiddle, **tin whistle**, wooden flute, and **uilleann pipes** (small, elbow-driven **bagpipes**) as well as the **concertina**, **button accordion**, **mandolin**, harp, and **tenor banjo**. Traditional Irish music is primarily melodic with a subtle but propelling **rhythmic pulse**. Because of this reliance on an often intricate melody line, harmonic accompaniment is a relatively new development in the twentieth century. Accompaniment is most commonly provided by piano, **guitar**, **bodhrán** (a handheld **frame drum**), and, since the late 1970s, the **bouzouki** or **cittern**.

Countermelodies and harmonies are uncommon in what practitioners consider strictly "traditional" music, although many younger Irish ensembles such as the New York–based touring band, Cherish the Ladies, increasingly incorporate such arrangements in performance. Dance tunes span a range of rhythmic meters and tempi: Those in **duple time** include **reels** (4/4) and **polkas** (2/4) as well as stately marches and **syncopated hornpipes**; tunes in **triple time** include **jigs** (6/8) and slipjigs (9/8). Other tunes include **waltzes** and slow airs (laments). Regionalism plays a role in repertoire: Irish traditional musicians from the north of Ireland, for example, play **highlands** (also known as "flings"), **mazurkas**, **schottishes**, and barn dances (see *Tom Doherty: Take the Bull by the Horns* 1993), while players from the southwestern counties of Kerry and Cork include upbeat **slides** in their repertoire.

Prior to the advent of modern technology, playing style was transmitted from player to player; in recent decades, however,

tape recorders and the recording industry have dramatically altered this process of dissemination. In the United States, playing styles are derived in large part from different regional styles originating in Ireland. For example, the Sligo fiddle style is one of the most popular among Irish American players today. This is due, in part, to the 78-rpm recordings made by labels such as Decca and Columbia in the early years of the recording industry of outstanding Irish immigrant musicians, including Sligo fiddlers Michael Coleman, Paddy Killoran, and James Morrison. Produced in the United States and sent back to Ireland by relatives and friends, these recordings popularized specific playing styles and repertoire for generations to come. Similarly, early recordings also served to immortalize and perpetuate individual playing styles of specific musicians such as button accordionist John Kimmel, uilleann piper Patsy Tuohy, flutist John McKenna, concertina player William Mullaly, and, much later in the 1960s, button accordionist Paddy O'Brien.

IRISH SONG

Like Irish instrumental dance music, Irish traditional singing (sean-nós) has been passed down orally from older to younger generations. Sung unaccompanied, sean-nós songs are a solo endeavor and feature intricate ornamentation that requires concentration on the part of an Irish-speaking audience, for the tale told (often in Irish) is usually long and complicated. Increasingly, contemporary sean-nós singers performing to American audiences select songs from both the Irish and English language repertoires and eliminate **verses**, shortening the songs to fit modern attention spans. Many sean-nós singers today were influenced by the virtuosic singing of the late Joe Heaney of Connemara, County Galway, who lived for many years in Brooklyn, New York.

Since sean-nós singing generally requires a command of the Irish language as well as excellent vocal control, there remain far fewer practitioners than there are Irish

See glossary for definition of boldfaced terms

instrumentalists and dancers. Among Irish immigrants in the United States, sean-nós singing was largely inaccessible to the general public due to the language barrier and so was bypassed in the revival of Irish music in the 1960s and 1970s. Instead, songs in English, backed with rhythmic accompaniment (most notably the guitar) took its place. This new style of folk singing was best exemplified by the Clancy Brothers and Tommy Makem.

By capturing the attention of an international audience, the Clancy Brothers and Tommy Makem spawned a new tradition from an old one. Eliminating most of the ornamentation found in sean-nós singing, the Clancy Brothers and Tommy Makem added instrumental accompaniment and performed their songs faster with a driving beat. They sang primarily in **unison**, which not only gave them their particular trademark as a group but also allowed for audience participation, thus increasing their appeal. Their early appearances on television (then a relatively new medium), coupled with their interest in political Irish songs, made the songs of the Clancy Brothers and Tommy Makem enormously popular, and they remain so today among Irish Americans.

Inspired in part by the Clancy Brothers and Tommy Makem, a folk-based singing style emerged beginning in the late 1970s. This style typically features a solo lead singer (sometimes with **harmony** vocals) and backup instrumentation, ranging from a single guitar to a complicated arrangement of various instruments. Often, the lead singer incorporates some of the simpler sean-nós vocal ornamentation into the delivery. The repertoire is typically in English and, on rare occasions, in Irish and consists of ballads and songs as well as recently composed pieces.

POPULAR IRISH AMERICAN MUSIC

Popular Irish American music is a less clearly definable genre of music than traditional Irish music given the vast array of

styles over different eras. In general, Irish American popular musics in the middle to late twentieth century have included a range of instruments, repertoire, and styles, ranging from big-band Irish to showband Irish to Celtic rock. Popular Irish American music, like its counterpart in Ireland, combines mainstream and Irish traditional instruments and incorporates harmonic and rhythmic accompaniment that reflect popular genres of the era. Some hybridized Irish American musical styles, particularly those popularized by composers/singers such as George M. Cohan (in the years before and after World War I) and Bing Crosby (during the 1940s and 1950s) easily worked their way into popular American culture. Today, the difference between some Irish traditional bands and popular Irish ensembles is difficult to discern as the lines between the two often blur, particularly as technology and media affect expressive culture on all levels.

Big-band Irish American ensembles were popular among Irish immigrants in New York, Chicago, Boston, San Francisco, Philadelphia, and other cities from approximately the 1930s through the early 1960s. These ensembles featured extensive horn and reed sections, amplified guitar and **bass**, piano, drums, and other instruments commonly found in American popular music. Some of the groups arranged parts in a similar style to the mainstream big bands such as the Glen Miller Orchestra, and most played cover versions of hits from these ensembles to suit the taste of their immigrant audience for the modern in addition to Irish and Irish American songs.

Beginning in the late 1950s, the big-band Irish genre was displaced in Ireland by a new style of popular music called "showband music." Showbands performed covers of popular music styles such as rock and roll, "skiffle," and country-western, plus standard *ceili* dance tunes and popular Irish songs. With strong rhythm sections and an emphasis on guitars and brass, showbands offered provocative showmanship, matching stage costumes, a versatile repertoire, and an occasional comedy act.

The showband craze arrived in the United States in the early 1960s. Performances by legends such as Brendan Bowyer and the Royal Showband sold out large dance halls in every major American city. Irish immigrants and Irish Americans formed local showbands and played in the dance halls where the Irish big-band sound had once been heard.

Like the Irish big bands, showbands incorporated a traditional Irish element into their performances: A set of ceili dances accompanied by an accordionist and a set of waltzes or polkas might be interspersed between light rock and roll, country music, and Irish popular songs. And like the big band music, showbands provided the Irish American community with a musical expression that was quintessentially theirs while reflecting the music of the mainstream. In 1965, Congress passed the Immigration and Nationality Act amendment which, in effect, cut off the steady stream of Irish immigrants to America. With no new audiences of young, unattached immigrants in search of a nightlife, Irish dance halls throughout the United States closed, and the heyday of the showbands came to an end.

Yet showband music has remained a popular form of entertainment in Irish America, particularly among the older generations. Showbands perform for wedding receptions, at dances and fundraisers, and for other community celebrations. Showband music remains the preferred sound at Irish American resorts in the Catskill Mountains, the Poconos, and other areas. Modern showbands typically feature an electronic keyboard sometimes equipped with MIDI technology, drums or drum machine, guitar, bass, and vocals. Often, the keyboardist doubles on the button accordion, if only to play the occasional ceili dance, waltz, or polka. Showbands appeal to their Irish American audiences because they offer some of everything—nostalgic and political Irish songs, modern American songs with a pop beat, traditional Irish tunes, and country-western music.

Beginning in the late 1970s, the Irish immigrant and Irish American communities in several cities—New York, Boston, and Chicago—saw the emergence of Celtic rock bands. Inspired in part by the Dublin-based band Horslips, Celtic rock groups combine Irish traditional instruments such as the uilleann pipes and the fiddle with **electric guitar**, electric bass, keyboards, full drum kit, and others. Celtic rock bands draw on a rock and roll aesthetic and perform Irish songs, originals, and Irish tunes with a rock beat. (The term "Celtic rock" distinguishes these types of ensembles from Irish rock bands such as U2 that are strictly rock bands from Ireland.) A modern cousin to the Irish showband, Celtic rock groups perform in many of the same venues, including Irish resorts, pubs, and music festivals.

The overall difference between showband music and Celtic rock is the degree of orientation to rock and roll, with Celtic rock bands favoring a harder rock (and sometimes **rap**) style. Additionally, showbands perform a diversity of musics while Celtic rock bands focus on Irish music and song adapted to rock and roll. Continuing a cultural tradition of political statement expressed through music, Celtic rock bands compose political songs that critique those in authority and power in Ireland and in Northern Ireland and comment on the life of illegal Irish immigrants in the United States (see *Black 47* 1993).

See glossary for definition of boldfaced terms

RECENT TRENDS

The Irish traditional music community in the late 1990s in the United States is thriving. Musicians of all ages—immigrants, Irish American, and non–Irish—attend week-long camps focused on Irish music and song, participate in myriad music sessions in both large and small cities, and flock to Irish music festivals. Both folk recording labels and major record labels are producing recordings by Irish individuals and bands at an unprecedented rate. Irish radio programming on both public and commercial radio gives extensive airtime to Irish traditional music as well as Celtic rock and other popular styles. Small and large concert venues

throughout the country, including Carnegie Hall, Kennedy Center, and others present concerts of Irish music, song, and dance. With the phenomenon of the Irish dance extravaganza *Riverdance*, the popularity of Irish cultural expression is clearly growing.

Over the years, Irish American popular musical genres have entertained their audiences until replaced by a modern style, one that is more in keeping with an evolving Irish American aesthetic and identity. That traditional Irish music has survived throughout the United States despite periods of unpopularity points to its inherent vitality as both an art form and as an important symbolic component of Irish immigrant culture. Irish music, both popular and traditional, continues to serve as an extremely visible vehicle for changing group identity. It is precisely this enduring sense of ethnicity and the fact that increasing numbers of non–Irish are attracted to Irish music that augurs well for its survival and creative adaptation into the future.

BIBLIOGRAPHY

McCullough, Lawrence E. (1974). "An Historical Sketch of Traditional Irish Music in the U.S." In *Folklore Forum* 7, no. 3 (July).

Miller, Rebecca S. (1996). "Irish Traditional and Popular Music in New York City: Identity and Social Change, 1930–1975." In *The New York Irish*, ed. Ronald H. Bayor and Timothy J. Meagher. Baltimore: The Johns Hopkins University Press.

Moloney, Mick. (1992). "Irish Music in America: Continuity and Change." Ph.D. thesis. University of Pennsylvania.

O'Neill, Francis J. [1910] (1973). *Irish Folk Music: A Fascinating Hobby*. Reprint, Darby, PA: Norwood Editions.

———. [1913] (1973). *Irish Minstrels and Musicians*. Reprint, Darby, PA: Norwood Editions.

Power, Vincent. (1990). *Send 'Em Home Sweatin': The Showbands' Story*. Dublin: Kildanore Press.

DISCOGRAPHY/FILMOGRAPHY

Black 47: Fire of Freedom. 1993. Produced by Ric Ocasek and Larry Kirwan. New York: EMI Records. CD.

From Shore to Shore: Irish Traditional Music in New York. 1993. Produced and directed by Patrick Mullins; co-produced and written by Rebecca Miller. New York: Cherry Lane Productions. VHS videotape.

The Clancy Brothers with Tommy Makem: Luck of the Irish. 1992. Shanachie Records (Columbia/Legacy) CK47900. Reissue of classic recording on CD.

Tom Doherty: Take the Bull by the Horns. 1993. Produced by Rebecca Miller. Green Linnet Records GLCD 1131. CD and audiocassette recording.

Wheels of the World, Vol. 1 and 2. Shanachie Records, Yazoo 7008 and 7009. Reissues on CD of archival recordings of legendary musicians from the early twentieth century, including Michael Coleman, Patsy Tuohy, James Morrison, and others.

IRISH TRADITIONAL MUSIC IN CHICAGO

L. E. McCullough

L. E. McCullough is a musician, teacher, composer, and author of articles, stories, poetry, plays, and music instruction materials, including The Complete Irish Tinwhistle Tutor *(1976). He has also served as the producer of numerous films, radio programs, and recordings, among them a 1978 anthology of Irish traditional music from Chicago coproduced with Miles Krassen for Rounder Records that was reissued on CD in 2001. The following essay is excerpted from the liner notes he wrote to accompany that CD, which is entitled* Irish Traditional Music in America, Volume 2: From Chicago *(Rounder 8261-6006-2)*

Chicago, Illinois, has for nearly a century and a half been a vital center of Irish musical activity. It was the fertile territory where the great collector and chronicler of Irish music in the late nineteenth century, Francis O'Neill, harvested the majority of the tunes that comprised his classic works. More recently, it has received renown as the city that nurtured the youthful artistic talents of Michael Flatley, Jr., arguably the most celebrated Irish dancer of the late twentieth and early twenty-first centuries.

By 1850 Chicago's Irish-born residents formed over 20 percent of the fledgling city's population. The majority of these early Irish emigrants congregated along the south branch of the Chicago River in housing developments built up around the brickyards, slaughterhouses, rolling mills, lumberyards, and other industries that made Chicago a manufacturing powerhouse. Conley's Patch, Healy's Slough, McFadden's Patch, Canalport, Canaryville, Bridgeport, Brighton Park, and the Back o' the Yards were strong Irish areas, and it was in these communities that Irish music, song, and dance flourished most vigorously in the late 1800s.

Occasional notices in the *Citizen* (a Chicago Irish newspaper of the late nineteenth and early twentieth centuries) indicate that Irish music played a prominent role in the public life of the Irish community during this period. On the night of the great Chicago Fire of 1871, **fiddler** Pat McLaughlin was providing the music for a dance in honor of a recently arrived Irish cousin; the McLaughlins, quite coincidentally, were tenants in the front of Mrs. O'Leary's house, and that was very likely a most memorable welcome party. There were several dance halls featuring Irish music and dance, some being formal affairs held at venues such as Finucane's Hall at 2901 South Archer, while others were impromptu occasions like the dances arranged by neighbors in the butcher shop on the northwest corner of Bonfield and Archer during the 1890s. Irish musicians and dancers were represented in the

two Irish Villages in the 1893 Chicago World's Fair, and many associations dedicated to political change in Ireland organized concerts, rallies, and picnics that included a wide range of Irish musical entertainment. Several noted Irish musicians attached to minstrel troupes and vaudeville companies frequently passed through the city and often supplemented their income by performing in Irish-owned saloons; pipers John Hicks, John Moore, Eddie Joyce, and Patsy Tuohey were a few of the most frequent and popular of these visitors. Undoubtedly, however, then as now, the bulk of Irish musical activity in nineteenth-century Chicago was concentrated in private homes at occasions such as weddings, wakes, christenings, and house parties.

This era might have faded into total obscurity had it not been for the efforts of Francis J. O'Neill, captain and later chief of the Chicago Police Department. A native of Tralibane, Cork, Ireland, O'Neill arrived in Chicago in 1873 at the age of twenty-four and began making the acquaintance of the city's Irish musicians. Along with another Chicago policeman, Sergeant James O'Neill (originally of Belfast), he set about notating the great store of music possessed by the city's Irish musicians. Their collection was augmented by tunes from the **repertoire** of the professional Irish entertainers mentioned above who visited the city.

By 1903, after nearly three decades of collecting from informants and relentlessly searching through old manuscripts, Francis O'Neill's *Music of Ireland* was published. Containing 1,850 pieces of music, including dance tunes, airs, and compositions by the harper O'Carolan, this work was followed in 1907 by *The Dance Music of Ireland: 1001 Gems,* an abridged version of the first book. Five more music collections appeared up to 1922, and two volumes of historical information on Irish music and musicians were also brought out by O'Neill, *Irish Folk Music, a Fascinating Hobby* (1910) and *Irish Minstrels and Musicians* (1913). Though he was an amateur who pursued his hobby solely because of a great love for Irish music and culture, O'Neill's work in collecting the mu-

sic and chronicling the Irish and Irish American musical milieu of his day stands as a monumental achievement in the field of Irish music. In addition to bringing a great deal of music to a vastly larger audience, O'Neill's books have given future generations their only vivid insight into the nineteenth- and early twentieth-century world of Irish music in America.

A focal point for Irish musical activity around the turn of the twentieth century was the Chicago Irish Music Club. This was an outgrowth of the frequent informal sessions held in the homes of O'Neill and his friends, and it included a vast array of outstanding performers. Pipers Barney Delaney, James Cahill, John Ennis, James Early, John Beatty, Adam Tobin, and John Canners, along with fiddlers John McFadden, Edward Cronin, Timothy Dillon, James Kennedy, John McElligott, Abram Beamish, and James O'Neill and flute players James Kerwin, Garrett Stack, Fr. Dollard, Fr. Fielding, and Francis O'Neill himself were among the club mainstays.

By 1920, however, most of the membership had died or retired from active performance, and, in O'Neill's words, "the most enjoyable, companionable and representative association of Irish musicians, singers and dancers ever organized in America" dissolved. A few wire cylinder recordings of McFadden, Delaney, and Early still remain and indicate that O'Neill's assessment was not at all exaggerated.

Though Francis O'Neill lived until 1936, the halcyon epoch of which he was so distinguished a representative can be said to have ended by the 1920s. The Irish and Irish American population of Chicago had reached a peak of over 225,000 by 1900, yet even at this early date, Irish music was noticeably beginning to lose its appeal to a large segment of the Irish American community. In his essays, O'Neill often alluded to the growing indifference with which aspects of Irish culture—particularly music—were being treated by the Irish in America, and there were many other observations of this trend reported in the contemporary Irish American press. O'Neill viewed the lack of proper

Liz Carroll

Please see the sidebar accompanying Chapter 24 in this volume for biographical information on Nick Spitzer. This essay is reprinted from the program guide for the Folk Masters 1995 concert series, held March 10–April 15 at the Barns of Wolf Trap in Vienna, Virginia.

Liz Carroll was born in Chicago in 1956 of Irish immigrant parents from County Offaly and County Limerick. Her father, a **button accordion** player, began teaching her Irish traditional music when she was five, and Liz also had the opportunity to hear her grandfather play during visits to Ireland. Although she studied classical violin for a brief period with a nun at her parochial school, local concerts of Irish music, sessions (informal Irish musical gatherings), and her family were her main sources of musical schooling.

Liz honed her skills through years of playing at meetings of the Irish Traditional Musicians Association and exposure to the music of veteran Chicago Irish musicians Johnny McGreevy, Joe Shannon, Seamus Cooley, Jimmy and Elenor Neary, and others. These experiences imbued her with a wealth of tunes, techniques, and stories, giving her a breadth and depth of musical and cultural knowledge possessed by few of her generation.

In 1975, after a series of stunning victories in the junior division of the All-Ireland Fiddle Championship, Liz, then eighteen, astounded the Irish music world both in the United States and in Ireland by winning the senior division championship title. In accomplishing this feat, she was immediately recognized as one of the outstanding Irish **fiddlers** of all time.

Liz Carroll's artistry flows from a deep sense

Irish American fiddler Liz Carroll photographed in the early 1990s
Photograph courtesy the Smithsonian Institution, Folk Masters

of connection and devotion to Irish music and culture. She says, "It's just one of those ingrained things, the kind of thing you keep going back to." Liz has never worked full-time as a musician, preferring to stay close to home in order to raise her children and to join in the many sessions that take place in homes and community gathering places in and around "County Cook." In 1994, she was awarded the National Heritage Fellowship by the National Endowment for the Arts.

Nick Spitzer

patronage, appreciation, and respect for the Irish musician as the chief problem and held misdirected social reformers, over zealous clergy, and greedy entrepreneurs as the three groups mainly responsible for the debased state of musical and cultural sensibility among the American Irish of the day.

There were other significant factors at work, too. The decline of Irish emigration to Chicago, the geographical fragmentation of Irish neighborhoods, the modification of cultural values and priorities that accompanies the emigrant's successful transition from "foreigner to native," and the chronic insta-

bility of American urban society in the post–Industrial Age all contributed to the increased remoteness with which Irish music came to be regarded by many Irish Americans. Despite the admonitions of O'Neill and other perceptive cultural commentators, Irish music, song, and dance would continue to recede into the backwaters of Irish American cultural consciousness for the next half century.

Notwithstanding these ill omens, the period between the two world wars saw a flurry of Irish musical activity in Chicago as several musicians made 78-rpm records for labels like Decca, Victor, Celtic, and Columbia. In

the 1920s pipers Eddie Mullaney, Tom Ennis, and Joe Sullivan, fiddlers Tom Cawley, Paddy Stack, Billy McCormick, Francis Cashin, Selena O'Neill (Francis' daughter), and Michael Cashin, flute players Paddy Doran and Tom Doyle, and pianist Frances Malone appeared on commercial recordings. While Chicago Irish musicians did not receive extensive attention from the record companies of the period, the seventy-odd sides featuring these performers provide an interesting assortment of styles and repertoire.

There was less recording activity following the onset of the Depression in the 1930s, but those that were made continued to be of considerable interest. In 1934 a recently arrived Irish dancing teacher from County Clare named Pat Roche presented the Pat Roche Harp and Shamrock Orchestra at the Irish Village section of the Century of Progress World's Fair. The band was one of the first American ensembles modeled on the Irish *ceili* band principle and, following a successful engagement at the fair, made several records for Decca. Included were Jimmy Devine and John McGreevy, fiddles; John Gaffney, **accordion**; Pat McGovern, flute; Joe Shannon, **uilleann pipes**; Eleanor Kane, piano; Pat Richardson, drums; and Pat Roche, **step dancing**. Within this assemblage were three teenagers who would continue to provide the foundation of Irish music in Chicago for the next four decades: John McGreevy, Eleanor Kane Neary, and Joe Shannon. Pat Roche, through his radio programs and organizational activities, also played a significant role in the city's Irish music and dancing activities into the 1980s.

In 1938 Eleanor Kane, fiddler Jim Donnelly, and accordionist Packie Walsh recorded for Decca, with one side featuring an outstanding piano solo by Kane. This was to be the last commercial recording of Chicago Irish musicians until the 1970s. Yet there were still a number of places where Irish music could be heard. Benefit dances for the Irish independence movement in the early 1920s always accepted the donation of talent by Irish musicians, and some welcome income was earned by musicians during the Depression by playing for open-air dances

or in private dance halls. Some of the venues boasted specialized types of dancing, such as the hall at Madison and Sacramento that hosted Kerry Sets, the hall at Root and Wentworth that featured Clare Sets, and the hall at Madison and California where the Mayo Set, or Plain Set, was danced. Gaelic Park at 47th and California was a large outdoor area that had separate platforms for Kerry, Clare, Mayo, and American-style group dancing. At various times during the 1930s, 1940s, 1950s, and early 1960s, Irish dances were held in halls or parks at 47th and Halsted, 51st and Halsted, 64th and Halsted, 69th and Wentworth, 69th and Emerald, 63rd and Kedzie, 79th and Aberdeen, Halsted and Diversey, the West End Ballroom at Cicero and Madison, and McEnery Hall at Madison and Pulaski.

Musical stalwarts of the 1930s, 1940s, and early 1950s included fiddlers Tom Fitzmaurice, Jimmy Neary, Jim Giblin, John McGreevy, P.J. Concannon (who hosted an Irish radio program for many years), Martin Wynne, Ann Cawley Scully, John McGinley, Jim McCarty, Anna McGoldrick, Dan Keogh, Tom Ryan, and Theresa Geary; accordionists Tom Rush, Tony Lowe, Paddy Kenny, Tim Gehene, Dan Shea, Wille Guerin, Jim Bresnahan, Tim Sheahan, Tom Treacy, Paddy Durkin, Packie Walsh, John Gaffney, Martin Hardiman, Tom Kerrigan, Mrs. McLaughlin, Nell O'Hara, and Terry Teahan; flute players Jim Rudden, Paddy Doran, Pat McGovern, and Frank Thornton; drummers Pat and Tom Richardson; pianist Eleanor Kane Neary; and pipers Eddie Mullaney, Joe Shannon, Denny Flynn, Joe Sullivan, Mike Joyce, and Mike Scanlon.

Other musicians participated in Chicago Irish musical affairs during these years and left their own legacy as well. Yet most musicians who recall the Depression, World War II, and postwar period are not overly nostalgic in their reminiscences. Though there was plenty of music to be heard, Irish music in Chicago had fallen to perhaps its lowest ebb of esteem within the Irish American community. Remuneration for performances was slight and infrequent when steady engagements were available at all. Few young Chicagoans had taken up the music, though those that did, such as McGreevy, Shannon, Kane, and fiddler Jim Donnelly's daughter, Mary McDonough, were certainly able to contribute significantly to the local music scene. Increasingly, Irish music seemed to retreat within the narrowing community of newly arrived emigrants.

The mid-1950s witnessed a new influx of musicians arriving in Chicago from Ireland in a wave that lasted until the early 1960s. Kerry fiddlers Paddy and Johnny Cronin, Galway accordionist Kevin Keegan and the Galway accordion player Joe Cooley and his brother Seamus (flute) were among the most widely acclaimed of the recent arrivals. Though only Seamus Cooley would remain in Chicago into the 1970s, each made a substantial impact on the city's Irish music community.

Inspired by the rise in Ireland of *Comhaltas Ceoltóirí Eireann* (CCE), the Irish Musicians' Association of America was founded in August 1956 by sixteen musicians attending a meeting at the Midland Hotel in Chicago. Frank Thornton was the first president, and by the time the first "Irish Musicians' Ball" was held on November 30, 1957, at McEnery Hall, sixty musicians had become active members of the Chicago branch. The organization expanded to twenty-two branches nationwide within the next few years but dissolved in 1964 due to an inability to resolve matters of organizational structure and procedure. However, the Chicago branch continued to operate and is now fully aligned with CCE.

Among the musicians active in the 1950s and early 1960s, besides those named above, were fiddlers Tom McMahon, Phil Durkin, Frank Burke, Mike Boyle, Pat Burke, Mike Shanley, Mossie Foran, Maida Sugrue, Una McGlew, and Jack and Eileen Fitzgerald; accordion players Pat Cloonan, Mike Madden, Martin Byrne, Jim Coyle, Tim Clifford, Tom Maguire, Tom O'Malley, and Des O'Grady; flute players Noel Rice, Tom Masterson, Albert Neary, and Kevin Henry (also an uilleann piper and former president of the Chicago

Irish Musicians' Association); pianists Nancy Harling and Maise Griffith; banjoist Bert McMahon; piper Dave Page; and drummers Billy Soden and John Smith. Several native Chicagoans also joined the Irish music ranks around this time, including fiddler Bob Murphy, accordionists John Murray and John Lavelle, flute players John Murphy, Pat McPartland, and Jim Thornton, and drummers Pat Gilhooly and John Cook.

During the 1970s, the numerous Irish music bars that had flourished along 79th Street and 63rd Street during the 1960s dwindled to a handful of meeting spots for weekend ceilis and sessions: Flanagan's Tavern at 65th and Kedzie, Hoban's Tavern at 63rd and Kedzie, and Hibernian Hall on West 63rd Street, which served as the meeting place for the Irish Musicians' Association and a weekly *Irish Hour* broadcast live on radio station WOPA by Martin Fahey, Sr. The Francis O'Neill Music Club, also affiliated with CCE, became active during the 1970s, along with the Emerald Music Club and Chicago Gaelic Society that sponsored monthly ceilis and sessions. Schools of Irish music instruction sprang up, and Chicago became a frequent host venue for the Midwestern American Fleadh Ceoil competition held each spring.

Chicago Irish musicians began performing with frequency for non–Irish audiences at folk festivals, coffeehouses, and college concerts locally and throughout the United States, including the Smithsonian Festival of American Folklife in Washington, D.C. American folk labels issued LP recordings of Irish music that included Chicagoans Joe Shannon, John McGreevy, Seamus Cooley, Terry Teahan, Noel Rice, Eleanor Neary, Kevin Henry, Frank Thornton, Jimmy Thornton, Maida Sugrue, Albert and John Neary, Frank Burke, and James Keane, Sr. Eighty-year-old Chicago uilleann pipemaker and Mayo native Patrick Hennelly was the subject of a National Endowment for the Arts research project from 1976 to 1977, and in 1980 Terry Teahan, who as a boy had been a musical pupil of the famed Kerry fiddler Patrick O'Keefe, published *The Road to Glountane,* a book containing sixty-three tunes by himself and six other Chicago musicians.

See glossary for definition of boldfaced terms

Most importantly, a number of talented, young, American-raised musicians emerged in Chicago during the late 1970s, several of whom would win All-Ireland championships and come to have national and even international impact on Irish traditional music of the 1980s and 1990s as soloists or group performers—fiddlers Liz Carroll, Kathleen Keane, Kathleen Rice, and John Cleland; piano accordionist Jimmy Keane; flute player/dancer Michael Flatley, Jr.; tinwhistle players Maggie Henry, Mary Mayer, and Johnny Harling; button accordionist John Williams; pianist Marty Fahey; guitarists Dennis Cahill and Jim DeWan; drummer Tom Masterson, Jr.; and percussionists Kevin Rice and Patrick Flatley, to name only a few. The local scene was also refreshed during the 1980s and 1990s by new blood from Ireland, with musicians such as Clare fiddler Martin Hayes, Fermanagh flutist Larry Nugent, and Dublin guitarist Pat Broaders using the city as a home base.

At the beginning of the twenty-first century, Irish music is well represented in Chicago's public cultural life. There are two annual citywide Irish music festivals (one sponsored by the City of Chicago mayor's office), two active CCE branches, two large multiarts cultural centers (the Irish American Heritage Center and a revived Gaelic Park), nine weekly Irish music radio programs, fourteen Irish step dance schools with forty-three branches, and fifteen sessions and pubs featuring Irish music and ceili and set dancing. The annual Chicago Feis has been held continuously since 1945 and, at close to 1,600 participants, is North America's largest.

The 1990s saw Chicago Irish musicians appearing on scores of commercial recordings and numerous Hollywood film soundtracks. Mark Howard's Trinity Dance Company pioneered an innovative music and dance fusion that presaged the format of *Riverdance,* and *Riverdance* star and *Lord of the Dance* creator Michael Flatley, Jr., along with Joe Shannon and Liz Carroll, were recipients of the prestigious National Heritage Fellowship Award from the National Endowment for the Arts.

The musical labors of Francis O'Neill have been commemorated in two 1997 works by Ossian Press of Cork: Nicholas Carolan's *A Harvest Saved: Francis O'Neill and Irish Music in Chicago* and *The Complete O'Neill Collection* edited by Liz Doherty. The O'Neill Irish Music Collection is archived at the Hesburgh Library at the University of Notre Dame in nearby South Bend, Indiana, and contains over 1,500 Irish music books and records along with the personal correspondence of Francis O'Neill.

O'Neill, who lamented at the turn of the twentieth century that the Irish of Chicago were in danger of forsaking their cultural traditions, would no doubt be pleasantly surprised.

BIBLIOGRAPHY

McCullough, Lawrence E. (1974). "An Historical Sketch of Traditional Irish Music in the U.S." *Folklore Forum* 7 (3):177–191.

———. (1975). "An American Maker of Uillean Pipes: Patrick Hennelly." *Eire-Ireland* 10 (4):109–15. Reprinted as "Making Uileann Pipes in Chicago," *Treoir,* 1976, 8 (2):18–20.

———. (1977). "Style in Traditional Irish Music." *Ethnomusicology* 21(1):85–97.

———. (1978). *Irish Music in Chicago: An Ethnomusicological Study.* Ph.D. diss. University of Pittsburgh. Ann Arbor: University Microfilms.

———. (1980). "The Role of Language, Music, and Dance in the Revival of Irish Culture in Chicago, Illinois." *Ethnicity,* Vol. 7, pp. 436–44.

———. (1981). "The Role of Irish Step-dancing in the Propagation of Irish Culture in the U.S." *Viltis* 39(6):5–7.

SELECTED RECORDINGS

Baal Tinne: About Time. 1991. Noel Rice, flute and whistle; Kevin Rice, bodhrán, percussion; Cathleen Rice, fiddle. Baal Tinne Records BT 01.

Chicago Irish Musicians. 1982. CIMA Records 82-513.

Fleadh Ceoil, '75. 1976. Michael Flately, flute. Dolphin Records DOLM 5013.

Hollow Poplar. 1976. John McGreevy, fiddle; Seamus Cooley, flute; Mary Cooley, vocal; Liz Carroll, fiddle. Log Cabin Records LC 8003.

Ladies on the Flatboat. 1977. Frank Burke, fiddle; Albert Neary, tinwhistle; John Neary, spoons. Log Cabin Records LC 8004.

Liz Carroll. 1988. Liz Carroll, fiddle. Green Linnet Records SIP 1092.

McGreevy&Cooley. 1975. Philo Records PH 2005.

The Noonday Feast. 1980. John McGreevey, fiddle; Joe Shan-

non, uilleann pipes. Green Linnet Records SIF 1023.

Sopin' Up the Gravy. 1975. John McGreevy, fiddle; Kevin Henry, tinwhistle/bodhrán. Log Cabin Records LC 8001.

Terry Teahan&Gene Kelly. 1978. Terry Teahan, concertina and accordion. Topic Records 12TS352.

Wheels of the World: Early Irish-American Music—Classic Recordings from the 1920s and 1930s. 1997. Tom Ennis, uilleann pipes; Michael Cashin, fiddle; Tom Doyle, flute. Yazoo Records 7008.

IRISH MUSIC FROM CLEVELAND

Richard Carlin

Richard Carlin is a writer and musician who produced about ten albums for Folkways Records in the mid-1970s. He is the author of several books, including The Big Book of Country Music *and, with his brother, Bob Carlin,* Southern Exposure: The Story of Southern Music in Words and Pictures. *He recorded three albums of Irish traditional music from Cleveland, all released by Folkways in the late 1970s.*

In the late eighteenth and early nineteenth centuries, when the first "folklorists" discovered the beauty of traditional music and song, the almost universal feeling was that these were the last in a long line of folk musicians whose work could be recorded. (At the time, songs were preserved for future generations using pencil and paper; later, advances in technology in the early twentieth century made audio recordings possible.) It was believed that the traditional music of the land would soon be heard no more, and so collectors tirelessly traveled through remote parts of England, Scotland, and Ireland in search of this music. At this time, little attention was given to dance music, which was still so commonplace that is was hardly classified as "ancient" or "folk" at all.

With each generation of folklorist and folk performers, new songs have been collected and entirely new areas of traditional performance have been "discovered" for the first time. And yet the feeling persists that folk music is dying, that few—if any—of the younger generation are interested in perpetuating a traditional art based on a culture that is becoming outmoded due to an increasingly industrialized and depersonalized society.

Collectors are just beginning to recognize the continuing tradition of folk music and folk culture within the large ethnic communities that exist in the inner cities of America as well as in select pockets in the countryside. The Irish, German, Slavs, Jews, Mexicans, Puerto Ricans, and countless others who came to the United States in search of employment opportunities, especially in the industrial sector, have found that their folk cultures have taken on an even greater meaning in their lives. Industrial society has not doomed folk culture to oblivion; if anything, it has intensified it.

The reasons for this are complex and deserve greater study. My own feelings are that folk music is an integral part of the popular culture of any given community. Music

serves a social function, both in the formal dance situation and the less formal family gathering. It literally brings people together in recognition of a common heritage.

THE IRISH IN CLEVELAND

Large groups of Irish immigrants began coming to the United States as the result of the infamous Irish potato famine of the mid–nineteenth century. It was only the last in a series of insults to the old way of agricultural life; indeed, there was little prospect for economic improvement in the homeland, and America beckoned strongly with its many jobs, abundant land, and the chance to escape a rigid, class-bound society. However, the Irish who came to America were greeted by a strong anti-immigrant backlash, the so-called "Know-Nothing" movement. While immigrants were at first welcomed to perform the backbreaking labor of laying rail-

road tracks, blasting coal mines, and digging canals—and to serve as surrogate soldiers in the Civil War for those able to pay their way out of the conflict—soon advertisements with the famous tagline of "No Irish Need Apply" began appearing in the newspapers.

Greeted by this hostility, it is not surprising that the Irish—like many other immigrant groups before and after them—banded together in small communities within the larger urban centers. It was also true that their housing choices were limited by a kind of de facto segregation; they would most likely begin living with relatives or friends, who, in turn, would know of other apartments or homes nearby that were available to those newly arrived from Ireland. And, limited by economics, they could hardly afford to buy homes in the better parts of town.

In Cleveland, the Irish mostly settled on the west side of town in a neighborhood

1 Tom Morrison (flute)
2 Paddy Killoran (fiddle)
3 Michael Coleman (fiddle)
4 Paddy Sweeney (fiddle)
5 James Morrison (fiddle)
6 Joe Heaney (vocalist)
7 Francis James O'Neill (music collector)
8 Tom McCaffrey (fiddle)
9 Tom Byrne (flute)
10 Patsy Touhey (Irish bagpipes)
11 Martin Wynne (fiddle)
12 Peter James Conlon (accordion)
13 Clancy Brothers (folk revivalists)
14 Tommy Makem (vocalist)
15 Hugh Gillespie (fiddle)
16 John McKenna (flute)
17 J P "Packie" Dolan (fiddle)
18 Michael Walsh (flute)
19 Tom Carmody (accordion)

known as Lakewood. During the nineteenth century, they were the second-largest immigrant group in the city, outnumbered only by the Germans, who generally enjoyed better jobs and more social prestige. By the mid-twentieth century, Eastern Europeans had become the dominant immigrant group in the city. However, the Irish remained a strong subculture, with their own bars and social clubs, an annual *feis* (a celebration of Irish food, culture, and dance), and private schools and churches that were for all intents and purposes strictly Irish.

However, the community is virtually invisible to outsiders, even others who live in Cleveland. There is very little promotion of Irish events beyond the community itself, whose residents are content to provide their own entertainment; others in the city, unaware or uninterested in the diversity of cultures within its boundaries, simply do not participate.

Cleveland, like many rustbelt cities, went through a particularly grim period during the economic recession of the mid-1970s and early 1980s. Early in the 1970s, the infamous Cuyahoga River fire—when the heavily polluted river that runs through the city caught on fire and burned for several days—seemed symbolic of Cleveland's economic malaise and spiritual exhaustion. Although the Irish were never among the city's most prosperous citizens, they were hurt even more by the flight of jobs; the many auto plants and steel mills that used to employ thousands of workers first cut back their payrolls and then shut down completely. Consequently, the once-active port, railroad yards, and truck depots where thousands of items were loaded and unloaded every day also slowed down.

When Cleveland made a comeback in the later 1980s and 1990s—thanks to clever public-relations efforts, the opening of the Rock and Roll Hall of Fame, and the general health of the economy throughout the country—the Irish community prospered, too, but not that much. It seems that, in good times or bad, the community perseveres, sometimes a little more vibrant, sometimes

Tom Byrne (flute) and Tom McCaffrey (fiddle) sitting on the sidesteps of Tom Byrne's Lakewood, Ohio, home. *Photographed in 1977 by Pam Hardman.*

a little more subdued. Although some Irish have become wealthy enough to move out of the city, most remain behind in a kind of economic limbo—not well off enough to leave, but not poor enough to slip further down the economic ladder into the slums.

LEADING MUSICIANS

Within the Cleveland Irish enclave, certain well-recognized "master musicians" have come to stand out as the most popular providers of entertainment at community functions. These musicians are not "professionals" in the sense that we recognize certain classical musicians (or even folk and popular performers) as professional entertainers. They all hold "regular" jobs and play music on weekends and evenings. Yet in another sense of the word, they *are* professional; they provide music for most of the important community functions. Music is an important part of their lives, perhaps more important than their day or night jobs.

While there are always a few musicians who achieve unusually high levels of skill—the most obvious example being **fiddler** Michael Coleman, who lived in the Queens Irish community in New York in the 1920s and 1930s and made dozens of legendary recordings—most are not virtuosos. A master musician will be recognized for many traits beyond sheer musical talent; good humor, clever presentation, and sheer nerve and determination all play a role in whether a musician emerges as someone the community recognizes as a master. There were some people on the music scene in Cleveland who had no musical talent at all; they served merely as promoters, lingering on the edges of the musical world, wishing to participate but knowing that they lacked the skills. Others were venerated for their past accomplishments; in his later years, fiddler Tom Scott was no longer able to play with the same capabilities he had possessed as a youth, but he was recognized for having been a great musician, one who knew the earlier generation of players and carried forward their techniques.

In Cleveland, the best opportunity to work regularly as a performer was at the local dance schools. Although only a few young people showed interest in becoming musicians, almost all were expected to study Irish dance. Dance has becoming an intensely competitive and important part of Irish youth; dance contests are held regularly, and attending dance school is expected as a means of maintaining ties to Irish culture. While recorded music could be played, it was far preferable to have live musicians who could interact with the dancers.

See glossary for definition of boldfaced terms

In the schools, a group of random **melody instruments** (such as flute, fiddle, or **accordion**), usually accompanied by piano, is enough to keep the young dancer's feet moving. The job is rather monotonous; there is much repetition of the same tunes or even **phrases** over and over while students master the steps. In competition, the model for accompaniment remains the ceidlih band—a 1950s- and 1960s-era innovation featuring a similar lineup of melody instruments accompanied by piano, sometimes **guitar** and electric **bass**, and drums. The military-style drumbeat is one of the most prominent features of the ceidlih band.

Another opportunity for music making comes at the session, or informal meeting of musicians to swap and enjoy tunes. This often occurs in a neighborhood bar or the basement of a neighborhood home. The sessions can run for hours, sometimes into the early morning. The home sessions that I attended were among the most relaxed and enjoyable ways of making music. Musicians would sit in a circle, and the emphasis was on sharing tunes; only rarely did one person play a solo. Instead, someone would start a tune and everyone else would join in. If you did not know the tune, you'd do your best to follow it; sometimes, if you were lucky, a more knowledgeable musician would play a phrase for you, on the sly as it were, so you could pick up some of the more difficult passages.

At the home sessions, there is always an emphasis on socializing as well as music making. After a few hours of tune swapping, the musicians put their instruments aside. The entire family in the house—who had gone about their own business during the music making part of the evening—assembles for tea, cakes, scones, and sandwiches. Jokes are exchanged, repeated, and retold; often over the course of an evening a single joke would be told five or six times, with someone saying, "What was that story about the sailor?" leading the teller to repeat the same joke all over again.

One of the stars of these sessions was fiddler Tom McCaffrey. A native of Mohill in County Leitrim, Tom learned to fiddle and sing from his father, a master fiddler and, as Tom says, "the pet of the family." Tom recalls that his father would often be absent from home for upwards of a week to play at weddings and local functions. Tom's father taught fiddle by what his son called the "alphabetic method"; students didn't read music but rather learned tunes by ear. Although he didn't elaborate further, this method probably involved using the letters of the alphabet (ABCDEFG) as stand-ins for the musical notes. Tom began to learn the fiddle from his father when he was eleven or twelve. After he learned to play, he was always in demand at weddings and dances. Not a flashy fiddler, Tom used short bow strokes to give his playing a jaunty, foot-moving feeling.

Besides his talents as a fiddler, Tom was a master storyteller and singer. With a warm personality and a keen talent for entertaining, he always stood out on the bandstand or in the session thanks to his wealth of jokes, songs, and stories. His **repertoire** was mostly based on music-hall and comedic songs of the turn of the century. Sometimes, he would recall only a fragment of the many **verses** of these comic songs. For example, the popular music-hall song "Phil the Fluter's Ball"—the tale of a classic evening of Irish dance and joviality—was reduced to just its **chorus** by Tom, who would sing the words along with the tune as he played it.

Tom also loved "recitations," the short, rhymed sayings that encapsulated typical music-hall humor. One of his favorites was "My Father Said":

My father said I should not go,
To see the sexy burlesque show.
When I asked him why, he said to me,
"You'll see t'ings there you shouldn't see."

But being young, I disobeyed,
and off I went, quite unafraid.
I sure saw t'ings I shouldn't see,
I saw my dad sitting next to me!

Before his retirement in the mid-1980s, Tom worked as a groundskeeper at a local high school in the Irish community of Lakewood. A bachelor, he tooled around town in his Chrysler Cordoba, a mid-level luxury car of which he was inordinately proud. When not working his day job, Tom often played in a semiprofessional dance band called the Emeralds. Their style was the classic 1950s–1960s-era ceidlih band, complete with the loud, regular, military-style drumbeat that wiped out many of the subtleties of rhythm usually found in Irish music.

However, in more informal settings he preferred to play duets with his close friend, Tom Byrne, a very talented flute player. Byrne was born in Gevagh, County Sligo, Ireland. When he was seven, he bought a **tin whistle** at a local fair for three pennies. Soon after, he had learned some of the popular marches, **jigs**, and **reels** from Sligo; he particularly remembers learning the "Swallow's

Tail" and "Miss McCleod's" reels early in his playing. Soon after buying the whistle, Tom was given an Irish wooden flute—with open holes—by an older player. He patched it up and has been playing ever since at dances and parties but also at home for his own amusement. Tom immigrated to Canada in 1948 and then went to Cleveland, where he bought a small, single-family home in the Irish Lakewood neighborhood. Short, stocky, and muscular, Byrne did hard physical labor unloading trucks downtown. He had eleven children, mostly daughters, who tended to his every need, bringing him cigarettes, drinks, and sandwiches whenever he called for them.

Tom's flute playing is marked by a wealth of ornamentation, particularly rolls (a cluster of notes played in a rapid fashion to **ornament** a key note in the musical phrase). He also uses his breath to accent notes and give variety to the tunes. He will introduce many **variations** into his playing and keenly listens to and interacts with the other musicians, echoing little phrases or responding to something that he hears.

The duo of "Tom and Tom" (as they were affectionately known) met in Cleveland in 1956 or 1957. Although Byrne was probably the superior musician, he was greatly inspired by McCaffrey; indeed, he played differently when in a large group or with another fiddler (even a technically better one). The excitement of their duets lay in the total sympathy between the two musicians and the slight variations that each is able to perform without destroying the unity of the melody line.

Most of Tom Byrne's children showed little interest in his music. They would join in the food and talk but not the music making that occurred every week in the basement of their home. They listened avidly to contemporary popular music, proudly showing their Fleetwood Mac and Kiss records to me. While many had taken dancing classes, particularly the girls, they did not seem to recognize the greatly talented musician who lived among them.

However, there were a handful of teenagers who were beginning to be inter-

Tom Byrne (flute) and Tom McCaffrey (fiddle) photographed in front of Tom Byrne's Lakewood house with Byrne's wife standing between them and his many sons and daughters assembled on the front steps.
Photographed in 1977 by Richard Carlin.

this country and hear the music only within the confines of a small community within a larger city.

Among the younger musicians, most were both players and dancers. Flute player Jimmy Noonan was mentored by Tom Byrne, who worked closely with him to show him the "tricks" of ornamentation and style. Noonan competed nationwide as a dancer and won many awards and trophies as a teenager. He took up the flute after several years of dancing and soon was confident enough to start his own school for fledgling musicians.

While the number of young people interested in traditional music seemed small, this may not have been that unusual. We have the impression that, a 100 or more years ago, the Irish hills were alive with music making—and perhaps they were. But it was probably always the rare person who took up music and kept at it throughout their entire life. Even musicians like Tom McCaffrey went for several years (if not decades) without touching their instruments. They were preoccupied with work, raising families, or simply fell out of touch with other musicians. And of all those who played music, only a small handful would achieve any level of talent; an even smaller subset would be recognized as masters.

The survival of this music despite all of these odds is a marvelous thing; and if the past is any guide, its continued viability into the next centuries seems a strong possibility.

DOCUMENTARY RECORDINGS

You can hear the music of Tom and Tom and their peers on the three Folkways albums that I recorded from 1977 to 1981 in Cleveland. The first volume (FS 3517) spotlights Tom and Tom as master musicians; the second (FS 3521) shows their work within the broader community and includes others who played with them; and the final volume (FS 3523) shows the next generation of musicians interacting with these older masters.

All the recordings were made either in Cleveland basements or in other informal situations; no attempt was made to "re-

ested in the older musical styles. Thanks to the Irish music renaissance that occurred in the mid-1970s as new groups like the Bothy Band and De Danaan made recordings and popularized the **genre**, it no longer seemed so dated or uninteresting. Even the older musicians were affected by it; Tom Byrne listened to Matt Molloy's solo records and learned tunes off them, so that the younger generation was influencing the older (just as the older, originally, had taught the young, closing a unique circle).

While the new young performers were not as expert as the old, they showed a remarkable sympathy for the traditional musical style. This is particularly remarkable when you consider that these young musicians are second- or third-generation Irish in

hearse" for the recordings. The overall effect is like eavesdropping on an afternoon of informal music making. The point is not to preserve perfect performances but hopefully to capture the community's music as it was made. All three records are available on special order cassette/CD from the Smithsonian/Folkways archive.

MUSIC TRADITIONS OF BEAVER ISLAND, MICHIGAN

Laurie Kay Sommers

Please see Chapter 11 in this volume for biographical information on Laurie Kay Sommers. The following essay is adapted from her 1996 book Beaver Island House Party, *for which Sommers relied extensively on the accounts of numerous islanders and the collections and field notes of the late Ivan Walter and Helen Collar.*

Beaver Island is the largest island in Lake Michigan, located nineteen miles off the northwest Michigan coastal town of Cross Village. The island sustains a year-round population of about 450, 35 percent of whom are Irish, and a seasonal population of around 4,000. Irish immigrants settled the island beginning in the mid–nineteenth century. They were preceded by Native Americans, some of whom still lived on Beaver and surrounding islands when the first Irish arrived, and by the Mormon colony of James Jesse Strang from 1847 to 1856.

Most of the Irish came via chain migration from the small, rugged island of Arranmore located off the northwest coast of County Donegal. At the time of peak emigration in the middle to late nineteenth century, most islanders were uneducated, devout Catholics who spoke Irish rather than English. Through the Depression, the island fostered an economy based on fishing, farming, and logging. Significant change began with World War II. At present the chief industry is tourism, and most jobs are in construction, real estate, and services to year-round residents and resorters.

The dominant music culture derives from the interplay between Irish immigrant culture, the occupational folksong traditions of Great Lakes schoonermen and lumberjacks, popular culture via the mass media, and the regional traditions of the Upper Great Lakes. Much of Beaver Island's musical interest lies in the scope and time-depth of its field documentation. Island material is the centerpiece of the premiere collection of early twentieth-century Great Lakes **ballads** and song, collected by folklorist and University of Michigan English professor Ivan Walton from 1932 through 1960. The Beaver Island portion of Walton's collection includes data from a joint field trip with Alan Lomax in 1938. Additional material was collected by island summer resident Helen Collar from the 1960s through 1996 and by the author since 1989.

The documentation reveals a fascinating history of music making, house parties, dances, and other home entertainment. The older Irish instrumental and ballad **repertoire** has been supplanted over time by classic country, square and **round dance** instrumentals, newly composed local ballads, Irish music learned from recordings, rock and roll standards, and songs by contemporary singer-songwriter Claudia Schmidt, who now makes her home on the island. This article, however, focuses on music making by Beaver Island Irish and their descendants.

REPERTOIRES OF MUSIC

Through the 1930s, Irish immigrant survivals distinguished Beaver Island from the surrounding region even though the islanders also readily adopted popular culture and regional traditions of the United States. Much interchange occurred on sailing vessels and in ports of the Great Lakes as well as in lumber camps, where islanders swapped songs with men from various ethnic and national backgrounds. Islanders also wrote a number of songs about local events and characters and continue to cherish their singers and songmakers, keeping copies of song texts or poems made up by a relative and handing them down from generation to generation.

The older singers recorded by Walton and Lomax sang unaccompanied ballads and spoke the last **verse** of their song in the Irish style. In later years islanders added **guitar** accompaniment and eliminated the more modal Irish repertoire. Today, the local Great Lakes ballad "Lost in Lake Michigan" is the only ballad from the Walton/Lomax collection still actively performed on the island. The old Irish ballads have been replaced by a new group of Irish songs learned from visitors, acquired during trips to Ireland, and heard on commercial recordings. Locally composed parodies or songs about island characters also continue to thrive. In addition, residents are writing new ballads—such as Barry Pischner's "Raymond" and "Big Bradley"—about Great Lakes shipwrecks of local interest. Perhaps the most popular song

Fiddler Patrick Bonner (1882–1973), pictured here at the King Strang Hotel, *c.* 1950s, played a repertoire of square dance tunes, schottisches, waltzes, jigs, and reels. *Photograph courtesy of the Beaver Island Historical Society.*

genre, however, is country-western, especially classic country from the 1950s.

The instrumental music recorded by Walton and Lomax was all dance music, and the Irish love of dancing continued on Beaver Island. The strong European influence on nineteenth-century American vernacular culture, combined with the cultural transplants of earlier generations of Irish and other European immigrants, meant that variants of Irish **jigs** and square and round dances already were established in the house parties, lumber camps, and community dance halls of the Upper Great Lakes by the time the Irish first arrived in the mid-1850s. The relative isolation of Beaver Island, however, contributed to a dance style that differed from the mainland.

The first generations of Beaver Island Irish were great **step dancers**. **Fiddlers**, mouth organ players, and even lilters provided the music, usually alternating jigs with square and round dances. Current dance styles include round dances, country **two-steps**, and a derivative of the old step dancing styles combined with the Polish-style **polka** called "jigging" or the "Beaver Island stomp." The country standard "Just Because" is a popular "jig tune" today. Music is provided by various combinations of guitar, electric **bass**, drum set, piano, and mouth organ. Fiddlers are highly prized, but no islander plays fiddle; they import one from the mainland when they can. Since the mid-1970s, most dances in Holy Cross Parish Hall have been organized by island piano, guitar, and mouth organ player, Edward Palmer. They begin with "On the Beach on Beaver Island," by islander Jewell Gillespie (a variant of "On the Beach at Waikiki"), and close with Danny Gillespie's rendition of "Danny Boy."

From the beginning, music and dance on Beaver Island occurred in association with holidays, paid-admission dances, and house parties modeled on Irish *céilis*. Since the 1940s, the tradition of "going around the island" in automobiles has replaced most older-style house parties. The key elements of storytelling, drink, music, and socializing remain intact. Holidays and family celebrations always have been occasions for dances. Today, the major island celebrations, St. Patrick's Day and Homecoming, both occur as benefits held in Holy Cross Parish Hall in St. James.

IDEAS ABOUT MUSIC

"It's not a song unless it's sad" is a prevalent belief among islanders. Americans in general selected the sad songs from the British ballad tradition, and the southern **hillbilly** music that grew out of these roots also featured mournful, lonesome themes. Not surprisingly, Beaver Islanders raised on the Carter Family and Grand Ole Opry radio broadcasts now sing sad country songs in lieu of the old ballads.

Ivan Walton captured another key island aesthetic, observing that the islanders retained the Irish "penchant for sociability; drinking, dancing, and singing seem to have been their chief source of enjoyment." This remains perhaps the most "Irish" characteristic on the island today. A good party lasts to the wee hours and is laced with plenty of drink and nostalgia. In a true "Beaver Island-style" party today, the musicians strive to create an atmosphere in which the elders can hear the tunes of their

youth, the island's veteran dancers will do a **waltz** or a jig, and the younger generation can learn island traditions. A core repertoire of country-western, round, and **square dance** tunes are now traditionalized as "Beaver Island music" and helps to define islander identity.

SOCIAL ORGANIZATION OF MUSIC

Major social occasions involve the entire community, although certain age and social groups hold their own parties. The island's overwhelming historic Catholicism led to friction with a small Protestant minority that affected patterns of socializing and music making during the earlier period; intermarriage and time have since broken down this division.

Most instrumentalists have been men. In keeping with prevailing social norms regarding women and **instruments**, women traditionally have played organ in church or chorded piano accompaniment. These norms of middle-class and religious respectability no longer hold such sway, but most dance band performers continue to be male. Two of the major historic singing contexts, Great Lakes sailing and lumber camps, were linked to male occupations, and thus Walton's field recordings, which reflected his interest in sailor songs, have predominantly male informants. Women more often sang at home for their families, for each other, or at house parties. Again, these gender distinctions are less strong today.

DOCUMENTARY RECORDINGS

The original Ivan H. Walton papers and sound recordings (1930–1958) are housed in the Michigan Historical Collections of the Bentley Historical Library at the University of Michigan in Ann Arbor. Copies of the Walton material plus the original Alan Lomax recordings from 1938 are housed at the Archive of Folksong, Library of Congress, Washington, D.C.

See glossary for definition of boldfaced terms

Island musicians
performing "Beaver
Island-style music" for
St. Patrick's Day, 1990.
left to right: Cindy
Edward Palmer (guitar),
Gillespie Brown (caller),
Dudley Stevens (fiddle),
Danny Gillespie (guitar),
and Rich Scripps
(electric bass).
*Photograph by Laurie
Kay Sommers, courtesy
of Michigan State
University Museum.*

BIBLIOGRAPHY

American Fiddle Tunes from the Archive of Folk Song. 1976.
Ed. by Alan Jabbour. Folk Music of the United States
series, Library of Congress. AFS L62. Contains three
songs by Beaver Island fiddler Patrick Bonner. Reissued on CD in 2000 by Rounder Records as Rounder
1518.

Collar, Helen. (1976). "The Irish Migration to Beaver Island." *Journal of Beaver Island History* 1:27–50.

Hendrix, Glen. (1980). "Songs of Beaver Island." *Journal
of Beaver Island History* 2:59–112.

———. (1988). "An Island of Fiddlers." *Journal of Beaver
Island History* 3:51–57.

Sommers, Laurie Kay. (1996). *Beaver Island House Party.*
East Lansing: Michigan State University Press, Michigan State University Museum, and Beaver Island Historical Society. Includes CD of the same title released
by Michigan State University Museum and Beaver Island Historical Society as BI001.

Walton, Ivan H. (1952). "Folk Singing on Beaver Island."
Midwest Folklore, 2, no. 4 (winter):177–185. Reprinted
in *Michigan Folklife Reader,* ed. C. Kurt Dewhurst and
Yvonne R. Lockwood (East Lansing: Michigan State
University Press, 1988).

RECENT BIBLIOGRAPHY/
DISCOGRAPHY/VIDEOGRAPHY

Compiled by Jennifer C. Post

BOOKS AND ARTICLES

Barrand, Anthony G. (1996). "Stumbling upon Lancashire Mill Culture in New England." In *The World Observed: Reflections on the Fieldwork Process,* ed. B. Jackson and E. D. Ives. Urbana: University of Illinois Press.

Bealle, John. (1997). *Public Worship, Private Faith: Sacred Harp and American Folk Song.* Athens: University of Georgia Press.

————. (1993). "Self Involvement in Musical Performance: Stage Talk and Interpretive Control at a Bluegrass Festival." *Ethnomusicology,* 63–86.

Berg, Wesley. (1996). "Hymns of the Old Colony Mennonites and the Old Way of Singing." *Musical Quarterly* 80 (1):77–117.

Bernhardt, Jack. (1996). *Cry Holy Unto the Lord: Tradition and Diversity in Bluegrass Gospel Music.* Montgomery, AL: Black Belt.

Blaustein, Richard. (1994). "The Oldtime Fiddlers Association Movement: A Grassroots Folk Revival." *Southern Folklore* 51 (3):199–217.

Bronner, Simon J. (1987). *Old-Time Music Makers of New York State.* Syracuse: Syracuse University Press.

Cairney, C. Thomas. (1991–1992). "'That evil fiddle': Scotch-Irish Folk Religion and Ethnic Boundary Maintenance in Southern Missouri." *Missouri Folklore Society Journal* 13–14:17–30.

Campbell, Gavin James. (1997). "'Old can be used instead of new': Shape-Note Singing and the Crisis of Modernity in the New South, 1880–1920." *Journal of American Folklore* 110 (436):169–88.

Carr, Joe and Munde, Alan. (1995). *Prairie Nights to Neon Lights: The Story of Country Music in West Texas.* Lubbock: Texas Tech University Press.

Carter, Thomas, with Sauber, Thomas. (1990). "'I never could play alone': The Emergence of the New River Valley String Band, 1875–1915." In *Arts in Earnest: North Carolina Folklife,* ed. D. W. Patterson and C. G. Zug III. Durham, NC, and London, England: Duke University Press.

Cauthen, Joyce H. (1989). *With Fiddle and Well-Rosined Bow: Old-Time Fiddling in Alabama.* Tuscaloosa: University of Alabama Press.

Cochran, Robert. (1996). *Our Own Sweet Sounds : A Celebration of Popular Music in Arkansas.* Fayetteville: University of Arkansas Press.

———. (1999). *Singing in Zion: Music and Song in the Life of an Arkansas Family.* Fayetteville: University of Arkansas Press.

Dalsemer, Bob. (1996). "Old Time Square Dancing on Ocracoke Island, North Carolina: Notes from Interviews with Ocracoke Island Dancers, September 13–15, 1992." *Country Dance and Song* 26:1–11.

Dugaw, Diane, ed. (1995). *The Anglo-American Ballad: A Folklore Casebook.* Garland Reference Library of the Humanities, vol. 1858; Garland Folklore Casebooks, vol. 8. New York: Garland.

Ellis, Bill. (1994). "Reinventing the Anglo-American Ballad: Dave Evans's Performance Style." *Southern Folklore* 51 (3):219–40.

Ellison, Curtis W. (1995). "Keeping Faith: Evangelical Performance in Country Music." *SAQ: The South Atlantic Quarterly* 94 (1):135–72.

Everts-Boehm, Dana. (1995). "'Oh, don't you remember': A Family Portrait of 'Babes in the Woods.'" *Missouri Folklore Society Journal* 17:17–31.

Fenster, Mark. (1989). "Preparing the Audience, Informing the Performers: John A. Lomax and Cowboy Songs and Other Frontier Ballads." *American Music* 7(3):260–77.

———. (1990). "Buck Owens, Country Music, and the Struggle for Discursive Control." *Popular Music* 9(3):275–90.

———. (1996). "Commercial (and/or?) Folk: The Bluegrass Industry and Bluegrass Traditions." *SAQ: The South Atlantic Quarterly* 94 (1):81–108.

Fitzwilson, Mary Ann. (1995). "With Hammers of Their Own Design: Scholarly Treatment of the John Henry Tradition." *Missouri Folklore Society Journal* 17:33–54.

Fryd, Vivien Green. (1995). "'The sad twang of mountain voices': Thomas Hart Benton's Sources of Country Music." *SAQ: The South Atlantic Quarterly* 94 (1):301–35.

Goddu, Theresa. (1995). "Bloody Daggers and Lonesome Graveyards: The Gothic and Country Music." *SAQ: The South Atlantic Quarterly* 94 (1):57–80.

Goertzen, Chris. (1996). "Balancing Local and National Approaches at American Fiddle Contests." *American Music* 14 (3):352–81.

Greenhill, Pauline. (1995). "'Neither a man nor a maid': Sexualities and Gendered Meanings in Cross-Dressing Ballads." *Journal of American Folklore* 108 (428):156–77.

Halpert, Herbert. (1995). "The Devil, the Fiddle, and Dancing." In *Fields of Folklore: Essays in Honor of Kenneth S. Goldstein,* ed. Roger D. Abrahams et al. Bloomington, IN: Trickster Press.

Hansen, Gregory. (1996). "The Relevance of 'Authentic Tradition' in Studying an Oldtime Florida Fiddler." *Southern Folklore* 53 (2):67–89.

Herman, Janet. (1995). "Music in a Dance Context: The Case of Contra in Los Angeles." *UCLA Journal of Dance Ethnology* 19:6–13.

Hollifield, Andrienne. (1995). "Family Tradition, Orality, and Cultural Intervention in Sodom Laurel Ballad Singing." *North Carolina Folklore Journal* 42 (1):1–34.

Hutson, C. Kirk. (1996). "'Whackety whack, don't talk back': The Glorification of Violence against Females and the Subjugation of Women in Nineteenth-Century Southern Folk Music." *Journal of Women's History* 8 (3):114–42.

Kahn, Ed. (1996). "The Carter Family on Border Radio." *American Music* 14 (2):205–17.

Kingsbury, Paul, ed. (1996). *The Country Reader: Twenty-Five Years of the Journal of Country Music.* Nashville, TN, and London, England: Country Music Foundation Press and Vanderbilt University Press.

Kisliuk, Michelle. (1988). "'A special kind of courtesy': Action at a Bluegrass Festival Jam Session." *TDR: The Drama Review* 32(3):141–55.

Krause, Rhett. (1995). "A History of Garland Dancing in America." *Country Dance and Song* 25:1–28.

Laufman, Dudley. (1992). *Dick Richardson: Old Time New Hampshire Fiddler.* Canterbury, NH: D. Laufman.

Lewis, George H, ed. (1993). *All That Glitters: Country Music in America.* Bowling Green: Bowling Green State University Popular Press.

Linscott, Eloise Hubbard, ed. (1993). *Folk Songs of Old New England,* 2nd ed. New York: Dover; London: Constable.

List, George. (1991). *Singing about It: Folk Song in Southern Indiana.* Indianapolis: Indiana Historical Society.

Marunas, Nathaniel. (1996). *Roots of Country: The Story of Country Music.* New York, NY: Friedman/Fairfax.

McLucas, Anne Dhu. (1994). "The Multi-Layered Concept of 'Folk Song' in American Music: The Case of Jean Ritchie's 'The Two Sisters.'" In *Themes and Variations: Writings on Music in Honor of Rulan Chao Pian,* ed. B. Yung and J. S. C. Lam. Cambridge: Department of Music, Harvard University; Hong Kong: Institute of Chinese Studies, Chinese University of Hong Kong.

McWhorter, Frankie. (1992). *Cowboy Fiddler.* Lubbock: Texas Tech University Press.

Milnes, Gerald. (1999). *Play of a Fiddle: Traditional Music, Dance, and Folklore in West Virginia.* Lexington: University Press of Kentucky.

Montell, Lynwood. (1996). "Absorbed in Gospel Music." In *The World Observed: Reflections on the Fieldwork Process,* ed. B. Jackson and E. D. Ives. Urbana: University of Illinois Press.

Morris, Alton C., ed. (1990). *Folksongs of Florida.* Gainesville: University of Florida Press.

Nusbaum, Philip. (1993). "Bluegrass and the Folk Revival: Structural Similarities and Experienced Differences." In *Transforming Tradition: Folk Music Revivals Examined,* ed. N. V. Rosenberg. Urbana: University of Illinois.

———. (1997). "Festival Committee of the Minnesota Bluegrass and Old Time Music Association: Musical Community." *Mid-America Folklore* 25 (1):14–35.

Oakley, Ken. (1999). *A History of Bluegrass in New York and Northeastern Pennsylvania.* Deposit, NY: K&C Publications.

Patterson, Beverly Bush. (1995). *The Sound of the Dove: Singing in Appalachian Primitive Baptist Churches.* Urbana: University of Illinois Press.

Peterson, Richard A. (1997). *Creating Country Music: Fabricating Authenticity.* Chicago: University of Chicago Press.

Pugh, Ronnie. (1998). *Ernest Tubb: The Texas Troubadour.* Durham, NC: Duke University Press.

Ritchie, Jean. (1997). *Folk Songs of the Southern Appalachians as Sung by Jean Ritchie,* 2nd ed. Lexington: University Press of Kentucky.

Rosenberg, Neil V. (1993). "Starvation, Serendipity, and the Ambivalence of Bluegrass Revivalism." In *Transforming Tradition: Folk Music Revivals Examined,* ed. N. V. Rosenberg. Urbana: University of Illinois.

———. (1993). *Bluegrass: A History.* Urbana: University of Illinois.

Sample, Tex. (1996). *White Soul: Country Music, the Church, and Working Americans.* Nashville, TN: Abingdon Press.

Sanjek, David. (1995). "Blue Moon of Kentucky Rising over the Mystery Train: The Complex Construction of Country Music." *SAQ: The South Atlantic Quarterly* 94 (1):29–55.

Sannella, Ted. (1996). *Swing the Next: A Second Collection of Squares, Contras, Triplets, and Circles in the New England Tradition.* Northampton, MA: Country Dance and Song Society.

Seymour, Chris. (1996). *Bluegrass.* New York: Friedman/Fairfax.

Sheaffer, John C. (1996). "The Thompsonville Strike: An Event and a Ballad." *Tennessee Folklore Society Bulletin* 57 (3):109–23.

Smith, Ralph Lee. (1997). *American Dulcimer Traditions.* American Folk Music and Folk Musicians, no. 2. Lanham, MD: Scarecrow Press.

Sommers, Laurie Kay. (1996). *Beaver Island House Party.* East Lansing: Michigan State University Press, Michigan State University Museum, and Beaver Island Historical Society. Includes CD.

Stebbins, Robert A. (1996). *The Barbershop Singer: Inside the Social World of a Musical Hobby.* Buffalo: University of Toronto Press.

Sweet, Stephen. (1996). "Bluegrass Music and Its Misguided Representation in Appalachia." *Popular Music and Society* 20 (3):37–51.

Tichi, Cecelia, ed. (1998). *Reading Country Music: Steel Guitars, Opry Stars, and Honky-Tonk Bars.* Durham, NC: Duke University Press.

Tribe, Ivan M. (1996). *Mountaineer Jamboree: Country Music in West Virginia.* Reprint. Lexington: University Press of Kentucky.

Tunnell, Kenneth D. (1991). "'Blood marks the spot where poor Ellen was found': Violent Crime in Bluegrass Music." *Popular Music and Society* 15(3):95–115.

Valle, Alf. (1995). "George Davis: Beyond the Singing Miner." *Southern Folklore* 52 (1):53–67.

Willis, Barry R. (1997). *America's Music: Bluegrass.* Franktown, CO: Pine Valley Music.

Wolfe, Charles K. (1996). *In Close Harmony: The Story of the Louvin Brothers.* Jackson: University Press of Mississippi.

———. (1996). *Kentucky Country: Folk and County Music of Kentucky.* Lexington: University Press of Kentucky.

———, ed. (1997). *Folk Songs of Middle Tennessee: The George Boswell Collection.* Knoxville: University of Tennessee Press.

———. (1997). *The Devil's Box: Masters of Southern Fiddling.* Nashville: Vanderbilt University Press.

Wright, John. (1993). *Traveling the High Way Home: Ralph Stanley and the World of Traditional Bluegrass.* Urbana: University of Illinois Press.

RECORDINGS

Sacred Harp Singing. Alabama Sacred Harp Convention. 1997. Library of Congress Archive of Folk Culture series. Rounder CD 1503.

Anglo-American Ballads, vol. 1. 1999. Library of Congress Archive of Folk Culture series. Rounder CD 1511.

Anglo-American Ballads, vol. 2. 1999. Library of Congress Archive of Folk Culture series. Rounder CD 1516.

Anthology of American Folk Music, 6 vols. 1997. Smithsonian Folkways/Sony Music Special Products SW CD 40090.

Brave Boys: New England Traditions in Folk Music. 1995 (1977). New World Records 80239-2.

Children of the Heav'nly King: Religious Expression in the Central Blue Ridge. 1998. Library of Congress Archive of Folk Culture series. Rounder CD 1506.

Choose Your Partners: Contradance and Square Dance Music of New Hampshire. 1999. Smithsonian Folkways CD 40126.

Cowboy Songs, Ballads, and Cattle Calls from Texas. 1999. Library of Congress Archive of Folk Culture series. Rounder CD 1512.

Crossroads: Southern Routes—Music of the American South. 1996. Smithsonian-Folkways SF CD 40080.

Doug and Jack Wallin: Family Songs and Stories from the North Carolina Mountains. 1995. Smithsonian-Folkways SF CD 40013.

Early Shaker Spirituals. 1996. Rounder CD 0078.

Folk Song America : A Twentieth-Century Revival, 6 vols. 1991. Smithsonian Collection of Recordings RD 046.

The Gospel Ship: Baptist Hymns and White Spirituals from the Southern Mountains. 1994. New World Records 80294-2.

The Hammons Family: The Traditions of a West Virginia Family and Their Friends. 1998. Library of Congress Archive of Folk Culture series. Rounder CD 1504.

The Mississippi, River of Song: A Musical Journey down the Mississippi, 2 vols. 1998. Smithsonian Folkways SFW 40086.

Pioneering Women of Bluegrass. 1996. Hazel Dickens and Alice Gerrard. Smithsonian Folkways SF 40065.

Railroad Songs and Ballads. 1997. Library of Congress Archive of Folk Culture series. Rounder CD 1508.

Roots of Country Music. 1988. Voices of the Americas. World Music Institute WMI-003. Audiocassette.

The Social Harp: Early American Shape-Note Songs. 1994. Rounder CD 0094.

Songs and Ballads of the Anthracite Miners. 1997. Library of Congress Archive of Folk Culture series. Rounder CD 1502.

Sounds Like Home: Connecticut Traditional Musicians. 1998. Hartford, CT: Institute for Community Research and Connecticut Public Radio. Traditional music of Connecticut ethnic communities. Program notes by John Dankosky and Lynne Williamson.

Southern Journey, 13 vols. 1997. Rounder Records CD 1701-1713. The Alan Lomax collection. Recorded in the field by Alan Lomax. *Voices from the American South: Blues, Ballads, Hymns, Reels, Shouts, Chanteys and Work Songs; Ballads and Breakdowns; Highway Mississippi: Delta Country Blues, Spirituals, Work Songs, and Dance Music; Brethren We Meet Again: Southern White Spirituals; Bad Man Ballads: Songs of Outlaws and Desperadoes; Sheep, Sheep, Don'tcha Know the Road?: Southern Music, Sacred and Sinful; Ozark Frontier; Velvet Voices; Harp of a Thousand Strings: All-Day Singing from the Sacred Harp; And Glory Shone Around: More All-Day Singing from the Sacred Harp; Honor the Lamb; Georgia Sea Islands Songs for Everyday Living; Georgia Sea Islands: Biblical Songs and Spirituals.*

Traditional Fiddle Music of Kentucky, 2 vols. 1997. Rounder 0376-0377.

White Spirituals from the Sacred Harp. 1994. New World Records 80205-2.

VIDEOS

American Patchwork: Songs and Stories about America. 1990. Alan Lomax. 5 vols. (60 min. each). Beverly Hills, CA: PBS Home Video. Vol. 1: *Jazz Parades;* vol.. 2: *Cajun Country;* vol. 3: *The Land Where the Blues Began;* vol. 4: *Appalachian Journey;* vol. 5: *Dreams and Songs of the Noble Old.*

Ballad of a Mountain Man: The Story of Bascom Lamar Lunsford. 1990. Donn Rogosin. The American Experience. 58 min. Alexandria, VA: PBS Video. North Carolina.

Bill Monroe: Father of Bluegrass Music. 1993. Steve Gebhardt. 90 min. New York: Original Cinema.

Bonsoir mes amis: Good Night My Friends. 1990. 46 min. Portland, ME: Films by Huey. Fiddlers Ben Guillemette and Lionel "Toots" Bouthot.

Chase the Devil: Religious Music of the Appalachian Mountains. 1990 [1982]. Jeremy Marre. 50 min. Newton, NJ: Yazoo Video.

Discovering American Folk Music. 1987. 21 min. North Hollywood, CA: Hollywood Select Video.

Dreadful Memories: The Life of Sarah Ogan Gunning, 1910–1983. 1988. Mimi Pickering. 39 min. Whitesburg, Ky.: Appalshop Films.

Dreams and Songs of the Noble Old: The Creativity of the Elderly. 1998. Alan Lomax. 60 min. Cambridge, MA : Vestapol, distributed by Rounder Records.

Earl Robinson: Ballad of an American. 1994. Bette Jean Bullert. 56 min. Alexandria, VA: PBS Video.

High Lonesome: The Story of Bluegrass Music. 1994. 95 min. Newton, NJ: Yazoo Video.

Legends of Old Time Music. 1995. 58 min. Cambridge, MA: Vestapol, distributed by Rounder Records.

The Mississippi, River of Song: The Grassroots of American Music. 1999. Elijah Wald. 240 min. (4 vols.) Bethesda, MD: Acord Media.

Musical Holdouts. 1990. John Cohen. 50 min. Berkeley: University of California, Extension Center for Media and Independent Learning. Music and lives of Americans who have maintained their ethnic and individual identities in their music.

New England Dances: Squares, Quadrilles, Step Dances. 1995. John M. Bishop. 29 min. Montpelier, VT: Multicultural Media (distributor).

New England Fiddles. 1995. John M. Bishop. 48 min. Montpelier, VT: Multicultural Media (distributor).

Shady Grove: Old Time Music from North Carolina, Kentucky and Virginia. 1997. 60 min. Cambridge: Vestapol/ Rounder Records.

Songs for Ralph. 1996. Paul Petrissans. 42 min. New York: Filmmakers Library. A musical tribute to Ralph Rinzler.

That High Lonesome Sound. 1996. 70 min. Newton, NJ : Shanachie. Three films shot in the 1960s: *The High Lonesome Sound; The End of an Old Song; Sara and Maybelle.*

Times Ain't Like They Used to Be: Early Rural and Popular American Music, 1928–1935. 1992. Sherwin Dunner and Richard Nevins. 70 mins. Newton, NJ: Yazoo Video.

Two Generations of Labor Singers. 1989. 28 min. Chicago: Committee for Labor Access, 1989. Utah Phillips and Billy Bragg.

The Unbroken Circle: Vermont Music—Tradition and Change. 1995. 59 min. Montpelier, VT: Multicultural Media.

GLOSSARY

A

a cappella Unaccompanied vocal music; singing without instrumental accompaniment.

Accordion A free-reed, bellows-driven instrument developed in the early nineteenth century. There are various forms of accordions; most common are the button accordion (with a keyboard made up of one or more rows of buttons) and the piano accordion (with a piano-style keyboard). *See also* Diatonic accordion.

Alabado A free-form lament of Arab-Spanish origin that is heard in Texas-Mexican communities of the southwestern United States.

Angular leap An abrupt jump between two intervals in a melody.

Antiphony See Call-and-response.

Ascending contour or **melody** A melody that generally rises in pitch over its duration.

Autoharp A musical instrument invented by C. F. Zimmerman in the late nineteenth century. It is tuned chromatically, covering about three and a half octaves. The strings are stopped by the player pressing down on "chord bars;" these bars automatically block all the notes except those found in a specific chord. Sold through mail-order catalogs and by traveling salesmen/teachers in the early twentieth century, the autoharp became a popular instrument for accompanying songs and ballads.

B

Bagpipe A common musical instrument found throughout Europe. There are many varieties made in different sizes with different features. The basic bagpipe consists of a large bag (sometimes made of the body of a goat or another animal) that is pumped to provide the air supply for one or more pipes. In the top of each pipe is a single reed that produces the sounds. The chanter is a long pipe with holes in it that produces melody notes; the drone pipes are shorter and play only a single, continuous note. *See also* Uillean (bag)pipes.

Bajo sexto A large-bodied, guitar-like instrument popularized in Mexico. It has a much deeper body than a standard guitar.

Ballad A song that tells a story. Ballads are usually long, and their main subjects are love and death.

Banjo (five-string) An African American–derived instrument featuring a skin or plastic head stretched across a wooden or metal hoop, with four long strings and one short "drone" string. The banjo was originally used in African American dance music and in minstrel music and is now commonly played in old-time and bluegrass music. *See also* Tenor banjo.

Barbershop harmony Traditional four-part harmonies developed by so-called barbershop quartets during the late nineteenth and early twentieth centuries. Barbershop quartets often featured an independent, and active, bass part. This style of singing was carried forward by gospel quartets and other popular harmony groups.

Barrel drum A drum with a long body that is slightly flared at its center, like the shape of a barrel. These drums can have either one or two heads and may vary in size from small to very large. The Japanese *taiko* and Puerto Rican *barile* are examples of barrel drums.

Bass An acoustic or electric four-string instrument used to play the bass harmony accompaniment to a melody.

Bass drum A large cylindrical drum of indefinite pitch with heads on both sides.

Batá drums Sacred drums (imported from Africa) that are played as part of Afro-Caribbean religious ceremonies. They have an hourglass shape with a head stretched across each end of the body. The drums are held vertically across the player's body, and each end is struck with one hand. Batá rhythms have been carried over into secular/popular musical styles from this region.

Bebop A style of jazz involving new harmonic concepts, rapid tempos, and small ensembles. It was developed in the 1940s and is especially associated with saxophone player Charlie Parker.

Big band The primary ensemble of the swing era of American jazz and popular music of the 1930s and 1940s. Big band music is scored for multiple trumpets, trombones, clarinets, and saxophones (melody group), while small groups usually employ, at most, one of each instrument. Usually the sections of the band perform alternately, in call-and-response style. In both big and small bands, the rhythm section is piano and/or guitar, drum kit, and double bass.

Big circle dance An Appalachian dance performed in a large circle. Couples pair off in sets of two to perform figures similar to those in square dances, then fall back into a big circle to perform larger group figures.

Blue note A note that is slightly flattened to give it a "bluesy" effect; often the third or seventh degree of the scale.

Bluegrass A style of music invented by mandolinist Bill Monroe based on old-time string band music, blues, and Western swing. Monroe put together a band that included the rhythms of popular music, the bluesy inflected vocals of African American music, and the tight harmonies of gospel and old-time church singing. The typical bluegrass band is modeled on Monroe's original group that featured mandolin, guitar, banjo, fiddle, and bass.

Blues A traditional African American musical genre. It is in 4/4 time, with a melody characterized by lowered third and seventh (blue notes), and has developed into a stereotyped, twelve-measure harmonic pattern. The term has also been used to describe any song that expresses "blue" or sad feelings.

Bodhrán *See* Frame drum.

Bolero Medium-tempoed dance in triple time, with intricate steps, popular in Spain, Latin America, and the Caribbean.

Bongo drums/Bongos Two small, shallow, single-headed drums that are played with the palms and fingers of the hands. Popular in Latin-Caribbean musical cultures.

Bottleneck A style of playing the guitar in which the guitarist places a glass bottleneck around a finger on the noting hand and slides it over the strings of the instrument, creating a sliding or whining sound. This is a common technique among blues guitarists, who use either a glass bottleneck or a metal bar (called a slide).

Brass band A band made up entirely of brass and wind instruments, popularized by bandleader/composer John Philip Sousa at the turn of the twentieth century.

Break dancing/Breaking A solo, urban dance style featuring elaborate athletic moves, including spinning, moonwalking, flipping, and popping (isolating certain parts of the body to mimic robot-like movement).

Broadsheet/Broadside ballad A single sheet of paper on which the text (and sometimes music) of a song was printed. Beginning in the seventeenth century, broadsides were popular as a means of spreading new and traditional songs.

Buck dancing *See* Clogging.

Button accordion *See* Accordion.

C

Cajun music A style of music that originated among natives of southeastern Louisiana of French descent. It often consists of dance music or lyrical songs sung in the local dialect (which is itself a mixture of English and French dialects). Typical Cajun bands feature fiddle, accordion, triangle, and guitar.

Call-and-response A vocal or instrumental style in which a short melodic line (the "call") is sung (often by a song leader) and then a second, "responding" phrase follows it (often sung by a group). In European and American classical music, the style is called "antiphony."

Caller A dance leader who "prompts" the dancers by calling out the figures before they are to be performed. Common today among square, contra, and big circle dances.

Calypso A Caribbean song form popularized in the United States during the 1930s featuring improvised songs of topical or humorous content with a syncopated beat.

Camp-meeting song A religious song associated with large nineteenth-century camp meetings, the purpose of which was to convert people to Christianity. Hundreds of congregants converged on a single spot to spend several days praying, sermonizing, witnessing, and exchanging and learning simple songs that were easy to sing by ear.

Canción A traditional love song of the Latino communities of the southwestern United States, Mexico, and Latin America.

Ceili Gaelic for "dance." Thus, any gathering where Irish dancing is performed.

Ceili or **Ceilidh band** An Irish dance band that combines traditional Irish melody instruments—fiddle, flute, bagpipe, and accordion—with a regular, heavy rhythmic accompaniment provided by piano, bass, and military-style drumming.

Celtic music Music of the Celts, the original inhabitants of Ireland and Wales; often used to describe Irish traditional music in general.

Chanson A short lyric song in the French language.

Chanter (1) A song leader. In the Native American tradition, the chanter (usually male) may also serve as the drummer who accompanies dancers. (2) The melody pipe of the bagpipe.

Chantey *See* Shanty.

Chanteymen Sailors who sing traditional shantys; also used to describe any sailors who work on a boat.

Chicago blues A style of urban blues that emerged on the South Side of Chicago after World War II, centering around performers such as Muddy Waters and Howlin' Wolf. Generally, Chicago blues is performed by a combo featuring electric guitar, piano, harmonica, and drums.

Chicken scratch music A common name (regarded by some as disparaging) for a type of dance music played by Native American and Tex-Mex bands that is derived from European styles such as quadrilles, waltzes, and polkas.

Chinese opera An elaborately staged and costumed musical theater tradition of China. Different Chinese regions have their own operatic styles, which are referred to as Peking opera, Cantonese opera, and so on.

Chorus (1) *See* Refrain. (2) A large vocal group made up of voices of different vocal ranges.

Chromatic scale All twelve divisions of the octave (not just the eight of the do-re-mi scale.) On a piano, for instance, the chromatic scale includes all of the white and black keys within the span of an octave.

Cittern A Renaissance-era string instrument similar to a guitar.

Clave rhythm The defining rhythm of much Latin-Caribbean music. It is a repeated two-bar pattern around which all other rhythmic patterns are organized. It goes "123-123-12 34-12-12-34," keeping an even pulse and stressing "1."

Claves Two sticks that are beat rhythmically together in Latin-Caribbean musical styles. *See also* Rhythm sticks.

Clog (1) *See* Clogging. (2) A dance tune to accompany clogging or step dancing, usually in 2/4 or 4/4 time.

Clogging Complicated step dances often performed by a solo dancer, with movement restricted to the lower legs and feet, while the remainder of the body is held straight. Similar to Irish step dancing and perhaps derived from it. Styles that involve keeping the feet close to the ground are known as "flat-foot clogging" or "flatfooting." Also called "buck dancing."

Coda An ending passage of a musical composition.

Combo A small instrumental ensemble.

Concertina A name loosely given to a wide variety of free-reed, bellows-driven instruments. The concertina played by German, Polish, and other immigrants in the American Midwest is really a form of button accordion. The Irish concertina is much smaller and plays a different note on the push and pull.

Conga drums *See* Tumbadoras.

Conjunto (1) A small ensemble, usually led by an accordion, popular in the southwestern United States and Mexico. (2) The type of music played by such an ensemble. *See also* Norteño music/*La música norteña.*

Contour Literally, "shape." The shape of a melody—whether it moves up or down gradually or in leaps—is called its contour.

Contra dance A New England form of couple dance, danced in two facing lines. The figures are performed by two couples and are similar to those found in square dancing. Chorus figures are performed by the entire line. Couples progress up or down the line as they become "active" (initiators of a figure) or "inactive."

Contradanza *See* Contra dance.

Contredanse *See* Contra dance.

Corrido A narrative folk song or ballad (often tragic and with elements of social protest) found among both Native American and Tex-Mex traditions in the southwestern United States and Mexico, its country of origin.

Cotillion A French ballroom dance of the late eighteenth and early nineteenth centuries that was popular in the American colonies as well as in England. It involved couples in square formations performing repeated figures and was a predecessor of the quadrille and square dance.

Cotillo *See* Cotillion.

Countermelody A contrasting second melody played simultaneously with the principal melody.

Counterrhythm A second rhythmic line played in contrast with the principal rhythmic line.

Couplet Two lines of a song's lyric that form a complete thought.

Cowbell A small, hollow metal bell—similar to those placed around the necks of cows—that is struck with a metal stick.

Csárdás A stylized Hungarian folk dance in 2/4 time that became popular in the first half of the nineteenth century. The melodies are noted for their minor keys and dramatic changes in tempo.

Cuatro A Puerto Rican guitar-like instrument, but with a smaller body and five pairs of strings.

Cubop A blend of Cuban rhythms and drums with bebop-style music. Pioneered by Dizzy Gillespie's bands of the 1950s.

Cycle (1) A group of songs or instrumental compositions that are usually performed together. (2) In square dancing, a group of four couples who form a single square. Also called set.

Cymbals Paired percussion instruments consisting of two brass discs that are struck together. They can be very small (for example, finger cymbals) or quite large.

D

Deejay *See* Disc jockey.

Descending contour or **melody** A melody that generally falls in pitch over its duration.

Diatonic accordion An accordion with buttons that play different notes when the bellows are opened (pulled) or closed (pushed). Sometimes called "push-pull accordions" for this reason.

Diatonic scale The eight-tone scale from octave to octave; the do-re-mi scale without chromatic tones.

Diddley bow Traditional African American one-stringed instrument. The string is made of hay baling wire stretched over two cans or jars and fastened horizontally to a wall or a board at each end.

It is plucked with the fingers of one hand. Different tones are produced by stopping the string with a small bottle or other slide.

Disc jockey An announcer who selects, introduces, and plays records, either "live" or on the radio. Commonly called a "deejay" or "DJ."

Disco Dance music of the 1970s noted for its loud, regular beat.

Dissonance In Western classical music, any harmony part that is based on seconds, sevenths, augmented, or diminished intervals. More generally, a harmony part that sounds unpleasant to the ear. "Consonance" is the term used to describe simultaneously played tones that are pleasant to the ear.

DJ *See* Disc jockey.

Dominant The fifth degree in the Western major or minor scale. Also, the chord built on this note.

Dorian mode A sequence of tones from one octave to the next, neither major nor minor, which can be sounded by the eight white keys of the piano starting and ending on "D."

Drone A continuous, unchanging tone that sounds throughout a musical composition or a portion of it.

Drop-thumb/double-thumbing (banjo) *See* Frailing.

Drum-rattle A skin-headed drum that features small rattles, either mounted on the outside of the instrument or along the rim of the drumhead itself, so that it can create both percussive and rattling sounds.

Dulcimer (Appalachian dulcimer or **lap dulcimer)** A three- or four-stringed instrument held on the lap. The strings run the length of the instrument over a fretted fingerboard, and the player frets the notes either with a small stick or the fingers while strumming the strings with a feather quill or pick. Not related to the hammer/hammered dulcimer.

Duple time/beat A rhythm that is divisible by two or with two primary accents.

E

Electric guitar An amplified guitar; the guitar's sound is enhanced through pickups that translate the sound into electrical energy that is amplified and broadcast over speakers. Amplification further allows changing the guitar's timbre.

Ethnography The systematic description of human culture.

Ethnology The scientific comparison of human cultures.

Ethnomusicology The study of people making music, all over the globe.

F

Fa-sol-la singers *See* Shape-note.

Falsetto An artificially high voice; often a male singer singing well above his normal range.

Feis An Irish competition/festival in which musicians and dancers compete for prizes.

Fiddle A bowed lute with four strings, ordinarily tuned GDAE like the European violin. Although fiddles and violins are now structurally more or less identical, fiddle players use different techniques and sometimes modify their instruments (flattening the arc of the bridge, for example) and play in nonstandard tunings.

Field holler An a cappella, African American work song.

Fiesta A religious celebration popular in Latino communities and among some Native Americans.

Fife A short, open-holed, transverse flute with six to eight holes.

Fifth The fifth scale degree; the related interval between the tonic and the fifth scale degree.

Fill An embellishing musical phrase, often improvised by an ensemble musician not responsible for carrying the main melody.

Finger cymbals Tiny paired cymbals that are attached to the fingers with small leather straps.

Finger pick To play a banjo or guitar with the tips of the finger or finger picks (metal or plastic extensions attached to the thumb or fingers to enable the player to produce a louder sound) rather than strumming across the strings with a flat pick held between the thumb and first finger.

Fipple flute A flute with a mouthpiece that has a plug with a notch at one end, such as that found on the recorder.

Flageolet A simple flute, often made from a reed or bone, that is blown from one end. It features four fingering holes and two thumb holes to vary the tones produced.

Flatfooting *See* Clogging.

Floating stanza or **verse** A common set of lyrics that moves from one song to another.

Folklife Study of the day-to-day lives of ordinary people in close-knit communities, with special attention to traditional ways of thinking and doing.

Folklore The oral and customary traditions of a group of people, including their stories, songs, recipes, clothing, holidays, architecture and use of space, and so on.

Foodways The traditional eating habits and cooking practices of a specific cultural group.

Form Musical structure; the way the musical design coheres as a whole.

Fox-trot Popular dance form of the 1920s and 1930s in duple time that has survived as one of the standard couple dances.

Frailing (banjo) The old-time style of playing the banjo that involves brushing

the back of the nail of the second or third finger across the strings while "catching" the thumb on the short drone string in a rhythmic pattern. Also called clawhammer, rapping, banging, thumping, or drop-thumb (a more melodic variation of frailing, where the thumb is used to pick notes as well as to hit the drone string). *See also* three-finger style (banjo) and two-finger (up-picking) style (banjo).

Frame drum A round drum with a shallow body. The rim of the drum is often made from a single bent piece of wood. Examples of frame drums are the bodhrán, which is used in Irish traditional music, and the tambourine.

Free reed A small, single reed—made of metal, bamboo, or some other material—that is held firmly at one end, usually in a frame. A Jew's harp is a simple free-reed instrument. Accordions, concertinas, the Japanese shō, and harmonicas are also free-reed instruments.

Freedom song Song performed during the civil rights movement of the 1950s and 1960s expressing the message of the movement.

Frolic An older term for a dance, often held at a private home, that might last all night long.

Funk (1) An African American popular music that developed in the 1960s from African polyrhythms and call-and-response textures. Funk music often uses a single chord or a few alternating, sometimes complex harmonies, through which clipped, syncopated lines emerge in the electric guitar and bass parts, drums and percussion, keyboards, winds (saxophones, trumpets), and vocal parts. Interjections by different instruments and voices, often repeated, is another typical element. Funk has been able to blend into successive styles, exerting influence on reggae, disco, hip-hop, and rap. (2) A roots movement in jazz during the 1950s that drew on blues, rhythm and blues, and gospel music in a reaction against increasingly abstract bebop and cool jazz styles.

G

Gaelic The family of traditional languages of Ireland and Scotland.

Genre A named type of musical composition and performance, such as jazz, blues, bluegrass, zydeco, and so on.

Gesangverein ("Singing society") A private, German American social club dedicated to choral singing, often of patriotic and sentimental songs, traditionally sung in German.

Gigue Originally a popular Baroque dance in a rapid tempo that was performed by men. In the Franco-American tradition, the gigue has evolved into a virtuosic solo step dance performed by both men and women. *See also* Jig.

Glide A smooth, rapid movement from one note to another, slurring over the intermediate pitches. In classical music, called "portamento" or "glissando."

Glissando *See* Glide.

Glottal stop An abrupt interruption of the breath by rapidly closing the glottis (the elongated open space between the vocal cords).

Gong A large, round, metal plate that is often suspended in a frame. It plays a single note when it is struck with a metal stick or mallet.

Gospel music Modern Protestant religious music that is more personal and informal than the traditional Christian hymn.

Gospel quartet A small ensemble of four or more singers who sing religious-themed songs in four-part harmony.

Gourd rattle A dried gourd that has been hollowed out and filled with seeds or small pebbles. When shaken, it makes a rattling sound.

Grace note An ornamenting or embellishing note, usually performed before the primary tone.

Griot An African storyteller; specifically applied to the master harpists of the Gambia who accompany themselves on a harp known as the kora while relating their political and cultural history.

Guitar A six-stringed instrument of seventeenth-century Spanish origin, successor to the lute. It was popularized among folk and amateur musicians in the United States in the late nineteenth century as an accompaniment for songs.

H

Habanera A traditional Latin-Caribbean dance form with a 3+3+2 rhythmic structure.

Half-tone or **half-step** The smallest interval in the Western scale; also called a semitone. For example, the interval C-C# is a half-step.

Hammer/hammered dulcimer A traditional instrument found in many regions of the world. It consists of a square or trapezoidal-shaped body with strings running across the length of the box. The strings are usually paired (i.e., each note is produced by two strings). The player strikes the strings with two small "hammers" made of wood (sometimes covered with felt). Unrelated to the Appalachian lap dulcimer, despite the shared name.

Hammond organ An electronic organ developed in the late 1940s that was far less expensive and much smaller and lighter than a conventional pipe organ and therefore appealed to smaller churches and home organists. Besides organ sounds, this instrument was also capable of producing some "special effects" electronically.

Harmonica A small, free-reed instrument. A series of reeds are mounted in small air chambers that are open at one end. The player either sucks or blows into these openings to make the reeds sound. By cupping their hands over the harmonica and opening or closing them while playing and by playing in keys other than what the harmonica is meant for, blues musicians have created many different timbres and effects. Also called a "mouth harp," "harp," or "mouth organ."

Harmonium A small reed organ. The reeds are set in motion by air from a bellows pumped by the player's feet.

Harmony Musical tones sounded at the same time. *See also* Melody.

Heterophony Two or more slightly different vocal or instrumental parts played simultaneously. Slight intentional variations in ornamentation and attack may account for some of the differences.

Hexatonic A six-note scale.

Highland fling The Irish name for traditional Scottish tunes played briskly in 4/4 time.

Hillbilly music The recording industry's pejorative, in-house name for early country music (c. 1923–1930).

Hip-hop African American popular dance music of the last two decades of the twentieth century that became the underlying musical basis for rap. While inheriting the strong beat of disco, hip-hop re-emphasized the backbeat of 1960s popular music and also drew upon house music of the late 1970s. It developed as sampling technology evolved, allowing musicians and producers to "sample" or record small excerpts from earlier popular songs. These small pieces were then electronically treated, looped (or repeated), and put one on top of another to form a dense musical texture.

Hoedown A community dancing party, originally in the rural American South and West, featuring square dances with calling and old-time music.

Honky-tonk A small bar or club featuring country music. Marked by the sound of electric guitars and pedal steel guitars, honky-tonk music emerged as a popular style in the late 1940s and early 1950s.

Hornpipe Since the sixteenth century, a dance and tune in 4/4 or 2/4 time. Originally played slowly to accompany step dancing, hornpipes are now often played as quickly as reels.

Hula Originally a form of religious dance from Hawaii; subsequently popularized as a show dance style.

Hurdy-gurdy A stringed instrument most commonly found in Eastern Europe and France (Brittany). The fret board is covered with an elaborate mechanism that allows the player to fret the strings by pushing down on a key (like the keyboard of a piano). The notes are sounded by turning a crank that activates a rosin-covered wheel that rubs up against the strings from underneath.

Hymn A religious song praising God.

I

Idiophones Musical instruments whose sounds are produced by striking or shaking a metallic, wooden, or other surface directly. Thus, idiophones produce their sound by the substance of the instrument itself. Cymbals, rattles, rhythm sticks, and triangles are examples of idiophones.

Improvisation The creation of new melody, lyrics, or harmony parts in the midst of performance.

Instrument A device that produces musical sounds.

Interval The distance in pitch between two notes. Intervals are usually measured from the lower tone to the higher. In the C major scale, the interval C-E is a major third.

J

Jam/jamming A dance competition held on the street; "jamming" is to compete with other dancers. *See also* Street dancing; break dancing/breaking.

Jam session An informal gathering of musicians to play tunes.

Jazz A number of popular musical styles invented by African Americans beginning around the turn of the twentieth century based on improvised melodies and syncopated rhythms.

Jew's harp A small musical instrument consisting of a metal tongue (or reed) mounted in a frame. The player holds it up against his or her open teeth, and, while vigorously plucking the instrument's tongue, breathes in and out to create a whirring sound. Also called "jaw harp."

Jig An Irish dance tune in triple time; also the rapid movement of the feet in a "jig" step.

Jubilee An African American religious song that has had different meanings over time and that may refer to (1) songs sung during the emancipation celebrations of 1862 and that refer to a liberation, (2) songs that are uptempo and rhythmic (such as "When the Saints Go Marching In"), and (3) the Fisk Jubilee Singers and their strong influence on a new singing style and songs written during Reconstruction. The Fisk singers and these new songs were important in the development of gospel quartets. Written in the context of freedom, not slavery, this music exhibited a different attitude and style.

Jug band An informal jazz group, often featuring homemade or inexpensive musical instruments, including the kazoo, washboard, washtub bass, and a large, empty jug. The jug player either blows or sings into its opening in a rhythmic fashion to create a bass harmony part.

Junkanoo music A style of vibrant, Bahamian percussion music performed

by costumed marchers (Junkanooers) at special parades and festivals that were originally held during the Christmas season but now occur at other times of the year as well.

K

Kazoo A small wind instrument featuring a thin membrane that is set into vibration when the player hums or speaks into one end of the instrument. A simple version can be made by placing a piece of tissue paper over a comb and humming through it.

Kitchen racket or **kitchen junket** An informal dance held in the home; the term was most commonly used in New York and New England for informal contra dances.

Klezmer A Yiddish term literally meaning "vessel of melody," it was the name given to Jewish American dance bands of the 1920s and 1930s who played a mixture of traditional and jazz-influenced music. Klezmer music has enjoyed a strong revival since the mid-1970s.

Konpas Haitian small-band music that incorporates elements of rock, jazz, disco, soul, and funk.

L

Ländler A couple dance in 3/4 time that originated in alpine central Europe in the early nineteenth century.

Leader *See* Song leader.

Lining out A term used to describe a style of hymn singing in which a group leader first sings a line of music and the leader and congregation then repeat the words to a different but related melody. The hymn continues in this way line by line.

Long bow style A fiddle technique in which several notes are played on a single bowstroke; smoother than playing "short bow" style, in which the direc-

tion of the bow is changed with the majority of notes.

Longways Dances performed in two long lines. *See also* Contra dance.

Lulus *See* Vocables.

Lute A generic name for a variety of plucked string instruments, most popular from the sixteenth through the eighteenth centuries. The body of the lute is shaped like half of a pear, with its neck turned back at a right angle. It usually has five sets of double strings, plus a single string for the highest sound, and they are plucked with the fingers. The mandolin is of the lute family, as are the Chinese pipa and the Japanese biwa. *See also* Guitar.

Lyric song A song that primarily expresses an emotion (e.g., love, loneliness, or anger). Lyric songs are shorter than narrative ballads. Usually in a verse-refrain format, a common structure in which one melodic part (a verse whose lyrics often change) is alternated with a repeated chorus or refrain.

M

Major The primary Western classical scale since the eighteenth century. A major chord consists of a first, major third, and fifth intervals.

Mambo A ballroom dance derived from the rumba. It appeared in Cuba during the 1940s and by the 1950s had spread to non–Hispanic audiences in the United States. The mambo uses forward and backward steps (beginning on the upbeat) to percussive polyrhythmic accompaniment.

Mandolin An eight-string, guitar-like instrument. The mandolin's strings are paired in four and tuned like those of a violin. Mandolin orchestras were popular in the early twentieth century. Today they have largely disappeared, but the instrument is featured in bluegrass music.

Maracas Popular Latin-Caribbean gourd rattles.

Mariachi A modern musical ensemble—often heard along the border between Texas and Mexico—consisting of vocalists accompanied by various stringed instruments, including guitars and violins and usually brass (trumpets) as well.

Marimba A wooden-keyed instrument with small resonators placed below the bars. It is played with a stick or a pair of sticks. A type of xylophone.

Matachina and **Matachines** *Matachina* are dances of conquest, originally Spanish in origin but later adapted by the Pueblo Indians; *matachines* are the male dancers who perform them. The matachines dance in two lines facing each other, often wearing elaborate crowns featuring long ribbons and carrying rattles. They may also perform circular dances around a maypole.

Mazurka A Polish dance style in triple time brought to the United States by immigrants beginning in the mid–nineteenth century.

Mele Chanted poetic texts that express the relationship of Hawaiians to everything around them (the land, the ocean, their gods, and all living things) and also serve as orally transmitted records of the legends and lore of the Hawaiian people, including family histories, plant names, place names, and medical practices.

Melisma Characterized by singing three or more tones per syllable of text.

Melody A succession of musical tones. *See also* Harmony.

Membranophones Musical instruments that produce a sound through a vibrating membrane, or skin head. Drums are the most common membranophones.

Merengue or **meringue** Characteristic Afro-Cubanesque song dance of Venezuela, Haiti, and the Dominican Republic. It uses four-line stanzas and refrain verse forms. Responsorial singing, polyrhythms, and 5/8 effects are layered over the basic 2/4 beat.

Metallophone Similar to a xylophone, but with metal keys instead of wooden ones.

Microtone Any interval smaller than the half-tone; often used to describe tiny divisions of a tone (such as 1/4 of a tone).

Minor The second most common Western classical scale, also known as the Aeolian mode.

Minstrel show A nineteenth-century American amusement in which actors and musicians mimicked African American dialect, music, and dance.

Mixolydian One of the Greek modes, rarely heard today in classical music, although still common in some folk traditions. Neither major nor minor, it is a sequence of tones that can be achieved by playing the eight white keys of the piano starting and ending on G.

Monochord A single-stringed instrument, such as the diddley bow.

Montuno The call-and-response section of Cuban son. It features a short, simple harmonic ostinato that forms the basis for call-and-response passages and solo instrumental improvisation.

Motown A type of African American popular music (created specifically to appeal to teenagers of all races) that was produced by the Detroit-based record label of the same name during the 1960s.

Music notation Any system of symbols for writing down music.

N

Narrative song A song that tells a story or relates history; a ballad.

Norteño music/La música norteña Contemporary accordion-based folk music of Tex-Mex origin characterized by stylistic simplicity and working-class themes. The style is known inside Texas as conjunto.

Note value The length of time or duration that a specific note is sounded. Also called "time value."

O

Octave The eighth or final scale step; the interval whose distance is eight diatonic tones, as from middle C to C above middle C on the piano.

Off-beat A beat that is normally not stressed or accented.

Old-time (1) The traditional songs and fiddle tunes of the southeastern United States. (2) Songs and tunes that were popular in the past but now are remembered by only a small group of musicians. (3) A term used by many European American cultures of the Midwest to describe the ethnic-based styles of social dancing and social dance music centered around waltzes, polkas, and often the schottische. Ballroom dances (such as the fox-trot) that have developed in more recent years are considered part of the "new-time" tradition.

Oral history (1) History that is passed from generation to generation by the telling of stories rather than through written texts. (2) A method of collecting history by means of interviews.

Oral tradition Songs, stories, and other customs that are passed down from generation to generation by imitation and by word-of-mouth rather than by being written down.

Ornament Formulaic decoration or embellishment of a musical tone.

Ostinato A melodic phrase that is persistently repeated (usually in the same voice part and at the same pitch) throughout a composition.

P

Panpipes A collection of reeds of different lengths that are tied together. The player blows across the top of the reeds to play different notes. Panpipes are found in many Pacific and Latin American musical traditions.

Parallel thirds A type of harmonic accompaniment in which the melody line is doubled by another part, two scale tones above it, in parallel movement.

"Pendulum-like" melody A melody that predominantly alternates between two notes.

Pennywhistle *See* Tin whistle.

Pentatonic scale A five-note scale, common in folk and traditional styles. On the piano, it can be obtained by playing the black keys only.

Phrase A short musical or lyrical thought; a portion of a melody.

Piano accordion *See* Accordion.

Pipa A short-necked, Chinese wooden lute.

Pitch The acoustical highness or lowness of a musical tone resulting from its frequency of vibration.

Play-party song A short, often nonsensical song sung primarily by children at informal parties to accompany a dance or a game involving physical activity (musical chairs, for instance).

Plena A Puerto Rican ballad similar to the calypso songs of Trinidad.

Polka A vigorous Eastern European couple dance in 2/4 time, introduced by immigrants to the United States in the mid–nineteenth century.

Polyphony More than one vocal or instrumental melodies sung or played at the same time.

Polyrhythm Two or more conflicting rhythmic parts played simultaneously.

Powwow A modern, intertribal gathering of Native Americans to perform traditional dance and song forms.

Pulsation A slight interruption in breath; a continuous revoicing of a note in rapid succession.

Q

Qeej A bamboo-reed mouth organ of the Hmong people of Cambodia. Similar to the Japanese shō.

Quadrille A precursor of the square dance, the quadrille originated in the ballrooms of France and attained its greatest popularity in the early nineteenth century throughout Europe, Russia, and the United States. It is performed by either four or eight couples and features five main figures (patterns of movement).

Quills See Panpipes.

R

R&B *See* Rhythm and blues.

Race records A term used by record companies to describe the special line of recordings marketed primarily from the 1920s through the 1940s to the African American audience.

Ragtime Originally a piano style with a regular, repeated bass line and a syncopated melody; later, any syncopated composition. Ragtime was developed by African Americans in the late nineteenth century.

Range In describing a melody, the overall intervallic distance covered between lowest and highest notes.

Rap A style of urban African American popular music characterized by (often) improvised, sung-spoken rhymes performed to a rhythmic accompaniment. Rap is frequently performed a cappella, with sexual, socially relevant, or political lyrics. The music itself became known as hip-hop.

Rasp/Rasping sticks A rasp is a small, notched piece of wood that is rubbed with a stick or scraper to make a grating sound. Rasping sticks are also notched in such a way that when they are rubbed together, they produce a similar effect.

Rattle A gourd, shell, or can filled with pebbles that makes a rattling sound when it is vigorously shaken.

Reel A fast Anglo-American dance tune, often played on the fiddle, in 4/4 or cut (2/2) time.

Refrain The repeated chorus of a song that alternates with the verse. Unlike the verse, the words to the refrain usually do not change. Sometimes a refrain is shorter than a chorus.

Reggae A popular Jamaican musical style that melds Western rock instrumentation with a loping, syncopated beat and often topical lyrics.

Repertoire The songs, dance tunes, or other musical pieces that are characteristically performed by an individual or a group of people.

Resonator An empty vessel—often a gourd—placed under a musical instrument to increase the sound produced.

Rhythm and blues (R&B) A generic term used to describe African American popular song styles in the late 1940s and early 1950s. Imitation soon led to rock and roll, the white equivalent of rhythm and blues.

Rhythm sticks Two sticks that are rubbed together to create a percussive rhythm.

Rhythmic pattern The patterns of beats that occur throughout a piece of music.

Rhythmic pulse The underlying beat.

Riff A short, memorable melodic phrase that is repeated throughout sections of an instrumental composition or accompaniment. *See also* Ostinato.

Ring shout Historically, a circular African American dance song expressing religious feeling. The song is half-sung, half-shouted as the dancers move slowly in a ring formation. Also called simply a "shout."

Rock and roll A popular white American style of the 1950s that was copied from

black rhythm and blues and featured a percussively heavy reinforcement of the meter (beat) played by combos consisting, minimally, of piano, bass, drums, and guitars, often with a single saxophonist or small wind section. Blues harmonic structures were common, but without the corresponding mood. By the mid-1960s, rock and roll had run out of steam, only to be revitalized and transformed into rock by the so-called "British Invasion" of musical groups that emphasized electric guitars and nonblues harmonic patterns. *See also* Rhythm and blues.

Rockabilly A musical style of the late 1950s and early 1960s that blended country music with rock and roll's sensibility, instrumentation, and heavily accented beat. The term was coined from a combination of "rock" and "hillbilly."

Round dance Any traditional dance that is performed in a circular figure. *See also* Big circle dance.

Rumba A syncopated Latin American dance form, originally from Cuba, that was popularized in the United States in the 1930s.

S

Sacred Harp, The The name of a religious songbook first published in the early nineteenth century; now applied to any song from this book or others in the shape-note tradition.

Salsa A vigorous Latin American dance form combining Latin rhythms with big band instrumentation. Based on the traditional Cuban son style.

Samba A Brazilian American dance style featuring a medium tempo and pronounced rhythms.

Scale A sequence of tones, arranged in ascending or descending order, and used in a characteristic way in a musical performance or composition.

Schottische An Eastern European dance that is a variant of the polka. It is per-

formed by couples in a circle, in 2/2 time, at a slower pace than the polka.

Scraper A small stick used to rub against another object to make a sound.

Scratching A technique used by disc jockeys in which records are spun back and forth while being played so that a percussive, scratching sound is created.

Sean-nós singing A traditional Irish singing style. Highly ornamented, it is particularly suited to singing songs in Gaelic but is also used for English-language songs.

Secular music Music without religious content; music performed for entertainment, not to express religious feelings.

Seísun Literally, "session." An informal gathering of Irish musicians.

Set A generic term for any square dance. The group of four couples who perform the dance are often described as a "set." Also called cycle.

Shanty A short lyric song sung by sailors to aid in their work or pass the time.

Shape-note A system of musical notation in which different scale notes are represented by notes of different shapes, including diamonds, circles, squares, and triangles. Singers can therefore learn their parts without "reading" conventional music by associating the shape with its scale tone (sung as "fa-sol-la," etc.). This method was used to promote music literacy and teach hymn singing to people both in the northern and southeastern United States. *See also* Sacred Harp, The.

Shellshaker In the Native American tradition, a turtle shell filled with small pebbles that is usually attached to the leggings or boots of a female dancer. The name "shellshaker" may be applied to the turtle shell or to the dancer herself.

Shō A Japanese musical instrument consisting of a group of thin bamboo pipes (each containing at its base a small reed) clustered around a small wind

chamber. The player blows into the chamber to sound the reeds. Small fingering holes at the base of each pipe are used to regulate which reed sounds. Variants of this instrument are found throughout Southeast Asia.

Shout *See* Ring shout.

Shuffle (step) (1) A walking step in which the feet are dragged slightly. (2) A syncopated beat.

Slide (1) Moving from one tone to another without a break; similar to a glide but usually covering a smaller range. (2) In reference to the guitar, the use of a bottleneck or metal bar to stop the strings; this technique is known as slide guitar. (3) In Irish music, a jig in 12/8 time, often in three or more parts.

Snare drum A small, two-headed drum of wood or metal, across the lower head of which are stretched several gut strings or strands of metal wire (snares), whose rattling against the head reinforces and alters the tone. The upper head is struck alternately or simultaneously with two drumsticks.

Soca Caribbean music that combines traditional calypso with disco rhythms and soul vocal styles.

Son (1) Generic name of indigenous songs of Cuba and neighboring islands, reflecting the influence of African rhythms and set usually in a strongly accented 2/4 time. *Son* was the principal form of Cuban popular music in the twentieth century and remains an important form of expression in New York's Cuban and Puerto Rican community. It is characterized by a two-part structure in which two or three verses (usually sung by a lead soloist but sometimes by a chorus) are followed by a call-and-response section known as the montuno. *See also* Salsa. (2) A traditional dance piece performed by Mexican mariachi musicians. It varies in style from region to region in Mexico, but is often fast-tempoed with raucous and sometimes improvised lyrics containing social commentary.

Song leader (1) In call-and-response form, the person who sings the melody first, unaccompanied ("the call"), to whom the chorus then answers or "responds." (2) Anyone who leads a large group in song, whether in a religious or secular setting (as, for example, during the rallies of the civil rights movement).

Soul music A term used to describe the gospel-flavored performances of popular African American singers such as Ray Charles and Aretha Franklin.

Spiritual A genre of popular religious songs, chiefly from the nineteenth century. Spirituals composed by African Americans during the slavery period are the best-known examples.

Square dance A traditional American dance form, usually performed by four couples in a square formation. Specific "figures" (dance patterns) are performed by the couples in succession, as prompted by a caller.

Squeezebox or **squeeze-box** A common name for any bellows-driven instrument, such as an accordion or a concertina.

Stanza *See* Verse.

Steel band A large ensemble of steel drum players.

Steel drum/steel pan A Caribbean musical instrument made out of the shell of an oil drum. Small indentations are made in the face of the drum. By striking in different areas with a metal or wooden stick, the player can sound different scale notes.

Steel guitar An electric guitar that is held, face up, on the player's lap (and is therefore sometimes called a "lap steel"). The instrument is tuned to an open chord and played with a metal bar that is moved across the fret board. Also called a "fry pan," because early models were small and thin; the small

body attached to a long neck resembled the common piece of cookware.

Step dancing A dance style of European origin that features rapid movement of the lower legs and feet while the remainder of the body is held rigidly. Similar to clogging.

Stomp dance In the Native American tradition, the term used for a variety of both secular and sacred dances in which the movement of the dancers' feet provides the rhythmic accompaniment. The percussive sound is often provided by rattles tied in bunches around the calves of the dancers.

Strathspey A Scottish dance tune named for the valley of the River Spey. It is characterized by its "Scotch snap" rhythm: a sixteenth note followed briskly by a dotted eighth note. In traditional Scottish fiddling, the sixteenth note is played with a slight upbow, followed by a sharp downwards stroke for the dotted eighth, giving the characteristic "snapping" sound. Played in 4/4 time, but slower than a reel.

Strawbeater In some traditions of the southeastern United States, a strawbeater would hold two small pieces of reed or straw and beat them rhythmically on the strings of the fiddle while the fiddler was playing. This would add a rhythmic texture to the fiddle's sound.

Street dancing A highly virtuosic, exhibition dance style, often performed on urban street corners. *See also* Break dancing/Breaking.

String band A group of musicians who accompany dances, usually consisting of stringed instruments such as banjos, fiddles, guitars, and mandolins. Non-stringed instruments—such as harmonicas—can also be heard in a string band.

Strophic Made up of stanzas or strophes; songs based on a repeated melody line that is used to accompany a series of stanzas.

Swing A style of big band jazz that was a major type of social dance music from the 1920s through the mid-1940s. Small swing groups featured improvisation, while the larger groups presented lavish arrangements of songs with interpretations that accented smoothness.

Symmetrical rhythm A balanced, or repeating, rhythmic pattern used consistently throughout a musical composition.

Sympathetic strings Strings that run under the neck (or in the body) of a musical instrument and thus are inaccessible to the player for either fretting or strumming. Instead, these strings vibrate "in sympathy" when the instrument is played; that is, they may vibrate when either the body of the instrument or the other strings vibrate. The Scandinavian hardanger fiddle is an instrument that features sympathetic strings.

Syncopation Accenting the off-beat; placing an accent on a beat that is usually unaccented.

T

Taiko A Japanese double-headed barrel drum, usually of great size.

Tambourine A small, shallow hand drum featuring a single head with small metal "jingles" placed in the frame.

Tamburitza An Eastern European folk lute.

Tango An Argentine dance form first popularized in the 1920s and 1930s that is marked by dramatic, strongly syncopated melodies.

Tap dancing A popular dance form of the 1920s and 1930s that has been revived over the past few decades. It is an elaborate form of step dancing in which the performer wears metal taps on the bottom of his or her shoes in order to emphasize the percussive sounds. Most of the movement occurs as the dancer alternates between tapping the front of the shoe and the heel; arm movements and other gestures are added for emphasis.

Tarantella A popular and energetic folk dance of Italian origin.

Tempo The rate of speed of a musical performance.

Tenor banjo A four-string instrument based on the original banjo but developed at the turn of the twentieth century specifically for playing accompaniment work in ragtime and early jazz. Tenor banjos were adopted by Irish musicians for playing melody as well.

Tex-Mex music *See Norteño music/La música norteña.*

Texture The interrelationship of the musical lines in a composition or performance.

Third The third scale degree; the related interval between the tonic and the third scale step.

Three-finger style (banjo) A more modern method of playing the banjo in which patterns are picked by the thumb and two fingers. This is also called bluegrass style because it was popularized by Earl Scruggs and other bluegrass banjo players.

Timbales Paired tom-tom drums mounted on a stand, popular in Latin-Caribbean dance music.

Timbre The characteristic sound quality of an individual voice or musical instrument; why a flute sounds different from a violin when they play the same note.

Tin whistle A small, six-holed, end-blown flute, popular in Irish music. Originally made of tin with a wooden mouthpiece, it is now more commonly made of brass with a plastic mouthpiece. Also called a "pennywhistle."

Tom-tom Generic term for African, Asian, or Latin American indigenous drums, of high but (usually) indefinite pitch. They may be played with the hands or sticks.

Tonic The first note of a scale and the pitch to which others in a composition gravitate.

Transcription A written version or notation of a musical composition.

Triangle A triangular piece of metal that makes a clanging sound when struck with a short metal stick.

Triple time/beat A rhythm with an accent every three beats.

Tumbadoras/Conga drums Tall, cylindrical, single-headed drums based on African models but popularized in Cuban dance music. They are played with fingers and palms of the hands and come in three sizes: The larger drum is called the *tumba;* the *secundo* is medium-sized; and the smallest is called the *quinto.* Usually, the tumba and secundo play one rhythmic pattern, while the quinto plays a counterrhythm.

Two-finger (up-picking) style (banjo) A style in which the banjo player picks upwards with the index finger, alternating or coinciding with a rhythmic downward pick of the thumb.

Two-step A popular and simple couple dance, found throughout the United States. It can be performed to any duple-time melody.

U

Uilleann (bag)pipes Irish bagpipes; unlike the Scottish version, they are driven by a small bellows that is held under the elbow and pumped. In addition to drone and melody ("chanter") pipes, they feature so-called regulator pipes that play chords.

Undulating (contour) Melody lines that seem to meander or wander without any definite goal.

Unison Two or more vocalists (or instrumentalists) singing (or playing) the same melodic part at the same time.

V

Variation Slight changes in the melody line, often occurring on its second statement or repetition.

Veillée A house party; the Franco American equivalent of a kitchen racket.

Verse The changing text of a song that alternates with the chorus or refrain. Usually, the verse is sung to one melody and the refrain to another one.

Vibrato A trembling, "vibrating" pitch; a slight variation in intensity in pitch creating a sense of vibration or fluttering.

Vocables Untranslatable but not necessarily meaningless syllables (such as "fa-la-la") that are sung to a melodic line in place or instead of words.

W

Waila A type of social dance music with European roots that has been incorporated into Native American traditions.

Waltz A European couple dance in 3/4 time, introduced by immigrants to the United States in the mid–nineteenth century.

Washboard A metal board used to launder clothes, which, when adapted as a musical instrument, is vigorously "rubbed" by the player, who wears thimbles or other small pieces of metal on his or her fingers. Also called a "rubboard."

Water drum A small, skin-headed drum made of a crock or vessel that is filled with water to alter its tone.

Well-tempered (or **equal-tempered**) **scale** The modern Western scale with twelve equal steps. The piano is tuned to this scale.

Western swing A musical style that developed in the Texas-Oklahoma region during the 1930s, led by fiddler Bob Wills. A marriage of old-time string band music with big band jazz, Western swing bands performed popular songs and blues in jazzy, up-tempo arrangements. Typical bands included fiddle, guitar, electric steel guitar, piano, drums, and often a small brass section.

Whistle A short, single-note flute, often made of a short piece of hollowed-out cane. The player blows into one end of the instrument to create a sound.

Woodblocks Small, square blocks of wood that are used as percussion instruments; they are usually paired and struck with a small stick.

Work song A rhythmic, repeated song, often in call-and-response form, used to coordinate a group of workers.

X

Xylophone A wooden-keyed instrument played with two small mallets. The keys are of different lengths, mounted on a frame or connected with strings, so that they can freely vibrate.

Z

Zither A stringed instrument with strings that run parallel to the full length of the body of the instrument. The Chinese ch'in (or q'in) and the autoharp are both zithers.

Zydeco A dance music of southeastern Louisiana that combines African American and Cajun styles. Alternately spelled "zodico."

INDEX

Page references in bold refer to a main essay or sidebar on that topic. Page references in italics refer to illustrations.

211

D